Cognitive Behaviour Therapy

3rd Edition

Cognitive Behaviour Therapy

Foundations for Practice

Frank Wills *with*
Diana Sanders

Los Angeles | London | New Delhi
Singapore | Washington DC

Los Angeles | London | New Delhi
Singapore | Washington DC

SAGE Publications Ltd
1 Oliver's Yard
55 City Road
London EC1Y 1SP

SAGE Publications Inc.
2455 Teller Road
Thousand Oaks, California 91320

SAGE Publications India Pvt Ltd
B 1/I 1 Mohan Cooperative Industrial Area
Mathura Road
New Delhi 110 044

SAGE Publications Asia-Pacific Pte Ltd
3 Church Street
#10-04 Samsung Hub
Singapore 049483

Editor: Alice Oven
Assistant editor: Kate Wharton
Production editor: Rachel Burrows
Copyeditor: Solveig Servian
Proofreader: Derek Markham
Marketing manager: Tamara Navaratnam
Cover design: Joni Strudwick
Typeset by: C&M Digitals (P) Ltd, Chennai, India
Printed by MPG Books Group, Bodmin, Cornwall

Library of Congress Control Number: 2012930408

British Library Cataloguing in Publication data

A catalogue record for this book is available from the British Library

ISBN 978–1-84920–564–1
ISBN 978–1-84920–565–8 (pbk)

Contents

Preface to the Third Edition

As we engaged in writing this third edition of our book first published in 1997, we have realised that cognitive behaviour therapy (CBT) is on the march – perhaps even 'at the double'. There have been numerous new developments and changes since we both trained in CBT in the early 1990s and the pace of change shows no signs of easing. It has been challenging to write an account of the model that retains its basic integrity but also reflects developing diversity within it. We were both trainees in one of the early cohorts of the Oxford Cognitive Therapy training course – a veritable engine room for CBT development in the UK. Even as we wrote the first edition of this book, *Cognitive Therapy: Transforming the Image*, in 1997 a major new development was evident in schema-focused therapy (SFT) and first attempts to address interpersonal and characterological issues. As we wrote the second edition in 2004–5, we had to think about how the transdiagnostic and metacognitive approaches and mindfulness-based cognitive therapy (MBCT) were to be understood and incorporated into a coherent model of practice. We were also noticing the first stirrings of acceptance and commitment therapy (ACT) and compassion-focused therapy (CFT) and contemplating what they had to say. Now as we come to submit this third edition in late 2011 we have seen yet more development in all these trends plus what we have called the 'late flowering' of the new behavioural approach. It is possible to see in all this diversity parallels with trends within the historical development of other models such as psychoanalysis and humanistic therapy. One can also recognise the same potential for schism and infighting and wonder if the overall integrity of CBT can be retained. Our approach has been to 'keep our powder dry' and not to over-react in the face of potential fracturing. We have no doubt that important points of development are raised in many of the new 'waves' of CBT and that they can be enthusiastically embraced, but they should not be uncritically embraced. There are other motives, including academic kudos, involved in developing new 'products'. Psychological therapy is such a fundamentally difficult activity that all of us sometimes think that if only we had one more theory or technique up our sleeves we would finally have it all sown up. We still, after 30 and 40 years of practice respectively, think this – life-long learning indeed! We have been very aware that alongside the production of 'waves' of CBT there has also been fearful consumer reactions that one will not be included in the 'latest thing' and suddenly find oneself passé, fallen and trampled down by rush of people literally running to avoid exclusion from the 'hot' conference workshop. This edition then focuses on retaining the integrity and parsimony of the original CBT approach whilst making appropriate assimilation from new developments from both CBT and other therapeutic models. We will return to these themes to assess how well we think we have managed this testing task in the Epilogue of this book.

A note on authorship: For this edition Diana has mainly contributed material on MBCT so that Frank has taken more responsibility for writing the rest of the book. Whilst both authors take responsibility for its overall thrust, there are inevitably small differences of emphasis at times.

ACKNOWLEDGEMENTS

We would like to acknowledge the following colleagues and friends who have helped us with this edition – some are 'the usual suspects', others new. We thank them with all our hearts: Sheila Brennan, Mo Chandler, Amanda Cole, Elaine Davies, Janet Gray, Alice Oven, Kim Richardson, Christina Surawy, Kate Wharton, Mark Williams, Annie Wills and, of course, each other.

PART I

COGNITIVE BEHAVIOUR THERAPY – THEORY, MODEL AND STRUCTURE

1

CBT: A Developing Model

Cognitive behaviour therapy (CBT), as developed by A. T. Beck and others, is built on the assumption that thinking processes both influence and are influenced by emotional and behavioural responses in many different psychological problems. Therapy therefore aims to modify cognitive, emotional and behavioural processes in an experimental way to test whether modification has positive effects on the client's difficulties. While clients may come to therapy asking for help with their negative thoughts, more often they come because they are feeling bad. Despite its focus on thinking, CBT is actually all about reaching and working with emotion. Cognitions and cognitive processes are emphasised because they can often provide direct and useful paths to relevant emotions. Furthermore, understanding specific thoughts, styles and processes of thinking can go a long way to explain negative feelings to clients, who may well have been experiencing them as incomprehensible and frightening. The way in which cognition influences emotion and behaviour is at the heart of CBT and the basis of both the early models, developed in the 1970s, and current theory and practice.

Since the first models evolved, both the theory and practice of CBT have been subject to continual and accelerating change and development. In this chapter, we look first at the foundational model of theory and practice and then at the subsequent developments leading CBT to what it is today. Such developments are now multifarious and include integration of the interpersonal and the therapeutic relationship within both the theory and practice of CBT. In addition, contributions have come from behavioural and cognitive theorists that have added new dimensions through increased understanding of the role of cognitive and emotional processes in psychological disturbance (Wells, 2009) and mindfulness in psychological change (Segal et al., 2002). After almost 50 years, the theory and practice of CBT are still developing, with what has been called the 'third wave' hitting the beach (Hayes et al., 2004). The chapter ends by looking at some of these new contributions, the 'third wave', bringing an experiential focus, mindfulness and acceptance to the practice of CBT.

FOUNDATIONS OF CBT

With his two major publications of the 1970s, *Cognitive Therapy and the Emotional Disorders* (1976) and *Cognitive Therapy of Depression* (Beck et al., 1979), Beck, and his colleagues, established what many now regard as the original model of CBT. The model contained a theory of how people develop emotional problems; a model of how they could heal disturbance; and a model of how further problems might be prevented. The links between emotion and cognition were initially most clearly demonstrated in the treatment of depression; opportunely because depression is often regarded as one of the most frequently presented psychological problems. The model was also supported by what was, for the psychotherapy field, an impressive range of research validation for both its underlying constructs and its outcomes.

The Thought–Emotion Cycle

A key aim in CBT is to explore the meanings that clients give to situations, emotions or biology, often expressed in the client's 'negative automatic thoughts' (NATs). The valuable concept of *cognitive specificity* (see www.sagepub.co.uk/wills3 for material on this and related definitions) demonstrates how particular types of thoughts appraise the impact of events on the 'personal domain' (all the things we value and hold dear) and thereby lead to particular emotions, as shown in Table 1.1. It is then possible to discern the influence that such thoughts and feelings have over behaviours – especially 'emotion-driven behaviours' (Barlow et al., 2011a). The appraisal of 'danger' to our domain, for example, raises anxiety and primes us for evasive, defensive or other reactions. The appraisal of 'loss' is likely to invoke sadness and mourning behaviour. An appraisal discerning 'unfairness' is likely to arouse anger and may lead to an aggressive response.

In themselves, responses to negative appraisals are not necessarily problematic and indeed are often functional: for example, we all know that driving carries certain risks and being aware of those risks may, hopefully, make us better drivers. Our specific appraisals of events may begin to be more problematic, however, as they become more exaggerated. If we become preoccupied with the risks of driving, and see ourselves as likely to have an accident, then the emotion of slight, functional anxiety becomes one of unease or even panic. Furthermore, if this feeling increases, the chances that driving ability is adversely affected also increase. Similarly, we may

TABLE 1.1   Key themes: cognitive specificity

Appraisal	Emotion	Emotion-driven behaviour
Loss to domain	Sadness, depression	Search, mourn, grieve
Threat to domain	Fear, anxiety	Fight, flight, freeze
Violation of domain	Anger	Attack
Expansion to domain	Delight	Praise

feel a certain comforting sadness about a loss in our life, but if we begin to see the loss as a major erosion of our being, we could then feel corrosive depression rather than relatively soulful melancholy. If the depression cycle goes on, we tend to become lifeless, lacking energy and enthusiasm, and are thereby less likely to engage in things that give our life meaning; as a result we become even more depressed. In another example, appraising meeting people as 'worrying' raises anxiety and primes evasion and defensiveness. If we become preoccupied with the risks of meeting people and making faux pas, then a sense of reasonable caution can become unease or even panic. Furthermore, if this feeling increases, the chances of our making faux pas may increase, which further increases our anxiety and so maintains the problem.

The essence of the model is that there is a reciprocal relationship between emotional difficulties and seeing events in a way that is exaggerated beyond the available evidence. These exaggerated ways of seeing things tend to exacerbate negative feelings and behaviour, and may constitute a vicious cycle of intensifying emotionally driven thoughts, feelings and behaviours (see Figure 1.1).

Critics sometimes wrongly regard CBT as being based on generalised formulae that claim people are disturbed by their thoughts. In fact, good CB therapists understand each client in a highly individualised way. Rather than reducing clients' mediating cognitions to formulaic sets of 'irrational beliefs', a CBT approach aims to understand why clients are appraising events in particular ways and why they feel the way that they do. In Epictetus' famous dictum – 'People are disturbed not by events themselves but by the view they take of events' – external and internal (i.e., thinking about something) events are important because they are usually the triggers that set off the whole cycle of reaction. The same event, however, may impact differently on different people because, first, each individual has a different personal domain on which events impinge. Second, each person has idiosyncratic ways of appraising events because cognitions, perceptions, beliefs and schemas will

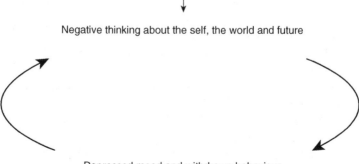

FIGURE 1.1   A vicious cycle of thoughts, feelings and behaviour

have been shaped by that individual's unique personal experiences and life history. The aim of CBT is to understand both the client's personal domains and their idiosyncratic way of appraising events. Additionally, when we look to modify cognitions, it is probably impossible to completely erase negative thoughts. Pierson and Hayes (2007) make a valuable point when they say that it is not so much that clients have to *replace* a negative thought with a more functional one, but they are able to *follow* it with a more balanced thought – learning to allow the thought 'I am a failure' to be followed by another thought like 'Hang on, that's not the whole story!'. Another account of the process of cognitive change comes from Brewin et al. (2006), who suggests that different cognitions are available at any one point in time but some – the more functional ones – are often difficult for depressed clients to retrieve. In this account CBT does not directly change cognitions but rather changes the relationship between different cognitions in such a way that more helpful ones are retrieved.

While, on a simplistic level, a person's thoughts and emotions about an event may appear 'irrational', the response may be entirely rational, given his way of seeing the world. As we look at new developments in CBT, we will see that it may be that the content of the thinking itself is not so problematic. It turns out that, perhaps in a good, democratic fashion, 'irrational' content is by no means confined to people with psychological problems. For example, the thoughts that are problematic for clients with obsessive-compulsive disorder (OCD) are shared by 90 per cent of the population (Rachman, 2003). OCD sufferers, however, pay attention to these thoughts in a different way. Non-sufferers can let them go: OCD sufferers cannot. Similarly, it seems that most people at times have the kind of intrusive thoughts that are a problem for 'worriers' (Leahy, 2005). People vulnerable to worry, however, will focus more time and attention onto the worries and will be less able to let them go (Wells, 2009).

Cognitive Distortions: Negative Thoughts

Cognitive themes are expressed in specific thoughts. Rather than thinking in literal sentences, such as 'There is a loss to my personal domain', such themes are expressed in situationally specific cognitions (e.g., 'He finds me dull') that, when added together, amount to a theme (e.g., 'People find me tedious'). These themes become elaborated and maintained by the day-to-day 'dripping tap' effect of the client's 'negative automatic thoughts' (NATs). Often the client is barely aware of these thoughts until they are highlighted. Beck (1976/1989) discovered the constant commentary of negative thoughts when a client became anxious while talking about past sexual experiences. The client, however, revealed that it was not the fact of describing these experiences that was causing the emotional pain but rather the thought that Beck would think her 'boring'. In depression, thinking has a characteristically negative and global tone centred on loss – not just of loved objects but of a sense of self-esteem and, crucially, for depression, a sense of loss of hopefulness about the world and the future. The triangle of negative views of self, of the world and the future comprise Beck et al.'s (1979) 'cognitive triad', in which the dynamics of depression operate.

In an early publication Beck (1976/1989) described a range of cognitive distortions, shown in Table 1.2. For example, the thought, 'I'm stupid', a common negative automatic thought in emotional disturbance, betrays 'all-or-nothing' thinking because it usually refers to a narrower reality – that people occasionally do some things which, with the benefit of hindsight, may be construed as 'stupid'. Depressed clients, however, will often go on to the globalised conclusion that this makes them a 'stupid person'. In this type of dichotomous reasoning, there are only two possible conditions: doing everything right and being 'not stupid' or doing some things wrongly and being 'stupid'. Thus the negatively biased person uses self-blame, thereby depressing mood even further in a vicious cycle.

In CBT, clients and therapists work collaboratively to identify and label negative thoughts and to understand how thoughts interact with emotions to produce 'vicious cycles'. These are the first steps that enable clients to understand their emotions. When clients detect specific thoughts, it can be useful to ask them what effect these repetitive thoughts will have on their mood. Many clients will conclude that such thinking is bound to get them down. Thus the simplest form of the cognitive behavioural model links thoughts and emotions most relevant – salient – to clients' situations. Therapists can then look at the degree of 'fit' between thought and feeling – does the thought make sense of the feeling? Looking at Table 1.2, if you had the thought, 'I will lose my job', would you be likely to feel anxious and worried? Clients may also have 'favourite distortions' – and this may allow them to take the helpful 'mentalisation' (being able to understand the mental state of oneself or others) step whereby they can say to themselves 'There I go – personalising things again!' As we will describe later such steps may be part of a wider ability to look at, defuse or decentre from negative thoughts from a new, more mindful position.

From Thoughts to Schemas

NATs are unhelpful cognitions closest to the surface of consciousness and may refer only to a limited range of situations. Beck recognised, however, that there were also deeper cognitions that incline the person to interpret wider ranges of events in relatively fixed patterns. Originally Beck used the term 'constructs' (Kelly, 1955) to describe deeper cognitive processes but then preferred the term 'schemas' used by earlier psychologists (Bartlett, 1932) to describe them.

Schemas are not, of course, all problematic. For example, Bowlby (1969) describes how children who have experienced satisfactory attachment and bonding to primary

TABLE 1.2   Common thinking biases

Type of thought	Description and examples
Black-and-white thinking	Seeing things in black-and-white, all-or-nothing categories, missing the 'grey' areas: '*I don't measure up*' (see Mary, p. 15) '*Everyone else gets it right*'
Mind-reading	Concluding that other people are thinking a certain way: '*People must think I'm really stupid*' '*Everyone thinks I'm boring*'
Crystal ball gazing	Looking into the future and making predictions: '*I will lose my job*' (see Keith, p. 11) '*She will leave me*' (see Ben, p. 12)
Over-generalisation	Seeing a negative event as an indication of everything being negative: '*I didn't get the job – I guess I'll never get another job again*'
Mental filter	Picking out a single negative feature and dwelling on it without reference to any good things which might have happened: '*I had an awful day, my computer crashed and I couldn't do anything for the rest of the day*'
Disqualifying, minimising the positive	Recognising something good in yourself or your life and rejecting it as invalid or unimportant: '*I'm a good mother to my kids but that doesn't matter, anyone can do that*' Or shrinking it inappropriately: '*I've been promoted at work, but it is not a top firm so it doesn't count*'
Magnification or 'drama queen'	Exaggerating the importance/significance of events: '*I've got a pain in my chest, it must mean I'm having a heart attack and am going to die*' '*I can't find my keys, I must be losing my mind*'
Emotional reasoning	Assuming that what you feel is true: '*I feel like a bad person, I must be a bad person*' '*I feel like I'm dying so I must be*'
Unrealistic expectations	Using exaggerated performance criteria for yourself and others. Using 'shoulds' and 'oughts' in your expectations of yourself and your demands of others: '*I should always be interesting when talking to other people*' '*I must keep going even though I'm tired*'
Name-calling and labelling	Attaching a highly emotional negative label to yourself or to others: '*Idiot*' '*Silly cow*'
Self-blame	Seeing yourself as the cause of a bad event for which you were not responsible: '*She's looking cross, I must have upset her*'
Catastrophising	Predicting the very worst: '*Nothing is ever going to work out for me again*' '*This lump in my neck must be cancer, the treatment won't work and I'll die a horrible death*'

caregivers will develop a basic set of rules or schemas that contain the inner working model that 'people can generally be trusted'. If people with 'trust schemas' meet untrustworthy behaviour in others, they are likely to think 'Something went wrong there, I may have to be more cautious in future', which is an adaptive response. When people with 'mistrust' schemas encounter untrustworthy behaviour, however, they are likely to conclude 'I was right. You can't trust anyone. I won't do so again', which is an overgeneralised and, therefore, less adaptive response.

Negative schemas are seen as underlying NATs. Unhelpful assumptions – conditional core beliefs – are operationalised into 'rules of living' and sometimes termed 'intermediate beliefs'. They are contained within schemas, are triggered by events and lead to NATs. Sometimes the assumptions persist after NATs and the other symptoms of depression have abated and may then be targeted as a method of preventing later relapse back into depression. Whilst these different levels of cognition are conceptually clear, in practice they are usually identified from client self-reports and therefore it is not always easy to know if the thought 'I am a failure' is truly a core belief or a thought that applies to only limited situations.

As CBT developed, schemas were given a more significant and autonomous role in therapy. It is important to remember when working with schemas that they are not concrete objects and may be better understood as 'schematic processes'. It has been difficult for CBT researchers to show the autonomous existence of these processes but the schema concept remains a useful one (Wells, 2000).

So far we have established that there are strong links between thought and feeling. We do not argue, as Beck did not, that they are *causal* links, but are best understood as two-way processes. Clients are likely to experience the links in this reciprocal way. Thoughts and feelings are often experienced as a unitary phenomenon, so it is likely that our labelling of 'thought' and 'feeling' is more a useful heuristic (speculative formulation to guide investigation and/or problem-solving) device for therapy than a truly knowable reality. Although our Figures and Tables are also heuristic devices and show clear relationships between thoughts and feelings, it is increasingly realised that the actual sequences are highly complex (Le Doux, 1998).

The Role of Behaviour in Disturbance

Problematic behaviours are best understood in relation to their role in reciprocal reinforcement in the vicious cycle by way of thoughts, feelings and actions. Thoughts and emotions have built-in action dispositions, so that behaviours may seem to come as instantaneous reactions – 'I could have kissed him'. Often, becoming aware of thoughts and feelings accompanying behaviour is helpful to clients, enabling them to respond with less automaticity and therefore less problematically. Equally, behaviours have independent effects on thoughts and feelings. 'Act as if' we felt confident can result in feeling more confident, so that a client can learn 'to act his way into a new feeling' (Izard, 1971: 410). Behavioural responses often play the role of final link in the chain, locking and maintaining the whole sequence of thoughts, feelings and behaviours into persistent, and unhelpful, patterns. This often happens because the concrete behaviours produce environmental consequences: see the examples of linked negative thoughts, feelings, behaviours and consequences that follow. In the first example, the sequence mainly affects the client's internal experiences, while the second has notably interpersonal affects.

CASE STUDY
Keith

Keith was a 40-year-old IT project manager in the Civil Service and had experienced recurrent dysthymia since his teenage years. His current depression had lasted for 2 years, since the threat that his work section would be outsourced. He worked hard but was isolated at work, often staying late and taking work home. He considered that his performance had deteriorated, making him vulnerable to redundancy. Keith's pattern is shown in Figure 1.2.

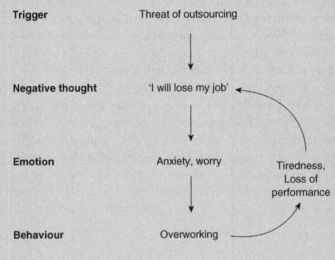

FIGURE 1.2   Keith's vicious cycle

CASE STUDY
Ben

Ben's mother died when he was 12 years old. He came to believe that 'Nothing lasts – people leave you'. Now when he meets potential girlfriends he feels anxious because he cannot help imagining them leaving him. He then tends to become 'over the top' – endlessly and dramatically declaring his love – with the ironic consequence of making his girlfriends uneasy and less likely to stay in the relationship. Ben's vicious cycle is shown in Figure 1.3.

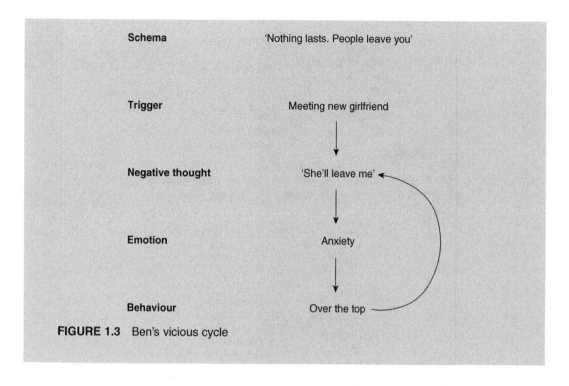

FIGURE 1.3   Ben's vicious cycle

Clients are often puzzled by their emotional and behavioural responses to situations – 'I cannot understand why I get drawn into doing that' is a common reaction. The whole cycle of thought, feeling and behaviour is made more concrete and understandable when therapist and client actually draw the vicious cycle onto paper or whiteboard. This can mark beginnings of formulation. Concreteness and clarity in formulation enhance the prospects of change. Formulating diagrams may be given to clients to take home and think about or work on, perhaps as homework assignments. The process of formulation is described in detail in Chapter 3. Formulation diagrams can extend to wider uses in therapy, including linking different parts of the vicious cycle to potential therapeutic goals and targets (see Figure 1.4).

Behavioural approaches in CBT have been refreshed by the 'new behaviourism', which has added strong new concepts and methods to our work: these will be described throughout the book and especially in Chapter 6.

The Original Model of the Therapeutic Relationship

CBT aims to be an accessible and practical mode of therapy, one that can be related to pragmatic common sense (Wills, 2009). One attraction is its immediacy, achieved by the way the model fits with the client's experience. Formulation often

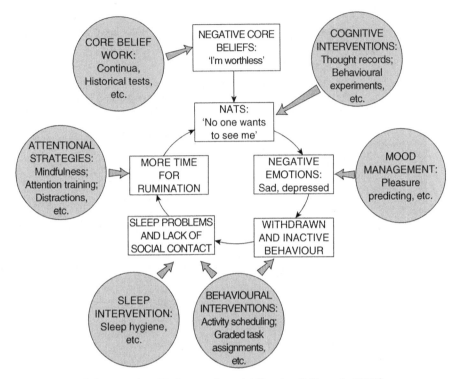

FIGURE 1.4   Vicious cycle with therapy targets (Dryden & Branch, 2011)

appears relatively simple and straightforward to students of the approach. CBT terminology may sometimes belie the complexities and sophistication of the model. It is congruence between the model and clients' experience, however, that enables the therapy to make sense to them. The basic therapeutic processes of CBT specified in early models and largely continued in recent developments involve three interacting elements: a *collaborative therapeutic relationship*, a *scientific, empirical method* and a *parsimonious form of therapy*.

In Chapter 3 of *Cognitive Therapy of Depression*, Beck and colleagues describe a view of the *therapeutic relationship* which draws heavily from Carl Rogers, stressing the 'core conditions' of 'warmth, accurate empathy and genuineness' (1979: 45). They add, however, that these conditions are not in themselves sufficient to produce optimum therapeutic effect. Trust, rapport and collaboration are also needed. It is the concept of collaborative empiricism that marks the point of departure from Rogers:

In contrast to 'supportive' or 'relationship' therapy, the therapeutic relationship is not used simply as the instrument to alleviate suffering but as a vehicle to facilitate a common effort in carrying out specific goals. In this sense, the therapist and the [client] form a 'team'. (Beck et al., 1979: 54)

The emphasis is on a working relationship: one that perhaps carries with it a little of the Protestant work ethic, and offers a contrast to therapies which stress the importance of 'being' rather than 'doing' in the relationship with the client – though with advent of mindfulness into CBT, this balance could be shifting. The nature of the cognitive and behavioural work to be undertaken is that of identifying and modifying unhelpful cognitive and behavioural processes respectively. More recently there has also been increased emphasis on the need for 'interpersonal sensitivity' in CBT (Wills, 2008a).

A second axiom of the therapy process concerns CBT as *a scientific and empirical form of therapy*. The client's problem is first collaboratively assessed, and then therapy proceeds from the findings of this assessment. As will be discussed in greater detail in Chapter 3, assessment involves full understanding of the presenting symptoms and underlying factors, allowing a clear direction for the therapy. The 'base line' of current functioning is established so that the outcome of therapy can be monitored, using tools such as the Beck measures for depression – the Beck depression inventory (BDI) – and for anxiety – the Beck anxiety inventory (BAI). By the time the usual allocation of around 12–20 sessions (for depression; 5–12 for anxiety) is coming to an end, the scores should be considerably reduced.[1] CBT can be regarded as a series of scientific 'single case experiments' (Kirk, 1989). The monitoring of therapy should not be determined by dogmatic use of tick-box scores, however: it also needs to take account of client feedback and other factors. A final aspect of the scientific approach is the *relatively*[2] standardised form of therapy. The degree to which the therapist appropriately stays with prescribed interventions and yet also applies them individually and artfully nearly always varies. Competence in the use of CBT skills is assessed using measures such as the Cognitive Therapy Scale (CTS) and its revisions (Young & Beck, 1980, 1988; James et al., 2000) – though much remains to be learnt in this area (Wills, 2010). Measures of competence ensure that CBT is conducted with *relative* consistency across different settings of therapy.

The third aspect of the therapy process is the relative *parsimony* (achieving the greatest benefit from the least effort) of CBT. Parsimony involves commencing work at symptom level and advancing to work on the level of underlying belief as appropriate: such as, when 'historical' issues keep coming up or when clients themselves want to work at that level. A typical example of parsimonious treatment is seen in the use of behavioural activation with depressed clients, for whom behavioural withdrawal is often a profound cycle which reinforces the maintenance of low mood and depression. Additionally, clients may initially be too depressed for cognitive 'insight' interventions. Therefore, CBT with depressed clients often starts at the behavioural level, moving to working on cognitions and underlying assumptions and beliefs when behavioural approaches have produced some improvement in mood (Fennell, 1989). Clients would typically be encouraged to schedule activities and then try to insert more 'achievement' and 'enjoyment' into their days. The overall aims of these behavioural tasks and experiments are to engage in constructive behaviour and to loosen the grip of 'depressogenic' thinking. Pleasurable activity is helpful in its own right but can also be used to test and disconfirm clients' NATs, such as 'I never enjoy things any more'. It is usually more possible then to address negative thoughts and beliefs directly as mood lifts.

The parsimonious approach is also evident in the recommendation that therapists start work at the most accessible level of cognition – that of automatic thoughts – and only later work at the deeper levels of assumptions, core beliefs and schemas. The great array of both behavioural and cognitive techniques gives flexibility to 'mix and match' therapeutic interventions. Good CBT should, however, always be carefully fitted to the needs and wishes of the individual client, and this allows therapy to proceed in a way that is highly interpersonally sensitive (Wills, 2008a).

THE DEVELOPING CBT MODEL

Since Beck's original cognitive model of psychological problems, a number of new ways of thinking about psychological processes have been integrated into CBT. One area of development concerns the integration of an interpersonal perspective into the model (Gilbert & Leahy, 2007; Wills, 2008a). Other developments have seen more explicit integration of work on 'transdiagnostic' cognitive processes into CBT (Harvey et al., 2004; Barlow et al., 2011a) and that of meta-cognitive therapy (Wells, 2009), acceptance-based and mindfulness-based models (Hayes et al., 2004; Segal et al., 2002).

Interpersonal Processes and the CBT Model

Various authors (Safran & Muran, 2000; Gilbert & Leahy, 2007; Wills, 2008a) have emphasised how the client's issues outside therapy can be worked through in the therapeutic relationship itself. They follow on from the earlier work of Guidano and Liotti (1983) and especially integrating Bowlby's (1969, 1973) attachment theory into CBT (Liotti, 2007). These approaches recognise the strong imperative for humans to relate to each other. Relatedness and affiliation have crucial survival value not only to the infant during the long period of dependency but also to all of us, as our lives are usually dependent on large degrees of social cooperation. Attachment behaviour is seen as a 'wired-in' propensity of human behaviour, evident right from the first moments of a newborn baby's experience. Infants quickly develop the ability to send and receive attachment-based communications with caregivers. Misattunements in attachment information, if persistent, can have a highly negative effect on development. A key process in attachment is that children seem to learn emotional regulation styles from caregivers (Leahy, 2011) – a factor that seems to inextricably link two key elements in 'emotionally sensitive CBT' (Wills, 2008a).

As a result of our imperative to relate, many core beliefs and assumptions about life and the world are likely to be interpersonal (Wills, 2008a). Attachment schemas are internalised and may become persistent, independently of subsequent experience. They can therefore become locked into a cognitive-interpersonal style.

CASE STUDY
Mary

Mary remembered her childhood as one in which she did not get the parental recognition that her siblings did. She summed this up in the core belief 'I do not measure up'. Consequently she developed a strong desire to please others during her childhood. Forty years later, she could not understand why work colleagues 'didn't respect her'. Her tactic was to try hard to please them and to win their respect. Unfortunately, as often happens with this tactic, it made her colleagues irritated and actually less respectful of her. Her overly pleasing behaviour was also evident in the therapy room, but here we were able to reflect on its nature and significance in a non-judgemental way.

As Harry Stack Sullivan (1954) pointed out, clients' attempted solutions may be part of the problem: that is, clients, understandably, try to counter unhelpful beliefs, yet in ways that only lead to their perpetuation. Therapists' assessments include appraisal of how pervasive these patterns are and whether they are replayed within the therapeutic relationship itself. Wills (2008a) suggests that therapists need to be aware of 'interpersonal signals', not only because awareness facilitates the therapeutic process but also because such signals can prove reliable guides to the contours of the client's interpersonal terrain. We turn again to Mary. The first time that the therapist met Mary, she asked a lot about his qualifications. The therapist made a standard interpretation of her actions: that they might conceal an anxiety about trust. In a later discussion, however, Mary explained that her inquiries were linked to her cognitive-interpersonal belief that 'People will only be interested in me if I am even more interested in them first'. In training on sales techniques, she had been taught that customers were more likely to buy from her if she showed interest in them first. A look back at the previous extract on her childhood shows how well this belief fitted into her existing cognitive-interpersonal schema 'I am only able to gain love and respect by pleasing people'. Wills (2008a) argues that interpersonally sensitive CBT is also founded on a thorough understanding of the therapeutic significance of 'felt meaning' and the deep emotions of affiliation. It should now be recognised that there was at least a grain of truth in criticism that earlier models of CBT were overly rationalistic and utilitarian in their approach, often seeming to view painful emotion as something to be 'brought under control'. There has, however, been a growing realisation in most forms of CBT that, as Beck has long said, emotion is the key to successful therapy and further that attempts to 'control' emotions often have unintended negative consequences. Even negative emotions such as depression can serve the purpose of directing attention to difficult areas in clients' lives; the problem is not so much that such emotions occur but that they persist longer than is helpful to clients.

The omnipresence of emotionally significant material in therapy can be linked to the importance of interpersonal schemas. These schemas are likely to have been encoded in highly emotional ways, so unless the therapeutic process activates these emotions, processing cold meaning alone is unlikely to have much therapeutic impact. Salient interpersonal beliefs may have been established in the client's earliest days and therefore influential material is encoded in non-verbal ways (see 'The Cloud' on pp. 231-2). Non-verbally encoded meanings may be left untouched by directly verbal interventions. This again highlights the role of the therapeutic relationship, especially as a context within which 'interpersonal signals' may be reviewed as possible samples of clients' interpersonal styles. The importance of interpersonal schemas and their role in the therapeutic relationship can now be more fully integrated into CBT. This changes CBT from being a therapy in which the therapist could appear as the stereotyped cool, detached, logic-chopping technician, to a therapy in which '*feeling* and thinking and behaving' are *all* central concerns. Therapists must have crucial awareness of how the clients' issues may be acted out in the 'here and now' of the therapeutic relationship itself, as well as in clients' lives outside therapy. Such awareness demands self-knowledge; awareness was emphasised more commonly in other therapies but is now also recognised in CBT (Bennett-Levy, 2001; Grant et al., 2004). A new impetus has also come from new behavioural models of how psychological change can be enhanced by clearer recognition of the therapist's interpersonally rewarding qualities (Tsai et al., 2009) and the benefits of 'disciplined personal involvement' with clients (McCullough, 2006).

In many ways, however, these new developments leave much of the original structure of CBT as it was. The difference lies in the quality of what goes on inside that structure. Although the interpersonal model of CBT is still developing, significant accounts of it are emerging as 'compassion-focused therapy' (Gilbert, 2009) and 'interpersonally sensitive CBT' (Wills, 2008a). Further description of all the strands of this developing approach to the therapy relationship in CBT follows in Chapters 3, 7 and 8.

Working with Cognitive Processes

CBT has developed new directions by adding to the previous focus on cognitive content (e.g., 'Something bad will happen') an additional focus on cognitive *processes* (e.g., spending unhelpfully long periods of time worrying that something bad will happen). CBT has increasingly elaborated on how these processes effect the development, maintenance and treatment of psychological problems. To some extent, this focus was evident even in Beck's early writing on 'fixation' (Beck, 1976/1989) and then in the highlighting of processes such as cognitive avoidance in anxiety, and in how rumination (continually thinking and worrying) maintains depression. Cognitive processes have moved more centre-stage as the roles of physiology in anxiety, and of meta-cognition ('thinking about thinking'), mindfulness and attention have been clarified. These new developments also chime in with parallel thinking on the need to enhance processes of acceptance, commitment and change, discussed in the final sections of this chapter.

CASE STUDY
Kevin

Kevin was a student nurse, prone to panic attacks. When he felt his pulse suddenly racing, he thought that he would collapse and believed that collapsing would lead colleagues to conclude that he could not do his job. Such catastrophic thoughts led to a growing sense of panic, with increasing physical symptoms to match. He then used safety behaviour: he sat down. After a worrisome half hour, the symptoms began to subside. Because he had not collapsed, he deduced that he had a 'near miss': sitting down saved him. This meant, however, that he could not learn that he probably never would have collapsed, and even if he had, this would not have led to the catastrophe he feared. His panic-inducing belief therefore remained intact to strike again another day. The role of physiology is also important in formulating depression, as the next example illustrates.

CASE STUDY
Jim

Jim reported that every morning he awoke feeling physically uncomfortable, stiff and 'down' and habitually thought 'Oh no, not another day feeling shit'. In response to his therapist's suggestion to 'postpone worry' until later in the morning, he found he could step back and monitor the feeling more closely, he realised that he often felt some bladder or bowel discomfort because he needed the toilet. When he went to the toilet and simply got ready for the day, he noticed that he felt less uncomfortable and 'down'. He usually forgot to return to his worry later and could then resist making negative predictions about the rest of the day. He also discussed his physical sensations on waking with his wife. Although she did not get such symptoms, she reported feeling tired in the early evening. As Jim felt better in the evening, he could redefine himself as 'different from' rather than 'inferior to' his wife. These two pieces of learning helped him to get out of the vicious cycle of depression.

Cognition and physiology

Physiological factors have always played an important role in the cognitive model, particularly in understanding anxiety (Clark & Beck, 2010). Models of anxiety have looked in greater detail at the way people interpret bodily cues (interoception), which has been shown to play a key role in panic attacks (Clark, 1986). People prone to panic attacks tend to make catastrophic interpretations of normal bodily symptoms. They are often prevented from learning that these symptoms are normal and benign by using 'safety behaviours' (Salkovskis, 1996). The following examples above illustrate how thinking about physical symptoms may be integrated into the cognitive behavioural model.

Metacognition

Traditionally, CBT has worked with the language (declarative) content of negative thoughts and beliefs. When new therapists first try cognitive methods, they often report the difficulty that the client may report being *intellectually convinced* that, for example, they are not 'stupid', yet may not be 'emotionally convinced' and thus will continue to 'feel as if' they are stupid (Dryden, 2006). This may be because traditional CBT methods that challenge the content of thought only touch the output of relevant cognitive processes, whereas it would be more effective to address the processes themselves to explore how people arrive at what they 'know'.

Metacognitive therapy includes analysis of the role individuals' thinking about their thinking plays in the development of psychological problems. For example, clients who are anxious usually have numerous negative, anxiogenic thoughts. What is of interest is not simply the content and meaning of specific thoughts, but the meaning of thinking in this particular way. Wells (2009) distinguishes between direct (type 1) worries, such as 'I will never be well again', and metacognitive (type 2) worries, such as 'Worrying like this will fry my brain'. As well as these negative metacognitive worries, problems can also be maintained by 'positive' metacognitive beliefs such as 'Worrying keeps me from nasty surprises'. Wells (2009) offers formulations and treatment plans based on a meta-cognitive perspective for a range of problems in depression and the anxiety disorders. The case of Sasha, a 43-year-old insurance clerk, illustrates this process.

CASE STUDY
Sasha

Sasha woke up worrying about the day to come, and went to bed worrying about what had happened in the day and what might happen the next day. Therapy initially focused on the distorted content of these worries, and helped her challenge her thinking. She reported that the process of evaluating her thoughts made sense in her head, but she continued to feel awful, worrying as much as ever. Therapy then moved to a metacognitive level, looking at the meaning of her worrying thoughts. She believed that not worrying would mean the things that got to her would be more likely to happen. Worrying alerted her to react quicker and would prevent terrible things happening in the first place. If she were not to attend to her worries, she might forget to do important things. Stepping outside her thought content to look at the meaning of the process was necessary before Sasha could begin to change her worry patterns.

Rachman (2003) and Salkovskis et al. (1998) offer similar analyses for clients with obsessive-compulsive difficulties, where clients believe that the fact they have 'bad thoughts' is in itself significant, proving something 'bad' about them. Bad thoughts are given enhanced significance and taken as indicating that something bad might happen, reflecting the client's excessive degree of personal responsibility for harm to self or others (Salkovskis et al., 1998). These clients often combine ritualistic behaviours, such as compulsive washing or checking, with 'neutralising', such as trying to stop the thoughts or replace 'bad' with 'good' ones. They are thus prevented from learning that the thoughts are normal, insignificant and harmless. As well as working on the specific content of thoughts, analysis of the meaning of thought processes is an additional effective and fruitful intervention.

CASE STUDY
Christopher

Christopher felt plagued with anxiety after walking past people in the street and imagining them slipping on the pavement and hurting themselves. He felt very guilty, believing that the fact he had those thoughts was as good as him wanting the accident to happen, and may even have increased the chance of accidents for which he would be responsible. If people were to slip and hurt themselves, he would not only be responsible for injury to them, but doubly responsible because he had failed to prevent catastrophe. Christopher tried to assuage his guilt by praying several times an hour.

Attentional processes and mindfulness

Shifts in perspective that help us to feel better often have a degree of mystery about them. One day we may feel preoccupied by a glitch in our lives that is going less well than we would like; yet another day we can think, as one client once put it, 'Well, it is a sunny day after all'. The ability to step back from negative thinking in a liberating way – 'decentering from' or 'defusing' it in the technical terminology – is one that comes and goes for most of us. The decentering manoeuvre, however, is particularly difficult to achieve when we are mired in the ruminative thinking so prominent in anxiety disorders and depression.

CASE STUDY
Sally

Sally suffered from a disabling combination of panic attacks and health anxiety. Interventions aimed to change the way she paid attention to her 'symptoms' at the start of the day were part of treatment designed to reduce the overall effects of these problems. Rather like Jim, presented earlier in this chapter, Sally often awoke immediately experiencing aches, pains and discomforts. She would then scan her body for other 'symptoms', often quickly reaching the conclusion that she had a major illness such as cancer. Attempts to counter this thinking via thought records proved unsuccessful, partly because the threat of cancer is a long-term one and so not easy to disconfirm. At this point, the therapist reflected on the way he himself handled this type of early morning feeling and suggested that Sally could try an experiment, during which she would merely 'notice' such symptoms on waking and postpone any serious evaluation of them until 10 am. Sally accepted the rationale for this manoeuvre: that if the aches and pains were only passing phenomena, they might well have gone by that time. This proved a revelation in that not only had such aches all but gone by that time but also on rare occasions when they did persist they were less serious and intrusive.

This relatively informal approach to attentional processes has been greatly supplemented in more recent years by the development of more systematic treatment approaches to problems of attention. In this book, we will particularly focus on mindfulness based cognitive therapy (MBCT) (Segal et al., 2002) and attentional training (ATT) (Wells, 2009), both discussed later in more detail. Mindfulness, drawing on the traditions of meditation and yoga, has developed ways of helping people view life experiences in less driven and more mindful ways. Attentional training has developed systematic ways of helping clients to shift their focus of attention while they are having negative experiences.

THE DEVELOPING MODEL OF THE THERAPY PROCESS

The scope of CBT is ever widening, both in terms of its application to an increasing number of difficulties and in terms of a wider use of therapeutic interventions within its overall structure. In this new scenario, the concept of 'formulation', described in detail in Chapter 3, becomes even more useful. If we think of the formulation as a map of client issues likely to be relevant in therapy, then we can see that it offers us many different points from which we may start and many different possible directions in which we may proceed. We could, for example, choose to proceed in the way of standard CBT and begin to work at the symptom level – the 'top down' approach. Increasing emphasis on working with emotions in CBT allows us to work in primary and direct ways with feeling, perhaps taking techniques from experiential therapies such as focusing (Gendlin, 1998; Greenberg, 2011). There is also a growing interest in working with emotions and imagery within a cognitive framework (Hackmann et al., 2011). Stopa (2009), for example, argues that imagery work has a special ability to access emotions and therefore is relevant to CBT, with many problem areas from anxiety symptoms to schema-focused issues. Beck & Emery (1985) described using imagery as a way of understanding the meaning that the client attributes to images or dreams, and also how reprocessing images can result in the development of more functional imagery.

As new ways of working in CBT evolve, rather than always starting with NATs, options to start elsewhere (e.g., with behaviours or emotions or at the deeper level of assumptions, core beliefs and schema) open out. Deeper cognitions may be less conscious than more surface-level NATs, so that this type of CBT may bear more resemblance to psychodynamic or emotion-focused therapies. The more explorative style of the schema-focused (Young et al., 2003) and 'constructivist' (Liotti, 2007) approaches put more emphasis on taking a developmental history and spending time working at that level. Assessment in CBT may now include more emphasis on historical and developmental analysis, allowing for more exploration of the origins of the client's core beliefs and schemas. This trend also allows many clients to tell their stories from the beginning, giving a bottom-up historical perspective on their difficulties.

In newer versions of CBT events in the therapeutic relationship may be used as markers, for both client and therapist, of unhelpful patterns that may be frequent outside therapy. Safran and Muran (2000) and Liotti (2007) have used ideas from both experiential and psychodynamic therapy to build cognitive-interpersonal perspectives for working with the therapeutic relationship. For example, if a client has had a poor attachment experience, then they may develop a core belief that 'people are not trustworthy'. They may carry that belief with them into therapy and 'incidents' may happen in which mistrust in the therapist will occur. In a similar way behaviour therapists have also stressed interpersonal processes – in this case related to interpersonal reinforcement (Tsai et al., 2009) and 'disciplined personal involvement' (McCullough, 2000, 2006) – that can be consciously used to enhance therapy.

Incidents when interpersonal issues surface offer golden opportunities to highlight the client's immediate 'hot' thoughts and schemas. Therapists can use the skill of immediacy to work with what is there in the room (Wills, 2008a) and interpersonal tangles resulting from such schemas can be worked through in the relative safety of the therapy setting, for example by what Young et al. (2003) call 'limited re-parenting'. New interpersonal behaviours can then be practiced in therapy sessions before being tried out 'for real' in the client's social environment.

CASE STUDY
Mary

Mary could see the origin of her 'people pleasing' and how it was driven by a lack of self-validation and self-esteem. She also identified an unhelpful assumption that 'I must work harder and harder to please people if I am ever to get respect and recognition'. Her people-pleasing style was sometimes active in therapy when she showed behaviour designed to 'please' the therapist. The therapist's supervisor advised him to look at how Mary could be more playful, first with her therapist and then with her colleagues. By saying things like 'I bet I really get up your nose sometimes', she could express empathy for others and, at the same time, get useful feedback from them. Mary's pattern was so ingrained that it took time for her to dare to experiment with being 'playful'. Yet eventually she did begin to get experiential and emotional disconfirmation of her belief. One day she refused to clear up the office. She sought feedback from a colleague by asking: 'I bet that surprised you, didn't it?' The colleague laughed and said that people would respect her more if she surprised them more often.

THE 'THIRD WAVE' IN CBT: THE NATURE OF CHANGE AND THE STANCE OF THE THERAPIST

It has been hypothesised that a 'third wave' of CBT has developed over the last decade or so, following on from the first, behavioural wave in the 1950s and 60s and the second, cognitive wave in the 1970s and 80s (Hayes et al., 2004). This has developed from clinicians questioning basic assumptions of previous CBT models:

Is change always a good thing? Is doing always better than being? Newer CBT models are developing methods based on acceptance to help clients to move between acceptance and change rather than automatically aiming for change. They are more likely to use experiential strategies, encouraging broader and more flexible client repertoires. There is more emphasis on therapists' interpersonal issues as well as those of clients. This wave is open to older traditions of mindfulness, spirituality, personal values and relationships (Teasdale, 2004). One intriguing issue is the slightly counter-intuitive role that a revitalised behavioural perspective plays in the new perspective. What does this mean in practice?

Hayes et al. (1999) have pointed out that although many people believe that they can 'get better' by changing negative patterns of thought and behaviour, these patterns are remarkably persistent and seem at times to defy rational analysis and treatment. CBT has perhaps had a default position of being overly rational in its treatment objectives, assuming that the client will want to take on board a therapy and model of change that makes so much sense to therapists. Clients may have considerable 'sunk costs' already invested in their old strategies and may even expect that therapists will design strategies that will confirm or at least be compatible with their own (Leahy, 2001). They may hope that significant others can be persuaded to do things their way and so may not be looking for a strategy based on them as active agents. Sometimes old patterns are based on lack of acceptance of problems, perhaps concealed by blaming another or in over-ambitious plans to transcend difficulties. Clients may not fully realise that change is hard work and takes a great deal of commitment. If CBT is undertaken in this spirit, it is likely to founder. Thus Hayes and colleagues (1999) have termed their approach to CBT 'acceptance and commitment therapy' (ACT). This approach demands subtle shifts in the role of therapists, including ensuring that both acceptance and commitment are tackled first before engaging in the more problem-centred and active aspects of CBT.

CASE STUDY
Don

Don came into therapy secretly resenting his partner's injunction that the only way he could save their relationship was to become a 'new man'. In the event, however, no matter how sensitive or how much of a 'new man' he tried to make himself, he could not succeed in making her want him back. Therapy had been subverted into a new version of the way he had always tried to 'win her back' before. Working on his patterns of thinking, feeling and doing *were* potentially helpful to him, and yet the goal for such work had been hijacked by his old pattern. When his therapist eventually realised that this 'putting on an identity' was not a productive strategy, it was difficult to convey this to him. It was only when Don discovered that his partner was having an affair, from even before therapy, that fury released him from this nonsensical strategy and he moved quickly thereafter towards psychological health and a new, much happier relationship.

Hayes et al. (1999) suggest that therapists who are over-reliant on rational change processes could develop a more nuanced understanding of irrational factors that can influence change. Therapists need strategies that help clients to fully accept their problems and to commit to experimentation with new styles of being. ACT therapists maintain that tracks leading to change are mined with behavioural and language traps and suggest many helpful ways of defusing such impediments throughout therapy.

A further aspect of the 'third wave' is the integration of mindfulness into CBT, not only in the form of explicit mindfulness practices such as those taught in MBCT (Segal et al., 2002), but in more mindful ways of conducting therapy. The complex relationship between acceptance, mindfulness and change is well conceptualised in dialectical behaviour therapy (DBT) for people with severe, long-term difficulties. DBT aims to teach people to examine, accept and change patterns of thought and behaviour using meditation and acceptance strategies in order to stay with, and sooth bad feelings and make informed choices about change (Linehan, 1993). MBCT is described in Chapter 8.

The full implications of these more strategic ways of thinking about CBT are still being worked through and embedded in the model. They suggest to us, however, a new angle on an old chestnut. How do we keep the clarity of the cognitive and behavioural models and yet at the same time make them flexible enough to be adapted to the differing needs of individual clients? The concepts of acceptance, commitment and mindfulness can help us to develop answers for questions long suggested for initial assessment interview (Wills, 2008a):

- What is/are your exact goal/s at this time?
- What other solutions have you tried with this problem?
- How hopeful are you that therapy can help you at this time?

CONCLUSION

Now almost 50 years old, CBT is no longer the 'new kid on the block' but is a well-established model of psychological therapy. It continues to show great vibrancy and a capacity to develop in sometimes surprising ways. CB therapists, but especially perhaps 'Beck and his group' (Wills, 2009), have always shown a capacity to listen to criticisms, and to change where appropriate. Although constructivist, schema-focused and attention-related models of CBT seem to have many differences from the original model, they also carry much of the older paradigm with them. For example, it is indeed debatable whether a true reading of Beck's earlier works does sustain the later accusations of being over-rational (Weishaar, 1993; Wills, 2009). It is probably more accurate to see the different ways of working as being on a continuum. Rather than replacing the old, newer approaches represent extensions of the original model that allow CBT to tackle a broader range of problems. The newer models have been put forward as being particularly appropriate for those difficulties with which the older model was not so successful – especially when clients have more intransigent anxiety problems, disrupted and traumatic histories and more fundamental personality issues rather than supposedly straightforward emotional disorders. It would be easy to get carried away by the excitement of the new, and dive headlong into the third wave, as if, as Paul Gilbert (personal communication) has put it, there was something terribly wrong with the first two. New developments are still consolidating and we look forward to their greater elaboration and secure location within the cognitive behavioural therapies. One particular challenge to the CBT community will come from the desirability of maintaining the relatively simple clearness and parsimony of the original model as it integrates new developments described above. We seek to respond to this challenge in this book. In the next chapters, we look at the core and well-established features of CBT: formulation and the therapeutic relationship.

FURTHER READING

The history and origins of CBT

Beck, A. T. (1976/1989) *Cognitive Therapy and the Emotional Disorders*. New York: Penguin.
Beck, A. T., Rush, A. J., Shaw, B. F., & Emery, G. (1979) *Cognitive Therapy of Depression*. New York: Guilford Press.
Rachman, S. (1997) The evolution of CBT. In D. M. Clark & C. Fairburn (Eds), *The Science and Practice of CBT* (pp. 3–26). Oxford: Oxford University Press.

New developments in CBT

Hayes, S. C., Follette, V. M., & Linehan, M. M. (2004) *Mindfulness and Acceptance: Expanding the Cognitive-behavioural Tradition*, New York: Guilford Press.
Crane, R. (2009) *Mindfulness-based Cognitive Therapy: Distinctive Features*. London: Routledge.
Wells, A. (2009) *Metacognitive Therapy for Anxiety and Depression*. Chichester: Wiley.

NOTES

1 One 'rule of thumb' is that the original score should have at least halved and have remained at that level for 2 or 3 months.
2 'Relatively' is a key word here – see later discussion in later chapters.

2

The Therapeutic Relationship and Interpersonal Sensitivity in CBT

> The CBASP (Cognitive Behavioural Analysis System of Psychotherapy) therapist must become a comrade to the patient ... Comrades are authentic people who are willing to interact on a reciprocal basis in ways that stand in explicit contrast to those of negative significant others. (McCullough, 2006: 47)

A main criticism of CBT from other therapeutic perspectives is that CB therapists pay little, if any, attention to the cornerstone of other therapies, the therapeutic relationship. Person-centred therapists view CBT approaches as being overly concerned with technique and method without taking into account the primacy of the relationship. Psychodynamic therapists dismiss CBT as not using the most important therapeutic tools of their trade, the transference and counter-transference in the therapeutic relationship (Persons et al., 1996). Somehow, many older writings on CBT give the impression that the therapeutic relationship is a mere container in which to do the real work, viewing difficulties and issues in the relationship as problems to be solved before getting on with therapy. The therapeutic relationship has been notable by its absence, at times seemingly dismissed.

These views are increasingly anachronistic and the idea that CBT does not pay attention to the therapeutic relationship may now be regarded as myth (Gilbert & Leahy, 2007; Wills, 2008a). Throughout psychotherapy, regardless of model or method, clinicians see therapy as an interpersonal and emotional endeavour, a far cry from the idea which some manualised forms of therapy might give of what Norcross describes as 'disembodied therapists performing procedures on Axis I disorders' (2002, p. 4). The development of therapy in general has provided many useful ideas that help us to understand the underlying processes of therapeutic change within the therapeutic relationship, processes that are now being actively integrated into CBT. As a result, there is a growing cognitive-behavioural model of the interpersonal process connected to the therapeutic relationship as well as a substantial focus on how to use the relationship as an active ingredient in therapy. Up until now, CBT authors have mainly focused on the role of the therapy relationship in working with 'personality disorders' and 'schema-driven problems', where the client's transference, the therapist's counter-transference and the experience of impasse in the therapeutic process all provide invaluable information for the facilitation of therapeutic movement. We will, however, argue that relationship issues can also be helpfully used to develop a more vibrant and emotionally engaged practice model for all CBT.

In this chapter, we examine how the therapeutic relationship has been viewed in the past, and how recent work on CBT has brought the therapeutic relationship more centre-stage. We describe how to build and develop collaborative relationships in CBT, and the similarities and differences between collaboration and other types of therapeutic relationship. We look at how clients' difficulties can be formulated to guide interpersonal exchanges in the relationship. We examine the problems that can occur in the relationship and ways of repairing therapeutic difficulties or ruptures.

Debates about the therapeutic relationship can be frustrating because it is often hard to get beyond clichés. Actually, the root meaning of the word 'therapy' is 'healing', so to say that there should be a 'healing' relationship in the endeavour of 'healing' people hardly gets us much further. Disagreements about the therapeutic relationship are often about different ideas of what makes for healing relationships, so that when critics say that CBT does not have a model of the therapeutic relationship they seem to mean that it does not have *their kind of* model. It may therefore be helpful to distinguish elements of the therapeutic relationship that are *involved in healing* and those that are *consciously healing in themselves* (Wills, 2012c). To get beyond clichés we must look more deeply at *how* therapeutic and interpersonal factors can be woven more fully into CBT, and hence how to enhance benefits that come from adding 'interpersonal sensitivity' into CBT (Wills, 2008a, 2009).

WHAT DOES CBT SAY ABOUT THE THERAPEUTIC RELATIONSHIP?

Traditionally, and in contrast to other approaches, the task of CBT has been defined as resolving the client's problems, as far as possible, using the tools of CBT rather than by using the therapeutic relationship per se. A good relationship had to be in place in order to do the work, and was seen as *necessary but not sufficient* for therapeutic change (Beck et al., 1979; Persons, 2008). The technical aspects of CBT have been considered its active ingredients. If the therapeutic relationship were a car, CB therapists would use it to travel from A to B, whereas psychodynamic or Rogerian therapists would be collectors, spending hours polishing and fine-tuning the vehicle. For many clients, particularly those whose problems are amenable to short-term work, a mode of transport is called for: it may be sufficient for the therapist to be warm, empathic, respectful and collaborative for the therapeutic work to proceed. For many clients, however, the therapeutic relationship itself becomes more crucial to healing. For these clients, commonly with core interpersonal conflicts (Beitman, 2003), it is likely that processes within the therapeutic relationship will prove rich sources of information for understanding them and their difficulties. It is also likely that there will be issues and difficulties in the relationship, and the travellers may well have to turn at least an occasional hand to mechanics.

It comes as little surprise that research in CBT supports what humanistic and psychodynamic colleagues have said: that the quality of the relationship is central. Various studies looking at the relative contribution of non-specific, relationship factors versus technical factors in therapy indicate the importance of both; a positive relationship makes a significant contribution to the outcome of CBT (Norcross, 2002). This evidence is sometimes used to support arguments for the equivalence of the different models of psychotherapy but this raises many unanswered questions, suggesting it may be a mistake to over-elevate the importance of non-specific factors (de Rubeis et al., 2005). It seems more likely that neither method nor relationship work in isolation, but that the combination of both is critical. Meta-analytic evidence is notoriously difficult to evaluate (Nathan & Gorman, 2007), and there is good evidence that it may downplay significant differences between therapies and, conversely, overemphasises the influence of 'common factors' (Butler et al., 2006; Clark & Beck, 2010).

Notwithstanding this fiendishly complicated debate, CBT authors have worked on ways in which therapeutic relationships can be used as active ingredients in their own right (Gilbert & Leahy, 2007; Wills, 2008a). For example, therapeutic relationships can provide arenas in which clients can identify and test beliefs about wider relationships, by practising alternative behaviours (Flecknoe & Sanders, 2004) and by learning and testing new ways of relating. As Persons succinctly says 'formulation-driven CBT is a synthesis of two views: the traditional view in CBT that the relationship is "necessary but not sufficient" to produce change and the newer (at least in CBT) view of the relationship itself as an assessment and intervention tool' (2008: 167).

THE CORE CONDITIONS

The general characteristics of the therapist that facilitate the application of cognitive therapy ... include warmth, accurate empathy and genuineness ... If these attributes are over-emphasised or applied artlessly, they may become disruptive to therapeutic collaboration ... We believe that these characteristics in themselves are necessary but not sufficient to produce optimum therapeutic effect ... the techniques in this book are intended to be applied in a tactful, therapeutic and human manner by a fallible person – the therapist ... A genuine therapist is honest with himself as well as with the client. (Beck et al., 1979: 45–49)

It is a commonly agreed assumption that the core conditions of any therapy, namely empathy, understanding, genuineness, respect, congruence and unconditional, non-possessive positive regard (Rogers, 1957), have to be in place for therapeutic work to proceed. If clients do not feel understood or respected, they cannot be expected to share their inner worlds with another and the idea of identifying and challenging their negative thoughts may seem too threatening. Leahy provides a valuable reminder of one of the key components of any therapy, being able to validate what is going on for the client: 'It is this aspect of the human condition, the recognition that we must learn to "weep for the plague, not just cure it", that is an essential component of meaningful therapy and meaningful relationships' (2001: 58). This view implies that therapists should be humble and eschew all tendencies towards omniscience. We need at times to recognise our fallibility and stand in the 'fertile void' with the client (Wills, 2008a). Sometimes human distress takes on an existential quality, so it can be comforting if another person can stay with us with good attention and at least attempt to understand our pain. Laing (1970), however, argued that even 'understanding' can pigeonhole some and limit others – a form of subtle aggression.

The importance of the core conditions was implicit rather than explicit in early models of CBT. This does not mean that Aaron Beck, for example, paid only token attention to these qualities. Throughout his work he stresses the importance of showing clients warmth, acceptance and respect, giving an impression of trust. Listening, summarising, reflecting, empathy, congruence, reflecting feelings, and all the skills that enhance warm encounters are vital to CBT, particularly in building therapeutic collaboration – enabling clients and therapists to work together to identify and resolve the client's difficulties.

These characteristics of the relationship influence outcome in CBT. For example, Burns and Auerbach (1996) focused on whether, and how, therapeutic empathy makes a difference in CBT, concluding that empathy has a large influence: a warm and trusting relationship can significantly enhance therapy and speed recovery. Keijsers et al. (2000), in a comprehensive review of empirical studies of the therapeutic relationship in CBT, identified two aspects of interpersonal behaviour clearly associated with a positive outcome. One is the group of variables associated with Rogerian therapy: empathy, positive regard, warmth and genuineness; the second, the perceived quality of the therapeutic alliance. Keijsers and colleagues point out that there is considerable evidence that CB therapists are just as supportive, perhaps even more so, than therapists using other models: 'There is no empirical evidence for the stereotype of the cognitive behavioural therapist as being more superficial, colder, or more mechanical in their contact with patients than of therapists from other psychotherapy orientations' (2000: 268). They also suggest that the fact that CBT may be quite directional does not adversely affect the outcome of therapy unless it is over-emphasised too early on. Outcome is improved if the client perceives the therapist as being self-confident, skilful and active. In a study on CBT training, a respondent makes this same point in more everyday language:

> I realized that you don't have to go in with hobnail boots on. Being directive is often just what my [drug and alcohol] clients need. Actually CBT does have the potential to be over-directive, and avoiding that is what it means to be an experienced practitioner. (Wills, 2006b: 8)

Therapists owe much to Rogers for steering therapy away from directiveness, but it is also perhaps time to distinguish more carefully between a 'directiveness' that imposes therapists' agendas and 'directionality' that allows therapists to use aspects of their knowledge base to negotiate direction with the client so that therapy does not become 'directionless' (Wills, 2008a).

Other relationship factors take into account the characteristics of the client and how these impact on therapy, such as clients' 'readiness': willingness, openness about problems, and predisposition to change and accept therapy as a means to do this (Keijsers et al., 2000). Thus, to consider what works in therapy we are always looking at interactions between the qualities of clients, therapists and therapeutic methods. The so-called 'common factors' across all the therapies (see Batchelor & Horvath, 1999) include the therapeutic relationship, the qualities of the client, therapeutic hope and expectation of change, and the technical aspects of therapy (Hubble et al., 1999). If clients perceive therapists as having positive attributes, this is likely to increase trust, inhibit drop-out, increase satisfaction, compliance with methods and make gains in therapy (Waddington, 2002). The relationship promotes hope and 're-moralisation' (Frank, 1971), which is central to effective therapy.

CBT also allows adaptation of the core conditions to maximise their helpfulness to individual clients: for example, too much empathy or warmth may be perceived as threatening to, say, a very depressed client, who may believe 'I do not deserve such caring' or 'No one understands me, why is the therapist pretending?'. Silences may be useful reflection time for many (Wills, 2008a: 152),[1] improving collaboration by allowing clients to take the lead, but could be anxiety provoking for others by reminding them of 'going blank' when teachers waited for answers. Hence, the value of formulating clients' needs so that therapists can modify the core conditions accordingly.

GOING BEYOND THE CORE CONDITIONS: DEVELOPING COLLABORATIVE CBT

> I certainly consider the therapeutic alliance as a common factor shared with other therapies. But I also believe that the shared and explicit focus on changing belief systems, reinforcing and refining reality testing, and developing coping strategies makes for a more robust therapy. (Beck, 1991: 194)

CBT uses factors that are common to many other therapies, but is more specific in how such factors are used. Alford and Beck (1997) argue that the active ingredients of many of the 'common factors' among various psychotherapies, including the therapeutic relationship, lead to cognitive change. CB therapists, however, aim to stimulate cognitive change by a more direct route. Cognitive change is achieved by developing collaborative relationships and collaborative empiricism. In the words of Beck and Emery:

> The cognitive therapist implies that there is a team approach to the solution of a patient's problem: that is, a therapeutic alliance where the patient supplies raw data (reports on thoughts and behaviour) ... while the therapist provides structure and expertise on how to solve problems. The emphasis is on working on problems rather than on correcting defects or changing personality. The therapist fosters the attitude 'two heads are better than one' in approaching personal difficulties. (1985: 175)

Collaborative empiricism helps therapists to 'get alongside' clients, so that the work of 'attacking' clients' problems will not be experienced as attacks on clients themselves. Again, in the words of Beck:

> It is useful to conceive of the patient–therapist relationship as a joint effort. It is not the therapist's function to reform the patient: rather his role is working with the patient against 'it', the patient's problem. Placing emphasis on solving problems ... makes him less prone to experience shame, a sense of inferiority and defensiveness. (1976/1989: 221)

What does this mean in practice? Beck and Emery (1985) spell out two implications:

- *The relationship develops on a reciprocal basis*: Therapists and clients are working together to reflect on the clients' ways of being and offer solutions for the difficulties they face. When clients cannot see ways forward, therapists offer different angles from which to view problems. Similarly, clients can offer other perspectives to therapists, including at times on the helpfulness of the therapists' behaviour. There is a feeling in CBT of setting out to journey and work together.
- *Avoid hidden agendas*: CBT is an explicit therapy. Therapists do not form hidden hypotheses and keep these to themselves. Instead, everything is put out 'on the table' as much as possible. If clients and therapists are working to different agendas, then it is unlikely that therapy will proceed smoothly. If therapists are trying to manoeuvre clients into seeing things from preconceived points of view (e.g., trying to get clients to be more logical) while clients simply want to feel valued and understood, again therapy will go askew. Instead, therapists are clear and explicit about what is in their minds. Clarity in therapeutic

thinking is an important therapist skill in CBT. Clarity allows both clients and therapists to know their aims and goals for moment-to-moment interactions, whole sessions and throughout therapy. Therapists admit mistakes, are open to suggestions and willing to go where the client wants to go, without colluding with difficulties.

A spirit of collaboration gives a reflective and interactive quality to sessions: the time that therapists and clients speak is ideally about equal; therapists share their thoughts about the client's thoughts, and ask for feedback. While both therapists and clients may ask questions, both work together, collaboratively and empirically, to find answers. Clients' thoughts, feelings and behaviours are reflected on, not interpreted.

The spirit of collaboration may be clearest when absent: for example, when therapists tell clients what to do or think; or come up with brilliant suggestions that leave clients cold. All therapy models have their characteristic strengths and weaknesses: the weakness of CBT is probably overly directive therapist behaviour. This is not usually authoritarian in intent, but more likely motivated by genuine desire for clients to get to better places, and at times can be helpful, but in general collaboration should come before didactic methods. Collaboration may also be absent when there are long silences in sessions; when, rather than representing meaning-laden pauses, silences leave clients high and dry, struggling with where to go next. In true collaboration, therapists help clients without being patronising or disempowering them. In developing good therapeutic collaboration, therapists should be warm, open, empathic, concerned, respectful and non-judgemental. Interesting debates are also opening out about whether there are times when therapists need to lay aside their traditional neutrality and use 'disciplined personal involvement' (McCullough, 2006).

Collaboration should be continuous and be expressed in the way we use our methods, discussed in greater detail in Part II of this book. At the first meeting we explain and discuss CBT and how we aim to focus on specific goals such as 'Being able to go out and see friends' or 'Get back to work'. Humble behavioural goals may seem less exciting than those of 'personal liberation' promised by some therapists but are usually closer to the phenomenological worlds of our clients.

Collaboration is built into the structure of sessions – effectively a 'rolling contract' is continually negotiated throughout (Wills, 2006b). Sessions are structured around agendas, discussions of homework and regular feedback. Summaries and reflection set a collaborative tone, with both therapist and client thinking about what is going on in therapy and asking about 'What went well?' and 'What are you taking away with you?'. Guided discovery through Socratic dialogue (GD/SD) is a collaborative method that enables clients to find answers and new perspectives without therapists appearing to be expert or directive. We should encourage clients to be active in therapy, and give the message that they have a central and equal role in making progress.

We share information and skills, aiming for clients to become their own therapists. Therapist statements to improve collaboration are:

- 'What shall we focus on today?'
- 'From my point of view it seems that … what do you think?'
- 'What question might you ask yourself right now?'
- 'Just to check we're both on the same wavelength, what sense do you make of what we've just been saying?'
- 'Where shall we go next?'
- 'What do you think?'

Some clients find active collaborative relationships a surprise, expecting that therapists will take a back seat and listen to whatever the person brings along, or conversely, see therapists as experts there to solve the problems. Therefore, it is extremely important to explain clearly and explicitly the ways in which CBT can work, and how teamwork is the best and most effective way of using the time, right from the beginning of therapy as part of 'socialisation' of clients. Clients' difficulties or reservations about such an approach can be discussed, so that they feel comfortable with and not surprised by this way of working. When working with more difficult interpersonal patterns, the relationship can become more central. These clients may, for example, have quite rightly found it difficult to trust key people during vulnerable periods of their lives. It is helpful to think that clients' attachments may be at least partly reworked within the therapeutic alliance (Gilbert & Leahy, 2007; Wills, 2008a). The adult attachment interview (Mikulincer & Sharer, 2007) offers useful questions to assess attachment profiles, such as asking for adjectives that clients might use to describe relationships with their mothers, fathers or other caregivers.

NEW APPROACHES TO USING THE THERAPEUTIC RELATIONSHIP IN CBT

Therapeutic relationships are not either in or not in place before the active therapy begins, but rather they are continually fluctuating, and these fluctuations can be actively used in therapy. Katzow and Safran (2007) describe a growing consensus amongst therapists of varying schools that recognises the imperative for humans to maintain relatedness. This imperative has survival value not only to the infant during the long period of dependency, but at all times. This means that the core beliefs and assumptions that people hold about life and the world are likely to be interpersonal. Gilbert (2007) has similarly highlighted interpersonal issues and concerns in his work on depression and shame. In practice, clients bring their interpersonal styles and difficulties into therapy, and these issues can be worked through in CBT just as in other models. For highly avoidant clients, for example, the whole therapy can be more about getting avoided issues onto the agenda than about finding clever solutions for those issues themselves (Wills, 2008a). Similarly, therapists bring their own beliefs and assumptions, making therapy relationships an interaction between clients and therapists, both influenced by the social and therapeutic environment, as shown in Figure 2.1. Safran and Muran (2000) argue that for therapists, mindful self-awareness plays a key role in dealing with situations where therapists and/or clients get stuck in interpersonal impasses. Mindful self-awareness helps therapists to acknowledge the stuck quality of the impasse and begin to disengage from it, and make informed interventions using immediacy (Wills, 2008a) and meta-communication, defined in Box 2.1 and illustrated in the client scenario below, in which client behaviour initially experienced as resistant became explicable in a different way.

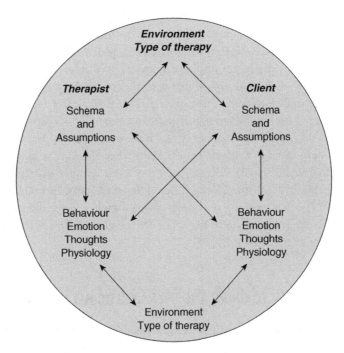

FIGURE 2.1   The therapeutic relationship

Box 2.1: Immediacy and meta-communication

Immediacy

The best way to share impressions about how people come across is by using *immediacy* (Inskipp, 1996), also termed 'you-me talk' (Egan, 1975) ... *relationship immediacy* reflects on the history of your relationship with the other person ... *here and now immediacy* uses reflections from relationship immediacy ... in the here and now with the client. (Wills, 2008: 48–49)

Meta-communication

[T]he practice of focusing on and communicating about the therapist–patient communication *as it occurs* in session ... a type of mindfulness-in-action. Through this process therapists become aware of their own feelings and actions, and make use of that awareness as they engage with the patient in a collaborative enquiry about what is going on in the therapeutic relationship. By exploring the patient's construal of events rather than continuing to react in a way that is consistent with the client's beliefs and past experiences, the therapist is able to *disconfirm* those beliefs and offer the patient a new relational experience. (Katzow and Safran, 2007: 98)

CASE STUDY
Carl

Carl could not follow instructions that the therapist gave him. When the therapist suggested either an in-session or homework task, he asked endless questions. Rather than clarify the task, these just raised further questions and difficulties, often resulting in the intervention being 'timed out'. The therapist became frustrated and found himself avoiding giving tasks because of the difficulty in explaining. The therapist's initial interpretation was that Carl was avoiding tasks. After supervision, however, he communicated his frustration and asked Carl how it seemed to him. Useful exploration followed when Carl reflected on the fact that his critical father often gave him incomprehensible instructions that could not be questioned and therefore often lead to humiliating failures in his father's eyes. This led him to the not entirely dysfunctional resolve to be more than usually active in clarifying what others wanted of him.

Motivation to maintain interpersonal connection is wired in, so much of it happens out of awareness. Like Carl, clients have frequently experienced difficult past or present interpersonal situations and develop restricted interpersonal repertoires. Such repertoires exert 'pull' so that the behaviour of others, including therapists, may be brought into 'complementary' responses by which the maladaptive interpersonal cycle is reinforced. In the case of Carl, the therapist is drawn into giving too much detail on tasks as the client himself continues seemingly to prevaricate. At these times negative schemas tend to amplify and perpetuate 'off-key' responses that drive clients' perceptions. Only when the amplifier is turned right up do others finally notice. There is not usually enough time in everyday life social situations, and perhaps few have the interpersonal skills to facilitate exploration of these moments: in therapy, both these conditions should be present. Therapists' immediate meta-communication skills would include: first, noticing the repeated negative cycle, 'This keeps happening, we are on a hook'; second, deciding how and when to put it to clients, 'Carl, I feel frustrated and wonder if we are going round in circles? What do you think?'; third, depending on the client's response, finding a way to work with the pattern, 'Perhaps we can explore how we both feel when this sort of thing comes up'.

Such interpersonal exchanges in therapy have often been discussed using the psychodynamic concepts of transference and counter-transference. Insights from other models can be gracefully received and used as valuable aids to formulating and treating clients in CBT. We examine these concepts in turn.

DEVELOPING INTERPERSONAL SENSITIVITY IN CBT: THE USE OF TRANSFERENCE AND COUNTER-TRANSFERENCE TO AID FORMULATION

The therapeutic relationship is an arena in which people behave according to their beliefs about relationships. If clients' ways of being surprise therapists, perhaps charged with emotions that seem out of context, or if the therapist feels 'pulled' into adopting a particular role with one individual client, it may that 'transference' is occurring. Translated into CBT terms, what happens in the therapeutic relationship is reflected in clients' core beliefs and assumptions and the mechanisms by which clients confirm these assumptions (Katzow & Safran, 2007; Wills, 2008a). The relationship is used as a guide to help understand and formulate clients' difficulties. Clients' reactions to therapists, and the therapy, while not forming the cornerstone of therapy, nor being deliberately provoked in CBT, provide 'a window into the real-world effects that the patient has outside therapy' (Leahy, 2001: 241) and can be seen not as obstacles in therapy but as data to set the compass of therapy by.

Leahy (2001) suggests that understanding and dealing with counter-transference is especially helpful in responding to 'resistance' to therapy. It has taken some time for CBT writers to really engage with these issues – perhaps fooled by our own propaganda that we are 'competent' to 'cure' all our clients in short order. This self-image can be especially powerful for those of us who harbour schematic doubts about competence, which may then be resolved by conducting 'power therapy' with clients. At worst CBT can seem like bulldozing clients and their problems into conformity. If clients, for example, have dependence schemas they may comply with our techniques on the surface only and therapists may be slow to notice this because of their own schemas. Leahy (2001) describes various types of resistance that are worth reading in full, but one type, 'validation resistance', can be highlighted because it is particularly relevant to a prominent downside to CBT: over-emphasising rationality and regarding client emotions as irrational. Even where CB therapists do not intend this, clients can still feel invalidated by the thrust of the model itself. Here Leahy (2001) recommends 'joining the resistance', aided once again by using the skills of immediacy and meta-communication to deal with the transference and counter-transference.

CASE STUDY
Jorge

Jorge had been complaining to his therapist for weeks about how bad life working in his college was. Having worked in a college, the therapist felt empathy but also thought it was time to 'move on'. Jorge had asked for therapy to 'retrain his brain'. The therapist initiated a Socratic dialogue that encouraged him to think about whether the people that ran his college really were the 'bastards' he described. At the end of this dialogue, Jorge wearily said 'You sound just like my Dean'. The therapist's first instinct was defensive, wanting to suggest that if Jorge were to get better, he had to shift his anger. Instead, with some effort, the therapist said 'I'm trying to find another way of looking at this but at times that must sound to you like I don't really get how bad you feel'. After a couple of minutes' silence, Jorge said 'Yes' – spoken ruefully but with a tone of thanks.

A crucial conceptual point that informs the way transference and counter-transferential interventions are framed is that there *may be* a link between clients' relationship styles in session and outside sessions. Persons' (2008) case formulation approach assumes that clients' behaviours and reactions to therapists may be influenced by their underlying problems but that clients might also have idiosyncratic thoughts and beliefs which may be driving their patterns. For example, being late for sessions or not doing homework may be driven by a number of different beliefs, such as those relating to extremely high standards, resulting in problems of disorganisation and getting things done on time; or by core beliefs of 'worthlessness', so that clients do not feel it is worth making efforts to try anything that might help. Other clients may fear dependency and so be unwilling to come to sessions on time, or work on tasks between sessions. Clients who have strong needs for advice and reassurance may have evolved specific but subtle behaviours, leading therapists to become 'friendly experts', giving advice, or doing all the work in sessions. Detecting tell-tale signs of 'transference' cognitions uses the same means as detecting in-session automatic thoughts: a sudden change in clients' emotional responses or non-verbal behaviours, such as shifts in gaze or rapid changes of topic.

While it is important to note these client reactions, it may not always be appropriate to work on them there and then, or indeed ever. It can, for example, risk that clients close down feelings and/or break off therapeutic collaboration. It may well be enough to simply notice what has happened and to 'file it away' for use on another day. This allows more evidence to accumulate and guards against premature interpretation, always a danger in therapy (Lomas, 1987). Therapists can develop helpful internal rules: for example, generally waiting for two or three instances of transferential transactions before raising them with clients. This often allows interventions to be discussed in supervision before trying them. It is worth bearing in mind that the way clients behave during sessions can be influenced by factors that are specific to therapy situations or connected to a particular session – including the possibility of therapist mistakes. Clients can be 'thrown' by interpersonal discussion, whereas therapists are more likely to 'know the form'.

The processes of schema maintenance, avoidance and compensation can also play a role in transference and counter-transference interactions. Behaviours associated with these processes perpetuate problematic core beliefs, as described by Young et al. (2003). Schema maintenance can affect the therapeutic relationship, where clients may test if therapists 'fit' their assumptions and beliefs – a process that a psychodynamic therapist might describe as a 'transference test'. For example, the belief that 'I'm boring' may lead clients to speak or behave in flat, boring ways, or selectively attend to tiny cues that therapists are finding them boring, thereby maintaining the belief. Clients with dependency issues may become passive in the therapeutic relationship, possibly evoking complimentary caring responses, which in turn maintain beliefs about the self. Clients with patterns reflecting schema avoidance may fail to do homework for fear of being 'marked' by therapists who may remind them of teachers. Schema compensation may lead therapists to mistake clients who cover up inadequacy with exaggerated self-worth as 'narcissistic'.

A good way to understand these processes is that clients' and therapists' interpersonal style can assume a real but unhelpful 'complementarity' (Kiesler, 1996). Kiesler (1996) devised the impact message inventory (IMI), which measures complementary patterns in the therapist/client dyad: for example, a dominant pattern 'pulls' on a submissive one. One common 'matching' pattern occurs when passive or uncooperative clients induce therapists to work hard and harder:

CASE STUDY
Kenneth

Kenneth was a jobbing actor. He was abandoned at an early age by his parents and brought up by his grandmother, who would tell him he was 'a poor old Joe'. He made great demands on his therapist yet hardly worked on his problems. Reflecting on how his grandma had 'saved him', Kenneth said 'She was a wonderful old thing but she was old and didn't have the energy for me at times. I learned that the only way to get attention was to make a lot of fuss'. He maintained that 'fuss and braggadocio' were the basis of his acting career – 'Though I can strut the part, I really almost never feel it.' It was some time before the therapist saw the contradictions of Kenneth's interpersonal style – until during a review of all the 'work' he had done in the therapy sessions, his supervisor simply asked 'And what work has your client done?'. To his chagrin, the therapist realised that he had hardly given that a thought.

The client's assumptions and beliefs about relationships may force the therapist into a 'damned if I do, damned if I don't' situation (Layden et al., 1993). Some clients, for example, may say that their therapists are 'too distant', but when their therapists move closer these clients might then say they now are 'too close'. This kind of feeling can also occur when working with clients whose life experiences mean that whatever others do is negatively misconstrued, resulting in a 'no win' situation in close relationships. In response, therapists can react in black-and-white ways, responding to clients' outbursts and irrational demands by eagerness to end therapy and discharge clients, labelling them as 'impossible to help'. Alternatively, at the other extreme, we might find ourselves becoming rescuers, going to unusual lengths to help clients or offering unrealistic assurances about our ability to help, inevitably leading clients to feel disillusioned or betrayed. Therapeutic relationships may bounce back and forth between over-distancing and over-involvement, mirroring the client's schemas and problems. Layden et al. (1993) describe a client who was sexually abused by someone she trusted and had learnt that it was extremely difficult to trust anyone; at the same time, she believed, from her early experience, that the only way to attain any kind of 'love' was to be violated in some way. In therapy, the client craved the therapist's affection but reacted with horror and distrust when the therapist showed signs of caring. When the therapist, in response to the client's withdrawal, acted in a more reserved way, the client jumped to the opposite extreme, perceiving the therapist as abandoning and neglecting her. Layden and colleagues (1993), describing clients with borderline features, stress that if therapists have powerful, anti-therapeutic reactions to clients, these will feed into their propensity for mistrusting the therapists. These clients can often 'zone in' on the slightest negativity in therapists' behaviours and may then test out therapists with difficult 'schema-driven' behaviours. In contrast, the process of disconfirming assumptions leads to therapeutic progress, so long as the disconfirmation is accepted and integrated by the client, allowing change in beliefs.

Using the skill of 'immediacy' (Wills, 2008a) to hold and discuss 'what-is-going-on-between-us-right-now' the client's responses can be explored: for example, saying to the client 'I'm feeling like I ought to be sorting this out for you'. Offered in a spirit of empathy and curiosity rather than judgement, such interventions allow exploration of what is going on; what the underlying beliefs might be – 'My therapist is never going to understand me, no one ever does' – and how they impact on clients' lives.

VARIETIES OF COUNTER-TRANSFERENCE AND CBT

Various types of counter-transference can be differentiated: *classical*, the therapist's transference to the client; *neurotic*, relating to the therapist's unresolved personal issues; *role*, the therapist's response to the role that the client has put him in; or *complementary*, where the therapists experience what is going on for and unconsciously communicated by clients. In CBT, counter transference is viewed as a valuable means of gaining a deeper understanding of therapeutic processes and of therapists' roles in them, as shown in the case study below.

CASE STUDY
Jill

The therapist found Jill an exacting client. She dutifully turned up for all sessions and assiduously did the tasks asked of her but resolutely failed to 'get any better'. As she had done her client duty, they both probably felt that this failure was the therapist's fault. Jill now became the classic 'dissatisfied customer' and complained about many aspects of therapy. As the therapist waited for her to arrive one morning, he found himself rehearsing his complaints against *her*, saying to himself 'You are *so* unrewarding!'. Armed with this clue to her style – and awareness that it triggered his not entirely functional need for approval – the therapist soon found a moment when the client's difficulty in rewarding others could be explored. To her great credit, she saw it straight away and was able to 'run with it'.

Much interpersonal communication takes place at a non-verbal level: subtle posture, eye contact, and tone of voice or muscle tension. Therefore, it can sometimes be hard to figure out why therapists react in certain ways. Therapists' bodily reactions, images or metaphors can provide useful clues to the conceptualisation. Diana once nicknamed one of her clients 'Malteser Man', because of her habit of buying Maltesers after sessions. On reflection, she realised that she perceived him as empty and sapping her energy. He filled his life with numerous medical consultations about his aches and pains. Having identified this feeling of emptiness, they began to formulate his problems in terms of beliefs around seeing life as 'hard work', 'It's too risky to get close to anyone' and 'The only safe place is work'. Imaging herself as a 'wise owl' served Diana well in identifying the client's need for reassurance. If, conversely, clients believe that no one can help, then they may well treat therapists with suspicion. A clue to this is if therapists find that they are trying exceptionally hard, and against all odds, to 'sell' the model to the client with 'estate agent' hats on. Supervision is the ideal place to explore these reactions to clients, and therapists often need help and support to work out the most therapeutic responses (Townend, 2005).

THE THERAPIST'S ROLE IN THE RELATIONSHIP

Deep interest in the interpersonal side of therapy is a relatively recent development in CBT. CBT models were originally developed for people with relatively short-term, discrete and specific problems. It was supposed that so long as the core conditions of the relationship were in place, the therapy could proceed without too much attention to the therapist. Some CBT models assumed that therapeutic relationship difficulties were mainly related to clients' underlying problems. However, as CBT develops for a wider range of problems, and with increased openness to emotional and interpersonal aspects of therapy, more interest is now focused on therapists' own functioning.

While examination of the therapist's own feelings and beliefs has always been explicit in other therapies, and personal therapy is seen as an essential training requirement, CBT also now pays more attention to explicit means of examining and working with our own psychological make up. Research has suggested that therapists' formulations based on their own feelings alone are not systematically related to what clients think or feel. For example, there may be significant differences between therapists' own estimates of their level of empathy, compared to how empathic clients experienced therapists to be (Burns & Auerbach, 1996). This gives emphasis to the need for frequent use of summaries and of immediacy in sessions, giving clients plenty of chance to tell therapists what they are actually feeling.

Work on the role of the therapist has developed in two main areas. First, a more explicit focus on therapist schemas in the work of Leahy (2007) and Padesky (in Kuyken et al., 2009), and second, Bennett-Levy's (Bennett-Levy & Thwaites, 2007) work on the role of personal therapy and reflection in CBT.

Therapist Schemas and Beliefs

There are a number of ways in which our schemas impact on therapy, and may cause recurrent problems in our therapeutic style or process. Leahy (2007) offers a list of 15 such schemas, including the need for approval, sensitivity to rejection and demanding standards, illustrated in the following supervisory discussions.

CASE STUDY
Ros (Counsellor)

I have worked on my own needs for approval. CBT demands more of clients and therapists compared to the person-centred model. I had this thing about asking clients to do homework. I thought they would see me as 'bossy' and that they would not like me. I'm realising that this is a useful sensitivity on my behalf but that I shouldn't let it stop me from giving homework where it would be helpful.

CASE STUDY
Meg (Nurse therapist)

I have put fear of rejection by clients as my big one. It is partly down to fear of looking incompetent in front of the doctors but it also taps into personal issues with confidence. I think it also pushes me to the self-sacrifice thing – you know, Nurse Bountiful will clean your bottom no matter how she feels today!

CASE STUDY
Phil (Psychologist)

I have been surprised by the degree of demandingness that comes up in some of my client work – come on, for God's sake, do your homework! I think that this can work out positively for therapy with some clients but for others it will just breed resistance – I am getting better at spotting it at least.

Phil's point is important – some of our schemas may impact positively on some clients but will 'mismatch' with others (Leahy, 2007). Some clients will respond to demands at some stages in therapy; Persons (2008), for example, argues for not setting the motivational bar for entry into therapy too low. At other times, if therapists are too demanding they may only build client resistance and derail therapy altogether. The need for such fine calculations further reinforces the arguments for interpersonal sensitivity, monitoring and on-going negotiation in CBT.

Therapists' schemas – as do clients' schemas – can offer good clues on why the overall strategies of therapy go off track. Leahy (2007) describes 'therapist schemas' that can militate against clear decisions on particular treatment issues. For example, sessions that repeatedly lack structure and focus and overrun may reflect therapist beliefs such as 'If I am structured, I will miss important things that the client has to say' or 'If the client gets very emotional, I have to stay with them until they feel better'. Core beliefs about being a caring person and seeing clients as needy and vulnerable may lead therapists to over-focus on empathy and allow clients to talk uninterruptedly, and not leave sufficient time for collaborative work on interventions. Padesky (1999; in Kuyken et al., 2009) describes how these attitudes are influenced by therapist beliefs, and Wills (2006b) refers to the influence of 'therapist heuristics' on learning CBT.

Other therapist beliefs include 'I should not feel bored when I am doing therapy', 'It is important that I like my client' or 'I have to cure all my patients'. Such rules are likely to interfere with therapeutic relationships: if therapists have particular feelings or thoughts that contravene their rules, then important feelings may be ignored or projected on to clients, rather than actively used and worked through in therapy. If, for example, therapists felt annoyed with clients but also believed they must never show or share this annoyance, they are more likely to think 'The client is being irritating: it is his fault so I won't let it affect me', rather than stopping and thinking what exactly is going on to provoke these feelings of annoyance.

If therapists have difficulty in empathising with certain client feelings, it may be because they cannot accept these feelings in themselves. For example, if clients are describing angry feelings towards a deceased friend, therapists may find these feelings difficult to accept if they similarly feel rage towards someone they have lost but believe that 'I shouldn't be angry'. Any strong thoughts such as 'I hate working with clients who are x' indicates that the therapist may have issues which may need looking at in order to work with that client group. If therapists are working with relatively new problems, or if they have just learned more about a problem, the long-suffering client may receive a mini-lecture on this particular disorder. The therapist's thoughts of 'I must show that I know about this problem' may lead them to try overly hard to look professional and knowledgeable.

CBT itself provides a number of tools that therapists can use to understand their role in the therapeutic relationship. These might include doing thought records to monitor what comes up for them with particular clients, observing and reflecting on work, listening to therapy tapes and identifying our own 'schema maintenance' behaviours, and trying out experiments to test out our beliefs, and take regular supervision focusing on process issues. Many CBT writers have stressed the importance of trying things out for ourselves. 'To fully understand the process of therapy, there is no substitute for using cognitive therapy methods on oneself', wrote Padesky (1996: 288). Judith Beck says that 'to gain experience with basic techniques of cognitive therapy by practising them on yourself before doing so with patients … and putting yourself in the patient's role affords the opportunity to identify obstacles that interfere with carrying out assignments' (1995: 312). Frank kept thoughts records every day for 3 months and discovered much about both their variable effects and how hard it can be to do them sometimes (Wills, 2008a). Padesky has developed training materials to enable therapists to identify and work with our own beliefs and assumptions (see www.padesky.com). All in all, we feel that we should, as Lao-Tzu advises in the *Tao Te Ching* (1993), 'yield and overcome' – in this case yield to our own fallibility in order to overcome the problems of therapist perfectionism. We should be ready to admit our mistakes, a gesture often appreciated by clients frequently burdened by a strong sense of their own fallibility. We have experienced clients to be generally very forgiving of our many eccentricities and failings.

Personal Therapy and CBT

In many counselling and psychotherapy traditions, personal therapy is seen as an essential requirement for training and practising as a therapist (Wilkins, 2006) and therapists rate this as an important aspect of training (Macran & Shapiro, 1998). Although it is accepted wisdom that personal therapy is useful, there has not been a great deal of research on its effect on subsequent therapeutic practice, nor on what learning mechanisms can explain its effectiveness (Bennett-Levy, 2006). In a review, Macran and Shapiro (1998) found that personal therapy improved empathy, warmth and genuineness, and given the importance of these factors in therapy, such improvements in themselves are likely to have a good impact on outcome.

In contrast, in the CBT community, personal therapy is not currently seen as an essential, or widely accepted, aspect of training. The British Association for Behavioural and Cognitive Psychotherapies (BABCP), while not insisting on personal therapy for accreditation, does stipulate that 'Therapists must ensure that they can identify and manage appropriately their personal involvement in the process of cognitive and/or behaviour therapy' and 'Therapists must have developed an ability to recognise when they should seek other professional advice' (BABCP, 2001).

Psychological therapists from other traditions have reported being somewhat mystified by this lack of interest in individual therapy. What they have gained from their own therapy – awareness and understanding of one's own issues and how these might impact on therapeutic relationships, the experience of being a client, a place to take difficulties which might arise during training or as a result of client work, material with which to formulate difficulties in therapy – are all seen as equally valid within CBT but have not until recently been explicitly fostered. In addition, we know that reflection is an important aspect of learning, and personal therapy provides the opportunity to reflect on both professional and personal issues. Part of the reason for the lack of focus on personal therapy may be historical: many of the 'old school' practitioners of CBT came from traditional behavioural traditions and clinical psychology, where it has not always been seen as essential or even relevant.

Given the belief in the benefits of personal therapy for therapists, it is rather baffling that there is little evidence for its overall effectiveness (Roth & Fonagy, 2004). This may be because of the way it has been implemented as a compulsory element in some training courses. This may not be a good enough reason to undertake therapy, partly because in real life therapy it is usually held as essential for clients to decide when the time is exactly right for this commitment. Other therapists have reported finding it difficult to work with a trainee who is 'just doing his personal therapy hours' – feelings of being inauthentic all round seem common. On the other side of the coin, we are also aware that undertaking therapy in this way has led to negative and even abusively exploitative outcomes for some trainees.

We are glad to report that the need for personal experience of therapy is increasingly recognised within CBT and that our colleague, James Bennett-Levy, has devised a method for facilitating such experience in a way that overcomes some of the difficulties described earlier by formatting it more for educational contexts. James has developed a training method called 'self-practice/self-reflection' (SP/SR), where trainees both provide and receive CBT with training partners and reflect in writing on the process of each session, thinking through the implications of therapy experiences for themselves, for their clients and for their CBT practice. Bennett-Levy found that SP/SR impacted on therapy in a number of ways. The trainees reported a 'deeper sense of knowing' of cognitive practices. They gained a deeper understanding of therapy, understood themselves better and demonstrated improvement in CBT skills (Bennett-Levy & Thwaites, 2007). Trainees also noted a re-emphasis on therapeutic relationship skills: the experience of being 'in the client's shoes' demonstrated starkly some of the anxieties and difficulties in making changes, even as high-functioning individuals, and served to emphasise how valuable are empathy, understanding, respect, tolerance and the guidance of the therapist (Bennett-Levy & Thwaites, 2007). The study found that SP/SR helped trainees develop self-reflection, enabling them to reflect both during and after sessions. We know that clients' perceptions of empathy are correlated with positive outcome; and if SP/SR leads therapists to be more empathic, as judged by clients, then it is likely to lead to better outcomes. Research into self-reflection and self-practice in CBT training confirms Bennett-Levy's findings, showing that trainees report substantial personal and professional gains from using SP/SR, reporting improved insight and self-awareness, and better understanding of the therapist role, the process of therapeutic change and the skills and methods of CBT (Chigwedere, 2010). Personal therapy or SP/SR may take a while to become incorporated within CBT training, but the intent to improve self-awareness in CB therapists is certainly increasingly recognised as a means of improving understanding of ourselves and of personal aspects of clinical practice.

USING THE THERAPEUTIC RELATIONSHIP TO PRODUCE CHANGE

Therapeutic relationships are powerful ways of working on the psychological difficulties that are the basis of the client's problems (McCullough, 2006; Persons, 2008; Tsai et al., 2009). Good therapeutic relationships can disconfirm negative beliefs about relationships learned early on (Katzow & Safran, 2007), and can offer the client a form of limited re-parenting, where beliefs can be directly challenged in relationships with therapists and clients can learn more appropriate and helpful relationship skills. In this way, the therapeutic relationships can be corrective experiences in their own right, particularly for clients with long-term difficulties (Young et al., 2003). Resolving alliance ruptures can provide a model to guide healing difficulties in other relationships. Wills describes how the relationship can be used to both identify and work through key client interpersonal issues evident from the formulation (2008a: 37). For example, clients who find it difficult to trust people in general can be encouraged to try trusting the therapist in small ways and observe the results, and may use these experiences as ways of learning new skills and developing new beliefs. Clients who have emotional schemas that make for difficulties in expressing emotion could test out the impact of describing their feelings about their therapists. For clients who believe that people always let them down, relationships in which therapists do their best to be trustworthy begin the process of challenging beliefs. Other ways of using the therapeutic relationship to experiment with relationship issues are described in Flecknoe and Sanders (2004). In the following case study the therapist reflects on how she used her initially unfavourable feelings about the client to construct a behavioural experiment, designed to help the client disconfirm some of the beliefs underlying her problematic patterns.

CASE STUDY
Alison

Alison would weep in sessions about how difficult everything was and how frightened she was of never being able to cope. In work with most clients this would evoke therapist empathy. However, with Alison the therapist would mentally walk away, feeling impatient and non-empathic toward her tears. Once she and Alison had established a good therapeutic relationship and worked well together, the therapist reflected how her calls for help had the opposite effect to the one Alison wanted, which in turn made her feel more desperate, and weep more. Alison's weeping, they conceptualised, was a cry for help rather than an expression of sadness. They then looked at how she might more effectively get the help she wanted, enabling her to test out therapist reactions to the changes in her in sessions, as well as her efforts to try different ways of behaving outside sessions. Gradually, weeping and wailing were replaced by more genuine expressions of sadness and fear, in turn leading to more genuine and helpful responses from others. For Alison, testing out new interpersonal behaviours within the therapeutic relationship was in itself an important arena for change.

It is easy for therapists – for whom experiences of interpersonal intensity in sessions are an everyday reality – to forget how unlike everyday life therapy can be. Part of the specialness of therapy comes from the fact that it is a place where things can be 'mulled over' in a way that people encountered in everyday life rarely have the skills to tolerate. In a way, for many clients, therapy *itself* is an on-going behavioural experiment. In contrast we have all also met 'therapy junkies' for whom sessions are so 'usual' that nothing much seems to happen in them. As we increasingly realise the importance of interpersonal awareness and responsiveness that are wired into human behaviour it is helpful to think how we can develop naturally rewarding therapist behaviours that reinforce client behaviours in the session – in a way that both aids and mirrors the therapeutic outcomes being aimed for (Tsai et al., 2009). McCullough (2006) argues that therapists need to be aware of their 'stimulus value' for clients: that is, well-delivered therapist feedback can have powerful effects. Both Tsai and her colleagues and McCullough stress that it is important for therapists to be natural and 'real' when offering interpersonal feedback: formulaic therapist clichés do not work.

CASE STUDY
Leo

Leo was a troubled client in his early twenties who had a tempestuous relationship with his father. He turned up for therapy in a raging mood one morning and almost knocked the therapist – not a notably small man – over as he barged into the therapy room. The therapist was shocked and upset by his behaviour and they exchanged quite sharp words before finally settling into the session. Leo later told the therapist that he was really shocked that he had upset him yet found this feelingly delivered feedback turned out to be a crucial turning point in addressing his deeper interpersonal issues.

CONCLUSION

Therapeutic relationships in CBT are now the focus of attention in their own right, based on interpersonal sensitivity and cognitive interpersonal models of the therapeutic process, as well as substantial work on how to use the relationship as an active ingredient in therapy. The cornerstone of CBT is the collaborative relationship, within which client and therapist work to identify and resolve clients' difficulties. Therapeutic collaboration is an empowering model, giving the message that difficulties are resolvable, and enabling difficulties to be addressed in a parsimonious, and empirical, way. We have described in this chapter ways in which the relationship can be understood and used, discussing concepts such as transference and counter transference within a cognitive behavioural framework and within the spirit of collaboration. In line with the empirical philosophy in CBT, the relationship can in itself be used to test out clients' beliefs and schemas, and provide an arena in which clients can practise new ways of being at the same time as testing deeply held interpersonal beliefs. This process may sometimes require levels of therapist self-awareness and skills that go beyond traditional therapist neutrality. As in all relationships, things do not always run smoothly, and difficulties can and do occur. In Chapter 10 we look at difficulties arising during therapy, and describe how to assess, formulate and work with difficulties. Supervision, self-awareness and high-quality training are crucial to enable us as therapists to work with process issues in CBT.

FURTHER READING

Gilbert, P., & Leahy, R. L. (Eds) (2007) *The Therapeutic Relationship in Cognitive-Behavioural Psychotherapies*. London & New York: Routledge.
Leahy, R. L. (2001) *Overcoming Resistance in Cognitive Therapy*. New York: Guilford Press.
Wills, F. (2008a) Using interpersonal skills in CBT, chapter in *Skills in Cognitive Behaviour Counselling and Psychotherapy*. London: Sage.

NOTE

1 For a wonderful literary account of the therapeutic value of silence, see Sally Vickers (2006) *The Other Side of You.*

3

Assessing and Formulating Clients for CBT

Mutual appraisal is a natural part of much human interaction. When therapists first meet clients, they seek to appraise the nature and extent of the problems clients bring (to assess); to understand the mechanisms that drive the problems (to formulate) before seeking to ameliorate those problems (to treat). Clients naturally also appraise therapists, and this can be formalised using rating forms such as those of Burns and Auerbach (1996). Assessing and formulating clients may be regarded as the 'pre-treatment phase' (Persons, 2008), though therapy can begin at any time: for example, a good initial telephone call may set up a therapeutic bond and lead to symptom relief as the client is 're-moralised' (Howard et al., 1993). The pre-treatment period usually lasts between 2–4 sessions. After that, there is a marked shift towards the more formal interventions that constitute 'treatment'.

This chapter will focus on key aspects of assessing and formulating and the relationship between them. Other aspects of 'pre-treatment', however, should be discussed first in order to clarify the whole context in which assessment and formulation take place. The verbs 'assessing' and 'formulating' are used to signal the fact that they are therapist *activities* constantly in process. The output of these activities should be regarded as provisional and open to revision throughout therapy. These activities include taking the concepts described in Chapter 1 and applying them to the situations of individual clients. As will be argued later, therapists should avoid preoccupation with the end product as some kind of perfectly correct 'true thing'; rather, it is the process of trying to understand what is happening to and with clients in a way that is helpful to them that really matters.

Two aspects of pre-treatment are particularly important. First, CBT sets particular store on a collaborative therapeutic relationship (Wills, 2008a) and this should be evident from the word go. Collaboration includes ensuring that CBT is 'suitable' for this client with this problem at this time. Collaboration also means that CB therapists may be less concerned with the absolute accuracy of assessment and formulation than with their helpfulness to clients. The chapter will therefore discuss helpful and 're-moralising' ways to communicate assessment and formulation data to clients. Whatever the form or style of assessment we follow, we should work in collaborative ways, explaining what we are asking, and why. Assessment sessions start with setting an agenda: 'I'd like to ask you about your difficulties and how they developed. I'd like to find out more about you, your past, family, work and so on. We'll then discuss how CBT works, and whether it is right for you. How does that sound?' The therapist can then start with an open question such as 'What brings you to therapy?', mindful that, on one occasion, this open question was answered by 'I came on my bike'.

Second, the 'pre-treatment' phase culminates in drawing up collaborative treatment goals to which clients can give informed consent. Clients therefore need to understand the rationale for each step of therapy. Persons (2008) recommends that clients, even when keen to give immediate consent, should be given at least some time to reflect on whether they really do want to 'sign up' for treatment. Therapists should, for example, describe what will be required of them and refer to any potential downsides of treatment. While we are now rightly keen to 'increase access to psychological therapy', we also need to promote maximum engagement with treatment. It is important to bear these factors in mind because the tone of treatment is set during assessment, and formulation and momentum for 'negotiating motivation' usually shifts away from therapists once therapy starts. The issues of client 'readiness' are nicely dealt with in the client materials for Module 1, 'Motivation Enhancement for Treatment Engagement' of Barlow and colleagues' (2011b) *Unified Protocol for Transdiagnostic Treatment of Emotional Disorders: Workbook*.

ASSESSING CLIENTS FOR CBT

Clients may arrive with a diagnosis that CB therapists, even if sceptical of diagnostic paradigms, will often review to determine if it can be safely accepted or whether other aspects may be significant. This might be termed a 'first client suitability check' – is a client with this problem a reasonable bet for CBT? As CBT is now widely applied and there is usually literature for CBT even with clients who have uncommon mental health problems, this does not necessarily rule that many clients out – though clients who are seeking 'personal growth' may struggle to use CBT. Most therapists are therefore likely to conduct a 'second suitability check' on whether CBT will help this particular client as a structured part of early assessment. It is also increasingly the case that CB therapists are likely to see clients' problems from a transdiagnostic perspective (Harvey et al., 2004; Barlow et al., 2011a).

Rogerian styles of therapy are wary of structured assessment (Tolan, 2006) and tend to receive clients 'where they are' by inviting them to 'tell their story' in their own way.[1] CBT is usually regarded as a more formal approach, and indeed CB therapists may well be following a predetermined structure for assessment. There are, for example, structured interview schedules relating to DSM (APA, 2000) diagnoses, such as the structured clinical interview for diagnosis (SCID). Other general schedules such as the adult intake questionnaire (Persons, 2008) or problem-specific ones, for example the OCD questionnaires (Rachman, 2003), can also be used. These schedules can be augmented by brief symptom measures such as the Beck Depression Inventory (BDI) (Beck & Steer, 1993). Formal methods, however, may not fit with either therapist style or client need. One therapist tried to administer a 10-page questionnaire to an OCD client three times without ever getting past the first page. We have observed Improving Access to Psychological Therapies (IAPT) programme triage workers asking preset lists of questions by telephone with great sensitivity and skill, simultaneously typing the answers directly into a database. Compromise between closed and open assessment can be achieved by using semi-structured formats of one's own design. The list of questions in Figure 3.1 and guided discovery questions can be adapted to, and used in, the assessment areas (see also Figure 5.2), both translated to the particular needs of therapists or clients. We were pleased to see the areas and questions in Figures 3.1 and 5.2 typed as crib sheets next to the telephone in the IAPT office referred to above.

Client suitability

CBT suitability criteria often include items such as 'ability to access thoughts and feelings' and 'readily make a therapeutic relationship'. Such criteria, however, often resemble those of psychologically healthy people, perhaps giving us cause to wonder if we may only see the 'worried well'. These criteria do give reasonable predictions about who will do well with CBT, but they may not tell us much about who *could* do well with CBT. We may only start to get a feel for that after several sessions (Wills, 2008a). Ilardi and Craighead (1994) suggest that it is often possible to make good predictions on outcomes of therapy from what happens in the first 4–6 sessions. Therapy reviews are discussed in Chapter 4.

Assessing current problems

Collecting a lot of detail about client difficulties can feel relentless. There are, however, good reasons to persevere, within reason. First, detail can become relevant later in therapy when the therapist needs to know, for example, how long it is since the client had a close relationship because it forms evidence on the negative belief 'I am unlovable'. Second, it can be difficult to return to items which clients are likely to assume that therapists know about – it may seem that therapists have not been listening. Third, detail on symptoms can be crucial in determining

1. Current problem

What is the problem? Give a recent, detailed example, collecting information on:
        Triggers to problem (external or internal)
        Thoughts
        Feelings
        Physical aspects
        Behaviour
        Environment

2. What keeps the problem going now?

What makes it worse? What makes it better?
Safety behaviours and unhelpful coping strategies:
        Avoidance
        Checking of symptoms or checking for danger
        Seeking reassurance from others
        Rituals
        Suppressing thoughts or feelings
        Worrying away at the problem all the time.
Hopelessness and lack of belief in change.
Other people in the person's life maintaining the difficulties:
        Lack of social support or
        Too much support and dependency.
Continuing life events and stresses.

3. How did the problem develop?

History of the problem.
What started it in the first place.
What was going on in the person's life at that time.
Is it lifelong or recurring?
Main life events and stresses.
Key themes in the individual's or family's life.
Ideas about underlying assumptions and rules.

4. Developmental history

Early life history, occupational and educational background.
Family and relationships.
Significant life events.
Themes within the family.
Medical and psychiatric history.
Previous therapy and reactions to this.

5. General health issues

Medication.
Prescribed or non-prescription drugs.
Alcohol, smoking.
History of dependency.

6. Expectations of therapy and goals

Ask about hopes or fears for therapy.
List key problems to work on.
Identify main goals for therapy.

FIGURE 3.1   Questions for gathering assessment information (to adapt to client need)

how they are best managed in treatment. Some anxiety symptoms must be tolerated for some time before any countervailing technique is likely to be worth trying (Clark & Beck, 2010). Acceptance of symptoms is therefore likely to be a helpful part in overcoming anxiety (Roemer & Orsillo, 2009). Knowing the intensity, frequency and duration of symptoms is important for any planned intervention. Such details establish a 'baseline' without which it is not possible to pick up the first signs of small improvement that often typifies psychological change (Wills, 2008a).

The importance of specific examples

Focusing initial assessment on specific examples of recent problematic functioning sharpens assessment and increases the chances of therapeutic impact in early contact – a factor known to improve the likelihood of good outcome (Persons, 2008). Such examples are usually focused on present time and problem-focused issues – in line with most versions of the basic principles of CBT (Wills, 2009). Such examples are usually uppermost in clients' minds although they have not usually been considered in detail. Exploring specific examples helps to establish difficult response patterns, typically in the form of vicious cycles of thoughts, feelings and behaviours. These patterns are intrinsically interesting, and identification usually helps to engage clients. We should, however, regard them as the most visible representations of wider strata of underlying issues and can note how vicious cycles might slot into formulations.

Use of specific examples is a good way of *bringing client issues live into the therapy room* as clients can start to feel distressed as they relate them. The presence of some distress is helpful because the therapist can discern what is most salient in the client's distress. Distress also opens up the possibility of emotional processing and healing even at this early stage. The therapist can facilitate this by getting the client to relate incidents in *first person, present-tense language*, illustrated in the following example:

> The therapist asked the client to use the present tense to describe his experience of anxiety while dealing with a car mechanic:

Therapist: So you're there … what are you wearing?

Client: I'm wearing my suit … smart … but not feeling my best … I feel tense and headachy …

Therapist: What can you see in front of you?

Client: The mechanic wiping his hands – smirking … his hands are oily – he's a skilled manual worker, not some office dude in a tie like me. He knows what he is doing but I feel a fool …

The client's negative automatic thoughts (NATs) emerge quickly and we get the sense that he really is *back there* as he talks; the emotional immediacy suggests that his description of the incident is germane to his main problems.

DISCUSSING THE CLIENT'S DEVELOPMENTAL HISTORY IN CBT

New models tend to develop in opposition to prevailing orthodoxies. Both humanistic therapy and CBT developed in contradistinction to psychodynamic models. This was especially true in how they saw the role of early experience in shaping later functioning – although Beck initially saw CBT as a new emphasis in psychodynamic therapy (Wills, 2009). CB therapists have, however, tended to show uncertainty, even guilt (McGinn et al., 1995), about being *snared* into unproductive exploration of past experience. We first look at positive ways of engaging with client histories, and second, discuss some less productive ways.

CB therapists are inevitably interested in clients' learning histories. They conjecture that NATs revealed in vicious cycles are influenced by deeper assumptions and beliefs that relate to early and later learning experiences. During Beck's interview with 'Richard' (Psychological and Educational Films, 1986), the client reveals much unhappy early childhood experience. Beck then simply asks, 'Oftentimes when people have those sorts of experiences they reach certain conclusions about life, what conclusions did you draw?' The client replies by giving near-verbatim reports on his core beliefs and assumptions. This seems like a perfect move for assessment: the client is engaged, the experiences reveal themselves as salient and material to the formulation that emerges. Such experiences might be explored with more detail and emotion later in therapy – and then by conscious choice with deliberate therapeutic purpose. In our experience, there are actually few clients for whom their history does not become relevant during at least some phase of the CBT process.

Exploring past experience does, however, have the potential to derail therapy, especially when CB therapists are drawn into what might be 'amateur psychoanalysis'. Hypotheses about the effects of childhood experience are usually speculative and complex. Therapeutic interaction can, however, turn them into reified over-generalisations (e.g., 'I am anxious because my mother was overprotective of me'). Actually, there is evidence that parenting styles do influence later propensity to anxiety, but they are neither mono-causal nor invariant (Chorpita & Barlow, 1998). Believing this can help clients – especially as an alternative to thinking 'I am anxious because I am a weak person'. The danger is not so much that clients hold an over-simplistic formulation but that therapists might do so and thereafter keep pressing the same intervention button. It seems best for therapists to remember that all formulations are socially constructed and therefore best held with a light touch. Problems can also arise when oversimplified formulations play straight into the clients' negative patterns. Clients may carry fears that their problems arise from central flaws that are 'in' them. Such negative beliefs can be particularly strong when there are family histories of psychiatric illness. This is another reason to hold historical hypotheses lightly. This problem has been well addressed by 'new behavioural' writing on depression and behavioural activation (Martell et al., 2001) with its emphasis on 'context'. From the perspective of compassion-focused therapy, Gilbert (2009) powerfully argues that if any of us had been born into certain difficult environments, the chances of significant psychological problems would have greatly increased. Many clients have, however, described experiences with other therapy by saying things like 'The therapist was only ever interested in my childhood and did not want to talk about my current problems'. Therapists should understand clients' histories, but must counterbalance this by understanding the nitty-gritty of their everyday lives in the environments in which they live. Finding out about the client's various behavioural patterns is often an excellent way of doing this (see Chapter 6).

Feeding Back Assessment Information to the Client

CB therapists are committed to eliciting feedback about therapy on an on-going basis (Wills, 2009). Ethical practice increasingly demands transparency from practitioners. We have, however, observed trainee therapists who spend so long giving rationales for procedures that they were left with little time to carry out those procedures. How then can we achieve a reasonable balance between giving the client information about assessment and overburdening them with too much? An obvious starting place is to ascertain what the client would like to know. In our experience, at the assessment stage this usually concerns three main questions:

- What is wrong with me?
- How much change can I reasonably hope for?
- How long will it take?

These are reasonable questions and therapists should give reasonable answers to them. They are, of course, complex questions and our replies need to be appropriately general: '… with other clients, I have found that … but I can't completely know that will be the same for you as yet …'. It is also necessary to be appropriately humble and provisional: 'This seems to be what it is … but we might find other things as we go along the way…'. It is often helpful to have reviews every six or so sessions during which assessment and the 'problem list' are revisited and revised accordingly.

Ending Assessment and Establishing the Problem List

Assessing the client is a continuous, provisional process, but clearly assessment activities eventually dovetail into formulation and then treatment proper. The construction of a problem list (Persons, 2008) marks a transition between these phases.

Problems emerge with greater clarity as assessment proceeds. Assessment should cover not only clients' problems but also their motivation and priorities: all three elements come together in the problem list. The list aims to include all the problems that are likely to be addressed during the therapy, usually in order of priority. It functions as an action template that in conjunction with the formulation template drives therapy and acts as a reference point for review. The problem list forms during assessment, crystallises in formulation and is periodically reviewed during treatment. Serviceable problem lists have the following features:

- they are agreed with the client;
- they have clear, unambiguous problems that can be addressed by interventions with known efficacy for them;
- they have problems that are measurable in valid and reliable ways so that progress can be monitored;
- they are prioritised in a way that allows reasonable hope of progress within the limits of the amount of therapy available.

Readers can check how these criteria map onto the problem list of a client, Alec, whose assessment and formulation are available on the author's Sage website (www.sagepub.co.uk/wills3). There are, however, likely to be many variations of the above requirements – to be exemplified here by discussion of situations where the principle of mutual agreement with the client might not hold. Therapist and client may not agree the exact nature and priority of all problems. Lack of agreement is not, however, a total barrier to treatment. For example, substance abuse may not be immediately apparent, and some clients show marked reluctance to acknowledge it. This can be difficult if therapists conclude that it is a central mechanism maintaining the problem and that progress is unlikely unless it is addressed. While client and therapist can 'agree to differ' for a time, this may only lead to more problems later (e.g. a feeling of 'abandonment' if the therapist decides that therapy is not viable). There are no easy solutions to such dilemmas but conscious clinical decision-making skills and supervision clearly can help, especially when therapists produce clear assessments and formulations.

FORMULATING THE CLIENT

Here we look at what is meant by 'formulation' in CBT, and the value of formulating. Therapists formulate at many levels and we start by looking at the 'basic level' or maintenance formulation, focusing on the clients' immediate problems in terms of interactions between thoughts, feelings, behaviour and biology within the context of their environments. We then go on to look at beliefs and assumptions that may 'run the show' and how underlying mechanisms fit into overall, longitudinal formulations. Some are generic, 'off the shelf' formulations, including transdiagnostic varieties (Barlow et al., 2011a). Finally, we discuss some of the hazards of using formulation addressing the role, pros and cons of using diagnostic systems and how diagnosis and formulation, together, can help understanding of individual clients.

What is CBT Formulation?

CBT formulations make sense of the origins, development and maintenance of clients' difficulties. They represent an overview that is essentially a hypotheses, open to testing and verification, arrived at collaboratively with clients, which then lead on to plans for monitored intervention and therapy (Persons, 2008). The idea of formulating clients' difficulties for therapy is not unique to CBT, but has been developed within other therapeutic models (Johnstone & Dallos, 2006). Formulation may indeed be a candidate for 'common factor' status in therapy (Wills, 2009).

Formulating is an active and continuing therapist task that aims to develop a working hypothesis to provide a 'map' (Persons, 2008) or overview of individual clients' problems and their origins. Such maps, made collaboratively with clients, are open to continuous modification, but act as useful guides on how to handle issues that crop up either in sessions or clients' lives outside therapy. When therapists formulate well it helps clients answer questions such as 'Why me?', 'Why now?' and 'Why doesn't the problem just go away?', as well as 'How can I get better?'.

What is the Value of Formulation in CBT?

Formulating is a cornerstone activity in CBT for a number of reasons. It provides bridges between CB theory and the practice, and helps make sense of clients' issues and difficulties. Formulation in itself is therapeutic, being a means of understanding, predicting and normalising what people experience. Formulating contributes to the structure of therapy and guides the choice of interventions and treatments. It aids collaboration and is a means of dealing with problems in the process of therapy. Therapists can also formulate their own feelings about the therapy (Persons, 2008). In these and other ways, formulation 'drives' the therapy.

- *Formulating makes crystal out of mud* by linking the theory and practice of CBT. CBT theory has been relatively clear and simple, though as we have argued, core complexities may now also be included. In practice, however, we are also dealing with the additional complexities of peoples' lives. Clients describe their problems as seemingly intractable, incomprehensible, unending and unpredictable. If clients' problems are well formulated, they become more understandable and predictable both to themselves and to therapists. Clarifying and differentiating between problems, defining apparently unrelated problems as part of one issue, or formulating a mass of issues into a smaller number of problems, helps clients to make sense of their problems and believe that change is possible. Clients are likely to feel understood and, by gaining a greater understanding of why they are the way they are, therapists can feel greater empathy towards them, thereby improving the therapeutic relationship. Formulating can be powerfully therapeutic by increasing clients' sense of control over problems, enabling them to predict future problems, thereby giving scope to avoid setbacks or relapse. Accurate formulations aid understanding of the picture for individuals rather than making generalisations based on a broad diagnosis – especially as part of a transdiagnostic approach.

- *Formulation focuses and guides therapy* and helps clients to choose from the many available strategies for seemingly unrelated problems that they bring to therapy. While one strategy might be to throw solutions at the various problems in the hope that one or more might prove effective, clients become discouraged when some interventions fail. For an individual whose anxiety can be conceptualised by a belief that relaxing and letting go is dangerous, learning progressive muscular relaxation to activate and challenge the belief may be useful. However, for another client who believes that 'If I'm anxious, I may die', relaxation may be counterproductive in that always relaxing when feeling anxious acts as a safety behaviour and prevents the client finding out that anxiety, while unpleasant, is not terminal. Formulation guides choice from the many approaches to anxiety and worry (Sanders & Wills, 2003).

  A more effective method is to base the choice of approach on an understanding of both the overt problems and the underlying mechanisms. Formulation is therefore a means of structuring and focusing therapy and enabling decisions to be made about the choice of intervention strategies and even which questions to ask when using guided discovery through Socratic dialogue (GD/SD) (see Chapter 5).

- *Formulation aids collaboration and helps deal with interpersonal problems during therapy*: Clients are actively involved in therapy by learning how to formulate problems and become their own therapists. An understanding of underlying mechanisms alerts them to particular attitudes and beliefs that might 'run the show', as well as teaching strategies for solving problems.

- Therapists formulate to understand and predict difficulties and 'off-the-ball' incidents in therapy, such as persistent lateness or non-attendance, or not doing homework. Such difficulties can be formulated in terms of the client's whole context, as understandable problems that client and therapist can work on collaboratively. Formulation helps clients and therapists to consider how particular moves and interventions may influence the overall pattern of therapy.

- *Therapists can apply the principles of formulation to their problems with clients*: By formulating our reactions to clients, we can work with difficulties that particular clients or clinical problems present (Persons, 2008). For example, perfectionist therapists may find themselves overly concerned with getting the technical aspects of therapy 'right' or using the 'right' methods even if it does not fully fit with the formulation or stage of therapy. Trying to do perfect, textbook CBT may mean we lose the sense of individual clients, and never risk forays into the murk and mess from which we may well learn something new. If therapists share the same, not altogether functional, beliefs as clients, then it can be difficult to predict difficulties or blocks in therapy, and therapists may unwittingly 'collude' with, rather than challenge, clients' assumptions. When therapists themselves find emotions difficult, believing 'I must be in control at all times', they are more likely to guide clients towards managing strong feelings rather than allow expression and explore their meaning. Having a formulation of our own views of clients' issues may be a way of avoiding such collusion.

Individual (Idiographic) Way of Formulating in Practice

Developing CB formulation is an on-going process throughout the course of therapy. It may start even before client and therapist meet. Therapists may have information about clients from referral letters, discussion with colleagues, knowledge about the problem based on training and experience, and information from contact with clients, such as telephone calls or difficulties in making an appointment. Likewise, clients will have an understanding of their problem based on their experience and knowledge, reading, surfing the net, previous experience of therapy and discussions with others. Therapists' and clients' assumptions about problems can be rich sources of material for formulation, or equally of misinformation, that needs revising.

Formulation is a shared process. At all stages, formulations are working hypotheses that may or may not be useful to client and therapist. We have seen how formulation aims to help therapists think about how things fit together, what might change and what the difficulties of change might be. Formulation also needs to have exactly the same functions for clients, hence CB therapists favour sharing as much of the formulation with clients as possible. In many instances, clients can be given a diagram or written account at an early stage of therapy to take away, 'play with' and reformulate as therapy proceeds and their own ideas develop. There are sometimes reasons not to look at full formulations until later in therapy: perhaps some clients might not follow it or, at the other extreme, some clients might treat them as excuses to 'intellectualise' problems.

Another reason to hold back aspects of formulation might occur when therapists have hypotheses about clients' underlying schemas, on which it may be counterproductive to focus on too soon, possibly because the issues raised would be too painful for the client to deal with all at once. In our experience, most clients are able to make good use of formulations in some form and we encourage therapists to err on the side of sharing. With these cautions in mind, a general principle is that sharing and discussing formulations in an overt and open way with clients is integral to the therapy process. It aids collaboration by introducing clients early on to collaborative empiricism.

Formulating Using Written Formats

CB therapists are never without pen and paper, and, ideally, whiteboards. They favour putting most things 'out on the table' and illustrate them in written formats. Formulations, often linked to key points of therapy, are illustrated, written onto a whiteboard and/or a carbon copy pad, during the session, for both client and therapist to take away and consider between sessions. There are many ways of formulating, such as by writing statements or by drawing vicious cycles, by pictures, metaphors or ready-made formulations with boxes to fill with negative automatic thoughts and underlying beliefs. Literally drawing out formulations as diagrams begins to trace out patterns and chains of different reactions in readily understandable ways and offers a means of finding points where interventions and change can start.

Information from assessment feeds the formulation process like data collection feeds data analysis in formal research: data is collated and categorised using the different orders and categories of assessment and formulation. Information from the client's history is matched with higher-order categories such as schematic functioning, core beliefs and assumptions. 'Here and now' material is matched with lower-order categories such as the 'vicious' and 'maintenance' cycles. In formulation there are also many middle-order categories, such as environmental and contextual factors. The requirement to formulate can seem daunting to aspiring CB therapists so it makes sense to allow a formulating process that builds up organically. A piece-by-piece process often allows organic formulation – which is always anyway provisional.

Formulating Clients: A Piece-by-Piece Approach

The process of formulating problems is usually described as a process of building what is known about clients into serviceable overall plans. It may, however, also be regarded as an excellent way to establish what is *not* known – *yet*. Formulations vary in content, from long narratives to short narratives and longitudinal and other diagrams (Wills, 2012a). Whatever the format, we can leave gaps – in narratives and in diagrams – for things we don't *yet* know. Trainees who castigate themselves for being 'incompetent' because they have incomplete formulations (Worthless et al., 2002) can challenge these negative cognitions by reminding themselves that all formulations are provisional and therefore incomplete and that gaps are normal and useful reminders about what next to ask clients (Wills, 2008a).

Piecemeal processes are, however, well served by systematic ways of scrutinising the pieces. Here we move toward full formulation in six steps, starting from the vicious cycle end of longitudinal formulation and working towards more schematic elements.

Step 1: Formulating at the level of vicious cycles of thoughts, feelings, behaviour, physiology and environmental factors

CB therapists look for typical response patterns to common problem situations. Standard CBT theory suggests that responses to trigger situations are mediated through cognitions, hence the key position of NATs in the vicious cycle diagram (see Figure 3.2) – interposing between triggers and emotional and behavioural responses. This inevitably oversimplifies such responses and may make it difficult for clients to understand, especially when they are not immediately aware of any negative thoughts. This lack of awareness may be due to the fact that the brain tends to process emotions more quickly than thoughts (Le Doux, 1996). This explanation may be difficult for clients to grasp, yet a more pragmatic view is hardly any less scientific – 'Let's see if we can experiment with different ways of thinking about this and see what happens'. Vicious cycles are probably most help-ful to clients when they have intuitive 'fit' with their experiences. Most people feel anxious if they have thoughts like 'I am so boring that no one could find me interesting'. When socially anxious clients have those thoughts at a party, they tend to make excuses and leave.

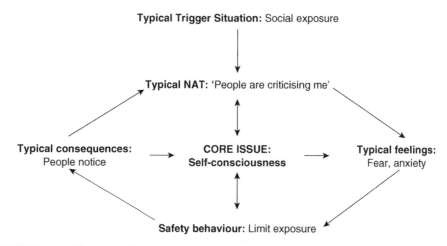

FIGURE 3.2 Vicious cycle in social anxiety

The process of testing the 'fit' of elements in the cycle also helps to generate therapist empathy for clients and clients' empathy for themselves. Therapists should, however, allow for idiosyncratic appraisals. Two clients encountered on the same day were both anxious about starting work with a new boss. One thought, 'I *won't* make a good impression on the boss' whilst the other thought, 'I *will* make a good impression on the boss but the others will see me as a goody-goody'.

Some care should also be taken to work through a range of possible emotional responses. Despite reporting anxiety, the client who fears his colleagues' reaction to how he gets on with a new boss may also report 'anger' as an emotional response. This is interesting and takes us to a different vicious cycle: for example, following the NAT 'They should not treat me like a *keener* – like the bullies at school', that would make sense of an angry reaction. At assessment and formulation these variations are noted with interest. In treatment, clinical decision-making is used to decide what to target and how to target them. Here, for example, we could challenge the anxiety making NAT with a cognitive intervention, or use an emotional intervention to facilitate expressing anger. If we have a full picture, either or both interventions are possible. Identifying behavioural responses helps clarify how their consequences may maintain the overall cycle. Socially anxious clients often try too hard to be inconspicuous – with ironic consequences of drawing unwanted attention (Wells, 2009).

Step 2: Understanding triggers

While many triggers seem conceptually straightforward, it is useful to be aware of some variations. First, there are *distal* (relatively distant in time or space) triggers and *proximal* (relatively near) triggers. For some people trying to make relationships is a distal cue that triggers a historical reaction of mistrust. A more proximal set of triggers with the same theme may, for example, include those involved in an attempt to relate to a particularly aloof person from a higher social class with an audience of colleagues at an office party. We notice that the first trigger is a general one but the second set of triggers is far more specific. As argued earlier, specific examples enhance understanding and increase the possibility of therapeutic processing. It is often helpful to ask questions about the specific moment that the negative cycle began. Knowing the specific moment helps therapists to get closer to the meaning driving client distress. For example, a client may report being upset by phone calls from an ex-partner as a general trigger but may be helped to find a more specific moment, such as when the ex-partner called without realising that it was the client's birthday – leading the client to conclude that 'It really is all over now, I will never find anyone to love again'. Therapists may find questions such as 'What was happening when the hurt really *kicked in*?' and 'What did that mean to you when that happened?' helpful in finding a specific moment of pain. For example:

Therapist: So, yesterday, it was difficult to write the essay. What went through your mind?

Client: I kept thinking 'I'm such a failure – a useless failure'.

Therapist: Did you notice when that kicked in?

Client: Well, I put all my stuff out – pens, books and all that. Then I just sat there staring at blank paper. I thought, 'You're a fake, thinking you're intellectual but producing Jack S—!'.

CASE STUDY
Jan

Jan, a female medical rep with social phobia, described being required to make a presentation to a group of doctors. She was anxious and preoccupied about this for several days beforehand, but had worked out strategies to get her through. Notice that the therapist has asked her to describe what is going on in the incident as though it is happening now.

Jan: My stomach is rumbling and I'm very nervous ... I am not too good with PowerPoint.

Therapist: What can you see in front of you?

Jan: Just tiers and tiers of people ... and I know they're all doctors and that they are all more clever than me ... Some of them are talking and others are looking bored – ... and I'm just feeling more and more nervous and panicky.

Therapist: And what is going through your mind?

Jan: I'm making a real mess of this ... they think I'm stupid ...

Therapist: So what happened next? What did you do?

Jan: I was just dying to get out ... I rushed through it as quickly as I could.

Step 3: Expanding the cycle: the role of behaviour

See also Figure 3.3. In this example, notice that from a behavioural angle Jan essentially 'cuts and runs' – in line with her belief that things are going so badly that she might as well 'call it a day' and so conserve her losses. From an interpersonal angle she has also cut off from her audience by avoiding eye contact completely.

Avoidance is a common and important safety behaviour that maintains anxiety, depression and other difficulties. Individuals may avoid going into situations just in case something bad happens: for example, staying in the house in case they collapse. Avoiding feared events may, in the short term, alleviate some anxiety. In the long term, however, avoidance prevents clients from learning how to deal effectively with situations, and neither will they learn that what is feared is unlikely to happen. Avoidance erodes confidence. Depressed clients avoid going out and doing things they previously enjoyed, believing that 'There is no point' or 'If I try to do something I won't feel any better, and that will just confirm there is something wrong

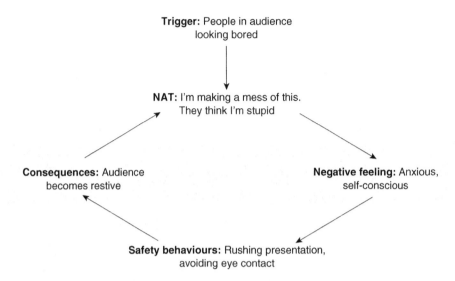

Trigger: People in audience
looking bored

NAT: I'm making a mess of this.
They think I'm stupid

Consequences: Audience
becomes restive

Negative feeling: Anxious,
self-conscious

Safety behaviours: Rushing presentation,
avoiding eye contact

FIGURE 3.3   Jan's formulation of safety behaviours

with me'. By not attempting to involve themselves in enjoyable activities, people do not get the chance to test out and disconfirm such beliefs.

When working on anxious behaviour it is important to determine the true status of hypothesised safety behaviours. The fact that distraction is sometimes helpful in dealing with negative thoughts leads to the question 'When is a behaviour a safety behaviour and when is it a useful way of getting through life?'. Many of us might feel nervous in situations like interviews, meeting partner's parents for the first time or giving evidence in court. It is quite reasonable and helpful for us to calm ourselves down by deep breathing, relaxing or by getting a good night's sleep. These strategies can all be either helpful coping methods or safety behaviours, depending on the individual's beliefs. Key questions that help us decide this dilemma are what the person believes would happen if they did not do these things, and whether they believe that such behaviours are the only ways of coping. If we know that whatever happens we will get through, and that once we start talking we'll get engaged in social events and no be so self-focused, it is likely that the anxiety will then recede and we can get on with the task in hand. This coping behaviour is now more a way of helping ourselves to feel better than a way of averting catastrophe.

Similarly, when very low, taking time out rather than attempting to deal with or fight situations may in some cases be adaptive or helpful. Taking an evolutionary perspective, depression and withdrawal may be appropriate responses when no change is possible, and the people are better off conserving their energy than wasting energy on fruitless attempts to change, or where submissive behaviour is valuable as a form of social defence (Gilbert, 2009). For example, in evolutionary terms, during long, cold winters, hibernation and not attempting to use any energy enhances survival. This does not mean that total withdrawal during depression is always a good thing, but it may help people to understand why we instinctively withdraw so they can be more compassionate towards their behaviours and become more active on a gradual basis.

Step 4: Adding physiology to complete the cycle

The fourth step in developing formulations is to include material on the clients' physical symptoms or somatic states. In anxiety, physical symptoms often predominate: the initial problem may be interpreted as 'There's something wrong with my body: I'm ill'. Formulating helps the client to explore how physical feelings interact and trigger off other components of the cycle, well illustrated by the cognitive models of panic and health anxiety (Clark & Fairburn, 1997). The following example illustrates how physical symptoms play a role in panic attacks.

The PWP records the sequence as illustrated in Figure 3.4.

CASE STUDY
Mavis

Mavis was referred to an IAPT service for low-intensity (LI) therapy for anxiety and panic attacks. She had not initially thought that she might be anxious, and did not know what a panic attack was. She had been feeling awful, with 'out of the blue' episodes of shaking, difficulty in breathing, a tight chest and tingling in her arms. She was extremely concerned that this was the beginnings of heart disease, and had been checked by a cardiologist, who diagnosed anxiety and sent Mavis off to 'sort herself out'. During initial phone contact her psychological wellbeing practitioner (PWP) asked Mavis to describe a recent example of feeling awful, in this case in the supermarket. The formulation proceeded as follows:

PWP: What was the first thing you noticed?

Mavis: I started to feel awful, really odd, completely out of the blue. I couldn't breathe, I started to get these pains in my chest and the tingling ... I felt quite shaky.

PWP: So, you were feeling really awful ... when you felt like this, what was going through your mind?

Mavis: Well, I know it's stupid since I know there's nothing wrong with me, the cardiologist said so ... but I really thought I was having a heart attack and this was it!

PWP: It sounds like you felt pretty bad, but you sound a bit embarrassed about what you made of it ... I guess it makes sense if you were feeling that bad.

Mavis: Um ...

PWP: So, you felt awful, chest pains, couldn't breathe, and you said to yourself 'I'm having a heart attack'. When you said that to yourself, how did that make you feel?

Mavis: Terrified.

PWO: And when you felt terrified, what was going on in your body?

Mavis: I guess it didn't help. I felt much worse.

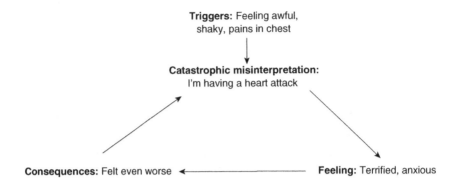

FIGURE 3.4   Sequence of panic attack

Step 5: Formulating environmental factors

All therapies aim to emphasise the unique qualities of the individual, and to understand the issues that each individual client brings to therapy in terms of an overall, holistic picture. Psychotherapy in general has been criticised for not paying sufficient attention to the wider social, environmental and cultural context in which the individual operates, and CBT is no exception (see Hays, 1995). Therefore, the formulation must always take into account the client's cultural background and environment (Tarrier, 2006). The context includes the client's gender, sexual orientation, ethnicity, family upbringing, social support or lack of, socio-economic circumstances, accommodation and employment status. We should also include in the environmental formulation positive factors in the person's life, such as good, confiding relationships, the ability to solve problems in the past and their financial status, which will facilitate rather than hinder change.

The nature and degree of reinforcement of positive behaviours are key aspects of an individual's social environment (Kanter et al., 2009). Socially isolated women with young children are at particular risk of depression; mental health correlates strongly with economic and gendered factors. Formulations must consider these, reminding therapists and clients that we do not operate in isolation, and therefore any change has to take into account the wider context (Gilbert, 2009). The cross-fertilising effects of different environmental events with personal history are shown in the case story below.

CASE STUDY
Jean

Jean presented as being profoundly depressed after a series of life events that would have tested anyone. The immediate trigger was being made redundant 'out of the blue' at her factory. Six months before, however, her husband suddenly disappeared and she discovered that he was an addicted gambler, had depleted all their money – debts that resulted in her losing her house. She had to move back to her parents and put up with an overbearing father. In response to her difficult childhood and father, she had worked hard and had built a viable life – until it was 'washed away' in a few months. A committed Christian, she compared her situation to 'the trials of Job' – it was hard to disagree.

Ways of formulating in CBT may be as varied as our clients, and require creativity on the part of therapists. Not all problems fit into vicious cycles or straight lines; for some clients, behaviour, biology or even thoughts may play little role. The challenge for therapists is to be sufficiently flexible and creative to develop a workable formulation with clients that takes into account what they say and believe, regardless of whether it fits into the CBT model in therapists' heads. A generic model, shown in Figure 3.5, integrates thoughts, emotions, behaviour and biology as well as environmental factors (Greenberger & Padesky, 1995). The model illustrates the impact of the different components on each other and means that wherever the client starts to describe his problems, the therapist can look at the other components and include these in formulations. The generic model helped to engage Jean in CBT.

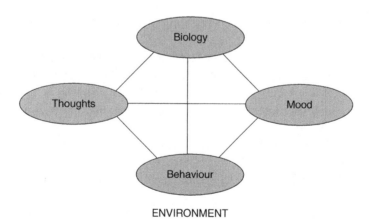

FIGURE 3.5 Generic model (© Center for Cognitive Therapy, Newport Beach, CA)

Jean: All my life I've had to 'dust myself down and pick myself up' – you wouldn't believe the things that have gone wrong. Before this I've always managed to come back, but not this time. I feel so down and think, 'There's no point – whatever I do I get knocked down again.'

Therapist: I guess anyone facing what you are would feel that way, but then feeling that way makes it hard to motivate yourself.

Jean: Yeah – The social worker said that I must apply to the council and to the housing association for a place but when I try to do the form I think, 'What's the point?'

Therapist: Well, thinking about that now, what is the point?

Jean: Well, I must escape my parents – that's really killing me. I feel like I'm 13 again … and I told you that my dad is so difficult and has always undermined me.

Therapist: I guess we can see how many things all combine to make it difficult for you and they all kind of interplay with each other – your social situation, the way you think and feel.

Jean: Yeah, I feel almost wrapped up in it all.

Therapist: [Summarising] I've drawn it up as you've been talking. [Shows her]

Jean: I see, all the bits connect together.

From discussion of this diagram, Jean decided to prioritise her housing application before trying things like job hunting, working out how to behave more proactively when depressed, and looking at her patterns of negative thinking.

All these various diagrammatic presentations are tying to show what 'underlying mechanisms' may be driving the overt symptoms (Persons, 2008). Persons (2008), in fact, prefers to use a short written statement rather than a diagram. This format and its rationale will be presented shortly, after we have considered how to factor-in the more historical elements that emerge as being related to the client's problems.

Step 6: Adding in schematic functioning and formulating unhelpful assumptions, core beliefs and schemas – a longitudinal perspective

After formulating links between thinking, emotions, behaviour, biology and environmental context, the next step is to formulate problems in terms of underlying psychological mechanisms, namely unhelpful assumptions, beliefs and schemas that relate to, and which 'drive', the problematic thoughts and emotions. Assumptions, beliefs and schemas can be understood in terms of the client's early and/or later experiences, and relevant cultural, biological and environmental factors. The client's fleeting thoughts may also be the immediate manifestations of deeper cognitive levels. If these thoughts are seen as concentric rings, then the core beliefs relating to early experience are in the centre and the assumptions and automatic thoughts are subsequent layers – which can be seen as three different levels of meaning, as illustrated in Figure 3.6.

It is, however, useful to scrutinise possible schemas, core beliefs and unhelpful assumptions and to assess the degree of 'fit' that they have with each other and with other aspects of the developing formulation. Assumptions are often rules of living in 'if … then' form, for example, 'If I can please, placate or avoid difficult people then I'll be okay'. Such assumptions may 'work' as strategies for managing a subjugation schema but are accidents waiting to happen – because they create anxiety about the

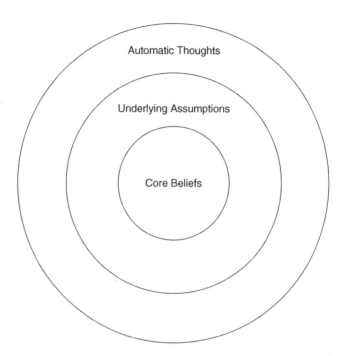

FIGURE 3.6   Levels of thoughts and beliefs (Padesky, 1995–2000. Cente for Cognitive Therapy. Reproduced with permission)

extent to which clients *are* placating people and also set up 'disaster' when placation fails. As Ellis might have said, this assumption offers an *inelegant* solution (Dryden, 1991). If clients have one schema rather than another, then a different fit between that particular schema and their assumptions would need to be elicited.

We can slot beliefs and assumptions into our formulation as they become apparent, maintaining a degree of scepticism towards the degree of causal power of client history that was advocated in assessment and continuing to scrutinise fit – now between all types of cognitions – NATs, assumptions, core beliefs and schemas. Construct validity and reliability for interpreting similar data across therapists have been found to be much lower for this level of the formulation than for the vicious cycle elements (Allen et al., 2009).

In practice, *identifying and formulating assumptions* often run in parallel with the development of a basic-level formulation but are developed more fully during later stages of therapy. Identification of assumptions involves exploring more general principles and themes involved in the client's problems as well as working with specific examples. Various sources are used to track down assumptions. These include the presenting problems, themes in therapy, diaries of negative automatic thoughts, questionnaires, the client's response to therapy or the therapist, and issues in the therapy process, and the 'downward arrow' – methods explored in Chapter 9.

Unhelpful assumptions may be dormant but triggered by particular types of event, or formed and active during low moods, disappearing when clients feel well again. If the client's life is going well, particular assumptions may hardly ever be triggered. If there is impending loss of an important person or the prospect of failure, then significant assumptions may be triggered. At these moments, clients not only deal with emotions that anyone would feel but also with latent negative feelings contained within the assumption. This double effect explains the strength of resulting feelings. Formulating underlying assumptions can help the client to understand these strong feelings better and thus be less frightened of them.

As noted previously, drawing out these patterns with pen and paper can help clients face and work with strong feelings and therefore move therapy forward. For example, some clients have the assumption 'If I go along with what people want of me I can placate them'. They can become good at placating people and even get things their way by stealth sometimes. Yet they rarely feel the satisfaction of asserting their needs and gaining things by the 'front door'. A typical chain of events connected with such an assumption was identified and drawn out on paper, as shown in Figure 3.7.

Some assumptions may be adaptive or socially acceptable and reinforced. For example, high standards and perfectionism may help some to do well in careers, at least during some periods. They may, however, cause problems when the assumptions do not fit with changes in the environment or the individual. In general, such assumptions work well when things go well – but not when inevitable downturns in fortune come along. For clients with chronic fatigue syndrome, for example, assumptions about doing well and not letting others down can inhibit recovery

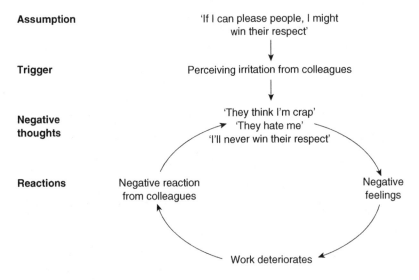

FIGURE 3.7 Formulating assumptions

from illness, leading to them 'pushing through' symptoms of exhaustion rather than allowing time to heal (Burgess & Chalder, 2005). Such assumptions can also underlie irritable bowel syndrome (Toner et al., 2000). For example, Shelley, who sought help with recurrent unexplained bowel symptoms, had extremely high standards for herself and her work and did well with her career, but became stressed and anxious as she got older, when demands of her family and natural decline in energy levels meant she could not maintain the same high standards in all areas. Her assumptions 'If I do well at one thing, I should do well everywhere' and 'If anything needs to give, it should be me' did not enable her to ease off at work and meant she kept on trying to be the 'perfect career-wife and mother' to the detriment of her health.

Formulating core beliefs and schemas brings the deepest level of cognition onto the map. While assumptions are 'if … then' conditional rules, core beliefs are absolute: 'I am bad' and 'Nobody can be trusted'. They are so negative and tyrannical that they are hard to live with. Core beliefs are not only about the self, but are also about wider concerns – about other people and the world. For example, beliefs such as 'People are never to be trusted' and 'The world is a dangerous place' may lead the individual to be over-vigilant and feel a heightened vulnerability. Core beliefs are more rigid and resistant to change than assumptions and appear from the outside as extreme, irrational and unreasonable. Hence assumptions develop that while in themselves may not be totally helpful or functional, at least mitigate the effects of the core belief 'I may be worthless but if someone loved me then I'll be okay'.

Core beliefs are relatively impervious to the impact of ordinary experience, and may be treated as facts rather than as beliefs. They may be expressed in very clear, simple, black-and-white language: 'I'm weak', 'It's always wrong to lose control'. The words may be child-like, representing primitive, undeveloped meanings that do not reflect clients' actual attributes. For some clients, what sort of person they are *not* is an important part of their core beliefs, for example, 'I am not a person who lets others down'. Negatively stated beliefs like this are sometimes easier to identify and may also be used to test out the dimensions of positively stated beliefs. They are often unhelpful and not functional, preventing the individual achieving many goals in life (Young et al., 2003).

Formulating core beliefs provides bridges between CBT and other forms of therapy that give prominence to the client's early experience. While early forms of CBT may have reacted against psychoanalysis by suspicion of exploring the past experience of clients, Beck always reserved an important role for past experience, specifically in the way that clients have drawn certain conclusions about life, other people and themselves based on their experiences (Beck et al., 1979). Therefore, as part of formulating the client's past experience, when reviewing the client's history, an important question for client and therapist to explore is: 'What conclusions do you think you drew about yourself, others and the world, based on what happened to you at that time?' These discussions may not necessarily involve vast amounts of time trawling through clients' history – clients can often answer the question 'What things that happened really sum up how it was for you at that time?' with a series of quite focused stories that contain signposts to schemas, core beliefs and assumptions.

Early Experience
Information about the client's early and other significant
experiences which may have shaped core beliefs and assumptions.

Development of Beliefs about the Self, Others and the World
Unconditional, core beliefs developing from early experience,
such as 'I am bad', 'I am weak and vulnerable', 'Others will always
look after me' or 'The world is a dangerous place'.

Assumptions or Rules for Living
Conditional statements, often phrased as 'if … then' rules, to enable the
individual to function despite core beliefs: e.g. 'If I am vigilant about my health
at all times, then I'll be safe, despite being vulnerable'; 'If I work hard all the time.
I'll be OK, despite being a bad person'.

Critical Incidents which Trigger Problems
Situations or events in which the rules are broken or assumptions are activated.

Problems and Factors Maintaining the Problem
Physical symptoms, thoughts, emotions, behaviours interacting in a 'vicious cycle'.

**Questions with which to monitor the progress of treatment based on this
formulation (Persons, 2008):**

1 Is the client following interventions discussed (monitoring his mood using a thought record, testing out alternative assumptions about the rules of relationships using mini behavioural experiments)?
2 Are the mechanisms changing as expected (are less catastrophic interpretations about being 'let down' developing and are more flexible rules of relationships developing)?
3 Do the mechanisms (negative thoughts) and symptoms (anger, depression) co-vary as expected (as more balanced thinking develop is he feeling better and are relationships running better)?
4 Are the symptoms remitting (less depression, less reported relationship problems)?
5 Are problems in the relationship interfering (does lack of trust or compulsive autonomy come up in sessions)?

FIGURE 3.8 Longitudinal formulation

THE FULL FORMULATION MODEL

While the approach described above sounds like putting together jigsaw pieces bit by bit, in practice it is more organic and flexible; formulation is a process running throughout therapy. The jigsaw is not – perhaps should not be – assembled too quickly. A large part of the process is about realising what you don't know and then asking about it. We would usually start with a basic-level formulation, putting together the pieces with the client, with the wider model in mind, thinking about underlying mechanisms might be driving the problematic experiences that have led the client to develop such beliefs about the self, others and the world. A longitudinal model of formulation (J. Beck, 1995) is illustrated in Figure 3.8. In contrast to this kind of diagrammatic formulation, Persons (2008) prefers a written statement and this is sometimes helpful in making us be more explicit about underlying mechanisms as diagram arrows can conceal a lack of clarity.[2] Persons (2008) also offers helpful questions to monitor formulation-based treatment. A written version of the same case questions with monitoring questions, follow the longitudinal 'map' in Figure 3.8.

Detailed formulations may be developed early on in therapy, or, for clients with more complex, long-standing problems, may evolve over many sessions (see Morrison, 2000). The detail in formulation can be helpful to clients, providing a substantial blame-free understanding of why they are as they are today, bridging past and present.

Using Ready-made (Generic) Formulations

CB theorists have provided an ever-increasing number of generic or 'off-the-peg' formulations, where the client problems have been seen to fall into familiar patterns, leading to the development of formulations which may well fit a range of people. For example, the model of panic (Figure 3.9) is well known, well researched and familiar (Clark, 1996) and an accurate description of the experience of panic attacks, and is therefore relevant and valuable to those who suffer from them.

Generic formulations guide the sense therapists make of clients' problems, supplemented by data specific to them, can be helpful to clients: they feel relieved that 'I'm not the only one – not mad after all'. Several generic conceptual models are referenced throughout the book. New models are continually developed; old models are revised in the light of clinical and research experience, for example metacognitive models, shown in Figure 3.10 and described in Chapter 5.

CBT is now quite far from being a young model, rather it is entering maturity. One feature of this stage is that it has been parenting a growing family of variant CBT-related approaches. This is testament to CBT's vitality but may lead to difficulty in integrating increasing numbers of new concepts from approaches such as schema-focused therapy (SFT), acceptance and commitment therapy (ACT) and

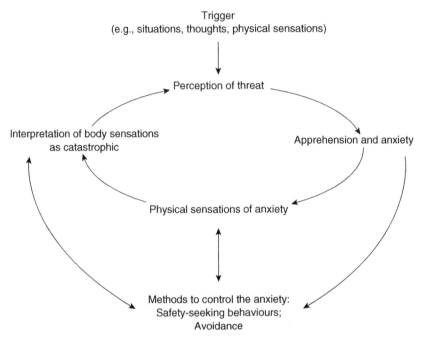

FIGURE 3.9   CBT panic formulation (Clark, 1986; Wells, 1997)

mindfulness–based cognitive therapy (MBCT) – to name but a few of the alpha-
betically challenging models. Wells (2006) offers interesting ideas on how to combine the simplicity of foundational concepts with newer and more idiographic
elements, by showing generic formats for linking material when formulating
anxiety disorders. Similarly, Barlow and colleagues (2011a) have now developed a
transdiagnostic formulation and protocol for a wide range of emotional disorders.

Jacobson and Christensen (1996) developed an approach that gives a particularly
clear illustration of the usefulness of formulating ways of change based on 'acceptance'. They designed an acceptance-based integrated couples therapy (ICT) model
developed on from their earlier behavioural couples therapy (BCT) (Jacobson &
Margolin, 1979). The earlier model was based largely on 'behavioural exchange':
couples would negotiate changing some aspect of their behaviour in exchange for a
similar response from the other. Subsequent research, however, suggested that even
when couples did this the resolution was subject to high levels of relapse in subsequent years. Jacobson and Christensen (1996) reformulated relationship difficulties
as frequently stemming from the partners' attempts to change each other's aversive
behaviours – resulting in a 'mutual trap' where both partners merely dug their heels
in more deeply. When partners could be more accepting of each other's aversive
behaviours, however, the atmosphere in the relationship improved and paradoxically truly consensual mutual change was more likely. An abbreviated short narrative
Integrated Couples Therapy (ICT) formulation is shown in the following case study.

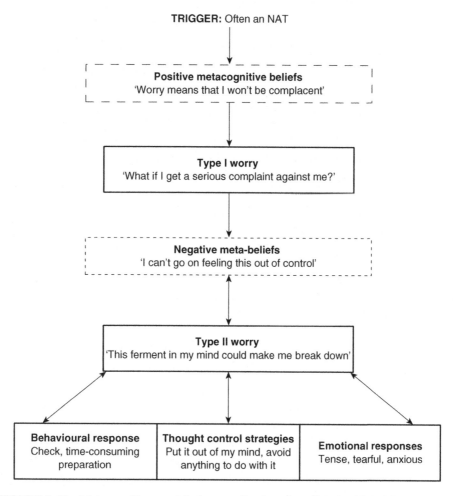

FIGURE 3.10 Metacognitive model of generalised anxiety disorder (GAD) (Wells, 2008)

CASE STUDY
Delia and Len

This couple came from very different families of origin: Len from a naval family with a 'clipped' and unemotional communication style, whilst Delia's family was warm but believed in having emotional arguments. For Len and Delia this difference became a highly problematic incompatibility that prevented them from discussing and resolving many important issues. They fell into a mutual trap wherein Delia tried to make Len reveal his emotions and Len tried to get Delia to be more rational. The more they tried to change each other the more they stuck to their original positions, bringing the relationship perilously close to falling apart.

Therapy based on this formulation used interventions that worked on Len's acceptance of Delia's emotional nature and Delia's acceptance of Len's rationality – an interesting breakthrough came when it emerged that his rationality and her emotionality were initially attractions to the other – but 'reinforcement erosion' had occurred as both partners began to find what they had originally liked could be 'too much of a good thing' after years of relationship. A therapy goal therefore developed around the need to refresh appreciation of these opposite qualities without 'devaluing their coinage'. A formulation based on the older 'behavioural exchange' concept would probably have focused on skill deficits in each partner, perhaps unwittingly reinforcing the 'mutual trap' that was now hypothesised as maintaining the conflict.

A range of approaches to formulation of mindfulness interventions is developing (Baer, 2006). Overall formulations oriented towards mindful interventions are based on the idea of bringing mindful attention to negative functioning so that this functioning is experienced from 'standing in a different place' (Segal et al., 2002) – mostly informed by a specific model of particular psychological problems (Teasdale et al., 2006). Approaches that integrate mindfulness and acceptance with traditional CBT-based formulation are now emerging (Ciarrochi & Bailey, 2008; Roemer & Orsillo, 2009).

Putting it Together for the Client: Sharing What You Know and Finding What You Don't Know

If therapy has been proceeding in a collaborative fashion, there should be no real surprises as formulations emerge. Many CB therapists make regular use of whiteboards to build up longitudinal formulations in the piecemeal way described above. It may be useful to remember, however, that diagrams use shorthand: the client is perhaps less likely to disagree because diagrams tend to under-specify the actual hypothesised relationship between elements in a diagram. For this reason, some CBT therapists have developed the practice of having both longitudinal diagrams and short narrative formulations, both given to clients (Wills, 2012a). Some do not find long narrative formulations particularly helpful, though occasionally a middle-level narrative is necessary. The process of combining diagrams and short narratives is illustrated in various case studies on the author's website link (www.sagepub.co.uk/wills3).

CASE STUDY
Alec

When Alec first looked at the formulation map, he pointed out that the arrow between his early experience and his subjugation schema did not explain what the link was. He defined this link as 'I so don't want to be like my brother that I keep my anger too buttoned down and this makes me agitated and anxious.' This idea was discussed and then added into the short narrative formulation.

TESTING ASSESSMENT AND FORMULATION

We have noted that there are varying degrees of inter-rater reliability for the different aspects of the formulation (Kuyken, 2006). It is unsurprising that this is so for schematic elements, and we have already argued for cautionary and light touch use of historical elements. Historical hypotheses are in any case very difficult to test. Though therapist agreement on formulating the more current level of symptoms is better, even here the results are not so overwhelmingly good to suggest less cautious use. Questions that test the formulation can therefore pay dividends:

- 'To what extent does the client agree with the formulation?'
- 'Is this formulation more convincing than rival explanations?'
- 'What significant issues in the client's situation does the formulation not explain?'
- 'Does formulation fit with other relevant information: measures, clinical reports and so on?'

CONCLUSION: COMBINING ASSESSMENT, FORMULATION AND EVIDENCE FROM ESTs TO DEVISE TREATMENT STRATEGIES

We noted earlier that problem lists solidify as formal assessment finishes and again as the preliminary formulation emerges. Problem lists often suggest probable goals for therapy because goals are often the 'flipside' of problems (Egan, 2002). Discussions on goal agreement are based on the key principle of collaboration and problem-focused therapy. Besides a degree of primacy afforded to the client's view, therapists use clinical wisdom and decision making, and knowledge of the evidence for empirically supported interventions (ESTs) in the problem areas (Persons, 2008) to steer therapy. These are complex and interactive factors that may become less, so as transdiagnostic formulation and treatments develop (Barlow et al., 2011a). A brief illustration of how various key factors operate is offered in Table 3.1 wherein the relationships between assessment/formulation, goal setting and intervention in the case of an individual client can be traced across the columns of the table.

The next step is to develop a treatment plan based on all that has emerged in pre-treatment. This involves considering which CBT interventions (described in Part II) may help ameliorate problems on the list. Therapists may sometimes not make sufficient allowance for other treatment elements, already or potentially impacting on the client's situation: a 'rogue intervention' element in one client's situation appeared in the form of a charismatic hypnotherapist. We have attended case conferences which identified that clients were engaged with up to 20 'helping agents' – including multiple therapists, doctors, social workers, community justice workers and others. Such conferences may suggest that the therapist presenting the case should withdraw from direct contact with the client and focus on helping the other 'treating agents' to liaise with each other. This surprising yet

TABLE 3.1 Alec's goal-setting using various sources of information

Assessment/ formulation	Client Factors	Technical interventions/ESTs
Nature/frequency/ intensity/duration of symptoms. Attitude to self. Functional analysis of specific situations. Nature/frequency/ intensity/duration of symptoms. Client history. Interpersonal behaviour in sessions. Response to therapist instructions. Response to marker events in therapy, e.g., reviews.	Problem list: 1. Lack of assertiveness 2. Low self-esteem 3. Anxiety symptoms 4. Depressive symptoms	Cognitive restructuring/Beck's (1995) CT. Fennell's (1999) application of CT to LSE. Compassion-focused therapy (Gilbert). Assertiveness training/CBT. Anxiety management/exposure treatment.
	Underlying mechanism/s: As Alec was brought up he had to cope with massive and unhelpful over-involvement by his brother. His mother was sympathetic but could not stand up to his brother to help Alec. Alec's confidence was undermined, especially when he needed to assert his wants and needs. The mechanism is continued today by his brother's behaviour and by any situations that remind Alec of the issues he faces with his brother.	Schema-focused interventions. Emotional processing of traumatic memories. Imagery restructuring. Narrative therapy.
GOAL SETTING:	1. To respond to trigger situations with more effective responses based on assertiveness. 2. To build a more positive image of self. 3. To use CBT to reduce anxiety score by at least 50%. 4. To use CBT skills to reduce depression score by at least 50%.	Use behavioural rehearsal and role-play to practice handling difficult assertiveness situations. Review new learning cognitive restructuring and compassion-based interventions to build self-concept. Use thought records and behavioural experiments to reinforce efforts to manage anxiety and depression better.

sound outcome becomes more possible when assessment and formulation considered all the psychological and environmental factors impacting on the client's wider social field.

FURTHER READING

Bruch, M., & Bond, F. W. (1998) *Beyond Diagnosis: Case Formulation Approaches in CBT*. Chichester: Wiley.

Eells, T. D. (1997) *Handbook of Psychotherapy Case Formulation*. New York: Guilford Press.

Persons, J. B. (2008) *The Case Formulation Approach to Cognitive Behaviour Therapy*. New York: Routledge.

Tarrier, N. (2006) *Case Formulation in Cognitive Behaviour Therapy*. London: Routledge.

NOTES

1 Thorne (2003: 21) tells the fascinating story of the experience in therapy that led Rogers to this view.

2 George Kelly found 'personal construct' theory after asking what the arrow between the S (stimulus) and R (response) diagram really meant (Bannister & Fransella, 1986).

PART II
CBT PRACTICE

In these chapters on CBT practice, after looking at beginning and generally structuring CBT, we will focus on specific methods of intervention. The first of the chapters on methods covers interventions aimed at explicit cognitive modification of automatic thoughts, beliefs and thinking processes. Subsequent chapters will focus on behavioural methods, emotional change, mindfulness and schema change respectively. The final chapter discusses process issues such as difficulties and endings. For each element of conscious intervention, we discuss how to choose specific methods and techniques according to the client's formulation, and how technical and experiential approaches are used in practice.

4

Beginning and Structuring CBT

CBT is, by reputation, characterised by methods and techniques. As well as the essential therapy tools of comfy chairs and tissues, CB therapists are armed with whiteboards, audio recorders, pens and paper, thought diaries, activity schedules, questionnaires and, in the case of the client with phobias, esoteric items in pots such as spiders or wasps. Perhaps the technical aspects of CBT led to the characteristic criticisms: that it is mechanistic, stressing techniques at the expense of emotions, concentrates methods rather than therapeutic processes.

Some of the early models of CBT *did* stress the verbal and rational at the expense of the emotional and interpersonal (Safran, 1998; Wills, 2008a), yet the more rational, verbal and behavioural techniques of CBT should not be rejected completely. The use of formulation in CBT, as well as more recent developments in the therapeutic relationship and the role of emotion, allow a more sophisticated approach, using a range of powerful tools of proven effectiveness so clients can understand and tackle their particular difficulties. Also there is growing understanding of how methods work, integrating both rational and emotional aspects in order to produce change, enabling people to think and *feel* differently. A careful formulation, within a collaborative therapeutic relationship, allows more mindful selection of approaches for individual clients. The selection takes account of both the evidence for problems in general and the client's specific needs. In addition, CBT helps clients to learn new skills that can be applied to different problems, and thereby to cope better with future difficulties. In other words, the therapy aims to provide people with a toolkit for life. The goal of CBT therapy is not simply to make clients think and behave differently or feel better today, but for many years to come. We are not simply fixing problems but also teaching ways of finding solutions (Padesky, 1993: 12).

Although there are longer-term versions of CBT such as schema-focused therapy (SFT), the default mode is still for relatively shorter-term therapy, and this gives an imperative to set the tone of CBT at the start and to stay on track thereafter. This chapter will therefore focus on setting an early tone for CBT by introducing CBT elements such as structure and rationale and then keeping on track by the conscious use of structure negotiated to the needs of the client.

THE PRE-TREATMENT PHASE

Matching Techniques to Clients' Formulations

> The whole of any system of psychotherapy is more than the sum of the parts. (Beck, 1991: 196)

In order to facilitate both rational and emotional change, CBT has evolved specific methods, such as guided discovery through Socratic dialogue (GD/SD), thought records, weekly activity schedules and behavioural experiments. CBT can also use methods from other therapeutic disciplines, such as imagery and metaphor, Gestalt techniques of role-plays and two-chair dialogues, and methods of mindfulness using aspects of meditation practice. Judith Beck (1995) clarifies the model's principles, one of which is that CB therapists can choose from a variety of therapeutic techniques as long as the model's basic principles are kept: the techniques should fit with the model of therapeutic change and be based on the individual formulation and 'cognisant of the objectives in the current portion of the session, in the session as a whole, in the current stage of therapy, and in therapy as a whole' (1995: 284).

Much development in CBT techniques has evolved in response to particular clinical problems. For example, the use of activity scheduling and thought records has proved to be valuable in depression; the hyperventilation provocation test has evolved to help disconfirm clients' fears in the treatment of panic disorder. However effective the techniques may be for general problems, the approaches should always be allied with clients' experiences in particular. It is easy for CB therapists to work systematically through the repertoire of approaches, or throw techniques at problems in the hope that one or other will work. A common observation of trainee CB therapists is that the approaches used in a session may be based on those learned the previous week. Thus, before introducing any 'trick of the trade' the therapist needs to ask:

- 'What is the problem here?'
- 'What kinds of things are likely to help?'
- 'How does using this approach fit with this person's individual formulation?'
- 'Am I just using this because I don't know what to do next or it's a new approach I've just learned?'

This is not to say that therapists cannot use general approaches for specific problems. For example, working through well-researched methods that have been shown to work with particular problems is reassuring to clients, giving the message that their problems are manageable and that a set of effective solutions is available. In addition, protocols developed for particular problems have proven effectiveness. But the introduction and use of techniques have to be matched to the individual, and 'sold' to the individual in terms of their formulation (Persons, 2008).

Emphasis on techniques in CBT raises questions like 'What happens if they don't work?' and fears that clients then feel even more hopeless and be put off CBT for life. The risk of engendering hopelessness highlights the importance of client–technique matching. The very depressed individual may be only too aware of negative thoughts, but unable even to begin to look for alternatives. Production of a thought record too early in therapy risks exacerbating the person's low mood, and we therefore more usually start with behavioural methods, aiming to help the person become more active. People with somatic problems commonly report that they have no negative thoughts, just symptoms (Sanders, 2006). In this case, introducing thought records may put the client off what the therapist has to offer. The introduction of techniques needs, at all times, to be a 'no-lose' experiment.

Information about how clients approach different therapeutic tasks can be valuable to the formulation, aiding the identification of underlying assumptions and beliefs. For example, if clients consistently agree that thought records would be useful but somehow do not do them, client and therapist can collaboratively work together to identify what is going on. Does it reflect the client's fear of 'failing' at homework tasks or their belief that 'Nothing will help so why bother?'. Is the client agreeing with the therapist in a passive way to prove that the therapy is rubbish?

When trying to figure out what might be the most appropriate way to match method to clients we can take note of:

- *What stands out in the client formulation?* – Such as especially noteworthy symptom features, signs of exaggeratedly negative thinking, emotional dysregulation, restricted behavioural repertoires, especially difficult social circumstances, or salient early history.
- *What stands out in the client's responses to items raised so far?* – Does the client show any facility to recognise thinking patterns? What is their 'emotional vocabulary' like? Are they doers or procrastinators?

For example, if clients can recognise ways of thinking and there is a central issue related to the way they think, then there are indications that cognitive work might be used effectively early in therapy. As noted earlier there is good reason to regard early symptom reduction as contributing significantly to overall therapy outcome (Ilardi & Craighead, 1994). Unfortunately, there are also likely to be paradoxical aspects to matching methods to clients. Measures like Epstein's cognitive experiential self measure (Epstein, 1998) and the Myers–Briggs type indicator (MBTI) (Bayne, 1997) discern differences between, for example, 'thinkers' and 'feelers' but the literature accompanying such measures often stresses the desirability of 'balance': 'intellectualisers' may need more feeling and 'intuitives' can benefit from more contact with their cognitive processes. It may not always be necessary to use an actual measure to assess these dimensions – most therapists can identify how clients balance between their emotional and cognitive processes. The key is how the client is experiencing and thinking about these things and it is usually possible to discuss it in a collaborative way with clients, using questions such as:

- 'Some people can rethink these negative thoughts but that seems difficult for you. Why do you think that is? Is it worth persisting with?'
- 'So the alternative thought does not seem to cut it for you – what else can we try?'
- 'You find it hard to "accept" the anxious feeling in order to overcome it, what happens when you try?'

THE IMPORTANCE OF STRUCTURE IN CBT

Both Aaron Beck (Beck and Emery, 1985) and Judith Beck (1995) have spelt out the principles of CBT and have included the use of structure as an important principle. Some of the other principles – a present time problem orientation, a preference for short-term work, using homework, collaboration, feedback, education and problem solving – cohere with the use of structure in a particularly powerful way (Wills, 2008a). These different attributes give a pronounced focus as CBT infolds. The initial stages of therapy start with contact between therapist and client, and then work through a formal assessment phase, towards developing a provisional formulation. Engagement in these stages involves introducing the client to a spirit of collaboration, working in a structured and focused way, and gaining feedback. Engagement in therapy is a key issue. Therapists engage clients with a collaborative working style that emphasises the use of continuous feedback, and gives clients a clear rationale for what therapists and therapy aim to do. This CBT style is taken into the assessment process, which aims to appraise not only the client's overall situation but also her capacity and willingness to engage with the model.

After the assessment phase, subsequent sessions follow a structure that familiarises clients with therapy and so promotes their ability to use it actively. Working in this way, we lay the foundations for the therapeutic work with the spirit of CBT present throughout. Table 4.1 is an overview of the CBT process as a whole, not as a rigid structure, but illustrating the process of the therapy through from assessment and formulation to using methods for therapeutic change and endings. In the following sections we focus on first contacts, engagement and goal-setting, and end with an overview of the essentials of CBT structure: agenda-setting, feedback, recording sessions and homework.

Frank's doctoral research investigated the problems trainees experienced whilst learning CBT and established that difficulties with structuring CBT sessions were prominent amongst such problems. Conversely, trainees stressed that the greatest gains to their practice came from being more structured and focused (Wills, 2006b, 2008b).

TABLE 4.1   Structure of CBT across sessions

Session number	Main focus
Assessment	Initial meeting: Collect information about problems, maintenance factors and background. Beginnings of simple formulation. Engaging client in CBT, showing collaboration. Education about CBT. First 'homework' (e.g., reading about CBT or diary).
1	Formulation: Building up a model. Engagement and socialising about how therapy works. Homework focusing on collecting information, e.g. thought diaries and/or activity diary.
2–4	Continuing formulation, engagement and socialisation: Working with information to start change, e.g., identifying negative thoughts and how to change these and/or activity scheduling in depression.
5–7	Using cognitive and behavioural methods to produce changes: thought challenging, beginning behavioural experiments.
8–9	As above, but beginning to identify and work with assumptions and rules. Testing out rules verbally and through behavioural experiments.
10–11	As above, introducing ideas of ending therapy. Looking at what client is learning and able to do outside sessions. Generalising learning to other problems and client's life.
12	Ending: Blueprint for ending. What client has learned and how to tackle future difficulties. Issues around endings.
Six-month follow-up*	Review progress, troubleshoot difficulties and solve future problems.
Yearly follow-up*	As six months. Dealing with final ending.

Note: *Follow-up sessions depending on the individual client and/or service setting.
Source: Adapted from Wells (1997) and Beck (1995)

The main cause of problems was that trainees, especially those trained in other models, often felt that structuring therapy was a bit like 'bossing clients around'. This view acted as a problematic 'therapist belief' (Kuyken et al., 2009). Rather than force trainees into something they do not believe in, it seems that CBT trainers would be well advised to allow trainees to 'play with' CBT first and explore the differences between being 'directional' rather than 'directive'. Greenberg (2011) makes an interesting point about conflict between 'following' or 'guiding' clients, suggesting that therapists should get in an optimum 'proximal zone' in relation to clients' development – being either too far ahead or too far behind will inhibit progress. These points suggest that finding a way of 'doing CBT structure' that is comfortable to aspiring therapists is a vital but variable factor in successful training. If CBT cannot be adapted to personal style and values, then dissemination will be limited.

INITIAL CONTACTS: WORKING COLLABORATIVELY AND GAINING FEEDBACK

Contact between client and therapist often starts before the first therapy session. Exactly how the first contact is made depends on the setting in which therapists work. Clients may call first to make general enquiries or to refer themselves. Either client or therapist may initiate contact after referral systems put them in touch. As this kind of contact is usually conducted on the telephone, it is often relatively brief and geared towards setting up the first face-to-face session. The first session then comprises formal assessment.

During initial contacts, collaborative work may consist mainly of taking an open stance towards the client: 'Is there anything about therapy, or about me, that you'd like to ask about or discuss at this stage?' In our experience, many clients opt to wait for face-to-face contact before engaging in such questions. Nevertheless, the opportunity has been offered and a degree of openness established. Some clients do raise valuable and important questions at this stage. Despite a growth in public knowledge about therapy in recent years, there are still areas of misunderstanding, raising questions such as 'Can talking really help?' and 'How long will the therapy go on?'. Although it is probably best to regard these questions as requests for information, therapists will also be aware of getting a glimpse of clients' world-views. While these glimpses are mainly noted and put aside for another day, there may be some occasions when useful therapeutic work can be done at an early stage. The following telephone conversation between Bill, referred for depression, and a counsellor in his GP's practice, illustrates how Bill's secondary appraisal of his problem, feeling stupid for feeling depressed, may interfere with his motivation to even get to the first face-to-face session.

Bill: I wonder if I'm wasting your time. I sometimes think that it's all so trivial …
Therapist: Sometimes it seems hardly worth bothering with?
Bill: I'm just letting things get to me, it's so stupid …
Therapist: Is that what you say to yourself about how you're feeling, it's stupid?
Bill: Yes, it is stupid really.
Therapist: Can part of you imagine not letting things get to you like this?
Bill: … Mmm … Yes, some days I can …
Therapist: Perhaps one thing we might work on is getting those days more often …
Bill: … Mmm … Yes [*uncertainly*] … it would be hard, though …
Therapist: Yeah, it may be hard … Worth giving it a go? … What do you think?

In this example, it could be tempting for a CB therapist to explore Bill's thoughts about being 'stupid', but the therapist does not dive in, rather he allows a more gentle exploration of what might be possible at this stage. During initial contacts, we aim to be as clear and explicit as possible about what is involved in therapy. An information sheet or booklet describing CBT, individualised to the setting, can answer many questions (Horton, 2006). The BABCP produces a leaflet called 'What Are Behavioural and Cognitive Therapies?' with basic information (see www.babcp. org), adaptable to individual work settings. A clear summary of what to expect is also helpful: 'I'd like to meet up for an hour to discuss what your current problems are.

I'll ask about your background and circumstances, and then we'll have a chance to talk over whether CBT is right for you at the moment. How does that sound?'

Beck et al. (1979/1989) stress the importance of gathering on-going feedback regularly, especially at the end of each session. Feedback is also a good 'marker' to end an initial contact, with questions such as 'How do you feel about the sorts of things we've discussed during our call?'.

Persons (2008) argues for the benefits of a clear, boundaried 'pre-therapy' phase. This pre-therapy phase consists of building a therapeutic relationship, assessment, diagnosis, initial formulation and treatment planning: all culminating in obtaining informed consent. She makes the point that the client may be 'desperate to get on with it' at this moment but that therapists should be wary of being pushed into 'starting' without adequate preparation, especially without getting well considered consent from the client. We may facilitate better client motivation by inviting clients to 'sign up' for various requirements. At first blush, this may offend our sense of wanting to increase access to therapy, but a nuanced pre-therapy phase can help us to get the best of both worlds – making it as easy as possible to start pre-therapy but require some motivation and commitment to get on to therapy proper.

GIVING A RATIONALE FOR CBT AND MAKING THERAPY RELEVANT

There are several different ways to give rationales for CBT, depending on the client and the type of problem. The key aim is to make it relevant to clients, so that they can see clearly what CBT has to offer for their particular issues at this particular time. Rationale giving varies from didactic to more organic explanations as therapy proceeds. In the didactic approach, the therapist explains the principles of CBT in a direct way, as a teacher might do with an evening class. This is particularly useful where the client has a clear problem and is likely to find the possibility of a stand-ard 'treatment' reassuring. For example, a client suffering from panic attacks may clearly match the 'textbook' model for both problem and solution. Therefore, the rationale may involve explaining CBT in terms of aiming to help the client get her fears into perspective, and to work on different segments of the panic vicious cycle. Working with depressed clients, therapy may be explained in terms of helping the client to break two vicious cycles contributing to the depression: low levels of activity and negative, depressed thinking. For many clients with 'diagnosable' problems, where more standard approaches apply, it is helpful for them to know that the problems are both recognisable and soluble using well-known formulas. In contrast, for clients with complex problems, rationales may need to be highly individual and develop an increasing fit with the client's situation as therapy proceeds. Events themselves may prove grist to the mill of organic rationales: a client may, for example, rush to get to the session and reveal thoughts about wanting more time for important things, and these ideas can be woven into a rationale.

Rationales are usually most effective when pitched at situations with which clients are familiar and where the therapy is clearly seen to match their needs. Judith Beck describes the process: 'the therapist explains, illustrates … the cognitive model with the patient's own examples … He tries to limit the explanations to just a couple of sentences at a time' (1995: 36). The therapist explores a situation that is characteristic of the client's problems, discussing the specific emotions and thoughts in detail. A common example is to ask clients what they were thinking about on their way to therapy. These thoughts are often rather anxiety provoking – 'Will I perform well?', 'What if he thinks I'm wasting his time?' – and can be easily linked to subsequent anxious feelings and behaviour. The method is demonstrated in the well-known 'Richard' videotape (Psychological and Educational Films, 1986), where Beck begins the session with a discussion of how Richard felt while waiting for the session to start.

Personal examples can be used to introduce clients to the basic CBT model, by asking how thinking such a way might make them feel, and how feeling such a way might make them think. Such an exploration leads on to a discussion of how focusing on the client's patterns of thinking might alter mood or behaviour: for example, asking 'What if you were to think x instead of y in that situation?'

In the dialogue below, Alan is a 39-year-old man who works for the Health Service. He refers himself because of what he describes as stress at work. The therapist has asked Alan to describe in detail a recent episode of feeling very low.

Therapist: So, think of a recent time when you felt really bad.
Alan: Okay, yesterday morning.
Therapist: Was that a typical morning, like you feel when you're low?
Alan: Yes, the same old story for me.
Therapist: Talk me through what happened. What was the first thing you noticed?
Alan: I was trying to get out of bed and get up. I felt, like, leaden. Heavy. I just wasn't going to make it. I felt, what's the point? I was thinking about how weak I'd become, how I used to be able to cope, and look at me now.
Therapist: So, you felt really heavy, leaden, and low?
Alan: Yes.
Therapist: And when you felt that, you had a number of thoughts: 'I'm not going to make it, what's the point? I've become weak, I used to be able to cope'? [*writes these down*]
Alan: Yeah, really negative.
Therapist: And how did thinking that way make you feel?
Alan: Crap, complete and utter crap. Like lying in bed all day.

We then use the example to illustrate the model. Note how Alan spontaneously goes into sentence-completion mode, showing that he recognises himself in the description of depression, which in turn encourages the therapist to move quickly into CBT work.

Therapist: The basic idea of this is that the way we see the world, see what is happening to us, has a big influence on …

Alan: How we feel.

Therapist: Yes. There are probably different ways of seeing things and some seem to help us more than others … If you're depressed, you seem to develop a kind of negative bias (*Alan*: [*nodding*] Yes) … not see some of the good things (*Alan*: Yes) … and focus on the bad. (*Alan*: Yes, that's me) Does that make any sense to you?

Alan: Yes, yes … I would think so … because I feel at one time I could take the knocks a bit more, … If anyone said I'd done something wrong then I could shrug it off quite easily.

The therapist recognises that Alan is sensitive to criticism, and asks for a specific example of when he felt criticised. Alan describes a meeting at which he had to present a report. He felt criticised and depressed, and this led to him taking two days off work. Reviewing the evidence of the comments that were made, however, revealed that these had been 80 per cent neutral, 10 per cent negative and 10 per cent positive.

Therapist: So there were an equal number of positive and negative comments?

Alan: I would say so … but, I don't know, I seem to grasp, take hold of the negative things more.

Therapist: Remember what we said before – a feature of depression is that you do over-focus on the …

Alan: Negative.

Therapist: I mean do you think it is possible that happened on this occasion?

Alan: It's possible.

Therapist: [*laughing*] You're looking at me incredibly unbelievingly!

Alan: No, no … it probably is what happened … it seemed though that they made more emphasis on the negative … or at least I thought they did.

In the above example, the therapist brings this opening phase full circle by referring back to the original rationale: 'what we said before'. The client's final comment expresses doubt about his appraisals – an indication that he is beginning to see them as hypotheses rather than facts. This constitutes a good 'base camp' from which the therapeutic exploration can proceed. Although it is only a first session, Alan immediately gains some symptom relief, which helps to engage him in therapy.

By contrast, the next dialogue offers an instance in which a laboured rationale quickly runs into the sand. The client, Beti, is 20 years old and a regular clubber. She is feeling suicidal, following a humiliating relationship break up. The therapist tries to offer her a rationale close to her experience.

Therapist: If you were going to a club with a mate and she thought, 'I've got to get off with someone tonight or it'll be a disaster', how do you think she'd be feeling as she went in?

Beti: Nervous. She'd be worrying if she'd meet someone.

Therapist: Yes, that's right. If you were with her and were thinking, 'I'd like to meet someone tonight … but if I don't, I can enjoy the music, have a laugh, whatever …' How would you feel?

Beti: More relaxed. Not so worried.

Therapist: So can you see that the way you see things does affect how you feel about them?

Beti: Mmm …

Therapist: And which of you might enjoy yourself more?

Beti: Depends on which one of us met someone …

Therapist: And which of the two of you might stand the best chance of meeting someone, do you think?

Beti: Well, that would depend on which of us was the best looking.

In retrospect, the therapist moved on too quickly from the client's uncertain response to his question about the effect of the 'way you see things'. Moving on did not allow Beti's doubts to be properly explored. The client's final comment, though showing an admirable realism, does perhaps indicate other areas that would need to be addressed. The need to address other areas would not rule out a CBT approach, but would suggest strongly that individualised packaging might be needed.

There are two important points to remember about giving a rationale. The first is to keep it brief and generally to keep to a 'three-sentence rule': therapists do not say more than three consecutive sentences during dialogues and constantly seek client feedback as they proceed. The second is that client queries about and objections to the rationale should be welcomed and openly discussed in an explorative way: we want clients to be convinced within their own frames of reference, not from the power of therapist logic. By asking for and discussing feedback, therapists start from the basis of collaboration and empiricism.

USING A PROBLEM LIST AND NEGOTIATING THERAPY GOALS

The 'problem list' is a concept that has been taken into CBT from behavioural therapy. It is usually developed in initial sessions as a simple list of the areas that clients find problematic in their lives and to focus therapeutic work. Clients and therapists usually keep the problem list in written form so that it can be used in reviews of progress during the course of therapy. A matching list of goals for therapy can also be negotiated at the end of the assessment. While problem lists define what issues are to be focused on, goals specify where the person would like to be at the end of therapy. It is a good chance for both therapist and client to check that they are working together with the same ends in mind, and that their goals are realistic.

Persons (2008) offers some good pointers on how to develop effective problem lists. They should aim to be comprehensive but not too daunting for clients; about

5–8 items seem ideal, especially if clients understand that this is a 'normal' number. Whilst problem list making should strive towards collaborative agreement, it does not imply that therapists passively accept clients' lists – care needs to be taken over problems such as substance abuse that are less likely to be reported because of shame. Sometimes the 'elephant in the room' should be acknowledged.

CASE STUDY
Will

Will was a patrician client who was suffering from a profound depression in the wake of a failed relationship. His usually immaculate appearance suffered as his depression deepened. It is said that one can always recognise the rich from their shoes – no matter how much they 'dress down' in other respects – and whilst Will continued to sport Gucchi shoes, his hair took on a distinctly unkempt ambience. The male therapist – not exactly a style icon himself – did eventually summon the courage to discuss this with Will. He was 'amused' by the discussion that led on to a focus on self-care, helping him to come out of depression and into another relationship.

It is also helpful to build a sense of priorities into the problem list. Problems that threaten life and limb usually take the highest priority. Threats to the therapy itself must also figure high on the list because 'it is hard to do therapy with people who don't turn up'. Generally speaking, higher priority may be accorded to 'best value' problems, where relatively quick gains that can build confidence are likely. One must also be aware of possible 'hazardous problems', which though important may be best tackled at another time because of their capacity to destabilise the client's life. An example follows.

CASE STUDY
Maria

Maria was a psychology student who had been feeling depressed for some time. She took a module on psychopathology during her final year and realised that she had some quite profound phobias that were probably underlying her depression. These phobias would normally be treated by exposure therapy, but by the time she presented for therapy it was just before her final exams. Her therapist explained that exposure could be very unsettling in the early stages and she decided that this was not a good time to begin. They therefore used a general introduction to CBT mood-management techniques to help in the short term and found information about specialist treatment available in the area to which she intended to move after her exams.

The best goals are *specific* and *measurable*. If, for example, someone comes into therapy with the goal of 'changing my life' or 'getting out of debt', then we need to specify exactly what goals could be met as part of therapy, and specify manageable and measurable steps such as 'Reducing the frequency of panic attacks so I can get out of the house and look for work', 'Stop spending money as my only way to comfort myself when I feel low'. Many people say that their goal is to 'feel better'. This can be translated into smaller goals, which can then be measured during the course of therapy, as the following illustrates.

CASE STUDY
Ann

Ann was a mature student of history. She had battled with anxiety for two years since starting the course, and at times felt too panicky to get to lectures. She had suffered from periodic anxiety since having leukaemia in her twenties but had always managed to cope on her own before, but now sought help from a student counsellor.

Counsellor: [*Summarising towards the end of the assessment session*] You have told me a lot about yourself today, and the anxiety you've 'battled with' for the past two years. We've talked about how it started and what's been keeping it going. It's really helpful to have a clear plan of where we're going in our work together, and what you'd like to get out of coming to see me – can we talk about that now?

Ann: Sure.

Counsellor: We'll first summarise the problems you're bringing today: panic attacks which you get every week or so.

Ann: Yes, depending on the pressure of my college work.

Counsellor: So, we'll write 'Panic attacks triggered by work pressure'? [*Ann nods*] … and 'Feeling anxious and uneasy a lot of the time'? (*Ann:* Yes) We'll add the consequences of the panic attacks and anxious feelings …

Ann: Not being able to get on with work when I feel anxious, and not getting to lectures.

Counsellor: Yes. [*Writing them down*] So, we have four main areas: panic attacks; feeling anxious; not getting on with work; and not getting to lectures. [*Shows Ann the list*]

Ann: Mmm, sounds a lot.

Counsellor: It must look daunting. What is really helpful too is to look at where you'd like to be as a result of therapy, what are your goals?

Ann: I'd like not to have panic attacks, or at least know what to do when I get them, and not feel so anxious all the time … just feel better, I guess.

Counsellor: So, we can write down 'Reduce frequency of panic attacks' and 'Know what to do when I do get panicky'. As to 'Not feel so anxious all the time', what would be different for you if you didn't feel so anxious? Can we translate that into a specific goal or two?

(Continued)

(Continued)

Ann:	I could get on with my work and get it in on time, at least most of the time, and I'd get to lectures rather than staying at home when I'm anxious.
Counsellor:	Our goals, therefore, are: 'Get on with work better'; 'Get my work in on time'; 'Get to more lectures' [*writes them down*]. What about 'Feeling better', how would we know you were feeling better? What would you be doing?
Ann:	I'd spend less time worrying about work and be able to go out and see friends more, and not have to agonise over work all weekend.
Counsellor:	A goal might be 'Going out and seeing friends at weekends'. More play time, perhaps? [*Ann:* Definitely!] Anything in particular you'd like to be able to do, that you're not doing because of the anxiety?
Ann:	I go to a salsa class but not for ages. That would be a good goal for me, I guess.

Ann's problem list and goals are shown in Table 4.2.

TABLE 4.2 Ann's problem list and goals

Problem	Goal
Panic attacks.	Reduce frequency of panic attacks.
Feeling anxious all the time.	Know what to do when I get panicky.
Not being able to go out when feeling panicky.	
Not being able to work.	Not feel so anxious:
Not getting work in on time.	Get on with work.
Avoiding lectures.	Get my work in on time.
	Go to lectures.
	Feel better:
	Not work at weekends.
	Go out more with friends.
	Re-start salsa dancing.

Goals need to be manageable and ones that can be met in or as a consequence of therapy. They need to be achievable within the timeframe of therapy, given service organisation or other constraints, and given the history and issues of particular clients. People with long-term problems who have received different forms of treatment and therapy may have over-ambitious goals, believing CBT to be an opportunity for a miracle ('I'm hoping you'll be the one person who can sort me out'). Other clients may have extremely small or negligible goals ('I don't know, really, I just came along because my GP told me to. I don't really expect anything to work'), reflecting hopelessness that anything can change. We therefore need to be realistic about what is possible, raising hope without being overambitious.

Notice that in Ann's goal list above there is a mixture of both goals that *reduce* problems and negative symptoms and goals that *build up* positive behavioural responses. Positive behaviours are known to be more productive and motivating to clients (Persons, 2008). Clients do not necessarily want to clear all the problems on the list and may instead go for more realistic goals, for example, reducing the intensity of certain negative symptoms. Formulation and goal-setting operate alongside each other and may well shift in tandem during therapy. The great strength of problem lists and goals is that they enhance parsimony in CBT: all parties are clear about the direction in which therapy is headed and can therefore work towards those goals rather than being side-tracked by less relevant issues. Goals are best reviewed regularly, and measured to see how far they have been met, or whether they need revising or breaking down into smaller sub-goals. The downside of problem lists is that they may exclude exploration of issues that may later prove essential. Some problems, especially perhaps those with personality or schema-driven dimensions, may only emerge later in therapy. It is therefore important to regard the list as not cast in stone, but as provisional and amendable.

In practice, therapists from different models may use problem lists and goals in different ways. Those with a leaning towards behavioural work may well use the problem list frequently. Others may get the feeling articulated in a Paul Simon song: 'The nearer your destination, the more you keep slip-sliding away', and be wary of over-focusing on 'problems' and failing to identify client strengths. Over-focusing on 'problems' may also hold the danger that one may miss new themes and issues. Where a therapist feels a strong ideological resistance to focusing on problems, it may be useful to examine what that discomfort is about. Equally, where there is a strong tendency to focus on problems at the expense of new material, it may be useful to try to detect in oneself any sense of discomfort with spontaneity. Thus, working with problem lists and goals requires balance between maintaining a structured focus and being flexible enough to move from the defined issues into uncharted territory as and when therapy requires. A useful rule of thumb for therapists is that, if therapy is moving off defined goals, it is important to check clients' preferences for continuing in this new direction, or getting back to the previously defined goals.

USING MEASURES

Once we have defined where we are going, it is helpful to have clear ideas about how we will know when we have arrived. Obviously, what clients tell us about what they are doing is an important measure, but in addition, more formal measurement process helps both parties to evaluate progress. Measures can help to keep us on track and to check on how useful therapy is proving. Most clients will happily fill out inventory forms that take a few minutes to complete, either before or at the start of the session. For some, it is actually helpful to have a sense that their depression can be contained or defined. It may help to inure them from blaming themselves for having symptoms if these symptoms are in some way legitimised. Measures can help people to communicate things that they might otherwise find difficult to say face to face, such as having suicidal thoughts or unacceptable physical symptoms.

The Beck depression inventory (BDI) was devised by Beck in 1961 and revised in 1978 and more recently as the BDI-II. The BDI is a 21-item self-report inventory that assesses emotional, cognitive and physiological aspects of depression. The BDI can be found in Beck et al. (1979), and a similar, self-scoring inventory is in Burns (1999a, 1999b). A manual giving guidelines on its use can be found in Beck et al. (1996). The BDI-II is better matched with current DSM (APA, 2000) criteria (Dozois et al., 1998), but some have argued that it is not so good for monitoring on-going weekly depression scores as BDI-I (Persons, 2008). BDI-II is subject to copyright but can be purchased from www.psychcorp.com or www.harcourtassessment.com.

The BDI and other similar measures are useful to CB therapists in various ways. First, the BDI, for example, gives an overall score that can be taken as an authoritative guideline to levels of depression.[1] Second, highly specific pieces of information can be quickly gleaned from it. For example, questions asked about suicidal thoughts and thoughts about hopelessness.[2] These questions offer a way into dialogue about self-harm and suicide, valuable for some therapists who find it difficult to initiate such discussion. Third, there are also questions about specific cognitions in key areas such as guilt and sleep disturbance. Many CB therapists would use the BDI at the start of most sessions with depressed clients. The development of the scores – usually in a downward direction, towards less severe symptoms – gives indications of how overall treatment is going, and decreasing scores enhance clients' motivation to continue.

There are measures for other problem areas such as anxiety (Beck et al., 1988; Wells, 2009) and obsessive-compulsive disorder (Clark & Beck, 2002). Measures such as the Hospital Anxiety and Depression scale (HADS) are widely used and easy to complete. The meta-cognitions questionnaire (Wells, 1997) is useful in highlighting beliefs about thinking, particularly where worry and rumination are part of the person's difficulties. Wells (2009) offers several rating scales, including those for panic attacks, social phobia and general anxiety.

Later in therapy, measures can be used to assess assumptions and beliefs. For example, the dysfunctional attitudes scale (Beck et al., 1991) is a 40-item scale with attitudes such as 'It is best to give up my own interests in order to please other people', 'It is shameful for a person to display weaknesses', 'I should be able to please everybody' and 'If you cannot do something well, there is little point in doing it at all'. The attitudes measured fall into the categories of: approval, love, achievement, perfectionism, entitlement, omnipotence and autonomy. Jeffrey Young has devised rather long – and potentially fatiguing to clients – schema questionnaires to measure early maladaptive schemas (Young et al., 2003).

Young and Klosko's book (1994) contains a shorter version that can often be a useful starting point for clients for whom schema-focused issues are evident. Measures of assumptions and beliefs are more appropriate later on in therapy once clients are fully engaged in therapy, and can make sense of where assumptions and beliefs fit into their therapeutic picture.

In addition to using formal measures, simpler methods can be invaluable, such as ones that ask clients to do a simple weekly rating out of 10 on problem areas. Similarly, we can develop our own measures. For example, one therapist and client devised an 'assertiveness at work scale' from a number of scaling questions about the sort of situations she often found herself in. Giving it to the client to fill out every week showed how well she was succeeding over the period of the intervention. Another client, Tracy, found it very difficult to say just how she was feeling, and found filling in questionnaires difficult. She devised a 'global yuch' measure, a 0–10 scale that she called her 'yuchometer', which gave useful feedback on how she was. Other measures can count the number of panic attacks and the times going out was avoided, such as for Ann earlier, or measures of the length of time someone could stay in a room without checking for the presence of spiders, the number of obsessional thoughts and so on. Some sessions may include specific, on-the-spot measures: for example, during therapy for phobias, the client repeatedly gives anxiety ratings during experiments to test what happens when in contact with their phobic object. In therapy with post-traumatic stress disorder (PTSD) clients subjective units of distress (SUDs), measured from 0–10 or 0–100, enable us to identify and work with 'hot spots' in trauma reliving. The list of measures is as long as the number of clients we see, and clients can be creative in coming up with their own ratings.

Another important way of using measures is in rating the degree of belief held in specific thoughts or assumptions, to be discussed further in Chapter 5. We can also use behavioural frequency measures: for example, the success with which a client has met specific goals, such as using a simple 0–10 measure of meeting the goal 'Engaging in previously enjoyed activities' (Grant et al., 2004), or for another client, we could keep a record of the number of times she has gone out with friends, handed in an essay on time, or gone to lectures despite feeling anxious.

CAUTIONS ABOUT MEASURES

Therapists have different attitudes towards measures. CBT therapists have the reputation of pursuing the therapeutic belief 'If it moves, measure it' sometimes beyond reason. When using measures, it is important therefore to be sensitive to clients' and therapists' expectations. Most measures are 'self-reports' and therefore have some 'demand characteristics': there may be a subtle subtext that implies that clients should show reducing scores over time. They can therefore lead people to feel temporarily unsettled or worse, particularly if presenting them with difficulties they try to avoid, or if high scores mean that they are not doing as well as they think they should. Once measures are regular weekly features of therapy, clients become more comfortable with them and understand more about their nature and purpose. Clients may be tempted to reduce their scores to convince either therapists or themselves that they are getting better. Clients sometimes exaggerate their scores to keep the 'patient role' or avoid ending therapy. Sometimes there can be misunderstanding about what exactly is being measured, as the following examples illustrate.

CASE STUDY
Ben

Ben had deep concern that he would go mad. After months of therapy during which his BDI score plummeted, he confessed that he had deliberately underscored on his BDI and BAI because he couldn't stand the idea that he might not be getting rapidly better.

CASE STUDY
Lorna

Lorna had regularly filled out depression and anxiety inventories. Much therapy was centred on her concerns at work. Several weeks passed before it emerged that she considered that she was filling out the inventory with the view that it was about her mood at work, rather than her general mood, as her therapist had assumed. As sessions were often on Monday there may well have been an in-built 'over-scoring' factor.

Both examples show that a degree of caution in the interpretation of symptom measures is warranted. Regular reviews of the purpose and meaning of using measures is therefore recommended. Therapists can usually feed back the general result of any measure to clients straightaway but add 'That is what the form says – what do *you* say?'.

There are clients who really dislike using measures. If there is no reasonable resolution to this difference, it is usually most helpful to either resort to a simple measure ('How do you feel out of 10?') or put the whole notion aside. Some therapists are suspect of the general notion of assessment and may therefore find the use of any measuring procedures foreign or objectionable, perhaps wondering if it is legitimate to use such measures outside the psychiatric domain with which they are associated. Some clients may refuse to fill out a BDI, perhaps because they fear what it will uncover (Persons, 2008). Measures may be off-putting to some, or the questions may seem irrelevant to their problems. Others report disliking measures as symbols of 'science' or of 'homework' – possibly linked to a degree of avoidance of unpleasant emotion. In practice, however, measures do have a place in therapy when they are used sensitively and collaboratively, and their limitations are accepted.

TREATMENT PLANNING AND INFORMED CONSENT

Persons (2008) defines the 'pre-treatment phase' as consisting of assessment, formulation and goal-setting. There is, however, one final task that might be considered the culmination of pre-treatment, and that is turning all that we have established so far into a treatment plan in line with the client's preferences. This step enables the client to make a fully informed decision about whether to undertake the therapy. As can be seen, the number of tasks that need to be taken to get us this far is considerable and we might already have had 2, 3 or 4 sessions, so if clients have stayed this far it is likely that they will stay on board. Careful phasing of pre-treatment gives a sense of proper preparation that should yield dividends but not all therapists want to have a formal sense of pre-treatment. We offer a brief form to guide on-going treatment planning in Figure 4.1 below.

GOALS What are our goals?	1. 2. 3. 4. 5.
THERAPY What type of therapy – individual, group, etc.?	
What methods will we use?	
How often will we meet – weekly, fortnightly, etc.?	
OTHER TREATMENT Is any other treatment involved – e.g. medication, etc.?	
Is there a need for any treatment intervention?	

FIGURE 4.1 Treatment planning form

KEEPING NOTES AND AUDIO-RECORDING SESSIONS

Recording sessions add to structure and collaboration in CBT. Keeping detailed notes, particularly during assessment, is valuable for both client and therapist, helping clients to feel that their concerns are being noted and understood. Making notes of salient points after sessions is useful, allowing the therapists to give simultaneous *aide memoires* to clients and to themselves. Such points often start on therapist's whiteboards and are then converted into 'takeaway' form in a variety of ways as photocopies, carbon copies and even mobile phone photographs. Therapy note-books or folders enable the client to keep notes and helps prevent the common scenario of key information becoming lost on scraps of paper (Beck, 1995). Clients are encouraged to bring notebooks along to sessions, to review gains in therapy. CB therapists often ask clients to make notes in their therapy books as reminders of important points that arise in sessions. They can use the book or file to collate general therapy materials, homework exercises, formulations and diaries – ready for on-going use after therapy ends.

CB therapists have a tradition of taping or digitally recording sessions and giving them to clients to listen to for homework. Tapes are invaluable to the process of therapy, improving what is remembered from sessions – even if it does include all the bits and pieces we wish we had not said. Recordings give oppor-tunities for repeated listening and reflection, essential to making sense of and learning from therapy, as well as giving clients useful feedback. For example, a client who believed she presented a muddled account of her difficulties was surprised at how clearly she had described them; another client may learn that while she states that she wants the therapist to help, she never really listens to what the therapist is saying. Recordings can also be used for therapist-oriented needs – such as to develop and monitor one's practice and for training, supervi-sory or accreditation purposes. Ethical guidelines for therapists usually require obtaining clients' permission and being transparent about uses, storage and eras-ure of recordings.

Occasionally, usually exceptionally, some clients and agencies may not accept the recording of sessions. Sometimes the sound of our own voice can come as an actual or predicted shock, and feed into a negative self-concept. This can lead to problems with recording but also to therapeutically useful exchanges and interventions.

CASE STUDY
Tracy

Tracy was initially reluctant to say anything when the tape recorder was running. She predicted: 'I know if I hear myself speak, I'll sound horrible and it will be embarrassing.' She knew she would then use it to 'beat myself up'. This proved useful in therapy in two ways. First, what she predicted about the tape fitted in with her general tendency to make negative predictions and, by listening to short extracts from sessions, her prediction could be tested. Second, her response to the tape was formulated as potentially valuable information for therapy, revealing her beliefs about herself. During the experiment of listening to the tape, Tracy also recorded her negative thoughts about listening to herself, which was then woven into the formulation. During the following session Tracy reported that she initially thought 'God, I hate my voice', but then found she got absorbed in the content of the tape and discovered that she only ever said negative things about herself.

Client sensitivities about taping highlight the need for ethical practice in this area. A form that allows the client to give consent to taping is offered in Wills (2008) and on the author's page of the publisher's website: www.sagepub.co.uk/wills3, follow 'Materials relating to CBT supervision and training'. A challenging aspect that has arisen for therapy practice in recent decades has been the rise of legal scrutiny of the helping professions. Both client and therapist need to be aware that there are circumstances in which tapes could be subject to subpoena in court cases. It seems almost inevitable that this will eventually happen, and that could result in widespread reluctance to use tapes in the way they have been in the past.

SESSION STRUCTURING

'Would you tell me, please, which way I ought to go from here?'

'That depends a good deal on where you want to get to', said the Cat.

'I don't much care where ...', said Alice.

'Then it doesn't matter which way you go', said the Cat.

'... so long as I get somewhere', Alice added as an explanation.

'Oh, you're sure to do that', said the Cat, 'if you only walk long enough'.

(Lewis Carroll, *Alice's Adventures in Wonderland*)

A key principle of CBT is that a structured, focused approach runs throughout each session as well as for therapy as a whole. Figure 4.2 illustrates a typical session structure (Wills, 2008a).

Although structuring can seem rather restrictive, it can be justified by the idea that clients are likely to have some preference for a reasonably focused type of therapy. Structure can be especially helpful in making best use of frequently limited time. In practice, most clients seem to like a collaborative and negotiated structure, especially because they can learn, follow it and understand its purpose.

---

1. Brief update and mood check – including measures;

2. Bridge from previous session;

3. Collaborative setting of the agenda;

4. Review of homework;

5. Main session items;

6. Setting new homework;

7. Feedback on session.

FIGURE 4.2   Structure of CBT within sessions

It is easy for therapists to forget what an uncommon experience therapy is for many clients. While it can sometimes be useful for therapy and therapists to be less predictable, predictability is generally a virtue for clients likely to be struggling with unfamiliar problems and changes. Equally, some clients find being structured aversive, and 'titrating the dose' of structure is a key interpersonal skill for CB therapists (Wills, 2008a).

The initial stages of CBT involve negotiating the structure and being clear with the client about what session format will be following. Suddenly introducing agendas and homework later on in therapy can leave the client puzzled. Giving rationales and explaining therapy are part of 'socialising' clients into therapy. Such socialising is best as a two-way collaborative process, with therapist and client learning how each other works and how they can adapt to work well with the other. As sessions proceed, there is less need for consciously overt structure: therapy begins to 'run itself'.

REVIEWING THE CLIENT'S MOOD AND 'BRIDGING' FROM PREVIOUS SESSIONS

The usual prelude to reviews of clients' mood is that they complete a BDI or other relevant measure as discussed earlier before each therapy session. Scores need to be interpreted with care and should generally be matched with a client self-report, asking the client: 'Your scores suggest things may be better. How has the last week seemed to you?' Usually clients' self-report match measure scores closely, but sometimes not: 'Well, I know the scores have come down but I still feel lousy, it doesn't feel better.' This material is often therapeutically valuable. Many clients have reported that Mondays are worse than others because of work. This can lead nicely to a useful agenda item: how to start the working week. It is also helpful to ask how clients remember the last session. This often tells how clients think that therapy is going in general but may also pick up some glitch in the client's experience of therapy that may have lingered since the last session.

SETTING AN AGENDA

Although the structure of sessions may be varied, agenda-setting is generally considered essential. The main purposes of setting an agenda are to maximise the use of time in the session and to ensure that key items are covered. Agenda-setting aids clients' memories of sessions. We know that memories about specific sessions are often quite limited, and will no doubt be aggravated by therapeutic 'clutter'. An agenda should help the session to begin collaboratively and maintain such collaboration throughout the session.

The content of agenda includes therapist and client items and there can be useful dialogue on what to cover and when to cover it. One deficit of the Rogerian model is that it may lead some client-centred counsellors to conclude that they have no right to raise things in sessions, denying them and clients the use of therapist insights and skills. Equally, however, therapists must ensure that they do not impose too many issues that they would like to talk about. This would be bad CBT, neither collaborative nor facilitative of the generalisation of therapy; that is, the process by which clients gradually learn to be their own therapists. Over the course of therapy, the client gradually takes more and more responsibility for agenda-setting. In the beginning phases we may say, for example, 'It would be useful to talk about how you've been during the week, and I've got some things I'd like to ask about, including how you got on with the diary. Is that okay, and is there anything you'd like to cover today?' Later sessions may start with joint negotiation of agendas: 'What shall we put on the agenda today?' We have, at times, to negotiate what is most important to cover if someone brings along many diverse issues (Grant et al., 2004).

REVIEW OF PREVIOUS HOMEWORK AND THE SETTING OF NEW HOMEWORK

Homework is increasingly seen as a factor that promotes efficacy not just in CBT but in other therapy models too – to the extent that many now consider homework-setting to be a new 'common factor' in effective therapy (Kazantzis & Ronan, 2006: Wills, 2008a). However, the idea of setting 'homework' may sometimes be difficult for therapists and clients alike, having overtones of the schoolroom. This is a useful sensitivity because some clients will experience being set homework in just this way. The very word may awaken old memories of bad experiences in schools or other authority situations.[3] This possibility should lead therapists to undertake an exploratory discussion with clients about why homework may be useful or agree an alternative word such as 'assignment', 'task', 'follow-up' or 'experiment'.

It is helpful to review clients' reactions to homework and the factors that can prevent them from doing it. It is demotivating for clients when they have gone to the trouble of doing homework and therapists either fail to follow it up or give it little time. This is why checking on the previous week's homework is included as an item on the session structure list. Equally, its inclusion later is a reminder to therapists to discuss homework-setting while there is reasonable time remaining in the session. This prevents homework becoming an appendage, thrown in as the client leaves the room. Homework is of central importance in CBT and as therapy progresses it can take on different aspects at different stages.

Appropriate homework-setting begins with simple tasks, moving to more complex ones in view of how clients proceed. Most therapists probably err on the side of simplicity: clients can, after all, ask for something more complex if the homework proves too simple. One regular homework task is to listen to tapes of sessions. Reading one of the many self-help CBT books or websites or a handout specific to the client's difficulties can also be valuable homework. Care should always be taken to read written material before assigning it, thinking about clients' frames of reference – sometimes books or pamphlets may unwittingly refer to some aspect of clients' situations that are disturbing to them. Devising a homework sheet is also valuable, influenced by the 'reformulation letter' concept of cognitive analytic therapy (Ryle & Kerr, 2003). Figure 4.3 gives an example of a homework sheet, which includes aspects of formulation, goals and homework.

MIKE

Reminder of the sessions: When you were a little boy, your dad was a difficult man who drank a lot. He was violent and abusive towards your mum and your brothers and sister. Your mum tried to look after you, but the situation was so bad that you got 'passed around' a lot to be looked after by others.

You came to believe: 'I don't belong anywhere'. You didn't have consistent care, and didn't learn how to look after yourself properly or how you feel about things.

Aims for therapy: To learn how to stand on your own two feet more, instead of relying so much on your wife. Another aim is to learn to take critical comments less personally, and not to strike out, especially at your wife.

The homework for this week:

1. Spot how you feel when you are being criticized: Write it down in your notebook.
2. Try counting to five before reacting to criticism. Write down how it went – how you felt, any difficulties, etc.
3. Listen to the tape and write down important points in your notebook.
4. Remember to bring the notebook to the next session.

FIGURE 4.3   Individualised homework sheet

SESSION TARGETS

Targets for sessions constitute the main part of the session and usually take up the majority of the time. The items that are worked on will be those already identified during the agenda-setting stage or issues that have arisen during the actual course of the session. It is not unusual for homework to become a central focus of the session. Working on session targets is where the main skills and techniques of CBT will be brought to bear on the identified issues. The direction of CBT tends to start at the symptom level and works towards the underlying issues as becomes necessary. Often the symptom-level focus will begin with behaviourally oriented work, such as graded task assignments, and then move on to identifying and challenging negative automatic thoughts (NATs). These techniques will be described further in Chapter 5. At a later stage in therapy, the work may tackle underlying issues by evaluating dysfunctional assumptions and modifying core beliefs via methods such as continuum work and positive data logs, described further in Chapter 9. The extent to which sessions have been tackling key session targets can be reviewed as part of the monitoring progress.

SESSION FEEDBACK

Feedback is an essential part of collaborative work, enabling us to focus our work on the specific needs of each client session by session. Open questions at the end, such as 'How have you found the session today?', 'Is there anything that was particularly useful?', 'Is there anything that was difficult or you didn't like?' encourage both positive and negative feedback. Each session starts with bridging feedback from the last one, particularly relevant when the tapes have been listened to and reflected on.

Most of us accept positive feedback more than readily, but have to do more work on ourselves to really want to know what clients do not like or did not find helpful about our therapeutic style. Yet it is crucial to be aware of negative and positive reactions because client negativity can easily bring therapy to an abrupt halt. Therapists may often need to look at their own NATs ('Ungrateful sod!'), dysfunctional assumptions ('If I work hard at therapy, I will be recognised as a great therapist') and maladaptive core beliefs ('I must be the perfect therapist').

Continuous feedback helps therapy to stay close to clients' needs so that a 'rolling contract' (Wills, 2006) between therapist and client develops. Continuous feedback and therapists' attempts to explain what they do by giving rationales for each move mean that therapeutic contracts are negotiated on a regular, on-going basis.

CONCLUSION

The early stages of CBT set the scene for the rest of therapy, with therapists actively involving clients from the start. Therapists explain the overall aims and structure of therapy, and of each technique. Each stage of CBT is properly introduced and negotiated with clients by asking for feedback from them about what they have learned as well as on what may have 'jarred' with them. Thus, we keep on track with clients, aiming to use therapy in the most effective fashion. This focus is facilitated by the structuring of each session around key activities, in ways that can be varied when flexibility is required.

Structuring CBT involves a critical set of sometimes under-appreciated skills. The cognitive therapy scale (CTS) (Young & Beck, 1980, 1988) and its major revision, the cognitive therapy scale revised (CTS-R), are widely used to measure competence in CBT. Both versions of the CTS are divided into 'general therapy skills' and 'CBT specific skills'. In Table 4.3 readers will see that the structuring elements listed above are well represented as skills in both categories.

The authors of both scales have produced helpful manuals on skill performance of the items shown (see professional resources on Beck's website www.beckinstitute. org, and in James et al., 2000), stressing that structure should always be done with 'exquisite sensitivity' (Beck et al., 1979: 66) to the needs of individual clients.

TABLE 4.3 The development of the cognitive therapy scale (CTS) items

1979 Checklist (Beck et al., 1979)	CTS (Young & Beck, 1980)	CTS (Young & Beck, 1988)	CTS-R (Milne et al., 2001)
2 Establishing agenda	1 Agenda setting	1 AGENDA SETTING	**1 Agenda**
3 Elicited reactions to session and to therapist	2 Feedback	2 FEEDBACK	**2 Feedback**
	3 Understanding	3 UNDERSTANDING	
18 Rapport	4 Interpersonal effectiveness	4 INTERPERSONAL EFFECTIVENESS	**5 Interpersonal effectiveness**
1 Collaboration and mutual understanding	5 Collaboration	5 COLLABORATION	**3 Collaboration**
4 Structured therapy time efficiently	6 Pacing	6 PACING	**4 Pacing**
6 Questioning	7 Guided discovery	7 GUIDED DISCOVERY	**8 Guided discovery**
10 Elicit NATS	8 Focus on cognition	8 FOCUS ON COGNITION	**7 Focus key cognitions**
11 Test NATS			
5 Focused on appropriate problem	9 Strategy for change	9 CONCEPTUALISATION	**9 Conceptual integration**
12 Identify assumptions	10 Application CB techniques	10 STRATEGY FOR CHANGE	**10 Cognitive techniques**
9 CB techniques		11 COGNITIVE TECHNIQUES	**11 Behavioural techniques**
		12 BEHAVIOURAL TECHNIQUES	
8 Assigned homework	11 Homework	13 HOMEWORK	**12 Homework**
7 Summaries	Overall assessment	Overall assessment	**6 Eliciting emotion**
Genuineness	Specific problems	Specific problems	
Warmth			
Accurate empathy			
Professional manner			

Encouragingly – and perhaps a good note with which to end this chapter – the authors note that:

> Raters [using the manual] should also be aware of level of difficulty with the particular patient in view. Therapists can do exactly the right thing but the client may still, for reasons of his own, not respond. (Young & Beck, 1980)

FURTHER READING

Grant, A., Mills, J., Mulhern, R., & Short, N. (2004) *Cognitive Behavioural Therapy in Mental Health Care.* London: Sage Publications. (Chapter 3.)
Persons, J. B. (2008) *The Case Formulation Approach to Cognitive-Behavior Therapy.* New York: Guilford.
Wells, A. (1997) *Cognitive Therapy of Anxiety Disorders.* New York: Wiley. (Useful first section on assessment and measures.)
Wright, F., Basco, M., & Thase, M. E. (2005) *Learning Cognitive Behavioural Therapy: An Illustrated Guide.* Washington: American Psychiatric Association.

NOTES

1 Usually defined as mild, moderate and severe.
2 The BDI manual recommends that positive responses to both these questions should trigger further enquiries about suicidal intent (Beck et al., 1996).
3 Some American clients have told me that the word 'homework' would be used in higher education in the US and so perhaps has less specific association with 'school' than in the UK.

5

Cognitive Interventions in CBT

> People are generally better persuaded by the reasons that they themselves have discovered than by those which have come into the minds of others. (Paschal, 1670/1995:10)

Identifying and modifying negative thinking are keystone activities in CBT. The changes brought about by cognitive interventions lie at the heart of the CBT enterprise. This chapter will begin by considering why such work is therapeutic and will emphasise the importance of 'emotionally felt' cognitive change.

The chapter will identify three distinct stages in cognitive interventions directed at changing negative thoughts and images: identifying, evaluating and modifying (Beck, 1995). Each stage has two phases: verbal and written (Sanders & Wills, 2005). The stages and phases can be used separately at different times but are essentially built up into quintessential CBT methods: guided discovery and thought records. Contrary to glib representations of this process, difficulties are frequently encountered during this work. These difficulties will be described and remedies suggested. Cognitive interventions directed at cognitive content are mainly phenomenological in that they involve describing and evaluating experiences. Evaluating cognitions essentially involves exploring the role that thoughts, images, memories and attention play in psychological functioning: how well do current cognitions fit with desired life goals, and how possible might it be to amend them? This can involve actively confirming or disconfirming thoughts and beliefs, using insights from the principles of science derived from Popper (1959). Popper, however, did not argue that this process leads to the 'truth', but rather to the idea that after inadequate explanations have been eliminated what we are left with is just the best current explanation – even that is likely to be dispensed with in time. The work involved in challenging negative thoughts has particularly benefited from vigorous techniques associated with Albert Ellis and rational emotive behaviour therapy (REBT) (Dryden, 2006). Less active interventions, such as being mindfully aware of thoughts, are becoming more frequently advocated as ways of promoting more nuanced sequencing of interventions. Therapists can help clients to step back to a more mindful position if they are getting stuck in challenging thoughts or to step forward to more active stances if they appear overly passive. Some clients respond better to exploring images in which vital cognitions are latent. Interventions at the level of imagery (Stopa, 2009; Hackman et al., 2011) and metaphor (Stott et al., 2010) have developed more depth and breadth in recent years.

Mindfulness and acceptance-based approaches have arisen from the realisation that the relevant experiences of psychopathology are not just linked to the content of negative thinking but also often involve cognitive and meta-cognitive processes such as memory and attention (Harvey et al., 2004). Furthermore, these processes seem to cut across traditional diagnostic categories suggesting that DSM (APA, 2000) labels may often be less useful to therapists than 'transdiagnostic' approaches to symptoms across various disorders. Worry, for example, is a prominent feature of many disorders. Worry has normal and functional aspects: we all need to be somewhat vigilant for future dangers. Problematic worry, however, occurs when we cannot 'switch off' these processes after their beneficial effect. Worrying then begins to dominate our attention in destructive ways, leading to experiences that are like continuously streaming 'videos' of negativity. Rumination plays a similar role in depression (Wells, 2009). The chapter will end by describing newer cognitive interventions that focus on the negative attentional processes, such as worry and rumination.

Although behavioural and cognitive interventions have been divided into different chapters in this book, readers should note that in practice they are often 'joined up': description of work with the cognitive intent of 'behavioural experiments' is in this chapter but could have been in Chapter 6. Equally, the methods for working with thoughts described below also involve the identification of feelings, dealt with in this chapter in connection with cognitive work but given fuller consideration in Chapter 7. It is perhaps a tribute to the increasingly joined-up nature of CBT that it is often difficult to know the best location for various concepts and methods.

HOW AND WHY COGNITIVE INTERVENTIONS WORK

CB therapists have traditionally turned first to scientific and rational methods to invite clients to explore how functional their thoughts, assumptions and beliefs are. These methods focus on ways of thinking known to play a role in psychological problems. Though the methods are mainly rational, we also know that they are unlikely to be effective unless they evoke and modify key emotions (Foa & Kozak, 1986). The idea of 'dual representation' (Brewin et al., 1996) – interplay between 'heart and head' in psychological functioning – is an ancient and familiar one. The relationship between cognition and emotion is complex and subject to different theoretical explanations: most of these, however, suggest that problem-free functioning is linked to establishing balance between the two factors. This balance can, however, show considerable variation. People who over-rely on emotions may show 'emotional reasoning' and not think things through as thoroughly as may be desirable. On the other end of the spectrum are 'intellectualisers', who may be out of touch with feelings and unable to ever trust gut instincts. Some clients present with pronouncedly flat affect whilst talking about their feelings – this may or may not be a sign of intellectualisation but is probably worth exploring.

Teasdale (2004) has identified different modes in processing information: a *propositional* mode that deals with essentially factual and specific quantitative knowledge and an *implicational* mode more concerned with evaluative and qualitative knowledge. The former establishes the 'facts of the case' and the latter establishes the personal meanings of those facts. Epstein (1998) also has developed a twin-track theory, suggesting that there are *rational* and *experiential/intuitive* information processing systems. He argues that optimal functioning is linked to the degree to which the two systems work harmoniously together. Clients who suffer from intense negative emotions do not use rational processing functions well because their psychological functioning has been 'flooded' by the experiential/emotional system. Cognitive techniques help such clients by reinstituting the basic steps of rational processing and re-teaching clients to use them in 'battle conditions' (i.e., when the system is disoriented by negative emotions).

It is a common experience when upset is followed by quieter moments of reflection: 'Wait a minute, did Kate really ignore me? Or was she just under pressure from elsewhere?' The more upset we are, the longer it takes us to take the natural steps of reality testing. Clients who are really emotionally disturbed, however, have lost touch with these rational processes in a more consistent way. They need the conscious and deliberative steps of CBT, especially reinforced by helpful written 'think steps' or other useful notes. This is not a position of a triumphal rationalism. The case is rather that thoughts and feelings need to work together in a balanced way. Intellectualisation (overriding emotions), for example, is as much of a problem in therapy as its opposite (emotional reasoning). Healing requires 'emotionally felt change': a *metanoia*, a change of heart, as much as a change of mind. Metanoia may be elusive and sometimes this is because language itself may hinder us from finding it. Pierson and Hayes (2007) contrast the process of the acceptance and commitment therapy (ACT) model with more traditional CBT by saying that whereas CBT aims to deconstruct negative language, ACT aims to deconstruct all language. They express the spirit of the 'third wave' in CBT well by saying:

> [A] person who says 'I am bad' and then changes it to 'I am good' is not now a person who thinks 'I am good' but a person who thinks, 'I am bad, no, I am good'. (Pierson & Hayes, 2007: 207)

Cognitive change may come less from change in the content of negative thought but more from changes in the thinking *processes* associated with negative thought – especially in the quality of attention that is given to it. In this perspective, negative thoughts may be better dealt with by defusion rather than by direct attempts at changing content. Part of this change may require some clients to be more aware and accepting of their negative feelings. Classically a humanistic activity, Chapter 7 will present a CBT perspective on working directly with feelings.

IDENTIFYING NEGATIVE THOUGHTS AND FEELINGS

Emotions move through our processing systems more quickly than cognitions. They travel along the 'low road' to awareness with cognitions way behind on the 'high road' (Le Doux, 1996). Clients often experience and express strong feelings in the body (e.g., the 'curled up' response of the depressed client). Most clients can express feelings verbally but some need help to find the words that best describe them (Wills, 2008a). Empathic CBT therapists pick up these verbal and non-verbal signals at the same time as attending and focusing on the NATs that arise in clients' accounts of key situations. Therapists are aided by knowledge of current generic formulations for various areas of psychological functioning. Westbrook et al. (2007) and Wells (2008) have, for example, provided a number of short readable chapters describing up-to-date formulations for key disorders. In contrast, Barlow et al. (2011a) have produced a transdiagnostic manual that gives a unitary approach to formulation and treatment of many emotional disorders. While recognising the utility of generic formulations, therapists also need to listen carefully for the individual thoughts that each client will report as variations on those generic themes. It is also essential for CB therapists to be sensitive to feelings by using well-developed listening skills. Good listening skills are essential for effective CBT practice and should not be forgotten by a misguided sense of needing to 'get on with things'.

Specific and transdiagnostic cognitive-behavioural maps for many problem areas are, however, some of the greatest strengths of CBT. Following Beck's (1976/1989) early lead that specific modes of thinking are linked to specific problems ('the cognitive specificity hypothesis'), an ever-increasing number of areas have been provisionally mapped (Clark & Beck, 2010; Barlow et al., 2011a). 'Provisional' here acknowledges that our maps are probably closer to those of explorers in the 18th century than today's Google Earth satellite maps. Even so, these maps are helpful to therapists and often suggest how to formulate questions to take us to key cognitions. In social anxiety, for example, we know that people become self-conscious and pre-occupied with negative evaluation in social situations (Wells, 2008), and this can guide our questioning. Here is a brief edited extract where the therapist guides a socially anxious client to report a difficult experience as if it were happening in the here-and-now. The therapist's framework of understanding is guided by research on how such clients think and pay selective attention to negative signals in difficult situations:

Therapist: What do you see in the room?

Client: Tiers of people … and they haven't dimmed the lights so I can see them all and they're in white coats … wearing their stethoscopes so I can tell they're doctors …

Therapist: What is going through your mind?

Client: (*Looking distressed*) They are not listening to me. They're bored … I am not making any sense here … they are cleverer than me ….

Therapist: How many people don't seem to be listening?

Client: About 4 or 5.

Therapist: About how many people are in the room?

Client: … about 50, I'd say.

Therapist: So about 4 or 5 people out of 50 don't seem to be listening to you?[1]

We can see here the start of a sequence of questions that lead further into the client's frame of reference. As this process unfolds, the client's feelings also come to the surface and therapeutic targets emerge in the form of the negative cognitions that may be modified. Sometimes merely identifying negative thinking in itself, without conscious modification, sets off a change process. Reflective discussion can stimulate change because it can help clients to reflect on and really 'hear' their internal processes of thinking and feeling for the first time. Certainly clients do often make comments like 'I know it sounds crazy but that is how it feels when I am low.' One can feel the tides of change flowing at such moments but it is still useful to underline the point by reflecting: 'So there is a type of thinking that goes with feeling low that isn't there when you are feeling better?' The therapeutic manoeuvre here comes from 'staying with' the negative material and letting it unfold, rather than pressing straight on to attempts to change. Later, and in Chapter 7, we will consider if evoking relevant emotions further accelerates this process (Elliott et al., 2004).

Therapists present rationales for CBT, helping clients to understand the link between thinking and feeling (Wright et al., 2005). Opportunities to begin this process come from spotting 'affect shifts' (when a client's mood intensifies during a session). A client may become tearful during discussion of a current or past difficulty, for example:

Therapist: It seems like you became upset when you mentioned your dad just now?

Client: Yeah [*pause and sobs*] … it is just so bloody sad … I didn't get to say goodbye to him and it was out of so-called loyalty to my mum. I really regret it now.

Therapist: Perhaps you thought 'I should have said goodbye' and then felt _?
Client: Yeah, really guilty ... angry too actually.
Therapist: And the angry thought is?
Client: Mum should have left it, she should have seen it was a special moment.

If helping clients to 'stay with' negative thoughts and feelings during the session proves helpful, then the client herself can go on to spot such moments in everyday life, and to record them in a simple diary. This can be a useful precursor activity prior to keeping fuller thought, behaviour or emotion diaries later.

Clients often report that they become more aware of NATs by hearing others, especially relatives, say them. It may be easier to hear the NATs of others than one's own at first – that skill may come later. For some, this valuable extra insight is hastened by recording others' NATs and then asking 'Do *I* have thoughts like that?'. This can make a useful early homework assignment.

IDENTIFYING NATs BY INTENTIONALLY INTENSIFYING EMOTIONS

Not all thoughts are 'in the frame' as we look for those involved in generating negative emotions. CBT therapists often use the term *hot cognitions* to isolate the thoughts that are most germane to the work of change. It can be difficult to identify hot thoughts because clients find them painful to bring to mind and may develop successful ways of neutralising them. Clients with post-traumatic stress disorder (PTSD), for example, sometimes exhibit a flat 'factually true' but 'emotionally absent' way of telling their trauma story. This often results from telling the story regularly to police, lawyers and medical staff who are mainly concerned with the facts. Therapists can help clients to give more emotionally engaged accounts simply by 'giving permission' for clients to tell them. At other times therapists need to be more active in eliciting them. This is particularly true in problem areas where there is avoidance of painful experience. With the previously described socially anxious client, for example, the therapist takes the active stance of asking her to speak in the present tense – as if the event were happening now. This intensifies the way clients articulate feelings experienced at the time of the event. Intensifying feelings helps clients to identify their thoughts in the situation more accurately and makes 'felt change' more likely.

EVALUATING THOUGHTS AND FEELINGS

Rating Strength

CB therapists frequently ask clients to rate the intensity of the emotions they feel in trigger situations and the extent to which they believe in the NATs they have identified. The way therapists make ratings is illustrated in the following extract.

They may also write down the ratings in a simple two-column record that mirrors the fuller thought record form filled out immediately or later (see Figure 5.1):

Therapist and Client are discussing the Client's reaction to an upsetting telephone call.

Therapist: So you felt upset after your dad's phone call. What was said?

Client: Basically he called to remind me not to forget to get a birthday card for my mum.

Therapist: So how did you feel about that?

Client: I felt really angry, you know, like he thought I might forget. I never forget. Why did he seem to think that I might forget this time?

Therapist: What is your theory on that? Why did he seem to think that?

Client: He has never trusted or recognised me as a competent adult. [*Very upset*]

Therapist: What's the feeling now?

Client: Sad, sad, … a bit forlorn, you know, it will never change.

[*Later* …]

Therapist: So there were two feelings – anger and sadness. Let's take them one by one and look at what's behind them? The angry one first – if 100 per cent were the angriest you have ever been, how would you rate how you felt then?

Client: Not too bad, irritated – 40 per cent maybe. I am used to it with him, you know.

Therapist: And the thought there seemed to be 'He shouldn't say that I will forget mum's birthday' … how much out of 100 do you believe that?

Client: It is just his interfering ways really … so not so much – about 30 per cent I guess.

They go on to identify that the sadness rating is much higher at 80 per cent, with a belief rating of 90 per cent for the thought 'He has never recognised me as a competent adult'.

Here the sad feeling and thought are established as more significant to the client and will therefore be tackled first. Note also that there are always choices in therapy: it would have been possible to regard the combination of sadness and anger as two sides of the same emotional coin – 'hurt'. Asking what hurt may be lingering under anger is often a good way to getting straight to the most relevant material.

Thought	Emotion
He thinks I'll forget mum's birthday He'll never recognise me as a competent adult	ANGRY (40%) SAD (80%)

FIGURE 5.1   Thought feeling ratings (Wills, 2008a)

Clients often reveal many negative thoughts and beliefs, but not all are relevant or can be tackled. As shown above, the process of rating feelings and thoughts can help to prioritise the most relevant material more accurately. Additionally, belief ratings carry two crucial meta-messages: first, beliefs vary over time, and second, they are not usually experienced in either/or (0–100 per cent) form. These messages prepare clients for the possibility that thoughts and beliefs have differing degrees of validity and utility over time. Ratings can also be used to monitor the progress of therapy in a similar way to the more formal measures described earlier.

EVALUATION WITH GUIDED DISCOVERY THROUGH SOCRATIC DIALOGUE (GD/SD)

Guided discovery (GD) consists of a series of CBT interventions that are designed to open the minds of clients who are stuck in limited and negative ways of seeing the world by helping them to be aware of other perspectives. The most well-known form of GD is via Socratic dialogue (SD). There are confusions about definitions of these terms, entertainingly described by Carey and Mullan (2004), but the use of CBT-oriented Socratic dialogue may best be termed 'guided discovery through Socratic dialogue' (GD/SD). Indeed, GD/SD may be defined as a generic skill ubiquitous in CBT (Wills, 2012b).

Socrates, an Athenian philosopher who lived around 400 BC, had an unwavering commitment to truth, arrived at through systematic questioning and inductive reasoning. He particularly set out to challenge pretentious fellow philosophers, and many of his dialogues show his questions reducing them to confusion. GD/SD aims to facilitate the client's ability to look at things from new angles. It primarily uses a question-and-answer format and particular combinations of different types of questions to help clients to see that the ways they think may exclude other possibilities. Anxious thinking, for example, exaggerates the seriousness and likelihood of feared consequences, and underestimates coping abilities. When depressed, we see things, past, present and future, in a negative light. GD/SD aims to guide clients to explore and test alternatives to come up with more measured ways of thinking. It is not about positive thinking – many human fears are real and need to be taken seriously – but GD/SD explores whether there are more helpful ways to see things.

Reading some CBT vignettes gives the impression that therapists always know the answers to particular problems, and ask questions that lead clients to these answers. In the best CBT, however, there is no one true answer:

> There are only good questions that guide discovery of a million different individual answers. … We can ask questions which either imply there is one truth the client is missing or which capture the excitement of true discovery. (Padesky, 1993: 11)

GD/SD should not consist of therapists persuading clients to see things from their point of view. Common mistakes include asking too many leading questions too soon, without taking time to explore why clients thinks the way they do. A question like 'Don't you think it would be more helpful if you did x?' may well close down the process of discovery. Instead, therapists need to be curious, cultivating metaphorical question marks over their heads. Clients' ways of thinking are often surprising and unexpected. Open yet directional questions, asked in a gentle and friendly manner, enable issues to be explored collaboratively. A useful question to clarify meanings is to ask 'What do you mean when you say x?' (Sage et al., 2006). This helps to define the often idiosyncratic meaning of a thought more clearly. Other useful questions are shown in Figure 5.2. A common sequence of four steps can be deduced from the way various authors analyse the process (Overholser, 1993; Padesky, 2004; Wills, 2012b):

1 Asking informational – especially analytic and evaluative – questions to uncover information outside the client's current awareness.
2 Accurate listening and empathic reflection.
3 Summarising information discovered.
4 Asking synthesising questions that help apply the new information discussed to the client's original thought or belief.

These questions essentially unpack the globalised negativity of NATs and then repack thoughts in more functional ways. This question sequence should inform GD/SD but be used flexibly. It can be tempting for CB therapists to become overly persuasive. Even when questions appear guileless they may be subtly directive. Socrates himself was accused of seeking to bamboozle his opponents by 'mock modesty'. As therapists practice CBT regularly, certain patterns in discussing NATs will become familiar to them, but it is less likely that clients will be as familiar with such patterns. CB therapists must therefore learn to put a break on the tendency to use knowledge to overpower clients. First, only clients can really know what will prove most persuasive to them, and, second, there is evidence that when they perceive their therapists as too persuasive, they become much more resistant to what therapists are saying (Heesacker & Meija-Millan, 1996).

Proponents of other therapy models often see CBT as overly directive, and there *do* appear to be therapist differences that can be arranged along a continuum from a 'discovery-based' style (e.g., Padesky, 1993) to a 'guidance-based' one (e.g., Ellis in Dryden, 1991). Wells (1997) strikes a more pragmatic note in suggesting that client-led exploration can be both desirable and yet at times too time-consuming. This pragmatic attitude may facilitate a more nuanced approach to finding the 'proximal zone' of the client's cognitive development – probably close to where clients experience just enough cognitive dissonance to motivate them to seek new perspectives.

GD/SD involves asking questions that invite the client to look 'outside the box' for additional information. These questions are Socratic because they have similar intent to Socratic dialogue. Socrates asked people to examine their assumptions yet hardly ever expressed his own opinions. He asked questions that made his debating partners think more deeply. These debates often ended in what is called 'aporia'[2] – a kind of confusion resulting from the abandonment of an old idea without altogether finding a new one. This state of mind is similar to that of the modern psychological concept of cognitive dissonance: ideas or facts that appear incompatible and irresolvable (i.e., are dissonant) produce the necessary discomfort that motivates people to adapt or shift their thinking: that is, discomfort motivates them to think out resolutions. Therapists should therefore learn not to be too alarmed when initial cognitive interventions lead to apparent confusion: over time confusion may motivate clients to think things anew – this 'hard won' change may prove more therapeutic to clients than being 'given' new ways of thinking.

A list of Socratic questions for both therapist and client is shown in Figure 5.2.

- What do you mean when you say x?
- What is the evidence that x is true? What is the evidence against x being true?
- What might be the worst that could happen?
- What leads you to think that might happen?
- And if that happened, what then? What would you do to cope?
- Have you been in similar situations in the past? How did you cope then?
- How does thinking that make you feel?
- Are you thinking in a biased way? (See Table 1.2) e.g., are you predicting the future or mind reading?
- Are you paying attention only to one aspect? What if you looked at it from a different angle?
- What would you say to a friend who kept on saying x to herself (e.g., 'I'm stupid'; 'I'm terrible')?
- Is there an alternative explanation?
- Is there any other way of seeing the situation?
- What are the advantages and disadvantages of thinking that?
- Is it helpful, or unhelpful?
- What would it mean to you to see things differently?
- Are you making decisions based on your feelings, or is reality telling you something different?
- What might you tell a friend to do in this situation?
- Is there something else you could say to yourself that might be more helpful?
- What do you think you could change to make things better for you?
- How would you like things to be different?
- What would you like to do instead?

FIGURE 5.2 Socratic questions

In the following example, the therapist uses the questions in an ordered sequence similar to the 4-step sequence described above to help the client to explore the difficulties summed up in his NAT 'My work is impossible'. A series of *analytic questions* (AQ) has already broken down this statement into key elements – the chief of which is that his boss is critical of his work and is 'dangerous'. The therapist now asks a series of *evaluative questions* (EQ) and *synthesising questions* (SQ) designed to open the client's perspective to dissonance and therefore further development:

Therapist: So, how is your boss dangerous, do you reckon? (EQ)

Client: Well, it means I'm out of favour; he won't give me any of the good work. I'm used to being one of the players. I might get left on the shelf now.

Therapist: You'd be left out. What is the worst that could happen with that? (EQ)

Client: I could lose my job … nah but that's not likely, I think. More likely I'd just be an old lag.

Therapist: An 'old lag'?

Client: … the guys hanging round for their pension.

Therapist: That's not you, but how would you cope if you were an old lag? (SQ/ EQ)

Client: I'd be fed up but I'd hack it I guess. I'd probably apply for other jobs.

Therapist: Would you find something? (EQ)

Client: Eventually, I guess.

Therapist: [*Summarising*] Let's gather that up. You were in your boss's favour but now you're not. You might now get left out and if that went on for long you might leave. How does that tie up with him being 'dangerous'? (SQ)

Client: No, no: not dangerous, just a bit cold. To be honest, I was always glad to be on his right side and now I'm not and I'm not sure where that could go.

Therapist: Okay but saying he is dangerous … how did that affect you? (AQ)

Client: I have been a bit paralysed, I think.

Therapist: Yeah, using the word 'dangerous' may act as an amplifier that adds to the anxiety and inhibits your problem solving. Maybe the problem is relatively straightforward: things have slipped with your boss and you're not sure how to put them right: those are problems we can work on. [*Summary*]

Client: Yeah, I think I have built up the fear and that's just got in the way really.

Therapists should not expect the identification of negative thoughts to go smoothly at all times. In practice a variety of problems occur and these require patience and creativity. If clients find it difficult to link thoughts and feelings, therapists can proceed more slowly and adopt more educational styles of work. This problem, others and matching solutions are shown in Table 5.1.

In order to use CBT methods well, the client should be able to distinguish between thoughts and feelings and see links between the two. In everyday language, however, people regularly say things like 'I *feel* like I will fail the exam' when this

TABLE 5.1 Problems and solutions for difficulties in identifying negative thoughts and feelings

Problems working with negative thoughts	Possible solutions
The client confuses feeling with thinking, e.g.: 'I just feel like I'm going to fail the exam.'	Reflect back to the client with the correct terms: 'So you think you'll fail the exam, I guess then you feel anxious?' Refer back to the terminological difficulty when the client has put it the right way round.
The client cannot identify a clear thought associated with distress, e.g.: 'I was on my own, I just started feeling anxious. I didn't seem to have a thought.'	Work back to a set of theoretical explanations and ask the client which one seems closest to his experience. 'When people are anxious they often fear something bad will happen. Does that ring any bells for you?'
The client's negative thought is a 'megaphone statement', e.g.: 'When my car failed, I thought "typical"!'	Reflect back and add a probe: 'So you thought typical … of your luck? Like fate is against you?'
The client's negative thought is in the form of a question, e.g.: 'Why it was me that was left out.'	Point out that the question could mask a negative thought and ask, if so, what would the 'negative answer' to the question be?
The client's negative thought is hidden in other material, e.g.: 'I was thinking about how my work had been going.' (In relation to feeling low.)	Make the thought/feeling link by asking, 'Does the fact that you were feeling low imply that you fear that your work hasn't been going well?'
The client cannot identify the negative feeling associated with the negative thought, e.g.: 'I just felt *yewk*.'	Go with the client's vocabulary in the belief that a more precise feeling is likely to emerge as therapy progresses.
The client cannot rate the emotion experienced.	Use an analogue scale: draw a line with the two extremes of emotion on either end and a mid-point, ask clients to indicate where their emotions would fall on the line.

Source: Wills, 2008a

statement confuses the fact that 'I will fail the exam' is a negative and predictive *cognition*. CB therapists can gently point this out to clients without sounding pedantic. The best way to do this is to work with examples in sessions, emphasising that it is the 'appraisal' (what the thoughts mean) that links them to 'hot' feelings. Other problems listed in Table 5.1 include the way certain figures of speech may mask cognitions: 'typical' in the third point, for example, masks the thought 'This is typical of my bad luck'. CB therapists can take educated guesses at what the underlying thought is, though they should be wary of engineering consent to their guesses. Some clients have difficulty identifying any kind of thinking and therapists can return them to the rationale-giving stage and build up understanding in simple steps or switch focus to behavioural work.

It should also be remembered that negative functioning is only part of the client's life. CB therapists probably tend to over-focus on 'the problematic' in formulation and interventions (Kuyken et al., 2009). 'Positive psychology' models (Seligman, 2003) may help us to balance this tendency by, for example, asking clients about exceptions[3] to periods of feeling bad:

Client: I get periods of feeling so stressed. I do a lot of work at home and when a difficult customer pisses me off, I get so morose ... the other day my wife said to me, 'You're having an Eeyore morning'. And I thought, 'Yes, you're right, I'm becoming a right misery guts.'

Therapist: Some mornings you feel like Eeyore – morose and depressed – but some mornings are you more sunny – like Pooh? (AQ)

Client: Yeah.

Therapist: So what happens then when a difficult customer calls? (EQ)

Client: Oh, I don't know, I just shrug it off, I suppose. I can be pleased to hear from them, pleased to give them a service so I just roll up my sleeves and get on with it.

Therapist: Okay, so it could be good to work out the thinking that goes with Pooh days and compare that with Eeyore days – aiming for more Pooh and less Eeyore? (EQ)

Client: [*animated*] Yeah, that would be good!

Therapist: We can also think whether Eeyore has any good points. Some people find him endearing. [*Summary*]

Analytic questions about 'exceptions' may be helpful early in therapy: they can set a positive tone and define goals in user-friendly terms (e.g., 'less Eeyore, more Pooh'). Writers from Marcus Aurelius (c.100 CE) to Carlson (1997) have noted our proclivity to 'sweat the small stuff' (i.e., over-react to the minor frustrations of life), and these can offer 'test situations' for trialling GD/SD skills with clients – perhaps safer places to start than the 'the big stuff'. Client and therapist can take one such frustration: work out the vicious cycles of 'bad' days compared to those of a 'good' day. What happens differently on these days? They can then think about how one could change so as to get more good days and/or less bad ones and if it would be worth the effort.

EVALUATING NEGATIVE THOUGHTS: TESTING COGNITIVE DISTORTIONS

All are familiar with the scenario in which one attempts to cheer up a thoroughly fed-up friend. All the things that were a joy to him seem now beyond the pale. Reminded of good things he does, he will tend to 'disqualify the positive' by saying 'Oh anyone could do that'. Beck (1976/1989) identified these 'cognitive distortions' and the way they exacerbate psychological problems. A degree of negative thinking is normal and non-problematic, but as negative feelings become more predominant, distorted thinking plays a major role in maintaining problems. Identifying the silent evaluative elements in negative thinking is aided by learning to spot cognitive distortions as they arise.

We have already seen a list of cognitive distortions with definitions and examples (see Table 1.2) to aid the process of recognising negative thinking. The list has expanded over time and sometimes trainees and clients may find them hard to use. They may contain too many overlapping concepts and require rather fine distinctions for easy use. Wills (2007) analysed the negative thoughts and cognitive distortions appearing in therapy notebooks and discerned four main subject areas: thoughts about the self; the self in relation to others; other people; and life/the world. He also discerned three main types of distortion: applying a negative label; making negative predictions; and making over-statements. These two dimensions are shown together in Table 5.2.

TABLE 5.2　Distortion types and domains of negative thinking

Distortions	About the self	About the self in relation to others	About other people	About life and/or the world
APPLYING A NEGATIVE LABEL: Attaching a highly negative and over-generalised label to oneself or others.	I am boring. I am worthless. I am a real Eeyore. Everything in my life is only ever half done. I am 'Billy No Mates'.	I just don't fit in. I don't measure up to the people around me. I have to placate people. Without a partner, I'm useless.	My boss is an idiot. He's a wee man in a big job. My wife is self-indulgent about her illness. My 4-year-old tries to wind me up.	The world is a cold, cold place. Life now is just a jungle. My workplace is full of sharks.
MAKING NEGATIVE PREDICTIONS: Making predictions about the future based more on how you feel than on what is knowable.	If I take the exam, I will just go to pieces. I will never find another partner. I will never get back to how I used to feel. I won't enjoy that now.	People will think that I am pathetic. No one will be attracted to me now. If I tell people how I really feel, they will just use it against me.	Girlfriends will always dump me. My colleagues will criticise anything I say in the meeting. If I ask people to help, they will let me down.	It will be downhill all the way from here. People won't be prepared to give me a chance. I'll end up an outcast if I screw this up.
OVER-STATEMENTS: Over emphasising the bad aspects of a situation and/or understating or ignoring the good aspects.	The fact that I lost that account means I'm incompetent. All my good work goes up in smoke in light of that failure.	Life without Sam is unbearable. I just don't know what to say in social situations. It's horrible if people criticise my work.	They never think about other people. People always put their own advantage first.	Life is pointless. There is so much violence and hatred in the world. Society is very unforgiving of mistakes.

Source: Wills, 2008a

A simplified list can help trainees and clients grasp the most important distortions quickly. The fuller list of distortions can be used later in therapy, as clients can identify them more readily. Some categories of distortion can be profitably linked to certain problems. *Catastrophisation* (subsumed under 'over-statement' above), for example, is frequently found in anxiety problems of all types.

There are other helpful approaches to identifying thinking biases (Harvey et al., 2004): self-serving bias, for example, may lead people to underestimate their own role in relationship breakdowns. Cognitive mechanisms such as 'limited search routines' may prevent people from searching widely enough to find appropriate evaluative evidence regarding their thoughts. In these circumstances, therapists must be prepared to be persistent and devise creative Socratic questions to uncover these factors.

EVALUATING EVIDENCE ON THOUGHTS: VALIDITY AND UTILITY

If there is one sentence that captures the spirit of traditional CBT, it would be 'What is your evidence *for* that thought/belief?' followed shortly by 'What is the evidence *against* it?'. Clients often come up with NATs that are malevolent accusations against themselves, so that CBT can have a resemblance to a 'defence attorney' (Leahy, 2003). Self-critical clients can be asked 'Is that (usually a minor indiscretion) really a *hanging offence*?' and 'Would that (self) charge (of being 'totally incompetent') *stand up in court*?'. Even clients who are lawyers can find it remarkably difficult to defend themselves: testimony perhaps to the compelling plausibility of negative thoughts. Albert Ellis advances a telling argument against any form of judgement on the self: 'The results are not yet all in.' Usefulness is established over a lifetime. Late goals change football matches. Churchill was still considered a political failure shortly before his 'finest hour'. Furthermore, the accusation 'I am useless' implies a judgement of the *whole self*, whereas usefulness and uselessness, in as much as the terms have any utility, emerge from many *separate behaviours*. This does not preclude the validity of judgements on some aspects of a person's behaviour.

These facts confront us with a striking aspect of reviewing evidence about NATs in CBT: all the relevant information is hardly ever completely available. This is true by definition of the kind of negative predictions that so often accompany anxiety: we can never know how a future event will actually turn out. The best hope is to estimate a range of probabilities for particular outcomes. Life in the universe remains frustratingly short of certainty. Clients who worry usually require more certainty than is available in life. They still, however, can look unconvinced when therapists suggest that life might be boring if outcomes were as certain as they would like them to be.

There are problems with estimating the relative strength of the quantity and quality of evidence: for example, one big example of incompetence usually counts for more than many small examples of competence. The therapist, however, has no choice but to look for detail and collect small evidence along with the big. Overall evidence is usually mixed and allows therapist and client to dispense with gross generalisations and promote more benign views of life than those usually held by people in the grip of painful emotions.

Evaluating negative thoughts requires subtlety and may raise profound, even existential, questions about what is most valued in life. Written materials can enhance the CBT process and as we turn to modifying negative cognitions, we begin by describing two of CBT's best known written methods: pie charts and thought records.

MODIFYING AND CHALLENGING NEGATIVE THINKING

Using Pie Charts to Look at Alternative Explanations

When clients' NATs over-focus on negative explanations of events, pie charts can help to gather and draw attention to overlooked factors that may be influencing the situation. For example, clients who are anxious about health may take a single symptom such as a headache and give it the catastrophic interpretation that it indicates a brain tumour. Such clients may be asked to brainstorm all possible causes of headaches and then each is given a probability rating. Often, the cause seen as the most likely when the client is anxious ends up being given a low probability. Pie charts can be useful when blame – of oneself or others – is an issue. Figure 5.3 shows a pie chart drawn after a client had the thought that her marriage break up was 'all my fault'. The client was then asked to describe all the factors that may have contributed to her situation and put them into a pie chart. The sizes of the slices of pie were based on her estimation of the influence of each factor they represented.

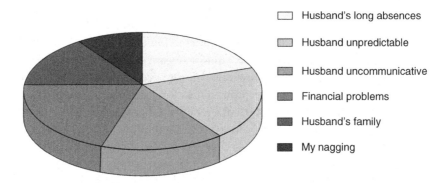

FIGURE 5.3   Pie chart (worked example)

A GD/SD process unfolds in pie chart work. The therapist begins by 'unpacking' the client's over-generalised view ('all my fault') with analytic questions that help the client to break this view down into a more differentiated set of sub-parts, whilst at the same time evaluative questions help the client to rethink and 'repack' the meaning implied by the separate elements ('I played a role but it wasn't all my fault'). To watch this process in action, see the DVD made by Simmons and Wills (2009).

MODIFYING AND CHALLENGING NEGATIVE THINKING: THE NATURE AND PURPOSE OF THOUGHT RECORDS

The thought record sums up many of the manoeuvres we have already described in the identification and evaluation of negative thoughts:

- It specifies trigger events that lead to negative thoughts.
- It describes the thinking, feeling and behavioural responses to those triggers.
- It evaluates evidence in relation to the negative thoughts.

The thought record also adds some final further elements to strengthen the possibilities of reframing the negative thoughts:

- It develops alternative, more adaptive thoughts or ways of thinking about such trigger events should they arise in the future.
- It summarises key elements of new alternative cognitive, emotional and behavioural response patterns in light of the review of the original such responses.

Grant et al. (2004) note that these processes enable clients to see the 'meta-message' that thoughts are mental events to be observed, identified and evaluated rather than regarded as absolute truths, thereby changing the self's relationship to the thoughts. Furthermore, using thought records helps clients to generalise skills in identifying and re-evaluating thoughts to other events, situations or life circumstances.

An example of a thought record is presented in Figure 5.4: the reader can cross-reference the bullet points listed above with the actual columns of the thought record. The client who completed the thought record shown was a well-qualified health professional who suffered from obsessional thoughts about contamination. Some of her main obsessions were fears of contamination coming from touching blood and other materials resulting from medical work. She met the criteria for both obsessive compulsive disorder (OCD) and the DSM classification 'Simple phobia: Blood' (APA, 2000)). The thought record shown is an exact copy of the original thought record completed by the client alone and then amended by therapist

Trigger	Emotion	NAT or image	Evidence for NAT	Evidence against NAT	Alternative adaptive thought	Outcome
Blood on money from cash point	*Anxious 80%*	*I have to wash my hands* *I have to change my clothes*	*Not hygienic*	*Infections are not transmitted this easily* *Probably very common*	*I should rationalise that the risk is negligible*	*Anxiety 60%*
Blood on money from cash point	Anxious 80%	I have got dangerous germs on my hands I could kill my son and husband	Germs are everywhere	Germs are only very rarely dangerous Blood infections aren't that hardy	I may have germs on my hands but they are almost certainly harmless	Anxiety 30% Resist washing hands/changing clothes

FIGURE 5.4 Example of a 7-column thought record

and client working together. The upper part of the form (written in *italics*) shows the clients first attempt to fill out a thought record for homework; the bottom part shows how the client and therapist reworked the form in the next session:

There are skilled and unskilled ways of completing thought records: clients *and* therapist must develop these skills. The way the client filled out the form in Figure 5.4 shows some misdirection and this meant that the thought record was not effective in helping her to manage her negative feelings better. The client reported that the reworked form made more sense and helped her to understand and feel better about her situation. This was the first thought record that she had completed and it is perhaps not surprising that the initial version misfired. Each section of the thought record is now reviewed, opening with a statement of the basic aim in each, followed by comments on each section of the original and reworked entries shown in Figure 5.4.

Trigger and Emotion

These columns establish specific triggers and the accompanying specific problematic reactions. The trigger situation here seems obvious but is not always so. The problematic reaction might reflect the syndrome or problem named in the client's referral: in this case, anxiety is very much part of the criteria for OCD.

In the upper part of Figure 5.4, the client makes effective entries in these two columns. She has found a 'specific' trigger that constitutes a 'moment' when the thought and emotion actually 'kicked in'. Sometimes thought records do not work because the client refers to a more general trigger in this section, such as 'My girlfriend finished with me'. Such experience is not really specific in the way we have defined but takes place over a number of days, weeks or months during which the client had many different thoughts and feelings. The therapist can encourage the client to make this type of trigger more specific by asking 'Which was the worst moment?'. This may produce an answer that can be translated into a specific trigger: 'When she didn't send me a birthday card, I knew then it was over for sure.' Getting the specific moment usually evokes a stronger emotional reaction and is more likely to evoke the most telling negative thoughts. The negative emotion in Figure 5.4 is clearly defined with a simple word for a primary emotion, but again we must be prepared to deal with clients who are not so clear in the way they identify feelings as this – see Tables 5.1 and 5.3.

NAT or image

The case has already been made for the importance of NATs and images[4] in the maintenance of psychological difficulties. As testing this thought will be a key part of cognitive restructuring, it is important that it is clearly defined in a way that can be tested. Therapists can be quite active in this process because there is already some reconstruction in the memory of thoughts so that they can legitimately work to define them further: in ways that clarify its underlying meaning and make it more testable in the thought record.

In Figure 5.4, the reported thought probably was close to what went through the client's mind but is actually more of a behavioural disposition[5] than an appraising negative thought. It is sometimes difficult to define 'hot' thoughts precisely but, if in doubt, the therapist should ask herself 'Does this thought explain the negative feeling?'. In this case, the answer must be 'no' because washing her hands would relieve the anxiety: it is a response to the anxiety, not the thought that evokes the anxiety. As they reviewed this thought record, the therapist asked the client 'Why did you think you should wash your hands and change your clothes?' The client answered 'Because I felt I had germs on my hands.' The therapist then asked a 'downwards arrow' question: 'And what was so bad about that?' She answered 'They could be dangerous. I could infect others … kill my son and husband.' These thoughts *do* explain the anxiety. Notice also that the client did not rate the strength of her belief in the NAT. The therapist did not ask her to do so because her rating of the thought now in the relative calm of the therapy session would not have reflected how she would have rated it at the time. This is a frequent problem with thought records that are not filled out in the heat of the moment.

Unless NATs occur in the session itself, retrospective reports of them are the best that can be done. Therapists can always encourage clients to fill out their thought records as soon as possible after the actual moment the thought occurs. This is not always practically possible, of course. Clients can be concerned that other people may discover their records and so they will therefore only ever fill them out when privacy is assured. When Frank kept thought records for three months, he devised a version that could be fitted into a small notebook and was surprised how often he could use it close to the time of incidents. Practical issues should be discussed with clients when setting homework: for example, fears about feeling more disturbed by clearer recognition of thoughts that once were vague. Some people find it hard to access their thoughts and some, even when they can, find it hard to report them. Some people find it easier to access images than thoughts. One client, for example, reported a depressed reaction to reading a job advertisement that led to a decision not to apply. It turned out that as she thought about applying, the client had vivid images of being rejected by the interviewing panel. She could describe this image in great detail, revealing rich undercurrents of negative meaning. She imagined the interviewers shaking their heads as they read her application. When asked what this meant, she said, 'They thought I had a cheek to apply and that I was wasting their time.' With such images in mind, it was hardly surprising that she failed to apply for the job.

Evidence for and against the NAT or image

The aim of reviewing the evidence for and against negative thoughts and images is to help clients to step back and reconsider them. The therapist can explore the degree of 'fit' between thoughts and feeling and then weigh the evidence for them. When people are emotionally disturbed they are likely to take negative thoughts as facts rather than interpretations or hypotheses. The hold of such thoughts on the client's mind needs to be loosened.

In Figure 5.4, the client produced good pieces of evidence in these columns but they were responses to the behavioural disposition and thus did not re-evaluate the negative thoughts. The evidence presented in the reworked version is similar to the client's original entries but *does* get closer to the underlying thinking. It is also more realistic: it accepts that there may be germs in public places but that the risk of harm is remote. The client later realised that the chances of infection were increased by skin cuts resulting from her excessive hand-washing.

Images can be reviewed in the same way: for example, the client who had the image about applying for a job could examine evidence about whether it was a reasonable estimate of what might have happened if she had decided to apply. In Chapters 7 and 9 we will review how 'replaying' the client's imagery can facilitate spontaneous processing of negative and traumatic emotions.

Alternative thought and outcome

Establishing alternative thoughts based on the evidence columns suggests other ways clients can think and behave when confronted by similar situations.

In Figure 5.4, the non-avoidant tone of the second version is more realistic and produces more decrease in negative emotion. The therapist strengthens the outcome column by initiating a conversation about 'dropping the safety behaviour' of hand-washing. This client agreed that she could drop hand-washing 'in her own space and time' – and did indeed stay faithful to that promise.[6]

Reviewing this thought record now, we notice that it is not wordy but comparatively parsimonious: that is, it has only a single situation and thought and does not amass a great deal of evidence. In many cases, the thought records may contain multiple entries for all the columns and this can feel cluttered and inhibit positive responses. Simple thought records showing clear links between thoughts and feelings usually work best. Sometimes clients' difficulties with obsessional lists making can interfere with simplicity as every nuance of every thought and feeling is recorded. Obsessional thoughts are harder to evaluate because they often concern 'risk assessment' and beg the question just how 'safe' one should be? Thought records do vary enormously in the amount of material they throw up. This example is a good one for our purposes here because it was parsimonious and therefore allowed focused discussion. Thought records, however, can sometimes be counter-productive for clients with obsessions and worries. There is now more interest about working with obsessional thoughts and worries by working with cognitive processes and this will be the subject of the final section of this chapter.

USING THOUGHT RECORDS IN PRACTICE

Thought records can be used more slowly and cumulatively by breaking up their various elements into smaller separate records, for example, with just a few columns at a time. Some clients need to build up slowly in this way – especially when an individual problem like appropriately labelling emotions arises. A slow build-up allows such clients more time to master the specific sub-skills of working with thoughts and feelings. When using the whole form, it is often suggested that the form (as per Figure 5.4) is given in two phases: the first phase consists of using only columns 1 to 3 for identifying triggers, feelings and negative thoughts open for entries, whilst the other response columns, 4 to 7, are blocked out for use later. The therapist should produce the form and explain it to the client, fielding questions as appropriate – with back-up guidelines available. Client and therapist should then fill out the form in the session, taking a recent incident in the client's life for a worked example. A collaborative stance is emphasised by encouraging the client to make the actual entries, perhaps running them past the therapist first. Working with thought records rarely runs as smoothly as in the textbooks. Most clients make some connection with their logic but are likely to report difficulties in getting them to really work. It is likely that therapist and client will encounter some of the problems described in Tables 5.1 and 5.3.

Clients' difficulties in responding to thought records are sometimes the result of pessimistic beliefs about therapy: a lurking suspicion that they might work for some but not for them. This belief can seem confirmed when they hit snags such as a thought record that leaves them baffled and feeling no better. The problems of the first three columns – identifying and rating thoughts and feelings – have already been shown in Table 5.1. Table 5.3 focuses on difficulties that arise in relation to generating evidence and alternative thoughts – covered in columns 4 to 7. The process supported by these columns strives for credible evidence and credible cognitive change.

Problems with Evidence

A major impetus to the growth of CBT was the recognition that the functioning of depressed clients was influenced by cognitive distortions. Obviously there are times when clients report severely adverse life experiences that are not at all exaggerated: life-threatening illnesses, for example (Moorey & Greer, 2002). The evidence about such events may well confirm negative thoughts. As well as expressing empathy and support, additional cognitive work could involve looking at ways in which the client's thinking is unhelpful to *them* rather than whether it is 'distorted'. For example, when working with clients with cancer, a CB therapist can help them think whether ruminating on how little time is left to them may get in the way of making use of what time is left. Therapists should approach this kind of dialogue humbly, opening themselves to the hard truth of the client's situation.

TABLE 5.3 Problems and solutions in evaluating and responding to negative thoughts

Problems	Solutions
Problems with evidence (Columns 4 & 5)	
Strongly adverse life events	Focus on empathic listening. Identify ways of thinking that may be making the problem even worse. Suggest it may be helpful to review how helpful these thoughts are.
The quantity of the evidence favours the negative The quality of the evidence favours the negative The client finds it difficult to evaluate a negative thought as anything but true (Negative evidence is more compelling or credible)	Discuss the balance of the evidence; where either the quantity or the quality of the evidence balances toward the negative, suggest an 'open verdict'. Use belief ratings: anything less than 100% indicates a degree of doubt that can be built on.
Problems with the alternative thought (Column 6)	
The client describes the alternative thought as having intellectual but not emotional conviction (head but not heart)	Go back over the whole sequence: check the exact wording of the NAT and the alternative. Recheck the quality of the evidence. Also suggest that emotional conviction does take longer and may take some time to 'bed in'.
Clients say things like 'Yes (I know I'm not really a failure) but ...'	Draw out the 'but' – often it is underlain by some unspoken fears or even by a mega-cognitive rule such as 'If I don't worry about this, I'll get complacent'.
Problems with the end result (Column 7)	
Client reports no change in negative feeling	Discuss need to use method over time. Write in a comment on how it could be different next time. If persistent, review focus; consider shifting to cognitive processes rather than content.

Source: Wills, 2008

Problems of evidence may also arise in other cases when clients' approaches to evidence give disproportionate weight to some factors rather than others. It can be helpful to weigh the balance of quantity and quality of evidence, sometimes settling for an 'open verdict'. The credibility of evidence to clients can be assessed by ratings of the key negative beliefs.

Problems with the Credibility of Cognitive Change

Clients often report that they believe the positive alternative thought with their heads but not in their hearts. It is actually in the nature of things that intellectual conviction often does precede emotional conviction and often this is just a sign that the client may need, in Ellis' words, to 'work and practice' (Dryden, 1991). It can be helpful to recognise that the credibility of alternative thoughts and beliefs may develop slowly. Views of self and life have developed over years, and it may take constant repetition of alternatives to produce change. Sometimes, however, these problems are a sign that the therapy is not on track and the therapist may use them to consider alternatives – especially working on cognitive processes rather than on content – particularly if the client has difficulty with intrusive thoughts, obsession, ruminations or worries.

Paul Gilbert (2009, 2010) suggests an intriguing rationale for developing cognitive work along compassion-focused lines. As neuroscience develops, it has become clear that there is a major area of the brain that is involved in 'calming' the whole person and that this is intimately involved in the quality of applying compassion both towards oneself and towards others. Paul began to develop compassion-focused CBT when he realised that unless a client can hear alternative functional thoughts in a compassionate voice it is unlikely that they will have much positive effect.

CASE STUDY
Rose

Rose's driven attitude towards her life led to frequent unproductive cycles of over-work and exhaustion. We worked on developing thinking that fitted with what we had both agreed was essential to her recovery – learning to 'pace' her activities. Whenever we evolved more 'easy-going' thinking – taking sensible levels of responsibility and not expecting too much of herself – it seemed not to touch her. Describing her teenage years, she reported that her parents had been loving but that there had been a period when her mum was desperately depressed. Rose herself was having major problems at that time but when her mother had turned to her for help in a very needy fashion, Rose realised that she herself could not expect help and would have to learn to comfort herself. Family problems were of such magnitude then that learning self-soothing proved very difficult.

CB therapists are now therefore keen to find ways of helping clients to experience compassion within themselves. Gilbert (2009) describes ways in this can be done, such as cultivating mindfulness and compassionate imagery. Unsurprisingly, these methods require highly congruent, compassionate behaviour on the therapist's part.

We must always try to empathise with clients who find it difficult to change. Thinking about how our own attempts to change virtually any aspect of our lives tells us that change is most frequently gradual and incremental. Therapists and clients can sometimes be too eager for immediate change. Sometimes it takes time and persistence for new ideas to sink in and come to conscious realisation (Leahy, 2003). Therapists should be wary of 'arguing' with clients when they seem to block new information out. It is better to acknowledge clients' doubts about the new information: 'So, the idea that you may actually be an okay person is simply not credible to you right now.' An ACT perspective – well oriented to the paradoxes of the human mind and the need to sometimes deconstruct and defuse its thoughts – is often helpful at such times. An ACT therapist might use a disjuncture like this to use a metaphor like 'passengers on the bus' to observe that it is only too typical of 'Mr Thought' to insist on staying on the bus when his absence would be highly desirable. Sometimes when you 'cheer-lead' for the positive, the negative seems to only dig in that much deeper. Anyone who has ever canvassed voters on their doorsteps will know that one.

It is important for CB therapists to take time to deal with client reservations and difficulties as thoroughly as possible in actual therapy time as the next move will be to ask the client if he can use thought records regularly at home. There is a good deal of evidence that clients who do homework regularly get significantly better results with CBT than those who do not (Kazantzis et al., 2005). If clients can bring one or more thought records, completed as homework tasks, to the next session, these are put on the agenda and given attention and time. Giving them proper attention is heartening to clients and respectful of the effort involved. Clients can feel afraid that their efforts will be judged negatively. They may find it helpful if therapists clarify in advance that spelling and grammar, for example, are not at issue.

As we fill out the final (response and challenge) columns of thought records, it is helpful to have more discussion about the therapeutic aims of this activity and how it may best be used. The prime aim is to help clients to develop more reflective relationships with their thoughts. This new perspective can raise the hope that clients can think more clearly and feel better in the shorter and longer terms. Sometimes clients can progress to generating new alternative thoughts during actual trigger events. Alternatively, they can use the technique in retrospect and thus prevent themselves from going into prolonged negative rumination. Frank found 'keeping them myself' instructive. First, he was surprised by the amount of negativity that came out of his head. Second, he found that thought records quite often made him feel better and clearer, helping him to get on with his day. Third, he noticed that they were sometimes ineffective in the short term but that often he would notice some effect later in the day. The experience emphasised the importance of persistence in keeping thought records. We would recommend the experience to all CB therapists. Having kept a record for oneself, therapists can ask clients to follow suit with more authority and understanding. Leahy (2003) emphasises the need for over-practice and over-learning. Hollon et al. (2006) also reinforce the view that CBT techniques do need persistence to achieve enduring effects.[7] This is because the sheer weight and persistence of negative thoughts mean that reversing them once does not banish them for life: 'one swallow' most definitely does not 'make a summer'. The best prescription for problems with thought records is to trouble-shoot in sessions but then to consider *increasing* practice rather than abandoning using them. It is perhaps necessary to also add a warning against dogmatic over-persistence: Bennett-Levy (2003) cautions that thought records, and perhaps cognitive restructuring more generally, can be a 'tedious' experience for some clients.

DEVELOPING CREATIVE USE OF THOUGHT RECORDS

The real aim of cognitive work is to stimulate alternative ways of thinking. We need also to be true to our principles of collaboration: getting the client to write down things in session and to keep them in their therapy book. It is helpful to fill out parallel copies alongside the client so that they can be studied before the next session. These notes serve as reminders of what was discussed in the session and sometimes therapists may see something that was missed or could be tackled in a different way.

Sometimes, however, CB therapists can be too keen to get clients to write down and/or challenge negative thoughts. It can be better to allow thoughts to 'hang in the air' and patiently wait to see what happens next. Therapists can try just writing thoughts on the whiteboard and inviting clients to 'contemplate' them. We have experienced some surprising client reactions to this – including clients laughing out loud as the 'absurdity' of the thoughts hits them. Some clients have also told us that they have on occasion been able to visualise thoughts written on the whiteboard when they are in a situation outside the therapy room and that this has helped them to rethink their reactions – a sign, perhaps, of some kind of helpful 'internalisation' of the therapy and the therapist (Power, 2010). Sometimes clients have picked up the board-marker and have amended the thought on the whiteboard – a self-efficacy to be welcomed.

CASE STUDY
Rose

Rose exhausted herself by her driven approach to her work in social services. She also described sitting all night with a distressed friend so that she felt 'completely wiped out' next day. As she explored her thinking round this incident, the therapist wrote one of her main problematic thoughts, 'I have to be responsible', on the whiteboard. After pausing to think, Rose picked up a board-marker and wrote next to the thought: 'If I burn myself out I won't be able to be responsible for anything!' The exchange led naturally to constructing a set of criteria for 'taking responsibility – within reason'.

Such shifts in thinking can be elusive and may occur in unusual ways. Frank once dreamt that his father was a client using a thought record. The final alternative way of thinking, however, was presented to him as a logo written on the side of a mug. His father loved his tea and Frank reflected that it might have been an evocative way to complete his experience of using a thought record. We could perhaps be more creative in our working ways. Once, after participating in an assertiveness training workshop, the presenter gave Frank an individualised badge that said 'I may not be perfect but parts of me are really nice'. He felt that this badge particularly spoke to his condition and treasured it for many years. As CB therapists do use coping cards with slogan-like adaptive thoughts, we have occasionally used the badge and T-shirt concept with clients – though it is helpful to discuss how other significant people in their lives are likely to react to them using such things.

We have identified over 20 different forms of thought record used by different CB therapists. They all include most of the steps indicated above, though they sometimes use different vocabularies and running orders. Many therapists use a version based on the 7-column thought record devised by Christine Padesky, though sometimes they find it helpful to use other formats with some clients. Some clients particularly like using Burns' (1999a, 1999b) self-help books alongside CBT and find it helpful to use his version of thought records, the mood log. We can customise CBT materials for the idiosyncratic needs of therapists and clients. Using the elements and language of the various thought records, therapists and clients can construct their own versions to best suit their needs.

EXPERIENTIALLY ORIENTED COGNITIVE METHODS

Behavioural Experiments

Bennett-Levy (2003) has suggested that behavioural experiments are often the most valued part of CB therapy for many clients. Whereas completing thought records can help clients to slow down and put things into perspective (Bennett-Levy et al., 2004), behavioural experiments can be more emotionally convincing: 'doing is believing'. Because clients often report 'procrastination' as a major problem, experiments that can be done during sessions can prove especially powerful because 'there is no time like the present'. Sanders and Wills (2003) discuss a number of behavioural experiments conducted outside the therapy room: for example, going to a zoo to overcome bird phobia. These activities may also have the benefit of developing other sides of the therapeutic relationship, where client and therapist can experience each other in ways different from 'business as usual'. Clients often report appreciating these activities, but they are also challenging and sometimes throw up unusual difficulties. One client became very upset during a behavioural experiment in a public place and this was a great embarrassment to him. It is helpful to plan how to handle such eventualities in advance: *forewarned is forearmed*.

Behavioural experiments should be collaboratively and clearly devised: the more precisely the client's negative belief is defined, the more this allows a clear hypothesis about the belief to be tested and the more effective the behavioural experiment will be. For example, an administrative assistant in local government, Julie, believed herself to be 'inadequate' and 'worthless'. Her fear of job appraisal was a key sign to her that she was inadequate. She considered that she was much more fearful than others. She agreed to test this belief by casually asking fellow workers how they felt about job appraisal. She was amazed that not only did most others share her fears but that some expressed them more strongly. This news forced her to review her opinion on the degree of her own inadequacy based on this criterion. In this case, the therapist had experience of working in local government and had good reason to suspect that the results would run this way. Therapists often, however, have to choose between encouraging open experiments and shielding clients from experiences likely to be negative. Even so, it is helpful to plan how therapist and client will react to an experiment that goes wrong.

Figure 5.5 shows a diary format devised by Bennett-Levy et al. (2004) – a text that offers many useful hints for devising behavioural experiments over for range of situations.

WORKING WITH COGNITIVE PROCESSES

Many have the thought 'I am so useless' at times when they fail at something they'd like to do. For most, fortunately, the thought eventually slides away and does not trouble them further. A person vulnerable to depression, however, might start to ruminate endlessly on this thought and remember incidents from their past that seem to bear it out. The question is, how can CB therapists help clients give more appropriate attention to such thoughts? Many of the newer CB approaches suggest that therapists and clients can develop more mindful and accepting ways of relating to negative thoughts. This way of thinking stresses acceptance of the idea that thoughts and beliefs are mental events and processes rather than reflections of objective truths. Apart from the more philosophical and spiritual aspects of this

Date	Situation	Prediction: How will I know if my prediction comes true?	Experiment to test prediction	Outcome?	What I learned
Monday	Standing outside the supermarket	I'm feeling so bad I am going to pass out. Unless I get out of here fast then I may be very ill (90%).	Stay in the super-market. Stop trying to do anything to control the anxiety and see what happens.	I felt quite uncomfortable but I did not pass out, or even need to sit down. I stayed there and was pleased with myself. The bad feelings went away after a few minutes. Found some nice new ice cream!	Stay with it, things are not as bad as they feel. Anxiety won't make me pass out. I enjoy things and feel good if I don't avoid and run away. Buy this ice cream again!

FIGURE 5.5 Example of a behavioural experiments diary (Bennett-Levy et al., 2004)

dimension, there is also the practical fact that emotions have to run their course to some extent so that it can be counter-productive to shut them down prematurely. For example, we can all think of people (including ourselves) who sometimes need to be left to calm down for a while before they can accept others' attempts to help.

Mindfulness and acceptance are being brought into CBT in a variety of ways: for example, mindfulness-based cognitive therapy (MBCT) is a group approach that will be described in Chapter 8. There is now also an impetus for CB therapists to find ways of operationalising these ideas in everyday practice, because they can be helpful to clients who are not in MBCT groups. Fennell (2004) describes how mindfulness can help with depression and low self-esteem for clients in individual therapy. She is clear, however, that bringing mindful techniques into everyday practice is not a question of learning new techniques but of importing the ideas, the spirit and therapeutic style from MBCT. ACT (Hayes et al., 2004) have also focused more on devising mindfulness and acceptance interventions that can be used in one-on-one sessions. There are a growing number of methods, developed in MBCT, ACT, metacognitive therapy and other models, that can be incorporated into CBT work.

The worked example for the thought record in Figure 5.4 showed the responses of a client suffering from intrusive, obsessional thoughts and phobias. The consensus amongst CB therapists is now that working with the content of such thoughts is often only partially effective. This is because the problems these thoughts cause are crucially influenced by the amount and type of attention that clients pay to them. It has been shown, for example, that almost 90 per cent of people report having thoughts similar to those that afflict sufferers of OCD (Rachman, 2003). The difference between these 'normal' and 'abnormal' obsessions lies in peoples' reactions to them. Most people dismiss the thoughts relatively easily, whereas for OCD sufferers such thoughts are so personally objectionable, carrying such profoundly negative meaning, that they attempt to suppress them. Unfortunately, this suppression works in a way that only succeeds in producing a 'rebound effect', making the thought ever harder to suppress.

Similarly with the problem of worry; the content of worry does not differ much between sufferers and non-sufferers. Worry is functional – up to a point. Most people need to be concerned about things that could go wrong in their lives and would be 'unprepared' for crises if they weren't. Leahy (2005) distinguishes between 'productive worry' and 'unproductive worry'. Butler and Hope (1995) describe how worry is productive when it leads us to take reasonable action about our problems, but is unproductive when 'ruminative worry' blocks adaptive responses.

METACOGNITIVE INTERVENTIONS

The emerging attentional perspective suggests that it is helpful to develop a different type of relationship between the mind and its worries, intrusions and obsessions. The way we think about our cognitive processes (metacognition) may determine how we can relate to these problems. Re-thinking our metacognitive

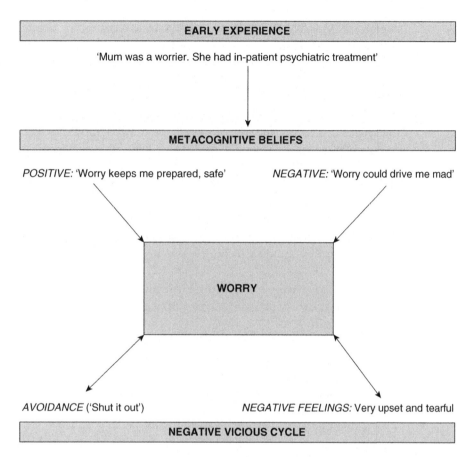

FIGURE 5.6　Metacognitive formulation of worry

beliefs can be a helpful first step in making such new relationships. Wells (2008) has suggested a number of helpful ways of changing the way we pay attention to negative thoughts: rethinking metacognitive beliefs, learning to vary our attentional routines and developing 'detached mindfulness' towards them.

Wells (2008) has now developed a complete metacognitive therapy (MCT), a variant CBT model. He offers formulations of depression and various anxiety disorders based on metacognitive concepts. He also offers suggestions on treatment approaches based on these formulations. Interventions include CBT techniques revised in the light of MCT formulations and also new interventions: attention training technique (ATT) and detached mindfulness (DM).

Metacognitive Formulation

As shown in Figure 5.6, metacognitive formulation begins in similar way to standard CBT formulation by indentifying trigger situations and negative automatic thoughts NATs. In MCT, however, the NAT is explored in a different way than in standard CBT. Instead of being regarded as containing problematic content to be modified, it becomes the kicking-off point for exploring a problematic meta-cognitive process that Wells terms the 'cognitive attentional syndrome' (CAS). The CAS is a toxic pattern of relationships between thoughts, emotions and behaviours that 'locks' the person onto negative thoughts in a type of fixated attention. The process involves the various types of metacognitive thoughts and beliefs described in previous chapters: positive and negative metacognitive beliefs and Type 1 and Type 2 worries. The following therapy dialogue illustrates an abbreviated version of an MCT assessment/formulation discussion and cross-refernces with Figure 5.6.

In the dialogue, the client has said that a recent episode of prolonged dysphoric worry began after she had the thought that she might have caused her child irremediable harm by shouting at him so much:

Client: I was cleaning the bath and it hit me like a ton of bricks and I just sort of stopped and felt dreadful, dreadful and never really got started again.

Therapist: What did you do and what were you feeling and thinking?

Client: Well I was on my knees cleaning and I just sat on the bathroom floor … and started sobbing … I felt upset, disturbed … that I was a terrible mother … a bad person … and then I thought about poor little Josh … I imagined him standing then looking all deprived … like one of those kids you see in the NSPCC ads …

Therapist: And when you felt like that did you think something bad could happen from feeling that way?

Client: Yeah I did actually – I could see myself in one of those ads – you know that I was an orphan kid, the damaged one – and I would end up in hospital.

Therapist: So do you think that worrying is bad for you in any way?

Client: Yeah definitely I am just like my mum – she was a real worrier – and she did end up in the psychiatric ward.

Therapist: So why don't you stop doing it then?

Client: If only it was that easy – I feel like it controls me more than I could control it.

Therapist: Can worrying sometimes be helpful in any way?

Client: My mum used to say, 'Always be prepared, don't let anything catch you out. Think ahead and plan for everything that might go wrong.' There is that to worrying – if you think things might go wrong then you won't be so surprised when they do.

Therapist: So worrying can have advantages but it also gives you problems.

Client: You can say that again.

Therapist: Do the problems make you do things to try to stop worrying?

Client: I have tried all sorts of things. I used to ring Bob at work but it is harder for him to take the calls now and he gets angry with me – so I just try to shut it out of my mind now. That day I was clenching my jaw so hard it ached for quite a while after.

Discussions like this focus on and reveal problematic metacognitive beliefs (such as 'If you expect things to go wrong then you won't be surprised if they do') that could well be maintaining the problematic pattern. These beliefs can be modified with methods similar to standard CB techniques reinforced by methods to help clients redirect patterns of problematic attention and other cognitive processes – especially ATT and DM.

Using ATT and DM in Therapy

ATT involves a series of instructions that help clients learn to shift attention between processing tasks. Wells found that sounds constituted a more effective focus for most clients, so therapists find a number of sounds in or near the therapy room that can be used for ATT practice. ATT constitutes the only focus for sessions for a limited period because it is important that the client gives undivided time and attention to learning it. Clients are asked to practice the technique between sessions. Research has shown it to be an effective way of helping clients to evolve new attentional routines that make them less vulnerable to repetitive worry and other negative symptoms (Wells, 2009). ATT exercises take about 20–30 minutes practiced in session and homework. The ATT phase is a discrete series of meetings separate from but sometimes parallel with other therapy work.

DM is:

> A state of awareness of internal events, without responding to them with sustained evaluation, attempting to control, suppress them, nor respond to them behaviourally. It is exemplified by strategies such as deciding not to worry in response to intrusive thoughts, but allowing the thought to occupy its own mental space without further action or interpretation in the knowledge that it is merely an event in the mind. (Wells, 2009: 71)

This type of attention is promoted by telling the client one of ten brief vignettes that they are then asked to reflect on. Vignettes illustrate how thinking and imagining are active processes that sometimes contain the seeds of making ideas seem more than they are. In the 'Tiger Task' vignette, for example, clients are asked to focus on the image of a tiger and merely then observe what happens in the mind. Many people experience that the image takes on a life of its' own. Clients are then asked to reflect on whether there is any similarity between this and the way that problematic thoughts and images form in their minds. DM vignette exercises take about 10–15 minutes each and are usually done once or twice in sessions during the early phases of MCT.

In contrast with other types of mindfulness, however, DM:

1 Does not involve meditation.
2 Does not require continuous practice.
3 Does not require increasing awareness of the present.
4 Does not use body-focused anchors for attention.
5 Involves meta-awareness of thoughts rather than present moment awareness.
6 Definitions connected to DM are more specific than those of mindfulness.
7 Separates mindfulness from detachment.
8 Is specific about suspending conceptual processing.
9 Is specific about suspending goal-directed coping.
10 Is specific about separating self from mental phenomena. (Wells, 2009: 79)

MCT has currently been applied to some of the most prominent anxiety and depressive disorders and has been shown to be an effective form of CBT (Wells, 2009).

CUSTOMISED MINDFUL ATTENTION METHODS IN INDIVIDUAL THERAPY

It is sometimes difficult to describe mindfulness in words. We have all known the relaxed feeling that can come whilst lying in the sun on a summer's day, but could we instruct someone to repeat our experience? Leahy's approach to worry, however, contains a useful set of 'think steps' that, in my experience, are helpful to clients trying to evolve a less enmeshed relationship with their own tendency to worry. There is value, therefore, in describing Leahy's 7-steps of mindful therapy for overcoming worry. Worry is an acute and persistent negative state linked to anxiety, especially to generalised anxiety disorder (GAD) (APA, 2000). Like Segal et al.'s (2002) mindfulness programme, Leahy's mindfulness steps are weaved in with more active cognitive steps focused on restructuring. The seven steps are shown in Figure 5.7.

In the steps designed to help clients learn to use mindfulness, the client is encouraged to develop 'mindful detachment', a state that strongly emphasises non-possessive awareness and radical acceptance: the spirit also suffuses the whole model. Step 2 is called 'Accepting reality and committing to change' and clearly mirrors aspects of Steve Hayes' ACT model (Hayes et al., 2004). Acceptance involves mindful acceptance of reality in the sense that it is desirable to move towards a way of accepting life as it is, not as we demand it should be. It is interesting that the mindful strategies associated with Leahy's acceptance step come *before* the more traditional cognitive intervention steps, such as the suggestion to challenge worried thinking. This order of precedence implies that it is important

1. Distinguish between productive and unproductive worry.

2. Accept reality and commit to change.

3. Challenge worried thinking.

4. Focus on the deeper threat.

5. Turn failure into opportunity.

6. Use emotions rather than worry about them.

7. Take control of time.

FIGURE 5.7   The 7-steps worry cure (Wills, 2008a)

for the client to develop a different type of relationship to their worry processes before starting to challenge the content of worrying thoughts. One of the important functions of worry may be to protect the client from other negative emotions (Leahy, 2005: 293). Disowning emotions in this way would mean that cognitive work could fail to evoke the appropriate emotions and would therefore fail to meet the criteria that would be needed for *metanoia* (emotionally felt cognitive change).

Therapists help worried clients become more mindfully engaged in the *present* moment because worry is oriented towards the *future* – involving the fear that catastrophes will unfold. Worry can also lead to depression, and depressed thinking is typically tied up with *past* failure. The therapist therefore helps the client to come to stay in the present moment by describing concrete experience and 'noticing' what is happening around him. This helps the client to feel better and is more likely to lead to problem solving (Wilkinson et al., 2011).

In the following example, necessarily heavily abbreviated client dialogue, we have followed some of the suggestions proposed by Leahy's (2005) for promoting the acceptance of worry. The therapist can introduce these concepts – gaining distance, describing what is in front of you; suspending judgement and, in imagination, fading out of the scene – and work them through with the client. The client, Bella, had many worries about her interactions with those closest to her. She had visited her brother before our session and had come away feeling preoccupied that she had upset him.

Therapist: Bella, can we hold this worry about Sam more calmly? You have read the Worry book, so we'll try to view the worry more distantly. The author suggests saying, 'I'm just having the thought …

Client: It feels silly.

Therapist: … Give it a go anyway?

Client: Okay then [*long pause*]. I'm just having the thought that I said something about dad that upset my brother and that he will fret all night about it ... Because I know him and how upset he can get ... [*Silence*] ... It is funny I can see him in my mind's eye, sitting there ... That was so vivid ... it is fading now.

Therapist: Okay, you're doing well. Let us take your mind away from that thought now and just tell me, what do you see in front of you now?

Client: [*Looking out of window*] I can see the garden and there is a bird hopping across the lawn ... it's got a worm ... and now it's flying off ... to the roof opposite ... It's puffing its chest out ... now it's in the sky ...

Therapist: Now back to the worry thought about Sam, but think about it without saying it is good or bad ... it is just a thought, neither good nor bad.

Client: I can see my brother again and I can see me saying what I said about dad ... My brother looks quiet, perhaps a bit sad.

Therapist: If this worry were a thing, what would it feel like?

Client: Like a lump ... but one that is now softening, melting perhaps ... I can see my brother again. He is sad and wistful maybe. I remember that he smiled as I left .... He probably will think about what I said but he'll be sad, not hurt. I mean it is sad about dad – but so is life, isn't it?

Therapist: Okay, life can be sad ... Your brother is now feeling sad, but can you fade yourself out of the scene and just leave him to it?

Client: [*Long pause*] I'm stepping away from him. I'm walking out of thinking of it like I walked out of the house. I'm thinking about him living his life and I can let him do it. I care for him but I'm not responsible for him. I can accept us both feeling low.

As mentioned earlier, it is hard to reproduce the quality of mindful functioning. Written down, these responses may appear trite. Dialogues that attempt to touch them have the feeling of poetry – a language that can capture feeling and meaning more fully at times (Teasdale, 1996). CB therapists have sometimes reported feeling uneasy about using 'touchy-feely' interventions like imagery and visualisation. The discussion shown above was slow and reflective and did not unfold as quickly as it is shown in the dialogue. It took some encouragement for Bella to find these words. Slowing down speech and increasing the reflective quality are important aspects of these mindful interventions. To some extent, a dialogue like this is trying to help client and therapist to make contact with the present moment in which they may even experience something of a transcendent sense of self. Leahy (2005) comments that worriers have often put themselves at the centre of the universe: not in an egocentric way but in a way that shoulders all its burdens. Bella found 'stepping back' particularly helpful and commented that 'There's a sense of peace in stepping back and letting life go on by itself'.

To gain distance – to 'decentre' from our thinking, to use the original CBT term (Beck, 1976/1989) – first we need to remember that a thought is just a thought. A thought is not reality. We can do this by using the formula 'I am simply having the thought that ...' and 'I am simply noticing that I am feeling ...'. We can bring our minds into the present moment by looking at what is around us and describing it in simple terms. We can also suspend judgement over our experiences and thoughts. Evaluation is only ever provisional, as Albert Ellis has reminded us (Dryden, 1991). Evaluation can tie up immense amounts of mental energy and yet finding what is really valuable in life can be elusive.

The final moves in Leahy's sequence involve 'taking yourself out of the picture'. This step is taken by imaging the world and life proceeding without you. This may sound scary, but it can also be liberating. The effect of these steps is to take the sting out of nagging worry. A key element is the slowing down and softening thinking processes by infusing them with calm and deeper, slower breaths. In Box 5.1 we offer a form of 'gaining distance' steps. Readers could try it next time they are stuck in a queue.

Box 5.1   Flowing through you like a river

1   Gain distance from your worrying thoughts by saying out loud (or writing down) 'I am having the thought that ...' and 'I am noticing that I am feeling ...'. Let the chain of thoughts and feelings run on as long as it wants.
2   Get to the present by describing what is around you in concrete, non-evaluative language.
3   Try also to take any evaluation out of any thoughts that crop up.
4   Think again about the situations that have evoked worrying thoughts and imagine yourself out of those situations. Imagine the situation, indeed the universe, going on without you.
5   Finally, imagine yourself disappearing altogether. Imagine yourself to be a grain of sand on a beach blown into the distance by a gust of wind.

CONCLUSION

In this chapter we have described some foundational and newer cognitive methods of CBT designed to help clients test whether thinking differently can make a difference for the better. The basic cognitive techniques help clients to change unhelpful thoughts and beliefs. Behavioural experiments may also be explicitly Socratic because they aim, like Socrates, to stimulate enquiry and experiential learning – 'the proof of the pudding is in the eating'. Finally, cognitive interventions to promote mindful attention present clients with choices about how they live at life's most basic level: moment-by-moment experience. Mindfulness-oriented interventions can range from discrete strategies for handling things like worry and other intrusive thoughts through to a programme of interventions such as MBCT. All the interventions described in this chapter may impact at any level of formulation. Mostly they impact on immediate experience and thus their impact may or may not be felt at the more enduring levels of cognition – assumptions and core beliefs. Tools and techniques designed to do that are discussed later in Chapter 9. As more subtle approaches to cognitive work have arisen, some have questioned whether basic cognitive restructuring still has a place in CBT (Martell et al., 2001; Longmore & Worrell, 2007). Whilst this has stimulated a useful debate, to our mind abandoning basic cognitive techniques would be premature. There is still much to learn about how we can promote best practice in cognitive methods. This debate is explored throughout this book and will be returned to in Chapter 10 in particular.

FURTHER READING

Leahy, R. L. (2003) *Cognitive Therapy Techniques: A Practitioners Guide*. New York: Guilford Press.
Leahy, R. L. (2005) *The Worry Cure: 7 Steps to Stop Worry from Worrying You*. New York: Random House.
Wells, A. (2009) *Metacognitive Therapy for Anxiety and Depression*. Chichester: Wiley.

NOTES

1 This is an extract from a CBT demonstration DVD/video (Simmons & Wills, 2006).
2 Originally in Greek *aporia* implied 'no crossing point'. The term has come to be used to signify an impasse in debate.
3 I am grateful to my colleague, Rosa Johnson, for suggesting this point to me.
4 Imagery work will also be described in Chapter 7.
5 It is in the nature of obsessions that the 'behavioural disposition' – in this case, the urge 'to do something' – comes to awareness first.
6 A graduated programme of delayed hand-washing subsequently made rapid progress.
7 With the possible exception of obsessional difficulties mentioned earlier.

6

New Behavioural Directions in CBT

> Human problem solving skills are considerable but they do not work well when they are used to 'fix' internal experiences – something else in needed. (Hayes, 2004)

It is sometimes forgotten that CBT itself is an *integrated* model of the behavioural and cognitive approaches to therapy. Rachman (1997) gives an excellent account of how the 'marriage' of those approaches unfolded. On the whole, it has been a harmonious relationship with both sides gaining much from the other. Behavioural therapy became a bit of a Cinderella in the immediate aftermath of the 'cognitive revolution' of the 1970s and 1980s but its adherents kept working away at their theory and practice and these efforts have now resulted in a 'late flowering' whereby behavioural approaches have risen to new influence in the wider cognitive behavioural range of methods. These developments are increasingly adding new directions to CBT practice that practitioners cannot ignore. They have some expected features – the elaboration of traditional behavioural interventions such as activation – and some less expected ones – such as behavioural perspectives on mindfulness and the interpersonal dimension of the therapeutic relationship. We will begin by describing foundational elements of current theory and practice and then focus on three new developments from behavioural theorist/practitioners:

1 The emergence of a refined approach to behavioural activation (Martell et al., 2001; Richards, 2010a).
2 The emergence of a set of acceptance and mindfulness interventions that draws on behavioural theory and practice (Linehan, 1993; Hayes et al., 1999).
3 A refined understanding of the therapeutic relationship from a behavioural perspective on how understanding reinforcement and reward processes can facilitate the therapeutic relationship (Tsai et al., 2009) and the use of 'disciplined personal involvement' in the therapeutic relationship during cognitive-behavioural treatment of chronic depression (McCullough, 2000, 2006).

FOUNDATIONAL BEHAVIOUR THERAPY THEORY

The two main strands of learning theory that have informed behavioural approaches in therapy have come from the classical conditioning tradition of Pavlov and the reinforcement tradition of Skinner. Classical conditioning was focused on understanding the antecedents of behaviour, whilst reinforcement theory focused on the consequences of behaviour. These two factors were pragmatically combined in the antecedents–behaviour–consequences (ABC) approach, also known as *functional analysis.* Functional contextualism stresses the need to understand the function of behaviour within its context. Different behaviours (e.g., substance abuse and intellectualising) may have the same function (i.e., emotional avoidance) in different contexts.

The Operation of the ABC Process

Clients often describe their overt behaviours as problematic in the context of their current life situation. Therapists would typically be interested in defining those behaviours quite precisely and identifying any regular triggers that might cue them off and the consequences likely to encourage or discourage their continuance.

A client, Jenny, for example, seemed to end up taking on more and more work tasks that she saw as beyond her purview. On closer examination it turned out that most of these tasks occurred late in the day when young male managers asked her to complete something 'before close of play'. Jenny smiled sweetly and accepted their compliments on what a 'brick' she was, complaining to her peers only after the manager left. Jenny was a single middle-aged woman and liked the young male managers' compliments but hated the extra tasks. More than anything she hated the uncomfortable tension that arose in her when there was any conflict between people near her. Further, there was history: Jenny's father was a domineering bully who not only treated her as a 'servant' but also overtly undermined her self-confidence.

Another client, Clive, had realised that his marriage was threatened by his sarcastic and aggressive behaviour toward his wife and daughters. Analysis of family rows precipitated by him showed that they predominantly occurred at teatime, especially on days that he was 'on call' when he would have to spend his evening awaiting potential call-outs. He felt that his wife 'nagged' him about tasks like paying bills and this 'drove him crazy'. His aggressive responses to his wife generally did 'shut her up' in the short term, but she withheld her affection and he tended to feel guilty. Another factor that may have impinged on this situation is that Clive's mother was an alcoholic who called him frequently and then 'went on' at him about her problems.

Figure 6.1 shows the ABC analysis of these problematic situations and adds in the 'sting in the tail' that motivates the client to seek help to change.

What happened before what happened	What happened	What happened after what happened
A: Antecedent	**B: Behaviour**	**C: Consequences**
Jenny is repeatedly approached to complete extra administrative tasks by young male managers late in the afternoon.	Jenny smiles sweetly and does the work but inwardly resents the number of the requests.	Jenny feels drained and taken advantage of but says nothing. The managers see no reason to stop asking her to do the tasks.
Clive's wife presses a point about family business in the brief window she sees him before he goes 'on call'.	Clive reacts aggressively to his wife and effectively 'shuts her up'.	In the short term, Clive gets the relative peace he needs before going on call. In the longer term, his wife resents his behaviour and has doubts about the marriage.

FIGURE 6.1   Example ABC analysis for Jenny and Clive

ABC analysis helps by offering a map for guiding behavioural interventions focused on antecedents and/or behaviours and/or consequences (Watson & Tharp, 2007).

Identifying and Working with Antecedents

After initial recognition of problematic responses, therapists can explore their triggers by asking a series of questions, such as those shown in Table 6.1. These questions focus on establishing various types of triggers, the most commonly encountered ones being vulnerable times of day, task factors that exacerbate stress, and interpersonal buttons that can be 'pressed' with undesirable outcomes.

Whilst these are interesting factors in their own right, therapists' main interest is likely to focus on how modifiable they are. Can Jenny, for example, be elsewhere towards the 'close of play'? Are there any managers who might be on her side if they were aware of how others exploited her? Could Clive do 'on-call' duties less frequently? Teatime stresses are common in many families, could anything be learnt from how other families organise themselves to help Clive and his family vary their routines to manage things better? Might it be helpful to review Clive's thinking about his wife's alleged 'nagging' in order to help him respond to her more temperately?

Notice that antecedents can be concrete external events (e.g., teatime) or internal events (Clive's thinking) – understanding them has great utility in *cognitive behavioural* analysis.

IDENTIFYING AND MODIFYING PROBLEMATIC BEHAVIOURS

Working on antecedents necessitates a preliminary identification of the problem behaviour. Frequently a more detailed and nuanced understanding of relevant behaviours emerges as antecedents are clarified. The first view of Clive's behaviour focuses on his anger, but a more rounded view puts this in the context that his wife does not pick her words and moments to approach him well at times. Therapist questions that discern the dimensions of behaviours and plumb their depths are also included in Table 6.1.

Therapists are helped to get a clearer view on how behaviours could be modified by finding out more about clients' wider behavioural repertoires. Are there some situations that Jenny, for example, could handle more assertively? Can she sometimes articulate what she wants and negotiate the accommodation of her needs alongside those of others? Can Clive think of times when he and his wife have stuck to routines that work for them and the children?

IDENTIFYING AND MODIFYING CONSEQUENCES

Behaviours that are rewarded or reinforced are likely to be repeated; those that are punished are less likely to be repeated. The technical behavioural language can help therapists here: especially to realise the slightly counter-intuitive power of negative reinforcement. For example, Jenny's non-assertion is strengthened by the fact that it helps her to avoid conflict. Clive's aggression does help him avoid his wife's 'nagging' – at least in the short term. Notice also the relatively ineffectiveness of punishment (Clive's wife's withdrawal of affection) only fuels his further resentment, though it may motivate him to think about seeking out help.

Therapists can explore the subtle dimensions of the consequences of the problem behaviour with the questions shown in Table 6.1. The subsequent focus for change is on whether changing those consequences can alter the general situation for the better. If Jenny can experience and survive conflict situations they might become less aversive to her. If Clive's wife were encouraged to 'keep going' in a more reasonable and negotiated way with her requests for Clive to pay bills on time, might this reinforce his determination to find a new way of resolving their difficulties?

TABLE 6.1   Useful questions when formulating ABC analysis

A questions	B questions	C questions
What happens just before you ...?	How exactly do you react?	How do you end up feeling? Any relief?
Were there any body sensations ...?	Any avoidance behaviours?	How do other people react?
Any thoughts?	Any safety behaviours?	Are there any longer-term consequences to you behaving that way?

BEHAVIOUR CHANGE AS A 'PERCENTAGE GAME'

If the history of psychotherapy has consistently overplayed the power of 'insight' as the engine of change, it has probably under-played the power of committing to graduated behaviour change by small steps. It is therefore often necessary to set a patient tone to much behavioural work. That tone is similar to that of the concept of a 'percentage game' in sport. In tennis, for example, the more you can hit the ball into testing areas of the opponents' court, the more likely they are to make mistakes. Only a relatively small number of points are actually won by spectacular shots.

The aim then is to get some forward movement in behaviour change and then to persist with efforts until 'critical mass' leads to momentum. One caveat is that we often take longer to achieve 'critical mass' than we hoped. Clients may not have clear pictures of their targeted behavioural goals and can be helped to form these images by descriptions that break overall targets down into small behavioural steps.

CASE STUDY
Tom

Tom desperately wanted to form a long-term relationship but experienced constant frustration with unsatisfactory dates. He judged himself harshly by saying 'There is something wrong with me – I am rubbish with women, obviously'. All this added up to a 'tough assignment' for change: finding this elusive internal 'fault' and then devising a super-change strategy to overcome it. In contrast, Tom's therapist suggested that they could define behavioural steps likely to contribute to successful dates and that Tom could use these to evaluate each occasion objectively. He could then find what he did well and where change might help. Tom identified the following behavioural criteria:

1   Greet his dating partner in a pleasant, open way.
2   Consult his partner on a plan for their time together.
3   Initiate topics of conversation.
4   Observe how interested his partner seemed in what he was saying.
5   Follow any leads of conversation she offered.
6   Make clear suggestions about following up on the date (if he was sure he wanted to).

He agreed to rate his next dates using these criteria. Important new learning emerged. First, he generally did these things well. Second, his nervousness made it harder for him to fully concentrate on signals coming from his dating partners. Third, when he was attracted to his partner, he went a bit 'over the top' by trying to act as in the rather unrealistic image of the 'man' he thought he should be rather than being the man he was. As he worked on these matters, he reported finding his dates more satisfactory.

The principles and practice of ABC functional analysis can be clearly seen as underpinning many key behavioural methods and will be evident to readers in the first of the major current behavioural interventions enjoying a revival in contemporary CBT: behavioural activation (BA).

BEHAVIOURAL ACTIVATION: AN INTERVENTION OF CHOICE WHEN WORKING WITH CLIENTS SUFFERING FROM DEPRESSION

Behavioural withdrawal plays a crucial role in maintaining depression. Withdrawal may begin as an understandable and, for a time, functional, 'hibernation' in a socially and emotionally 'cold climate'. A prolonged withdrawal associated with depression, however, can quickly turn sour – with a series of highly negative effects on the client's life. These negative effects include physiological lethargy and atrophy of social skills, social isolation and the shrinking of support networks. Increased negative rumination leads to new depths of negative feeling so that the risk of suicide increases. Poor cognitive functioning leads to poor decision making, affecting many client contexts, including work. It is therefore not surprising that 'activating' depressed clients has been a therapeutic aim since the earliest times – an 18th-century physician even suggested giving melancholic patients scabies to get them moving. Lewinsohn's (1974) behavioural approach to depression developed around the same time as Beck et al.'s (1979) cognitive approach and was referenced in Beck's work. The main thrust of Lewinsohn's work was to increase the *level* of activity – in particular to increase the number of pleasant experiences without which other types of more sophisticated change were unlikely to be effective. More recent versions of BA (Martell et al., 2001) have been more oriented towards a functional analytic interpretation of depressed behaviour, influenced by Ferster's (1973) description of the environmental reinforcers of depression. This account crucially emphasised the role of avoidance in depression: as Guidano and Liotti (1983) wryly note, there is no one more active than depressed persons avoiding something they do not want to do. Functional analysis typically uses the ABC concept described earlier. In this framework, therapists do not make assumptions about what behaviours might prove rewarding for clients but rather, in collaboration with them, deduces what these might be from individual assessment of clients' current and former life circumstances.

CASE STUDY
Doreen

Doreen, an Afro-Caribbean mother in her forties, was depressed following separation from her husband. She was assigned to a newly employed 'low intensity' IAPT worker for BA. Doreen had previously been active in church activities in her community so that her worker reasonably thought that she would be positively mobilised by re-engagement in such work. Doreen's lack of interest in doing this was interpreted as being due to her depression. Supervision from a more experienced colleague, however, led to re-assessment and reformulation of the situation. It turned out that Doreen had moved to her husband's neighbourhood when they got married. His relatives, who lived locally, blamed her for the failure of the marriage. They also were active in the same church groups, and this made them purgatorial for Doreen. This new understanding refocused intervention in re-engagement with similar activities elsewhere.

Using an ABC format in the reformulation helped the therapist to realise that the consequences of Doreen's attempts to resume former activities met with punishment and her propensity to stay at home was negatively reinforced by avoiding critical scrutiny by her husband's relatives. The IAPT workers also needed to ascertain that Doreen's negative mood was not making her feel more critically scrutinised; in fact, her view was supported by a vivid account of a friend who had observed a relative 'dissing' Doreen in the local shop. These incidents also illustrate the interpersonal aspects of BA where the activities often either link clients into or exclude them from the social environment (Simmons & Wills, 2009).

Ferster (1973) also suggests that it is important to understand how some negative behaviours are reinforced in depression; in particular, how 'complaining' can be subtly rewarded by friends and family. At first, people surrounding depressed clients tend to sympathise, but may unwittingly reinforce the complaining style that some depressed people take on. Initially, complaint may win attention. Over time, clients' friends and relatives come to experience it as 'moaning' and find that only when they agree with the client will the 'moaning' end. Their agreement may, however, be insincere and they may subsequently avoid the client. By the time clients realise this it may be too late. As supportive social networks play a big part in restraining depression, the loss of them can play a major role in maintaining the problem. Therapists therefore often focus BA on developing clients' skills in connecting with supportive social environments. Therapists can usefully monitor their own feelings about the client: we will explore later in this chapter whether it is possible to use therapists' awareness of clients' *clinically relevant behaviours* (Tsai et al., 2009) and *disciplined personal involvement* (McCullough, 2000, 2006) within the therapeutic relationship to therapeutically useful ends. The fact that BA interventions have proved to be effective in the treatment of depression (Martell et al., 2001) has led to some tensions between the behavioural and cognitive wings of CBT. The late Neil Jacobson undertook various 'dismantling' studies of CBT in which its various components were tested separately for effectiveness. These studies suggested that behavioural and cognitive interventions were roughly equivalent in effect. These results may, however, be regarded as rather undermining cognitive approaches because behavioural interventions are typically more cost effective as they involve less intensive staff input and training. Even previously cognitively oriented researchers have accepted the fact that BA should be given renewed emphasis in CBT (Hollon, 2001). Others assert that BA has not yet demonstrated the same 'enduring' change as cognitive therapy (Dobson et al., 2008). The interpretation of Jacobson's research, however, is often stated in the form 'cognitive interventions do not really *add* anything to behavioural interventions', so that the question 'Do we really need to challenge negative thoughts?' (Longmore & Worrell, 2007) is now raised. Many CB therapists remain cautious in response to this question and query whether dispensing with cognitive interventions in this way may be 'throwing out the baby with the bathwater'. It is also important to note that relatively little is yet known about what the active ingredients of BA are (Martell et al., 2004). Additionally, it has always been difficult to completely deconstruct the entangled relationship between thinking, feeling and behaviour (Carey & Mansell, 2009). Nevertheless, along with similar challenges from acceptance and commitment therapy (ACT) (Hayes et al., 2004), there is no doubt that this perspective does have implications for even the most cautious CB therapist.

DOING INTERPERSONALLY SENSITIVE BA

Whilst it is important to explore the depressed client's current behaviours openly, it remains true that our understanding of depression is well enough developed to suggest a number of fruitful lines of enquiry about the behavioural element of depression, expressed in the following questions that can be usefully put to depressed clients:

> 'What are your current activity levels at home, in work and at leisure?'
> 'How do these levels compare with your life previous to your depression?'
> 'What pleasurable activities do you still manage to keep up?'
> 'Are there things that you should perhaps be doing which you are now tending to avoid?'
> 'How does your depression seem to affect significant others in your life – at work, in your family or in other important relationships?'

Therapists can enhance these questions by suggesting that clients complete ABC forms for particular target problems. Figure 6.2 shows an ABC form for Doreen. These data can be used to establish a 'baseline' from which improvements in clients' activities can be assessed. On a more qualitative level the data can also be sifted for clues on the client's deeper life values, helping to ground therapeutic effort in what is most important to them. Therapists should, however, remember that depressed clients may have impaired memory and therefore cannot always supply much detail. As we move into the intervention phase, clients can keep some kind of behavioural diary to follow up on what has been gathered in the assessment questions. Diaries often make useful and relatively easy-to-complete early homework tasks, though the level of demand regarding completion needs to take cognizance of the way the depression is likely to impact on the client's cognitive and writing abilities and current level of motivation. Clients can bring diaries – perhaps as part of an overall 'therapy book' – and can work together with therapists to convert the relatively simple data of a daily record into the refined format of an ABC chart (Figure 6.2) and/or activity schedule (Figure 6.3).

For some, behavioural work seems rather humble and even 'dry': that is, technical, detached and concerned with humdrum day-to-day reality rather than the seemingly more exciting 'depths' of other models of therapy. A key skill in the art and science

What happened before what happened	What happened	What happened after what happened
A: Antecedent	B: Behaviour	C: Consequences
Having felt low after her separation, Doreen attempts to re-engage with local life by going to the corner shop. Her sister-in-law happens to be in the shop, glowers at her and makes a disparaging remark.	Doreen blushes, leaves the shop without buying anything and heads for the safety of home.	In the short term, Doreen feels 'safe' but also more fed up because she 'just can't go anywhere now'.

FIGURE 6.2   Example ABC analysis for Doreen

of BA, however, is to combine its essentially simple and clear technical interventions with an appreciation that life and its mysteries are lived out in minute-by-minute existence. The flavour of this more subtle work is illustrated in the two client examples below.

CASE STUDY
Ceri 1

Ceri was a busy architect who became trapped in a cycle of working long hours in a competitive firm that emphasised 'keeping ahead of the opposition'. He was gay, with an apparently supportive partner. His father had been remote and decidedly homophobic but had reacted surprisingly well to Ceri's coming-out. Though the relationship with his father did come to healing resolution, it left Ceri with life-long habits of secrecy. Problems of tiredness, overwork and depression became exacerbated by him hiding in his office, accumulating work and not asking for help in sorting it out.

CASE STUDY
Rose 1

Rose was a social worker in her early thirties, who exhibited a 'driven' attitude towards her work. Rose described her parents as 'formidable'. Her mother's formidability was especially meaningful to her, as the mother had been a helping professional who aspired to the 'highest of standards' and seemed to oblige her daughter to follow. Rose's diary revealed that she was working between 80 and 90 hours per week and she refused to succumb to minor illnesses until the holidays. Like Ceri, she found it hard to share her feelings – especially her sense of vulnerability. Rose struggled to manage these pressures until a boyfriend that she'd had high hopes for 'dumped' her. She plunged into depression and had to take time out of work with the ubiquitous 'stress' diagnosis.

Although there are new features in the current approach to BA, it has retained substantial elements of the older methods, including 'pleasant events' (Lewinsohn &

Graf, 1973) and 'activity scheduling' (Beck et al., 1979), and these are utilised as initial interventions. Figure 6.3 shows the ABC form, the information from which fed into a subsequent discussion and activity schedule for Ceri.

**CASE STUDY
Ceri 2**

Ceri laughed – for the first time during therapy – when the therapist said how he was stuck in his office was reminiscent of 'Rapunzel'. He laughed again when asked if he was 'ready to let down his golden hair'. Discussion of his activity schedule revealed that there was a long-standing office tradition that senior partners, such as he himself, joined an extended morning coffee break by 'milling about' in the coffee room. There was an informal norm that various members of staff could approach each other for brief informal consultations. This was always a 'flaky area' for Ceri, who frequently doubted his own ability to manage his own work, never mind anyone else's. Ceri finally realised that he was avoiding this and becoming cut off from the support it offered. Not only that, but he also realised how meagre were the returns he was getting from his ruminative isolation.

What happened before what happened	What happened	What happened after what happened
A: Antecedent	**B: Behaviour**	**C: Consequences**
Ceri is at work and realises that it is 11 am – about the time he would have normally gone to 'network' with his colleagues in the coffee room.	Feeling nervous about going down, Ceri decides he will give it a miss today – perhaps tomorrow he will feel more like doing it.	Ceri calms down again but this has now been going on for weeks and it is getting harder to resume going to the coffee room. His colleagues are beginning to wonder if something is wrong.

	Monday	Tuesday	Wednesday
0600–0700	Sleep	Sleep	Breakfast
0700–0800	Breakfast	Breakfast	Getting ready and travelling to Cardiff
0800–0900	Getting ready for and travelling to work	Getting ready for and travelling to work	Getting ready for and travelling to work
0900–1000	Office working alone	Office working alone	Office working alone
1000–1100	Office working alone	Office working alone	Office working alone
1100–1200	Coffee brought to desk	Coffee brought to desk	Coffee brought to desk
1200–1300	Lunch alone in room	Lunch alone in room	Out for lunch alone

FIGURE 6.3 Example ABC analysis and activity schedule for Ceri

CASE STUDY
Ceri 3

Ceri responded rapidly to a BA intervention focused on increasing engaged behaviour at work and increased rest and relaxation at home. His BDI dropped from severe to moderate/mild after six weeks. At first he found it difficult to take the initiative socially, and the therapist found himself being directive in this phase. As Ceri improved, however, the therapist detected a veiled truculence in some of Ceri's responses, culminating in Ceri saying in an exasperated way, 'I can work this sort of thing for myself, you know!' The therapist took this as a 'relationship signal' and discussed what was going on between them. Ceri explained that he responded to his father's demands by being autonomous. Though he had lost some of that during the period of depression, he felt ready to pick up at least some aspects of old positive values again now.

Ceri's vignettes illustrate not only the ubiquity of interpersonal aspects of even the most structured ways of doing therapy, but also demonstrate a good behavioural principle – that of 'fading' – in this case starting to reduce the intensity of therapy at the appropriate time. The therapist was behind Ceri's proximal zone of development, failing to notice that Ceri no longer needed the reinforcement of directive structuring that had been helpful to him earlier. This is a good illustration of the need to 'titrate' the dose of therapy structure (Beck et al., 1979: 123). Neither should therapists feel incompetent because of such oversights: therapists' abilities to negotiate corrective adjustments in response to client signals have powerful therapeutic effects (Safran & Muran, 2000) and are therefore vital therapy competencies.

CASE STUDY
Rose 2

There were features of Rose's depression that were suggestive of chronic fatigue syndrome (CFS). She felt, however, that she did not have this problem and her doctor supported her view. Having considering this in supervision, the therapist decided that approaches to either problem would be remarkably similar and therefore decided that it was wise to be pragmatically transdiagnostic about the 'label'. At home and work she needed to experiment with pacing her activities and resting until she found the balance that worked best for her. Initially, Rose went for shorter rests and carefully planned social activities. One problem with curtailing late-night social activities came from her feeling that she was losing the chance to meet a partner. This feeling was amplified by rumination on the fact that her 'biological clock was running' – she was keen to have children before she 'got too old'. Further analysis of her responses to social situations also revealed that she would 'go along but not participate' because of her NAT 'I'm a rubbishy flirt'. Exploring how she came over in sessions, therapist and client conceptualised her shyness as an attractive quality that could be used positively. This was one factor that did eventually help her to engage in a good long-term relationship.

The new approach to BA stands at an interesting point of development. Having evolved in almost accidental fashion from dismantling studies of CBT (Jacobson & Gortner, 2000), it has ironically perhaps now been subject to further such studies, some of which suggest more elaborated versions of BA add little to its briefest format (Hopko et al., 2003). It may, however, be that, like Erasmus' bridge,[1] dismantling itself has unknown affects and that logic of dismantling studies have limited transferability beyond the controlled world of clinical trials. In the vignettes offered, thoughts and beliefs frequently became apparent in client and therapist interaction. Whilst it is true that during these moments it would be hard to say that 'the intervention' was focused on cognition, all that therapists know about cognition cannot help but be communicated to clients. It remains true that we do not really know exactly how BA works or what combination of its various components works best for different clients (Hopko et al., 2003). The research on BA has been outcome-based, and there have been few case studies showing how it works out in individual cases. Much of the literature reads as if clients responded rationally to rational therapist suggestions, and one sometimes wonders 'Where is the blood, sweat and tears that seems to occur when we do BA?'. Clinical researchers often think that dismantling studies are the obvious places to find answers to these questions, yet their implications may seem far from clear to practitioners in everyday practice.

BA has played a major role in the IAPT project. Richards (2010a) describes how BA has slotted into 'low-intensity' work and describes a parsimonious six-stage process for implementing BA from a low intensity, usually telephone-based, perspective. The intervention has showed up well in the early research on the project, and the large-scale nature of the project also means that we are likely to learn a lot more about another assumption that often fuels this debate: that BA will prove easy to disseminate and train people in.

Another intriguing aspect of BA is that it follows a behavioural tradition that has been extremely skeptical of 'labelling' clients with internal deficit models of 'psychopathology'. It regards the existence of an internal entity called 'depression' as 'unproven' at best, and suggests that when clients believe this it may tie them further into rumination and what ACT therapists might call 'cognitive fusion' – now often focused not only on internal worries but on how they can be eliminated. Thus the treatment for depression works 'from the outside in' rather than from 'the inside out'. Clients are encouraged to be more active even when they don't necessarily 'feel like it', on the basis that activity itself is associated with positive emotional response in depressed clients. Even here, however, we need to consider contextual variations: some clients will drive themselves into 'avoidant exercise' (i.e., 'flogging oneself' in the gym to avoid sad thoughts). This is usually counterproductive because it has a rebound effect. This marks a good point to further our exploration of the new behaviourism by describing behavioural aspects of ACT.

BEHAVIOURAL APPROACHES TO MINDFULNESS AND ACTION

Steve Hayes was raised in California and considers himself 'a child of the Sixties' (http://bigthink.com/stevenhayes, accessed 8 October 2011). He entered clinical psychology and trained in cognitive and behavioural methods. He leaned more towards the behavioural approaches and began researching and extending Skinner's (1953) radical behavioural work on language development. Sometime in the 1970s he suffered problems with panic and found that the cognitive and behavioural methods of those times were not helpful to him and so began to look at other methods, especially humanistic- and Buddhist-oriented ones. His research on language and his experiences of seeking help for his own panic led him to develop relational frame theory (RFT) and ACT respectively. Both developments influenced each other and have contributed to what is now called 'functional contextualism' (Hayes, 1993), characterised by an emphasis on understanding behaviour according to its functions in the context in which it occurs.

RFT posits that human beings learn to respond to language according to both the content and *context* of the language: that is, on how language relates to other things in the environment (i.e., to relational frames). A child who has experienced pain at a dental surgery can learn to associate pain with the street that leads to it. This relatively arbitrary cue may lead a child to conclude that 'the World is a dangerous place'. As all learning is additive, some trace of this learning will always remain, and this may be why cognitive restructuring can be so difficult.

Behavioural models have a history of being radically skeptical about language and 'self reports'. Now ACT adds an additional layer of radical scepticism: about restructuring internal 'self-talk'. This insight is at the heart of ACT. Hayes and his colleagues have, unlike many earlier behaviourists, taken on board language and thoughts. Rather than having no interest in thinking, they, like more orthodox CBT colleagues, identify negative thinking as part of the problem in psychopathology, but they see the nature of this problem differently. The problem is not so much that the thinking is 'wrong', distorted or erroneous, it is that no language is ever quite what it seems to be (Hayes with Smith, 2005). Furthermore, tackling psychological problems by focusing the client on the fact that the thought is distorted *may* worsen things because it can lead clients to think they must 'get rid of it' and, as Hayes has often said, 'If you don't want it, you have got it'. Thus clients can become more fused and entangled with their negative thinking, as in the ironic results of thought suppression (Wegner, 1994). The fact that the word 'may' is put in italics in the penultimate sentence is important and lies at the heart of the argument about the role of acceptance in current CBT practice. If we had written that cognitive restructuring *does* or *usually does* lead to further fusion of negative thoughts, then we are moving towards the position of Longmore & Worrell's (2007) suggestion that it is not necessary to do cognitive restructuring in CBT at all, as previously discussed. If we had written *does sometimes* lead to fusion, then ACT might merely be accorded a minor position in CBT practice. The fact of the matter is that we really do not know the true extent that cognitive restructuring might increase thought fusion. ACT's place in CBT is likely to be significant but cognitive restructuring is likely to stay in the model. Hayes has ensured that there will be a lively debate on how and why acceptance or restructuring may be used in phased or parallel ways, and this will in the long run supply us with a more flexible clinical skill repertoire. O'Donoghue and Fisher (2009) provide one of the few discussions on what potential criteria for making such distinctions might look like. Whilst acknowledging that we are only at the start of figuring out this question, in Figure 6.4 we combine their suggestions with some that flow from our own work in Table 6.1.

These last few paragraphs, given that they are written about behavioural aspects of ACT, may have struck readers as saying a lot about thinking. We have commented before that it is increasingly difficult to locate material in watertight categories when writing on CBT. Let us think back to the earlier section on ABC functional analysis for a moment and remind ourselves that a more sophisticated

---

1. Does the research literature suggest that there might be evidence particularly favouring acceptance or restructuring of negative thoughts in this problem area?

2. What does the client think might be the better first intervention choice?

3. How has the client responded to acceptance and/or restructuring interventions so far?

4. Could the thinking trigger behaviour with very negative consequences for the client or for others? (May be unwise to accept it.)

5. Can the client distinguish between accepting the thought and accepting that thought as true? (Establish before fostering acceptance.)

6. Is the negative thought a response to a situation that could be changed? (If it cannot be changed, acceptance is favoured.)

7. Is the thought linked to important memories? (Best accepted.)

8. Is it possible to combine acceptance and restructuring? (Especially, for example, accepting the feeling of anxiety as a base camp to explore and question from.)

Adapted from O'Donoghue and Fisher (2009).

FIGURE 6.4   Questions for acceptance or restructuring of negative thoughts

approach to behavioural work recognises that thinking is a behaviour subject to antecedents and reinforcement from its consequences – in positive, negative and punishing ways. By extending Skinner's work on language, Hayes and his colleagues have been applying functional analysis to internal speech and thinking. An additional behavioural angle is evident in the ACT focus on 'values and committed action', as Hayes et al. (1999: 250) put it: 'During the latter phases, ACT takes on the character of traditional behaviour therapy ... behaviour change is a kind of willingness exercise, linked to chosen values.' This phase is illustrated in the case of Pavel below.

ACT is raising some of the most fundamental issues that face the development of the CBT model today. We consider that most CBT therapists can be ready to think about these challenges and to learn at least some skills from ACT. Hayes himself actually encourages such use of the ACT 'scaffold' to explore one's practice, and he and his colleagues are also evolving an 'open-learning community' of resources to support such learning (www.contextualpsychology.com): a model of practice development that, incidentally, would in our view be of great utility to the wider CBT community, as Hayes et al. put it:

> In the cognitive behavior therapy (CBT) tradition relatively little has been written about how to produce greater progress *within* an empirical approach. (Hayes et al., In Press: 3)

A full discussion of ACT is obviously beyond the scope of this book, but we offer some brief thoughts on what appear to us to be particularly fruitful aspects of the model that can inform and extend the practice of CBT practitioners (see also Ciarrochi & Bailey, 2008). We have already offered some discussion of defusion techniques in Chapter 5, and would like now to discuss the way ACT is contributing to developing the adoption of mindfulness is CBT: ways of helping clients to 'come into the present moment' as a further antidote to fusion and to facilitate 'psychological flexibility' in their responses to their life situations. All the early interventions in ACT are designed to promote *psychological flexibility*, while later interventions gradually help the client move towards 'valued and committed action' for change – the subject of a second focus here.

COMING INTO THE PRESENT MOMENT

It has been observed many times that it is hard for human minds to stay fully focused in the present moment. Many of us know the experience of trying to meditate with the hope of finding our way to a blissful fully present moment of nirvana, only to find minutes later that our mind has drifted into a mundane future concern – what are we going to buy for tea at the supermarket later? Alternatively, our minds may have drifted back to a past concern – what did Cassie mean when she made that rather pointed comment about my work today? Thinking about such concerns tends to activate our internal 'problem-solving' mechanisms and this can be helpful if it takes us to some viable solution relatively cleanly. Problems, however, can occur when no obvious solution arises, leaving the thoughts to cycle uselessly around our minds. This is not yet of course rumination and we can remember that according to Jon Kabat-Zinn, minds 'wave' back and forth quite normally. Furthermore, it is neither possible nor desirable for us to stay in the present moment all the time – we need to reflect on the past and make plans for the future sometimes – but healthy functioning is probably enhanced by the balancing act of being able to come into the present moment sometimes. We have already detailed how cognitive processes such as rumination, obsession and worry are increasingly 'in the dock' as problematic influences in psychological health. ACT theorists have hypothesised – in a quotation that will be echoed in the next chapter on mindfulness – that:

> Psychopathology is caused in large part by the tendency to become entangled in thoughts, taking thoughts literally and remaining in a problem solving mode even when that is not helpful. (Hayes et al., In Press: 18)

'Coming into the present' is easy to say, but when working with clients it is necessary to remind them that it is 'not so easy to do'. Another starting point lies surely, as psychodynamic therapists have particularly been arguing, in the mindful presence of therapists (Hick & Bien, 2008). Beyond that, most mindfulness methods in psychological therapy do seem at least somewhat dependent on using exercises. One simple one is to ask clients to look round the room and identify an object on which they can focus, and to begin that focus after taking a few moments to be aware of their breath. This can be especially effective at times when clients are distressed in sessions after contemplating some aspect of their situation. After holding focus on the object in the room for a period of time that is reasonable for that client (we find that about 5–10 minutes suits most clients), therapists can then invite the client to return attention to the thing that had been disturbing before and see if anything in his mind has shifted. Most usually clients have become calmer and less fused with the problem so that we may see the first inkling of some more helpful response. The idea of being radically skeptical about the extent to which words represent reality is a useful consideration in this aspect of therapeutic work. The manoeuvre of coming into the present moment is not achieved or easily described by words, and practitioners often seem to use hand movements in a non-conscious way that may offer non-verbal support for the notion. ACT therapists make considerable use of the more poetic language of metaphors and working images, such as 'passengers on the bus' already cited. These metaphoric exercises can sometimes become too wordy, and this can make them backfire. A client once observed about an ACT 'white room' exercise: 'I knew where the exercise was trying to take me and I was just determined not to go there!' It may be then that we can use other peoples' metaphors, but mainly as inspirations to find our own. I therefore conclude this section with a case example in which client and therapist stumble on a metaphoric exercise that proves helpful.

CASE STUDY
Pavel 1

Pavel and his family were deeply religious. His father had fled from his East European homeland during World War II. Pavel was diagnosed as having OCD and was troubled by fantasies about wanting to harm other people, especially when he was in church. These experiences were very difficult because they seemed to deny all his most deeply held values. They became so difficult that he had stopped going to mass – a matter of deep regret to him. During one session, he had a fantasy about harming the therapist. Pavel was encouraged to surface this thought and 'stay with it' for a while … When the distress and shame became overwhelming he was encouraged to switch his attention to an object in the room … which happened to be a hand-bell that the therapist used in mindfulness groups … Pavel was then reminded of following the sound of bells to church services when he was a boy … and then the candles in the church and the feeling of safety and security that he associated with the church … The therapist remembered an ACT exercise that involved remembering a transcendent moment in life and bringing it fully into the present in the session ('The Sweet Spot Exercise', Wilson & Sandoz, 2008) and used its spirit to build up the feeling of being 'freed up' from the fantasy in a way which will be elaborated in the next extract from this therapy.

VALUED AND COMMITTED ACTION

> The primary aim of ACT is to embrace necessary suffering in order to increase one's ability to engage in valued living. (Wilson & Sandoz, 2008: 92)

The role of values in change has been a common feature across many of the new behavioural approaches emerging in CBT and can be seen in BA (Martell et al., 2001) and functional analytic psychotherapy (FAP) (Tsai et al., 2009). Clients' values are likely to be related to what reinforces their behaviour. They may also have an intimate relationship with problems because they link to the possibility of pain – frequently underlain by loss of valued assets, including a sense of our own worth. Neither is the work of values ever completed: one might aspire to become, for example, a 'good son-in-law' as part of family values, but one does not arrive and stop at that status but will need to keep re-asserting it as new situations in new life arise.

CASE STUDY
Pavel 2

Pavel saw his family as being at the centre of his life and his religion. He saw his obsessions as questioning his worthiness to be a husband and father. He had fantasies about harming his wife's mother and found these nonsensical but profoundly disturbing. We pursued work along the lines suggested by Rachman (2003): helping the client to reconsider whether obsessions are actually significant. In general, Pavel became increasingly able to regard these thoughts 'as just thoughts', but what seemed to make the crucial difference for him was when he realised that they did not in any case interfere with his ability to act in the ways that showed his usual courtesy, concern and affection for his mother-in-law. A helpful sense of certainty about this was enhanced after discussion of the many things that he did in his role in the family and how these reinforced his values.

Hayes (1984) has described a behavioural and language-sceptical view of 'self', where self is not a thing but a series of behaviours and thus, rather like Pavel's family values, has to be continually reaffirmed in action. The problematic internal verbal processes of avoidance and fused cognition can predominate over other sources of stimulus control, causing further cognitive fusion and avoidance, widely regarded as behaviourally harmful. The therapist was aware throughout the work with Pavel that 'working too hard' on the obsessions could easily exacerbate them. Discussion of values and the positive sense of validation that accompanies it helped at times to shift from an overly 'problem-solving' focus of the work to a broader set of questions that helped him reach for a fuller view of his life rather than his life being dominated by obsessions. It also was a prelude to a sudden shift in therapeutic activity.

CASE STUDY
Pavel 3

It turned out that over his lifetime the subjects of Pavel's obsessions had shifted in content several times. So it was not altogether surprising when he reported that the fantasies about harming others had ceased, and indeed did not come back. Neither did any other obsessions take their place, but rather some compulsions, that had been present but not previously reported, now became therapeutic foci. Pavel worked as a security man in a local factory; his job involved a good deal of checking doors and windows. Whereas he had previously lacked commitment to undertake an 'exposure and response prevention' (ERP) treatment for this, his renewed optimism and sense of affirmed values now enabled him to show 'committed action' in doing this work, and he made significant progress.

Twohig et al. (2006) report on a randomised trial in which ACT elements proved effective with OCD without any use of exposure. Hayes et al. (In Press) argue against taking this result as an argument for neglecting proven behavioural interventions in ACT – as Ost (2008) asserted might be true of ACT – and Hayes has frequently asserted that ACT is a behavioural model. Hayes et al. (1999), however, do not offer guidelines for integrating more traditional behavioural work, implying that they have still to be fully developed – and they repeated this statement in the new edition of the text (2004: 250). Twohig et al. (2006) and Hayes et al. (In press) perhaps do now show that this work is underway, but as yet we still await its fuller realisation.

One final question about ACT might be contemplated, as described in Box 6.1.

Box 6.1: Pavel's Good Question

When discussing the idea of valued goals with Pavel, he really surprised the therapist by saying, 'I have a problem with that – Hitler had valued goals, didn't he?' Given that the SS had detained his father during the war, this question really gave the therapist pause for thought. He said that he supposed that one had to accept that ultimately one might not approve of some peoples' values and goals. He reflected though that he had been able to discuss some clients' racist ideas but had made his different view clear. Pavel could eventually articulate that his valued goals would have to coincide with his religion. The therapist was never sure how well he dealt with the question, and when he looked at the therapy texts, he could not help noticing how most of the clients seemed to articulate very 'Californian' goals.

Answers on a postcard please.

NEW BEHAVIOURAL PERSPECTIVES ON THE THERAPEUTIC RELATIONSHIP

Functional Analytic Psychotherapy (FAP)

Charles Truax (1968), a research colleague of Carl Rogers, wrote an interesting paper suggesting that Rogers was perhaps not quite as non-directive as he imagined himself to be. The paper analysed one of Rogers' well-known recorded interviews from the behavioural perspective and suggested that Rogers, probably not consciously, had positively reinforced client responses that fitted with his theory and negatively reinforced those that did not. Reading this article and watching the interview may lead readers to conclude that the analysis is not entirely fair – although they may also think that Truax's general insight was correct. Therapists almost certainly do reinforce differential client responses; the question is whether this insight can be used in the service of therapy. Having turned to a non-CBT source to begin with, let us proceed by looking at another. Psychodynamic therapy has always rested quite heavily on the idea of 'parallel process' (Casement, 1985). Parallel process suggests that clients are likely to bring aspects of their problematic functioning into the therapy relationship. Thus clients reporting problems with chronic anger are likely to display that to their therapists at times. More subtly, if this anger is driven by a covert lack of trust in people, that mistrust is also likely to show itself at times. If we take away the psycho-analytic overlay from this idea we have a strikingly simple yet highly useful idea: that clients are likely to offer up examples of their problematic attitudes and behaviours in the 'here and now' of the therapy session.

Many therapists are likely to have had the experience of discussions with clients about their problem 'out there' that feel repetitive, disowned and stuck' ('Oh no – not this again!'). Most have also had the experience of how that problem suddenly can become 'live' in the therapy room: for example, the therapist cannot quite suppress a yawn and the client says in a hurt way 'I guess I'm just boring people to death'. If we put this second factor (the likelihood of samples of clients' problematic behaviours occurring in session) together with the Truax's insight, we have the possibility that clients' behaviours can be reinforced positively or negatively or even punished (live behaviour modification) in the therapy session. This is exactly what is explored and elaborated in FAP (Tsai et al., 2009) and, as we will see later, such thinking is also evident in a developing view of the therapy relationship in the Cognitive Behavioural Analysis System of Psychotherapy (CBASP) (McCullough, 2000, 2006).

Kanter et al. (2009), FAP therapists, suggest that BA can be practiced in a way that is not really based on the reinforcement principle because therapists usually have no control over the reinforcement process in client environments 'out there'. Therapists essentially often suggest that clients go out and try things in their environments – where they may or may not be reinforced. Furthermore, there are inevitable time delays before those things are tried and reinforced or not. Clients' efforts to try new behaviours in their own environments may, of course, be reinforced by their therapists when clients come in the next time to report them, but again there is the time delay problem. The more distant in time reinforcement becomes, the less well reinforcement works and the less 'natural' it is. Kanter et al. (2009) do not present the idea of therapist reinforcement as an alternative perspective on BA but as an additional one. Instructional control and suggestions about what the client can try 'out there' are effective, but we should also be looking for opportunities to enhance cheerleading with in-session reinforcement where possible. The FAP perspective offers some useful guidelines for doing this.

In FAP, clients' in-session behaviours that represent a parallel process are termed 'clinically relevant behaviours' (CRBs). The in-session behaviours that are linked to problematic patterns are called 'CRB1s': an example would be a depressed client's tendency to withdraw and be passive. Outside sessions this pattern would show itself as a pervasive withdrawal from friends, work and leisure. In sessions it might show itself as detachment from and passivity in therapeutic interaction. These tendencies may become evident to therapists with a sudden realisation like 'I am doing all the work' and with a gut feeling of 'wading through treacle'. We have already discussed the value of awareness of these internal therapist body–and–mind clues and how they can be successfully mobilised by the skill of *immediacy*. The first move is to use immediacy to draw the client's attention to the fact that the problematic behaviour is now manifest in the session. This task requires sensitivity as it can easily suggest criticism and put the client on the defensive. The behavioural reinforcement principle comes into play with the idea of a second type of CRB (CRB2), which represents a more positive and functional alternative to the CRB1. The depressed client, having been very withdrawn, suddenly shows engagement: an opportunity for the therapist to do something rewarding like saying 'It is great when you are really engaged like this'. From a behavioural perspective, reinforcement theory tells us that the most efficient formula for positive behaviour change comes when the problem behaviours become detached from any factors that might reinforce them and when alternative functional behaviours are reinforced as soon as possible after they have happened.

CASE STUDY
Michiko

Michiko was a Japanese American bank employee who became depressed whilst working in the UK. She was isolated and prone to ruminating on her situation – and worried that the time she had ruminated meant that she would not complete her work. In one session, Michiko launched into a long depressing monologue on her depression, her unfinished work and the disasters that would follow. The monologue became hypnotic – there was no eye contact and Michiko swayed as she spoke. The therapist felt his heart sinking and his energy fading. He suddenly saw that Michiko was speaking her ruminative routine out aloud and live in the session. The therapist said, 'I hope that it is okay to observe that I find my mood is sinking as you say this and I see that you are swaying and your voice has become like a dirge.' The therapist briefly mimicked what Michiko had been doing. She smiled in recognition and came into contact with the therapist. The therapist noticed some vitality in this contact – and saw some shine in her eyes – and said, 'It is just so much nicer when we are in contact like this'.

Looking at the above scenario from a behavioural perspective, we can see something valuable has happened. The client's CRB1 (her withdrawal and detachment from life) is identified and brought to her attention. This is helpful in several ways. First, such behaviours have become so habitual that the client does not notice them any more and does not, therefore, usually perceive the aversive responses they trigger in significant others. Second, it is extremely difficult to get this kind of feedback in the world outside therapy. Therapy should be an exceptionally safe environment in which such learning can occur. Indeed, we could argue that therapeutic sessions are the ideal and the most fitting setting for such work. In the above example, the converse of the problematic behaviour is engagement: we see this in the 'small' behaviour of regaining eye contact with Michiko, but we also see the value of this 'small' thing in the presence of shining light in the client's eyes. When trainees hear of using immediacy in this way, it seems risky to them – Michiko could have felt belittled by the therapist mimicking her. As we become more experienced, however, we realise that it is not possible to do completely risk-free therapy and also that these are usually highly rewarding experiences for clients, therapists and for the therapy: it seems almost what therapy is most created for. It does occasionally backfire – but what therapy technique worth its salt does not have that potential? 'Catching' therapist errors can also be turned to therapeutic profit. In FAP we have a framework in which the benefits and risks of immediacy can be more precisely thought about. Rather than being a separate model, FAP has the ability to enhance any form of practice, and Bob Kohlenburg and his colleagues have already written about 'FAP-enhanced behavioural activation' (FEBA) (Kanter et al., 2009) and 'FAP-enhanced cognitive therapy' (FECT) (Kohlenburg et al., 2002) – well worth the attention of those interested in exploring the widest possible applications and styles of CBT, offering exciting possibilities as we look at how the 'third wave' models are developing and contributing to the overall practice of CBT.

DISCIPLINED PERSONAL INVOLVEMENT IN COGNITIVE BEHAVIOURAL ANALYSIS SYSTEM OF PSYCHOTHERAPY (CBASP)

James McCullough has developed the cognitive behavioral analysis system of psychotherapy (CBASP) as a form of therapy that is specifically targeted at chronic depression: where client problems are persistent and where suicidal tendencies occur frequently. He argues that many previous treatment modes, such as Beck's cognitive therapy, were not specifically targeted to deal with chronic depression. A particular type of problem seems to occur more frequently in this treatment domain: the therapeutic relationship can be threatened by what often seems like a fundamental lack of the interpersonal skills in the client, often connected to not registering the impact of their highly negative behaviours on others, including therapists.

McCullough offers a developmental explanation of the poorly developed social skills in these clients by arguing that some behaviours of chronically depressed clients reflect Piagetian preoperational cognitive functioning: when children have not learnt to make links between different causal events. Such cognitive functioning may result from the effects of chronic depression itself or it may be linked to certain aspects of developmental deficit resulting from childhood traumas acting as an underlying vulnerability factor in clients' lives. The result is that clients do not connect their behaviours with the consequences they produce in their lives. The lack of interpersonal connection is a chronic condition that aggravates the problem in severe depression and typically leads to helplessness and hopelessness. Furthermore, it leads to interpersonal deficits in clients' lives that maintain psychological problems.

The aim of CBASP is to help clients enter into more mature interpersonal communication where they learn and use more formal operations in interaction and so understand the impact of their own behaviours on significant others – and in the prime instance of the therapist. McCullough suggest methods to help the client learn these skills, such as situational analysis, briefly illustrated in the case example below. The case example also illustrates the main focus of our discussion here: the use of what McCullough calls 'disciplined personal involvement' in this work. Both areas of work draw heavily on the behavioural concepts of reinforcement and punishment. He advances the interesting argument that for these clients, motivation to change is often crucially achieved by the therapist's skilful use of negative reinforcement, for example, by not seeming to just tolerate clients' aversive interpersonal behaviours.

McCullough uses interpersonal analysis to examine aspects of relationship context in which CBASP interchanges take place in similar ways to that described by Safran and Muran (2000). The 'pull' of clients' negative behaviours elicits matching responses from therapists, using the concepts from Kiesler's (1996) impact message inventory (IMI) to offer categories such as 'dominant' that would pull on other categories such as 'submissive'. A competent therapist, however, could probably work this out without needing to use an inventory. This review of the mismatching of client and therapist roles can be seen as a form of transference formulation.

Mismatching creates problems between therapists and clients as discussed in Chapter 2. This idea is revisited here using an example where aspects of CBASP theory and methods were used.

CASE STUDY
Shahin

Shahin was a severely depressed hospital doctor who had taken extended sick leave after becoming unable to function in her post. Her therapist thought that the first session had gone well and that a good alliance was developing. He was therefore quite thrown when Shahin's feedback was that she said she had not learnt anything 'from all that boring CBT stuff with arrows'. Reflecting later, the therapist realised that she had hit one of his buttons: feeling that he should be a good therapist who helps everyone he saw. At the start of the next session, when he shared his reflection with her, she was shocked and became distressed, criticising herself for 'upsetting him'. They had an uncomfortable period before they were able to work this through. The therapist found it hard not to 'shut down' this interaction by reassuring her, but eventually they did reach a helpful point: she really did want help but had given no thought to what helping her would be like for other people. Later they were able to use McCullough's (2000: 107) situational analysis exercise to re-analyse that first meeting by comparing her desired outcome ('to bring the therapist 100 per cent on line to help her') and the actual outcome ('almost wrong-footing the therapist and undermining his confidence').

Later analysis of interactions with this client showed that the lack of ability in thinking about how to bring her therapist on board was probably related to the strong pessimism that this client experienced as part of her depression. It was of sufficient strength to provoke transference and counter-transference reactions; the subsequent discomfort was pronounced and could easily have led to a break-down in therapy. The therapist felt that his willingness to surface his vulnerability saved the situation on this occasion. Once the client had found herself in a safer place – where her 'mistake' had been 'caught' and rectified after it looked likely to take her down a familiar road that led to no help – she had experienced a tremendous sense of relief. It is this type of 'negative reinforcement' that McCullough holds to be the vital curative element in these types of therapeutic exchange, once again showing the ubiquitous usefulness of the ABC analysis with which this chapter opened.

CONCLUSION

Behaviour therapy was by reputation even less interested in emotions, spirituality, interpersonal exchanges and the therapeutic relationship than CBT later became accused of. This chapter, however, has shown that there are interesting new developments in all these areas and behaviourally oriented therapists are showing that they have much to contribute. Yet we find that these developments can be related back to the basic behavioural theory of functional analysis and ABC formulation.

It is important, though, to add some words about the standing of this work in terms of the degree to which its efficacy is empirically supported. We have already mentioned the solid evidence that supports behavioural activation (Martell et al., 2001) and some aspects of ACT (e.g., Twohig et al., 2006), though, as ever, there are dissenting voices (Ost, 2008). CBASP has been shown to be effective for chronic depression (McCullough, 2000). These developing models amount to early stage work, hardly surprising given their relatively recent vintage. Persons (2008) usefully points out that it just may be that CRBs will not occur in all sessions, so that FAP may need to be assessed by some more specialised mode of research than the straight RCT.

All in all, these new behavioural models contain much of interest for the current generation of CBT therapists, especially those who consider that the empirical supported therapy movement only provides half of what we need. There will be more discussion at the end of this book on how the integrity of the current model of CBT practice, given all these increasingly diverse developments, can be maintained.

FURTHER READING

Hayes, S. C., with Smith, S. (2005) *Get Out of Your Mind and into Your Life: The New Acceptance and Commitment Therapy*. Oakland, CA: New Harbinger.
Martell, C. R., Addis, M. E., & Jacobson, N. S. (2001) *Depression in context: strategies for guided action*. New York and London: Norton.
McCullough, J. (2001) *Skills Training Manual for Diagnosing and Treating Chronic Depression: Cognitive Behavioural Analysis System of Psychotherapy*. New York: Guilford Press.
Tsai, M., Kohlenburg, R. J., Kanter, J. W., Kohlenburg, B., Follette, W. C., & Callaghan, G. M. (2009) *A Guide to Functional Analytic Psychotherapy: Awareness, Courage, Love and Behaviourism*. New York: Springer.

NOTE

1 It is said that Erasmus once made a bridge without nails but when later engineers took it apart to see how he did it, they were unable to rebuild it without nails.

7

Emotional Interventions in CBT

> Emotion is the horse that pulls along the cognitive cart. Emotion provides direction and motivation for cognition. Emotion without cognition is a horse without a cart that will run wild and aimlessly. But cognition without emotion is a cart without a horse, which will simply sit going nowhere. (Power, 2010: 149–150)

Throughout the history of psychology and philosophy, debate on the relationship between reason and emotion has been hotly contested. A sense of opposition between the two factors has often resulted in advocacy for cognitive *mastery* of emotion, sometimes with counter-productive results (Power & Dalgleish, 2008). CBT can easily be interpreted as advocating unhelpful mastery of emotion, as indeed many critics have argued. We have previously argued against the idea that CBT does not deal adequately with emotion (Wills & Sanders, 1997; Sanders & Wills, 2005), but we have now come to the conclusion that there are significant problems for CBT practitioners in this area and that more needs to be done to address it in both theory and practice. These problems, we believe, are:

1 Consideration of emotions has been too narrowly focused on those associated with psychiatric diagnoses (e.g., anxiety and depression).
2 An over-emphasis on *mastery* of negative emotion and not enough emphasis on accepting positive aspects of emotion.
3 Insufficient appreciation of the subtle flow of emotions as they move and change independently and in tandem with cognitions.

Fortunately, considerable resources are now becoming available to us to address these issues. Some of these resources come from outside the CBT model: concepts from emotion-focused therapy, for example, can be helpfully integrated into a more emotionally grounded version of CBT (Greenberg, 2011). From within CBT there has also been a resurgence of interest in methods for working directly with emotions (Leahy, 2011); a transdiagnostic model for emotional disorders (Barlow et al., 2011a);

meta-emotional skills (Power, 2010); emotional regulation skills (Leahy, 2011); mindfulness interventions to help accept painful feelings (Hayes et al., 2004; Williams et al., 2007; Orsillo & Roemer, 2011); emotional processing in trauma work (Smucker, 2005); using validation and self-soothing skills (Robins et al., 2004); and compassionate interventions to defuse and heal extreme negative emotions (Gilbert, 2010).

This chapter will begin by discussing the nature and function of emotions. This will include revisiting our earlier discussion of the somewhat complicated relationship between thinking and feeling, this time from the perspective of emotion. It will particularly consider emotional dimensions of the 'dual process' model of mental functioning: an approach that is now commonly shared by a number of converging therapeutic models. Building on the assumptions that the main function of emotion is to give people information about the current state of their being in the world, the chapter will then discuss how therapists can work with a spectrum of emotions from the essentially functional to more problematic manifestations.

Whereas CBT has sometimes given the impression that it wants to eliminate negative feelings, for example by 'swatting' negative thoughts (Power, 2010), this chapter explores the notion that even 'negative' emotions have positive aspects and therefore often first need to be accepted before any work for change can begin. As Greenberg (2011: 78) notes, 'One cannot leave a place until one has arrived at it', an idea echoed in ACT when Luoma et al. (2007: 49) quote Steve Hayes' well-known dictum 'If you don't want it, you have got it'. Mindfully paying attention to uncomfortable emotions can be helpful in this regard and the 'motive power' in emotions may subsequently trigger relatively spontaneous and helpful 'processing' of them. Alternatively, more maladaptive emotions may need to be addressed more actively. There are different approaches to doing this and here we describe a representative selection of methods, including emotional regulation, a generic form of emotional-cognitive processing and self-soothing. Processing methods have been particularly helpful in working with traumatic and shame-based emotions and some examples will be drawn from such situations. Finally, extreme emotional reactions are prevalent in certain client problem areas and can be hard for both clients and therapists to handle. Methods of emotional regulation and self-soothing have been shown to be effective with extreme emotions, especially when twinned with validation of clients and, implicitly, validation of their emotions. In these situations, it is particularly helpful to see extreme emotions as being driven by desperate attempts to fulfil unmet needs.

THE NATURE AND FUNCTIONS OF EMOTIONS

Emotions are a complex set of psychological and body states that involve feelings, behavioural responses and thoughts. They are usually experienced quite briefly so that a different term, 'mood', is often used when they become enduring, negative and disabling, when they may also be described as 'chronic'. Feelings often occur below the level of consciousness, so again another term, 'affect', is used for the more conscious aspects of emotion. Emotions may be best understood as acting as forms of information that tell people that there is something significant happening inside them or in their environments and that this may need their serious attention. Fear, for example, draws attention to possible threats in the environment and therefore has at least some survival value. In this sense even very negative emotions can be functional and it is usually important for therapists to help clients foster acceptance of emotions as a first step. Attempts to suppress emotions may well have the ironic result of reinforcing them (Wegner, 1994).

Emotional reactions occur much faster than more deliberative cognitive processes, though it is hard to explain certain emotional reactions if it is not assumed that there is at least some fleeting and perhaps non-conscious element of *appraisal* – the key explanatory concept of cognitive accounts of emotion. Emotions are also *motivating*, having built-in behavioural or 'action dispositions'. We move towards things when we experience them as good and move away from them when we see them as bad: approach and avoidance. These reactions can happen so quickly that we can only identify the sequence in retrospect. From a physiological viewpoint, emotions also seem to move round the body and may change form and meaning as they do so. To some extent, what we say about our emotions may never quite fully express the visceral experience of feeling them. All in all, it seems most reasonable to assume some kind of complex reciprocal interaction between emotions and thoughts. This is why therapists must accept that clients often correctly report experiencing feelings apparently without any thoughts going with them.

When emotions and cognitions are acting in harmony, humans sometimes react instinctively and at other times more reflectively. Emotions guide and protect humans, though they may run out of control. They also seem to play a key role in helping humans to identify their needs. Hunger is a good example. Physiological processes are deeply involved, triggering many different bodily reactions as well as psychological ones. The feeling of hunger is also highly effective in mobilising the appropriate action disposition of foraging. Similarly, anxiety seems to activate awareness of danger and the need to act to ensure safety.

A convincing argument can be made that fearful and sad emotions may form different elements of a more generic 'negative affect'. Negative affect itself may, however, be orthogonal (running at right angles) to a generic positive affect. The importance of this for therapists is that decreases in negative affect do not necessarily lead to increases in positive affect, and vice versa. Separate strategies might be needed for working on these two activities. There are persuasive theoretical and practical reasons (Power & Dalgleish, 2008) for working therapeutically round five basic emotions: fear, sadness, anger, happiness and disgust. Complex emotions can be seen as involving mixes of these basic emotions: obsession-linked anxiety, for example, seems to involve a mix of fear and disgust. Emotions have been linked to evolutionary processes since Darwin wrote of them. Oatley and Laird-Johnson (1987) make the case for seeing them as strongly linked to goals, especially to transitions between different valued goal states. For example, clients may have set high store on maintaining a relationship so that if that relationship is threatened, they will feel highly anxious and fearful. At the point the relationship is lost, they may easily *switch* into sadness and depression. The cognitive appraisal element here is very similar to that employed in Beck's concept of 'cognitive specificity'. The identification of common processes underlying different emotions has led to increasingly powerful transdiagnostic cognitive-behavioural formulation and treatment (Barlow et al., 2011a).

We have discussed various 'dual process' models (Teasdale, 1996; Epstein, 1998) of the link between emotion and cognition in previous chapters. A similar model has been described by Power and Dalgleish (2008). They agree with Le Doux (1996) that there are two routes – a 'high road' (cognitively mediated) and a 'low road' (direct emotion) – involved in the generation of emotions. Sometimes these routes act in harmony and synergy but sometimes they are in conflict and this can be a major factor leading to emotional problems. Sometimes CBT diagrams and formulations can seem to suggest that there are linear relationships between cognition and emotion. Clients, however, are more likely to be aware of the emotion first and much less aware of the cognition. Thus a cognition reported by a client may be an artefact of an emotion.

PROBLEMS WITH EMOTIONS

Some conflicts between the operations of the different routes involved in emotion are caused by the fact that emotions are typically triggered more quickly and strongly than cognitions. Strong emotions are especially attention fixating – this is, after all, what these 'emergency signals' are designed to do – so that they can overwhelm and disrupt the cognitive system. The speed of emotional reactions sometimes means that subtlety and accuracy in the perception of personal needs are sacrificed to urgent assessment of basic need. The result of these mutually interfering processes is that the cognitive mind starts to function less effectively, making the characteristic 'errors' of those gripped by negative emotions. Fearing anxiety produces more anxiety. Anxious clients typically become hyper-vigilant for danger and begin to over-interpret possible environmental threat signals as indicating clear and present danger.

This takes us back to the need for balance in emotional-cognitive processing.[1] Ideally, the cognitive system helps to make realistic appraisals of risks detected by the emotional radar. People may or may not then decide that the situation *is* dangerous enough to justify action. On the other hand, if emotional reactions to threat register only weakly, then the cognitive system would not get the chance to process them. These factors will inhibit normal processing of negative feelings.

According to Leahy et al. (2011) there are two other major problems that prevent normal processing: avoidance and negative interpretation of emotions. Not only can the emotional and reasoning systems go out of balance, they can sometimes act independently of one another. This can be scary and lead to avoidance of emotions that therefore cannot be processed. Furthermore, memories may be encoded in body emotions out of conscious awareness so that, in Bessel van der Kolk's (1994) memorable phrase, 'the body keeps the score' in trauma. In post-traumatic stress disorder (PTSD), the body may be 'tricked' into reacting as if the trauma were happening now even though the mind 'knows' that it is not happening.

Another key area in PTSD concerns the roles that the interpretation and meaning of traumas play in maintaining trauma-based emotions – and this fact seems to confirm the relevance of cognitive appraisal in the generation of emotions. After trauma a person's world can be 'shattered' so that people who previously thought of themselves as 'strong' cannot accept the weakness they experienced during traumas (Ehlers & Clark, 2000). Victims' inability to 'accept' what happened and to give new meaning to their suffering – especially in the relation to what traumas mean about the self – inhibits their ability to process them successfully. This again emphasises the role of thoughts and beliefs in therapeutic work with negative emotions.

EMOTION AND COGNITION

From time to time, a debate arises over whether cognition has a primary influence over emotion or vice versa. Although it is possible to still find some early statements in CBT that imply cognitive primacy in emotional problems, a more widely held view is that expressed by Beck and Emery:

> In essence, far from being a *cause* of anxiety disorders, cognitive processes constitute a major mechanism by which the organism adapts itself to the environment. When a variety of factors interfere with the organism's smooth operation, it becomes the mechanism through which anxiety disorders … are produced. (1985: 86)

Appraisals do not *cause* emotions but do inevitably play an important role. Debate limited to a simple linear model of how cognition and emotion relate to each other will, however, be unproductive. As implied in the above quotation, a more helpful perspective is that of a network model in which cognitive, emotional and other processes are intertwined with each other. The commonsense notion of 'heart and head' fits well with many current notions of psychological functioning, and a number of CBT theorists have applied similar concepts to CBT theory and practice. Some tracks in the mind are associated predominantly with 'heart' functions such as emotion and experience, and others with 'head' functions such as cognition and thinking.

These tracks may work in tandem or against each other. We have all known the experience of conflict from situations such as where one says 'My heart says yes but my head says no' (or vice versa). Epstein (1998) and Greenberg (2011) make similar distinctions in 'emotional intelligence' that, for them, is characterised by the emotional and cognitive tracks in the mind working in harmony with each other.

Power (2010) discusses how the idea of the two routes to emotion can be integrated into CBT. CBT theorists have tended to show how clear use of cognitive strategies helps clients access their analytical minds when they are overwhelmed by emotion. Current humanistic theorists have tended to move away from the unreserved trust in emotions that characterised their earlier models to a basic trust in emotions when considered with emotional and cognitive understanding using reflection (Greenberg, 2011). Rennie defines reflexivity as:

> Our ability to think about ourselves, to think about our thinking, to feel about our feelings, to treat ourselves as objects of our attention, and to use what we find there as a point of departure in deciding what to do next. (1998: 3)

What emerges from these converging ideas about emotion and cognition is the possibility of a more 'emotionally sensitive' version of CBT practice, which, given the vital interpersonal functions of emotion and the fact that 'emotional coaching' seems to be a key function involved in attachment (Leahy, 2011), sits nicely alongside what we have already described as 'interpersonally sensitive' CBT practice.

APPROACHES TO WORKING WITH EMOTIONS IN CBT

'Emotionally-sensitive' CBT practice retains established cognitive and behavioural interventions but would implement them within the following guidelines to:

- recognise emotions that are not included in the DSM (APA, 2000);
- avoid attempting to 'over-power' unhelpful emotions with cognitions;
- facilitate healing unhelpful emotions via various types of emotional processing and emotional regulation.

Issues arising from the above are illustrated in the following brief case example.

CASE STUDY
Jane 1

Jane was a 'stressed' and depressed (BDI = 28) doctor. At assessment, she described much negative self-criticism and summed up her situation as 'I feel unrecognised, put upon and unloved, … I am angry'. When asked if she could 'stay with her anger', she put out a long string of reasons *why*

(Continued)

(Continued)

she was angry. When asked a second time to 'come back to the feeling of anger', the same thing happened. The therapist noticed that she had avoided the *feeling* of anger, and reflected this to her. She described how her 'strictly' religious parents encouraged heated arguments about religion and politics, but would not tolerate any expression of personal anger. At the end of the session, Jane said that the revelation of her 'forbidden anger' had been a major insight for her and that was what she wanted to explore. If she could find a way to express her anger healthily, it might do much to put her situation right.

Reflecting on this session, the therapist realised that he could easily have ignored the anger and challenged the thoughts underlying Jane's depressed symptoms. Yet working with her unexpressed anger brought energy into the session and was clearly what she herself wanted to do. The therapist had gone with the angry feeling that was expressed without precluding exploration of sadder feelings later.

Emotional sensitivity involves not talking *about* emotions but encouraging clients to feel them and then being prepared to run with the most salient emotions in a transdiagnostic fashion. Our aim here is to explore what this would look like in CBT practice. In the following sections, we first consider assessment and formulation of emotions in CBT, and then describe emotion-focused CBT interventions within a sound therapeutic relationship.

ASSESSMENT AND FORMULATION OF EMOTIONS IN CBT

Emotions are very varied, so that any blanket prescription on how to work with them should be viewed with caution. Earlier we noted how functional and adaptive emotions could be: even ones such as anxiety that we tend of think as negative. We know from clients, however, how easily emotions can slip from being functional to maladaptive. A client can be wistfully sad and gently melancholic about a loss in life one day, only to become suicidal suddenly a few days later. The emotion has taken on a different tone and quality and needs to be dealt with differently.

Many clients show strong emotional and cognitive avoidance as part of their symptoms, and this is understandable because negative emotions often hurt. Sometimes anger is a *secondary* emotion, covering a primary emotion of hurt or sadness. Sometimes emotions can appear *instrumental*, designed to articulate a need in an indirect way: as when some people cry to get others to respond. All these situations represent different aspects of emotional functioning. The following steps are therefore often helpful to the therapist during assessment of emotions:

- Identify what the client's current problem emotions are.
- Decide whether these emotions are healthy or unhealthy.
- If unhealthy, are they primary, secondary or instrumental?

Identifying Emotions

It should be evident by this stage that CB therapists like good questions that help to open out significant areas of psychological functioning. Good questions for exploring emotions are shown in Figure 7.1.

The answers to these questions would help us to know what kind of *emotional schemas* a client might have. Leahy et al. (2011) describe emotional schemas as being organised patterns in the mind that contain various visceral, emotional and cognitive elements: including 'meta-emotional' information, feelings and personal and cultural rules about emotions themselves, often adopted as part of the client's learning history (Chorpita & Barlow, 1998). Leahy (2003) has developed a questionnaire, the 'Leahy emotional schema scale' (LESS) and scoring guide, to identify schemas from his hypothesised 14 emotional schemas. This helps the therapist to assess the client's working rules about emotions: evidence of a *controllability* emotional schema, for example, indicates that the client has a pervasive fear that emotions, in general or in particular, can easily run out of control. The emotional schema concept has some similarity to recent descriptions of schemas and modes by Aaron Beck (Beck, 1996). Identifying emotional schemas will help us to understand familial influences on the way clients experience and use emotions (Chorpita & Barlow, 1998).

Primary emotions are relatively pure and basic feelings, whereas *secondary* emotions may hide or suppress primary ones. A classic example of a more fundamental emotion hidden underneath is expressed anger hiding hurt. People, especially men, often express their hurt through anger. This can be problematic as it can mean that the primary emotion is never processed. As with anxiety, the first therapeutic step therefore is often to acknowledge the presence of the primary emotion, whatever that is. There is an aspect of the need to 'name' a problem or emotion before it can be healed that has ancient spiritual roots (Whitehead & Whitehead, 2010). Most therapists have skills for helping clients to identify and formulate emotions but some clients

---

Primary adaptive emotions:
  'What is this feeling telling you about your life?'
  'Is there some health in this feeling?'

Primary maladaptive emotions:
  'Is this your feeling at rock bottom?'
  'Does this feel like a familiar and stuck emotion?'

Secondary emotions:
  'Does there seem to be another more important feeling that lurks below the one you have talked about so far?'

Instrumental emotions:
  'Is this a feeling that you show to get people's attention?'

FIGURE 7.1   Questions for exploring emotions

can still struggle, sometimes because they lack an emotional vocabulary and this can sometimes reach the problematic level of 'alexithymia', a sort of emotional blindness in which the client can't get any handle on naming the relevant emotion.

We can think of emotions as dimensional (on a continuum, for example, between happy and sad) or categorical (happy *or* sad). Experiences of emotion often seem to have both dimensional and categorical aspects (Persons, 2008). The five basic categorical emotions – sadness, fear, anger, happiness and disgust – are solidly recognised in emotions research (Power, 2010). It is also helpful to think in terms of an emotional palette that allows mixing of emotions. The mixing of sadness and disgust, for example, seem implicated in the generation of an emotion (shame) that appears frequently in therapy (Gilbert, 2009).

Clients will often report 'just feeling bad' and cannot say more. Such a feeling may be understood as a general 'negative affect' in which a melange of negative feelings may be mixed and in which more positive emotions may be 'deactivated'. Clients may have idiosyncratic words for emotions: one client referred to her negative feeling as 'head fog'. Therapists should use clients' own words for their emotions, adding the term into any formulations, perhaps alongside the more usually used words.

Self-monitoring emotions can be a helpful aspect of assessment. Various exercises have been devised to help clients to develop a 'vocabulary of feelings' and other aspects of the client's approach to emotions that make up their emotional schemas. A number of emotion logs, diaries and records can be found in the literature (Leahy, 2003; Persons, 2008; Power, 2010) and a generic format that can be elaborated for a multiplicity of purposes is offered in Figure 7.2.

Emotions: Healthy or Unhealthy?

Diaries can help clients to understand the distinction between healthy and unhealthy emotions, which are defined here:

- *Healthy emotions* may be negative but have a sense of freshness and newness. They are less related to 'old stuff', easier to express and push the client in a definite direction without interfering with the client getting help.
- *Unhealthy emotions* are negative but old and familiar. They often relate to old history, feel 'stuck' and are hazily expressed. Clients may 'harbour' them by becoming pre-occupied with their expression. Rather than leading to helpful processing, they may begin to show destructive effects, including inhibiting clients from getting proper help.

Keynote questions that can tease out these different types of emotions were shown in Figure 7.1. Identifying the most salient emotions, whether they are primary, secondary or instrumental, influences the selection of interventions. Primary adaptive

	Monday	Tuesday	Wednesday	Thursday	Friday	Saturday	Sunday
Anxious							
Guilty							
Angry							
Sad							
Fearful							
Excited							
Happy							
Proud							
Compassionate							
Regretful							
Disgust							
Jealous							
Interested							
Other _____							
Other _____							

FIGURE 7.2 Emotions diary

emotions often respond to 'light-touch' processing, whereas primary maladaptive emotions, secondary and instrumental often require more deliberative strategies. We describe below the selection and use of methods to respond to these different aspects of emotions.

CBT INTERVENTIONS FOR EMOTIONS

Therapists normally precede interventions by offering rationales. A rationale for working from an emotionally more informed CBT perspective could be:

> A unique aspect of therapy is the way it can help you to gain access to the web of all those emotions and thoughts that built up from significant things that have happened to you. If you can tolerate the discomfort of doing this, the chances are that you can relearn to feel some of those emotions and thoughts in ways that can work better for you.

The options for direct interventions with emotions open to therapist and client may be summarised as follows:

- If negative emotions are *primary* and *adaptive*, our aim is to facilitate clients to access, express, reflect on and process them. To achieve these aims we can use acceptance-based and mindfully oriented emotional processing methods.
- If emotions are *maladaptive*, then more deliberate strategies may be needed: cognitive or schema restructuring, described in Chapters 5 and 9, or more active emotional-cognitive processing, emotional regulation, distress tolerance and self-soothing.
- If problematic emotions are *secondary*, the aim would be to identify the underlying primary adaptive emotions and use interventions for such emotions listed above, dealing with any problematic remains of the secondary emotion after.
- If emotions are *instrumental*, therapists can use interpersonal interventions to explore how the client can articulate needs without using covert strategies.

The general aim of emotional work is to get back to dealing with primary adaptive emotions. For example, the man who covers hurt with anger may be encouraged to work with his anger in order to acknowledge and get back to the hurt, whilst the woman who cries to get sympathy can be encouraged to acknowledge her actual needs and work out how to ask appropriately for them to be met.

Whether clients are generally experiencing too much or too little negative emotion affects subsequent emotional intervention. Clients generally complain of experiencing too much negative emotion, and we know that too much of some emotions (e.g., anxiety) prevents successful emotional processing of fear (Foa & Kozak, 1986) so that in this instance the emotion has to be regulated to at least the point where processing becomes possible. Equally, however, clients should feel enough emotional processing immediacy in expressed emotions, otherwise processing them will be under-powered.

The picture is complicated by the fact that it is possible to have too much positive feeling (e.g., the excessive 'high' of bipolar clients) and too little negative feeling (e.g., suppression of disgust and fear may prevent acceptance and processing of negative experience). We have already noted that the emotion that is most evident may not be the most active one: cultural and 'genderised' (Power, 2010) inhibitions, for example, can play a role in making feelings about vulnerability or anger not 'acceptable' so that they 'switch' into other emotions. This can easily derail therapy by laying a false trail of emotion. Emotions can also be somatised (so that depression, for example, is expressed only via endless physical complaints), for which the client may believe there is more socially 'legitimate' help.

If emotions are identified as relatively *healthy*, then clients can generally be encouraged to accept and welcome them in: to let the emotions come, do their work and then recede. Therapists may not need to be too active in this process. If healthy emotions are flowing, they are often self-correcting. As emotions move, clients seem naturally to reach out for new, more healing meanings nested within them. Clients can be encouraged to give the process proper time and attention so that they can stay with, dwell and reflect on the feeling. Therapists can help to clarify points of meaning, perhaps reaching back to thoughts and beliefs identified in the overall formulation.

When *unhealthy* emotions arise, there can be more threat towards the therapeutic alliance, especially from client hostility. Therapists can feel fundamentally challenged by client negativity so that supervision often plays a vital role in 'getting through' it.

Instrumental and secondary emotions are generally *unhealthy* and therapists may have to discern what is going on beneath them before productive work can begin. 'Stuck' emotions can also become unhealthy and though they do sometimes respond to acceptance, they often require additional more deliberative processing, as described later in the chapter in the case of Bez, or more cognitive approaches or emotional regulation techniques such as self-soothing and imagery based compassion, illustrated by the cases of Lorna and Glen.

Therapists need to be emotionally sensitive not only in relation to the effect of negative emotions on therapy alliances, but they should also be aware of relatively normal feelings such as those of potential loss when therapy ends. It is important, especially in longer-term therapy, to at least offer the client the opportunity to talk about their feelings about this and to be able to articulate any feelings of our own.

INTERVENTIONS WITH PRIMARY ADAPTIVE EMOTIONS

Acceptance and Mindfulness with Emotions

Accepting approaches to negative emotions have been associated with mindfulness practice – one of the most exciting developments in CBT. At first look, linking science-based CBT and mindfulness, strongly related to Buddhism, may seem surprising. Yet the link has long been there. Aaron Beck practices meditation regularly and had an intriguing dialogue with the Dalai Lama.[2] The wider range of strategies linked to mindfulness is dealt with in the next chapter but here we will examine a highly practical application: helping clients to manage anxiety. This involves using the AWARE strategy described by Clark and Beck (2012: 142). This strategy is a five-step process that involves the client learning to:

1 Accept the anxiety
2 Watch the anxiety
3 Act with the anxiety
4 Repeat steps 1–3
5 Expect the best

The reader is recommended to read the full version of the strategy. Looking carefully at the steps, we can see, however, that the client is being invited into a revolutionary new relationship with her anxiety. Anxiety has probably been regarded as a harmful, negative state to be avoided and suppressed at all costs. We know also that, paradoxically, this avoidant and suppressing approach actually empowers anxiety. So instead of avoiding the anxiety, the client is invited to accept and even embrace it.

Acceptance opens clients up to what emotions have to teach them. Once the anxiety has been accepted, it should be 'watched' and acted with rather than suppressed: a case perhaps of 'Feel the fear and do it anyway' (Jeffers, 1997). This also results in the client having a different relationship with the anxiety: 'riding the waves' of it and shifting from the 'worried suppresser' to the 'detached observer'. The last step adds a cognitive finale to the procedure, giving the message that it is wise to expect the best because what one fears most rarely happens.

The AWARE strategy can be used in various ways: for example, as a behavioural experiment to test the effects of staying with the emotion of anxiety rather than trying to make it go away. Clients often think that the emotion will get out of control if they do not suppress it. Ironically, suppression and avoidance seem more often to make anxiety rebound in an even stronger form. Another use of the AWARE strategy is for clients to use it by themselves at home. Many clients find it helpful to use AWARE in this way. We usually introduce it in session by asking the client to close their eyes and get into a relaxed state by using progressive muscle relaxation, and then read out the AWARE strategy script in a gentle voice. This often has a helpful impact on clients and they can practice it at home without undue problems. It is also helpful to reinforce the method by coming back to using it in session, especially if an anxiety attack spontaneously arises during the session, and as part of exposure sessions. Some clients have reported that AWARE has been a mainstay tactic for dealing with anxiety attacks and has also helped to develop more mindful approaches to anxiety symptoms.

Wills (2009) argues that the AWARE procedure is evidence that a strain of mindfulness was evident in the even the earliest models of CBT. We are now accumulating practice wisdom in this area as mindfulness is being expanded to many different problem areas (Baer, 2006). Orsillo and Roemer (2011) describe an approach that expands methods like AWARE to delineate a 'mindful way through anxiety'.

Focusing

Focusing, in the therapeutic sense, has different faces. Primarily it is an attitude towards personal experience with many similarities to mindfulness (Elliott et al., 2004). Mindful attitudes towards experience aid processing and healing negative emotions. It is also an attitude that has been operationalised into a skilled therapeutic activity that can be used to enhance therapeutic work and contact (Gendlin, 1981). Its therapeutic utility has led to expansion into a model of therapy (Gendlin, 1998). There are also 'focusing communities' which facilitate its practice between members as a normal part of psychologically healthy living. Focusing has also been given a privileged position within the wide range of methods in emotionally focused therapy (EFT) (Greenberg, 2011) and the closely allied process-experiential model (Elliott et al., 2004).

The use of focusing in CBT can be thought of as being located near the mid-range between skilled activity and whole approach. One aspect of the process of EFT that closely matches the process of CBT is that it has been at pains to specify phases, stages and steps in the description of its interventions. Elliott et al. (2004) offer the following helpful format for learning and practicing focusing.

The first phase is 'clearing a space for attentional focus difficulties' with six stages:

1 Identifying a marker for the need to clear space.
2 Attending to the internal problem space.
3 Listing concerns.
4 Setting aside concerns (partial resolution).
5 Appreciating the cleared internal space (mid-level resolution).
6 Generalising the cleared space (full resolution). This phase has also developed as a stand-alone intervention for helping clients with traumas (Leijssen, 1996).

The second phase is 'experiential focusing for an unclear feeling' and also has six stages:

1 Identifying a marker for the need to focus.
2 Attending to the unclear feeling.
3 Searching for and checking potential descriptions.
4 Feeling shift (partial resolution).
5 Receiving (mid-level resolution).
6 Carrying forward (full resolution).

The above terms and sequence are illustrated in the client vignette below. Specified stages offer a general structure for work but should not be followed slavishly.

We last heard of Jane when a difficulty in expressing anger was identified. Further exploration of this issue revealed that she had major difficulties expressing a wide range of negative feelings because restricted beliefs about expressing emotion had been inculcated by her family and had been thus incorporated in an emotional schema with the theme of forbidden emotions.

CASE STUDY
Jane 2

Jane and the therapist were exploring her ideas and experiences of emotions, consciously trying to find a good 'working distance' from which she could work with her feelings. The therapist used the example of grief in a rationale for expressing emotions. Jane suddenly burst into uncontrollable tears, explaining that though she had lost her mother many years ago, she had lost 'my father in 2008, my brother in 2009 and my daughter (who had left home to go to university) in 2010', adding 'It is so hard dealing with all this alone'. She described how her father had regularly phoned for 'fireside chats', offering detailed advice on all aspects of her life. Jane felt ambivalent about this 'advice' – partly liking her father's 'patriarchal wisdom' but partly feeling that it signalled that 'he thinks I cannot deal with things myself'. Her brother had played a crucial role in putting her father and his intrusive advice into perspective – they would laugh together about *Moses' latest pronouncement*.

Jane's feelings appear to jump all over the place. When asked if she thought staying with her grieving feelings might help with her other difficulties, she said that she had sometimes tried to 'park' her other feelings so that she might allow herself to grieve but had never been able to do so.

CASE STUDY
Jane 3

Jane then used the 'parking' metaphor to help to 'clear a space' for grief by putting her anger and depression elsewhere. She chose to put her anger and depression into an imaginary freight container in the garden of the house where sessions took place. She mischievously told her therapist that she intended to leave them there as long as she could. Reaching for her unclear feeling and bodily felt sense, she said 'Something is missing' and reported sensing a heavy grey lump on her chest. Searching for a descriptive 'handle' for this body feeling, she settled on 'I am missing something'. There was no further felt shift in that session (though some came later), but there was useful reflection in that Jane could articulate that the loss of her brother and father was more than the loss of the sum of their parts but that there was a further, deeper loss of 'the family': she was now the only member of her nuclear family still living.

The therapist learnt valuable lessons from working with Jane and her rich and varied emotions. Sometimes to clear the way for more orthodox CBT work – in this case cognitive interventions in relation to her depression – therapists have to be prepared to work with other connected emotions. Understanding Jane's emotional schemas and being able to focus on her bodily felt grief and anger prepared the way for working with her depression. Jane always remembered the day that she wept openly for the first time in the presence of someone outside her immediate family as the day that her recovery from depression began.

Sometimes this kind of work can result in dramatic emotional-cognitive shifts – such as will be illustrated in a following extract on therapy with a client with PTSD – but other times the shift is more straightforward but nevertheless a significant part of client change. The fact that clients' chosen words act as 'handles' in focusing indicates that there is a cognitive element even in this emotional form of processing.

INTERVENTIONS WITH MALADAPTIVE EMOTIONS

Maladaptive emotions are often associated with abuse, trauma, hopelessness and shame (Greenberg, 2011). Greenberg has described client process 'markers', especially a sense of 'split' emotion that indicates their presence. The interventions described here (processing, using compassion and self-soothing) all begin with elements of mindfulness and focusing before moving on to include more deliberate interventional elements.

Emotional Processing with a Cognitive Focus

Focusing uses the time-honoured therapeutic concept that client issues should not only be identified and worked *with* but also be worked *through*. The expression 'working through' is a commonplace one in psychotherapeutic discourse yet may be understood differently. Various strands of meaning in 'working through' can be organised into the following steps:

1 Identifying difficult feelings.
2 Holding a feeling in open awareness.
3 Allowing the feeling to develop into a new form.
4 Reflecting on the changing meaning of the feeling.
5 Staying with the developing feeling and meaning until they coalesced into a new form.

Other terms used in psychotherapeutic discourse for all or part of this pattern of psychological development have been 'accepting feelings into awareness', 'emotional reprocessing' and 'cognitive reprocessing'. We consider that they can be operational-ised in CBT in what might be called 'emotional-cognitive reprocessing', a generic set of therapeutic manoeuvres that has similarity to eye movement desensitisation and reprocessing (EMDR) (Shapiro, 2001). Another way of seeing this sequence would be as an extended period of reflexivity working on various dimensions of the emotional schema (Greenberg, 2011; Leahy, 2011). We illustrate emotional-cognitive reprocessing in the next section with an actual case example concerning a client, Bez, with PTSD, highlighting relevant therapist skills for each of the above steps.

Identifying Emotions to be Processed

The main methods to identify emotions use the basic counselling skills of listening and empathic reflection. Careful listening allows the therapist to hear that certain words are 'feeling words' and are discernible because they are often delivered in a different register than more factual discourse. Some expressions seem to 'hang in the air' because they are redolent with meaning and emotion. Sometimes evident in a change in tone of voice, at other times they can be detected by the presence of an unusual emphasis, phrase or metaphor. Some research suggests that hearing such communication registers in distinctive physiological responses (Greenberg, 2011). Simple reflection is often a good way of testing whether what you think you heard as significant is indeed so to the client. For CB therapists there is also a second layer of empathic listening that comes from training the ear to hear patterns of cognition that we know are linked with certain types of emotion. This might be thought of as 'advanced cognitive empathy'. It comes from knowing, for example, that anxiety may be linked to thoughts that will over-estimate danger and under-estimate the client's capacity to cope with it (Sanders & Wills, 2003).

Difficulty sometimes arises when clients cannot identify or name feelings. Another difficulty has been called the 'think/feel confusion' dilemma. This dilemma is partly linguistic in that it is a language convention to say things like 'I feel like I am going to fail the test'. 'I am going to fail the test' is, however, actually a thought: a prediction, in fact. 'I feel' probably points to a feeling of anxiety. 'I feel anxious because I think I am going to fail the test' makes complete sense but is a bit long-winded. CB therapists know what the client means but are also keen that clients can identify the thought and feeling elements. Linking thoughts and feelings is therapeutically helpful because the client can use knowledge of such links to work on changing his feelings by changing his thinking. The conventional language is, however, easily understood so that it can seem pedantic to get the client to restate it. Confusion between what is emotion and what is thought may hamper clients' ability to work with thoughts and feelings and to do thought records. A good way to clarify this point is for clients to use written exercises such as thought records piecemeal and work on inserting the different elements into the correct columns with the therapist backing up with explanations of the thought/feeling link. Sometimes a thought/feeling link chart as shown in Figure 7.3 can facilitate this.

Accepting Traumatic Emotions into Open Awareness

Bez referred himself at the instigation of his employer, who thought that he was in constant 'great distress'. This 'distress' was a melange of several different negativities.

CASE STUDY
Bez 1

Bez worked for an NGO that supplied emergency aid in war zones. He functioned well whilst 'in country' but back at home he suffered intense anxiety, violent tempers and depression. He was a former soldier and had served in military operations during urban unrest. His employer recognised his PTSD symptoms and persuaded him to go for therapy. He was a reluctant client at first and, like many PTSD sufferers, showed tendencies to avoid thinking or feeling anything about his problems and symptoms. He reasoned that he couldn't have PTSD because he had coped so well in war zones. The therapist did not argue the point but helped Bez to bring his emotions into open awareness, by using relaxation and by instituting a 'safe place' procedure.

When I feel … (e.g.)	I tend to think …
Angry	He should not be like that!
Sad	?
Anxious	?
Worried	?
Other: _____	?

FIGURE 7.3 Linking feelings and thoughts

When strong emotions may be stimulated by therapy a 'safe place procedure' should be employed. Clients are encouraged to bring to mind a real or imaginary place where they feel safe so that they can access the feeling of safety if talking emotionally about a trauma which produces overwhelming feelings during sessions. Clients can be trusted to name their own version of this before processing begins, as they can before exposure therapy. Therapists can then introduce the idea of bringing the most troublesome emotions into awareness. Therapists should encourage clients to get as close to a non-fearful and mindful sense of awareness with as little evaluation as possible. Bez described arriving at this sense of new awareness of his emotional hurts by saying:

I began to realise that I had these wounds [*moving his hand over his chest*] all over my body. The wounds were not physical but they were deep and open. I had ignored them but now I thought, 'My God, I have been wounded. I need to find healing.'

As in the AWARE process, trauma clients may be invited to allow emotions to come and then to 'just watch or notice' them, monitoring and 'noticing' whether they are rising or falling in strength. The client may stay in this process as long as is tolerable: usually it *is* tolerable because holding emotions often leads them to subside naturally. If they do not, therapists can take clients to their 'safe place' or end the procedure by talking about low-key matters until they resettle. Whichever way the session has gone, client and therapist should review the experience. If successful, they can plan to use it again and/or the client can try to develop it as home practice (see Figure 7.4). If not successful, they can discuss whether to try again and, if so, what amendments would be helpful.

---

1. Identify the excluded feeling.

2. Discuss the possible reasons for exclusion, e.g., family rules about emotion etc.

3. Discuss the pros and cons of allowing the emotion in.

4. Ask clients if they are willing to try feeling it ('to see what happens') but make it clear that clients can come out of the feeling by simply asking to refocus on something else.

5. Encourage clients to stay with the feeling without evaluating it.

6. Ask clients to indicate when they have 'had enough' and finish accordingly.

7. Review the experience and reconsider any emotional rules identified in step 2.

FIGURE 7.4   Bringing excluded feelings into open awareness (Wills, 2008a)

CASE STUDY
Bez 2

Bez found he could use this way of letting his distress in and then watching it with detached mindfulness: at least during therapy sessions. He did report on-going problems outside sessions and also began to talk about traumatic experiences when a soldier.

At this point the therapeutic focus switched from anxiety management to a more specific form of emotional-cognitive reprocessing.

Holding the Experience and Allowing it to Unfold (Reprocessing)

The switch in focus came as Bez spontaneously began talking about specific combat experiences – the kind of emotional jump in narrative that characterises processing work.

CASE STUDY
Bez 3

Bez described how his buddy was killed whilst they were on patrol. As Bez described the scene, a remarkable and scary transformation came over him. His voice became a strained and hoarse whisper. He sweated heavily and shook so violently that water appeared to come from his head like a fountain. The therapist understood that he was processing trauma memories and indeed was psychologically back in the combat zone.

Therapy for 'emotional processing of fear' (Foa & Kozak, 1986) is most therapeutic when there is emotional *reliving* (i.e., of the original experience) alongside new information and cognitively restructured meaning. Descriptions of the pioneering work of Dr Rivers with World War I shell-shock victims read in uncannily similar fashion (Rivers, 1918).[3] Re-processing work can enable clients to feel something like the fear of the original situation and simultaneously access new information regarding the event (e.g., that the situation was, or is now more benign than it feels). It is also recognised that the re-stimulated feeling of fear can reach such intensity that it blocks processing: hence the therapist emphasises a secure therapeutic relationship and uses a 'safe place' method.

As clients 'view' these traumatic events, there may be a cinematic dimension to processing. Some clients have described watching traumatic images as if a film were being projected onto the wall. Therapists can encourage this feeling as an aid to processing, whilst also asking questions such as 'What can you see?', 'Who is there and what are they doing?', 'What does the image seem to mean?' that promote processing of the meaning of the event. Therapists ask clients to explore the meaning of the events they are reliving and can get them to identify the core beliefs that they seem to symbolise (Ehlers & Clark, 2000; Shapiro, 2001).

Bez identified the beliefs 'The world is full of evil men' and 'I too am an evil man'. In this case, the first belief makes sense in light of his experience, whereas the second suggests an as yet unknown area of experience possibly relating to another trauma. At this moment, Bez was experiencing feelings so intense that they could have blocked effective processing. The proof of the pudding is, however, in the eating and at the end of this session Bez reported himself to be exhausted but relieved. However, he continued to report considerable problematic symptoms between sessions, suggesting another area of trauma. From their early experiences of working with abreaction, Freud and Breuer (2004) developed the 'talking cure' informally referred to as 'chimney sweeping': clearance of blocked and trapped feelings so they could then flow naturally. The analogy is apt and is similar to the EMDR term 'channel clearing'. The idea of channel clearing implies that there are usually several, related, channels that need to be cleared. In CBT, we would conceptualise these different channels as having different meanings with links to different networks of feeling, beliefs, sensations and behaviours.

Trauma stories in their raw unprocessed state are characterised by fragmentation and haziness (Brewin & Holmes, 2003). Increasing clarity and coherence of the story is associated with healing. It seems that traumas often nestle within each other and so reprocessing may turn out to be like peeling away successive layers. Sometimes one peeling back reveals new and unexpected layers of trauma and meaning, and thus it was with Bez.

CASE STUDY
Bez 4

Bez returned after his emotional session saying that he had concluded that the death of his friend was not the original cause of his trauma and that there was 'something else'. He was at first reluctant to say what this was, but eventually he revealed that he had lost military discipline the following night and fired a plastic bullet directly into a crowd of rioters. The 'rules of engagement' were that soldiers shot plastic bullets into the ground so that they would not kill – as they could if shot directly at people.

Reflecting on Changes in the Meaning of Traumatic Events

Over several weeks therapist and client kept returning to this traumatic memory of the night of the riot. The therapist helped Bez to relax, use his safe place, and then asked if he felt ready to return to the traumatic event. The traumatic focus had now shifted to the night after Bez's friend was killed: when he shot into the crowd of demonstrators. The central point in the retelling of the story was always the moment when he shot into the crowd, but now memories surrounding that moment gradually returned in greater detail. This is a normal, healthy aspect of retelling and filling out trauma stories.

'Staying with' the Feeling Until a Major Shift (Accommodation) Occurs

Therapists and clients need to persist in 'staying with' traumas because there may be more elements to be processed. Therapists can feel that healing is developing

> **CASE STUDY**
> **Bez 5**
>
> Bez now remembered more about events surrounding the incident: the situation in the city – the early days of a civil war, the people involved and the training they had (or not had, more accurately) to deal with the situation the soldiers were in. He now saw that his 'badness' was less central to events than he had believed. As a soldier, he was part of a much larger social-political context with many points of badness and goodness. He also talked about his adolescence, reflecting that he had become a soldier 'quite unthinkingly'. He was still unhappy and troubled by all this but both he and his therapist felt that his stuck and bad memory was now developing and moving. Bez said, 'It's strange, I still find it horrible but I feel as if fresh air is getting in there now.'

but may never be sure when they have reached the end point of the treatment. The frequent shifts in material whilst working with PTSD add an extra dimension of unpredictability.

> **CASE STUDY**
> **Bez 6**
>
> Bez kept going over the same old ground of the trauma story. His therapist was unsure whether any further progress could be made, though Bez believed it would. Then he remembered a small detail about the operation that evening. As he was climbing into the troop carrier that had taken him to the riot, an officer looked into the vehicle and said 'This is our chance to get our own back'. Bez was sure that the officer referred to his friend's death and signalled a semi-official encouragement to hurt rioters that night.

The therapist felt sure that they had arrived at an important point: the knowledge that Bez had been part of a political–military system responding to social turbulence had previously been of impersonal relevance to him, whereas the officer's intervention was personal and especially significant in that command structures of armies require soldiers to follow orders. He could now begin to forgive himself and to see himself as a 'small man in a big conflict' and a man who was 'not wholly evil' but subject to the same terrible dilemmas and pressures as other men in these situations.

CASE STUDY
Bez 7

Bez never regarded the officer's remarks as an excuse. In fact, he also remembered that a sergeant, whom he respected more, had seen him fire the rubber bullet into the crowd and had given him a severe dressing down, adding 'Never mind what the officer said!'. Nonetheless, the tectonic plates of meaning had shifted and Bez now moved on to other traumatic events that had occurred when he was a member of a violent adolescent gang. He never returned to war experiences again: that particular chimney was perhaps finally swept clean. Therapy came to a premature end when Bez's NGO sent him to a war zone. There was follow-up therapy by email. The fact that he went to a war zone again was significant because his boss had vowed not to post him abroad again until he was coping better at home. Bez continued to be well, planned to marry and to cease his foreign travels.

PROCESSING SHAME WITH IMAGERY

When the therapist asked Bez to name the worst feeling experienced during processing his trauma, he named it as 'shame'. Shame is a frequently reported feeling in therapy, especially when trauma and childhood abuse arise. CB therapists are increasingly addressing emotions not in the DSM (APA, 2000): for example, shame. Gilbert (2009), for example, has developed a thorough going conceptualisation of shame from a cognitive perspective. Shame often has a strong visceral sense of being contemptuously looked down on by others as being flawed and inferior, linked to the primary emotion of disgust. Its behavioural disposition is, like depression, to shrink or withdraw. Clients often need to undergo some kind of 'de-shaming' process by developing an increased sense of internal empathy: what Gilbert has called the 'compassionate self'. Some clients are particularly ready to engage with emotions via imagery, often an ideal medium in which to heal distress, shame and the 'threatened self' (Stopa, 2009). Therapists can use imagery to help clients recreate vivid and emotionally felt scenes (Hackman et al., 2011). These might be historical events but might also be imaginary scenes that contain the key meaning elements involved in the clients' shame experiences. Scenes can process automatically as described earlier but sometimes, painful images keep 'looping'[4] and then it is helpful to give the process momentum by introducing 'imagery re-scripting'.

CASE STUDY
Lorna

Lorna always felt estranged from peers at school. Partly in response to this, she became what she called a 'self-conscious and nerdy' girl. Unfortunately, her classmates reacted by calling her 'Dyke'. She did not understand this word but knew it was a put-down. She was ostracised, culminating in being surrounded by classmates chanting 'Dyke, Dyke, Dyke'. She could never face this jibe without showing hurt, and now saw that she was powerless to stop it until the group decided it had hurt her enough. Even her one class friend had joined in the chanting. Years later, in therapy for persistent obsessional worry, this scene kept coming back to her. She and her therapist decided that it contained unprocessed shame and connected to her current anxiety. They used an imagery exercise in which she was able to reconstruct the experience in startling clarity. The image, however, remained stubbornly unchanged and her distress remained high. Therapist and client therefore began to re-script the scene, seeing it as part of a television programme in which a commentator reconsidered the motives of those involved and revealed what had happened to them since. In the 'programme', the friend who betrayed Lorna was interviewed. The girl explained that she had been scared not to join in with the chanting and that since, she had tried to make it up to Lorna in various ways. Lorna remembered ways in which this friend *had* signalled that 'she didn't really mean it'. Lorna also remembered that the ringleader, who had come from a difficult background, had since developed alcoholism. Lorna occasionally saw this woman and recognised an unspoken understanding of these facts flowing between them.

Lorna subsequently reported that the imagery re-scripting had been particularly meaningful to her and had, with other parts of the therapy, helped her to overcome her recurrent anxiety symptoms.

Gilbert (2009) has developed a linked series of therapeutic foci from depression, to shame and then to compassion. Compassion-focused therapy (CFT) features many of the new developments in CBT already described, including acceptance, mindfulness, interpersonal sensitivity and emotion sensitivity. This section on shame ends with a case illustration showing an emotion-focused exercise from CFT for a client who frequently felt troubled with shame-based feelings.

CASE STUDY
Glen

Glen took part in 'granny-knocking' when he was 8 years old. He and a friend had knocked on the door of an old lady and ran away before she could answer. Unfortunately, the lady had died during the night after one such incident. Glen then felt guilt and shame about his behaviour, fearing that he had contributed to the lady's death. This fear had faded but had recently resurged after having doubts about whether he was doing the right subject at university. Cognitive restructuring seemed not to help him come to terms with this memory, partly because it was impossible to establish whether the incident had played any role in the lady's death. During imagery exploration of his feelings about this memory, he could feel compassion, first for the old lady, then for his friend and finally even for himself. He realised that guilt had the effect of reminding him of his values but that for fallible humans, the importance of such values may only be learned by acute disappointment when our behaviour negates them.

Gilbert (2009) has linked his ideas on compassion to different neuro-cognitive pathways involved in developing internal ways of soothing ourselves. Marsha Linehan (1993; Robins et al., 2004) has also made valuable contributions to that area.

Self-soothing and Extreme Emotions

Extreme mood swings are a feature of borderline personality disorder (BPD). There is also a tendency to swing in relationships between 'idealisation' and 'devilisation' of significant others. Thus clients with borderline symptoms may approach potential partners in an intimate way, only to recoil sharply as they fear that they are getting too close. This is confusing and difficult for partners to read. They often decide that the relationship is not worth their effort and reject the client, thus confirming their 'abandonment schema'. As many of these clients have experienced abusive child-hoods, they often have both 'emotional deprivation' schema and 'mistrust' schema. These schemas act as antagonists, on the one hand, driving the client to move close to others, but on the other hand, to keep a wary distance. The elements of this formula are difficult to reconcile and are almost guaranteed to keep the client in a constant state of volatile emotion.

Although interpersonal mood swings are a feature of BPD, other clients display this pattern without justifying a full diagnosis. In any case, strategies that help clients deal with these situations as they arise will be helpful to many clients. Linehan (1993) has described an overall approach to BPD as 'dialectic behaviour therapy' (DBT). We cannot give a full description of this model here, but we can profitably draw on two of her key strategies that impact on extreme emotional swings: *validation* and *self-soothing*. One reason why validation is important to survivors of traumatic abuse is that they have been in very invalidating environments. Linehan (1993; Robins et al., 2004) sees her validation concept as being 'dialectical' in that it tries to be neither wholly change-oriented nor wholly acceptance-orientated. If therapists put too much stress on change, clients are partly invalidated in that clients are not accepted as they are. On the other hand, over-emphasising acceptance may be taken as saying that their pain must be tolerated. Leahy et al. (2011) extend the validation concept into his emotional schema work as validation involves being 'Okay to be who I am and feel like I do'.

To some extent the therapist's attitude oscillates between these two attitudes, though middle ground can be found by stressing that clients' responses to their situation *do* make sense of their life situation as it was then. It is also helpful to acknowledge the grain of truth in clients' extreme reactions to their current life situations. Such clients often have an uncanny ability to detect negative therapist responses. Since working with them can be difficult, it is just as well for therapists to acknowledge the kernel of truth in these observations too. Accepting strong emotional responses that may swing from one extreme to another can defuse the client's cycle of avoidant and emotionally suppressing reactions, which exacerbate their negative emotions. It should also be borne in mind that borderline features invariably result from invalidating environments. Sroufe (1996) shows that children's ability to develop control over their emotions is influenced by parents' abilities to do so. Children who have not been soothed consistently find it difficult to self-soothe. There is an element of 're-parenting' when therapists can create a calm, soothing environment for the therapy.

Clients can then practice 'distress tolerance' strategies: identifying and at times avoiding triggers, using calming breathing techniques, distraction, self-soothing, improving the moment and focusing on the pros and cons of staying the same and changing (McKay et al., 2007). Here we focus on self-soothing skills.

The skills of self-soothing are essentially about comforting oneself, as well as nurturing and being kind to the self. It is important to note that clients may have had little previous experience of being soothed and comforted in ways such as those a mother might use to 'kiss better' a child's sore leg. Parental soothing gradually builds up knowledge of how wounds, internal and external, can be healed and soothed (Kahn, 1991). Soothing is a very visceral matter. Touch has especially powerful healing effects. The smell of baking can carry the experience of 'someone is baking a cake for me' and the meaning 'the baker cares for me and thinks I'm special'. Self-soothing techniques often use the sensory modalities, listed here with examples:

- *Smell*: Experience the smell of baking.
- *Touch*: Stroke a friendly animal. Put on clothes that feel good next to your skin.
- *Hearing*: Listen to some soothing music, music associated with good times. If near some flowing water, that sound can be soothing.
- *Taste*: Now eat the cake or some other sensuous and textured food.
- *Vision*: Look out over a favourite view or painting.

The idea is to help clients enter into another sensory-emotional modality, moving away from the pain of extreme negative emotions into a more comforting modality. Therapists can sense that clients are moving into a painful area, and it can be helpful to acknowledge this and ask if they really want to go there. It may be appropriate to move closer to them with a gentle presence and ask them to make eye contact and return to the present moment. This immediate response is only possible in the present moment of the session. Greenberg (2011) describes how 'splits' between sources of soothing and agitation occur in some clients so that 'two chair' techniques can be useful in self-soothing work – showing that EFT draws from the Gestalt tradition.

Self-soothing using sensory modes can be practiced in session and then used by the client outside sessions. The list above obviously contains limited examples and therapists can help clients to generate their own lists of self-soothing activities. It is also wise to anticipate idiosyncratic reactions: for example, some clients might make a cake and then become self-critical if it does not seem as tasty as the ideal, so that fall-back plans can build more safety into this work. Some clients feel that they do not deserve to be soothed or to feel pleasure: sometimes because of family or personal beliefs. The general principle is to generate diverse responses so that if one does not work, the client can simply try another. The meta-message is that there *are* things that can be done to overcome feelings of helplessness; they will not work perfectly every time, but at least clients will have things to try. It is also impor-tant for therapists to keep reflecting on the experience of using self-soothing. Humanistic therapists have argued that 'changing emotion by emotion' can be more effective than changing emotion by cognition (Greenberg, 2011). It is possible to see self-soothing interventions as working mainly in this way so that CB therapists can at least have an open mind on this question – remembering the adage 'different strokes for different folks' (Ivey et al., 2011). As we are evidence-based practitioners, we can be open to what might work best for different clients.

POTENTIAL DIFFICULTIES FOR CBT INTERVENTIONS WITH EMOTION

There is a danger that the emphasis on cognition in CBT may lead to incomplete treatment of emotion. As Power (2010) says, therapists cannot just 'swat' emotions and negative thoughts with other 'functional alternatives'. It is easy to over-apply certain well-known CBT generic formulations that may not fit with the idiosyn-cratic worldview of an individual client: not all clients, for example, have panic attacks accompanied by the kind of propositional 'catastrophic misinterpretations' described by Clark (1996). We have argued before that there may be significant numbers of clients who experience panic at times of developmental transitions (Sanders & Wills, 2003) – especially relationship breakdowns – so that a protocol for treating panic that did not allow consideration of other emotional and inter-personal issues might fail.

If therapists do not focus on the client's most salient feeling, any attempt at cog-nitive transformation may prove superficial or premature. For example, clients may fear negative evaluation in particular situations. They might complete a thought record and be convinced that people in that situation are not making such evalua-tions. The anxiety may, however, mask a deeper fear of evaluation itself, and this may relate to shame-inducing experiences. The anxiety could mask anger at the unfair-ness of evaluation or actions by others that have limited clients' proper preparations. Thus cognitive change could represent a change of words (semantic change) but may leave the schema itself untouched. The edge of the feeling has been weakened but the emotion is still unacceptable – a type of change sometimes described as 'defensive restructuring'.

This problem has been partly addressed within CBT theory: Ellis, for example, advocated 'elegant change' (deeper philosophical change) as opposed to change of the inferences on the periphery of deeper cognitive change (Dryden, 1991). Deeper philosophical change should allow the client to live a fuller life with little need for defensiveness. This emphasis on deep change is also reflected in the values work of ACT. CB therapists can overcome these difficulties by helping clients to generate cognitive change with more emotional conviction. This becomes more possible when they can stay with and dwell in both their own feelings and those of their clients. A generic method that can help in ensuring the emotional relevance of therapy interventions is that described above as 'processing' in its varied guises.

CONCLUSION

This chapter has made the case that in order to be effective, CB therapists have to develop emotional intelligence and meta-emotional skills and apply them to therapeutic interventions and to their own functioning, especially in the therapeutic relationship. This can involve finding ways of working round clients', and therapists' own, emotional avoidance, sometimes helping the client to find and really feel the core feeling, and sometimes helping the client to manage emotions when they seem overwhelming. This does not involve abandoning cognitive or behavioural methods but ensuring that all such interventions are emotionally grounded. Although the importance of emotions has always been stressed in CBT, there are significant areas where it is easy for CB therapists to stray into premature closure and other errors in handling emotions. The best way for CB therapists to avoid these pitfalls is to commit to more reflexivity in relation to their own emotions and from that to build an emotionally grounded version of CBT.

FURTHER READING

Foa, E., & Kozak, M. (1986) Emotional processing of fear: exposure to corrective information, *Psychological Bulletin*, 99: 20–35.
Gendlin, E. (1998) *Focusing Oriented Psychotherapy: A Manual of Experiential Method*. New York: Guilford.
Gilbert, P. (2009) *Compassionate Mind: A New Approach to Life's Problems*. London: Constable Robinson.
Greenberg, L. (2011) *Emotion-focused Therapy*. Washington: APA.
Leahy, R. L. (2011) *Emotional Regulation in Psychotherapy*. New York: Guilford.
Power, M. (2010) *Emotion-focused Cognitive Therapy*. Chichester: Wiley-Blackwell. Especially Chapter 5 'Too Much Emotion', and Chapter 6 'Too Little Emotion' (pp. 79–124).
Rivers, W. (1918) The repression of war experience, *The Lancet*, 2 February. (Available as free download at http://net.lib.byu.edu/estu/wwi/comment/rivers.htm)

Stopa, L. (2009) How to use imagery in cognitive-behaviour therapy, chapter in *Imagery and the Threatened Self: Perspectives on Mental Imagery and the Self in Cognitive Therapy* (pp. 65–93). London: Routledge.

Whitehead, E. E., & Whitehead, J. D. (2010) *Transforming Our Painful Emotions,* Maryknoll, NY: Orbis.

NOTES

1　Processing theories in CBT and emotion-focused therapy (EFT) are remarkably similar. I use the term 'cognitive-emotional' in discussion of cognitions and 'emotional-cognitive' when exploring emotions. A more thoroughgoing analysis of the similarities and differences has yet to be written.

2　A film of this discussion is now available as a free download at: www.tpccg. com/beck/MeetingofTheMinds.html

3　Also described in Pat Barker's brilliant novel, *Regeneration* (1992).

4　More research is needed on why certain people seem to 'loop' during processing. One cause of looping that I have encountered is on-going pain. As one client put it to me, 'How can I come to terms with this when the pain is with me every single day?'

8

Mindfulness and the Third Wave Developments in CBT

Throughout the book we have emphasised how CBT is an evolving and changing form of psychotherapy. Starting with its roots in classical behaviour therapy, various stages or 'waves' (Hayes et al., 1999) have developed different ways of working and conceptualising problems. Standard, traditional models involve active working towards change: challenging thoughts, changing behaviours, finding different beliefs about the self and others. Many forms of CBT, including standard short-term models and longer therapy focusing on core beliefs, are effective. However, CBT has its inherent problems. Although CBT is very effective for episodes of depression, relapse is a significant problem and many people who have experienced one episode of depression are particularly vulnerable to repeated episodes. People with long-standing, complex and profoundly painful difficulties may not find CBT helpful, and physical problems such as severe, chronic pain require additional or different approaches.

Third wave therapies, described throughout the book as well as in this chapter, challenge some of the basic assumptions and models of previous ways of working: Is change always a good thing? Is active movement away from pain better than staying with and accepting experience? Third wave therapies involve, at the core, changing individual's relationship to thoughts and experience through acceptance, compassion and mindfulness. The newer approaches include mindfulness-based stress reduction (MBSR), mindfulness-based cognitive therapy (MBCT), acceptance and commitment therapy (ACT) and dialectical behaviour therapy (DBT), which includes mindfulness as a means of helping people to regulate emotion.

The ideas embodied in mindfulness, acceptance, moving towards experience rather than trying to control or change it, are hardly new. Many spiritual traditions, primarily Buddhism, have long known how meditation, and awareness of the present, can reduce suffering. The new models are taking on such ideas and methods, without specifically adopting Buddhist terminology or traditions (Baer & Kreitmayer, 2006), an integration of Buddhist concepts and methods with modern psychological principals and approaches.

This chapter describes mindfulness and its impact on CBT, including ways in which the concepts and methods of mindfulness are integrated with traditional CBT to produce different methods of therapy that are proving to be effective for a number of people for whom traditional CBT is less valuable. The chapter is a brief introduction, a taster, to what is a fast-growing area in psychology, neuro-physiology and psychotherapy. Sources of further information are given at the end of the chapter and in the appendix on CBT Resources, but for those interested in exploring mindfulness further, the best way forward is through trying it for your-self and attending experiential workshops and groups. The starting point for the chapter is the story of how the search for a form of therapy to prevent relapse in depression led to the development of MBCT. The so-called 'green book' by Segal et al. (2002) is a highly readable account of this journey, summarised below.

DEVELOPING MINDFULNESS AND CBT FOR DEPRESSION

Depression has a chronic and persistent nature, and high rates of relapse. When people recover from depression, they face the additional challenge to stay well. Episodes of sadness or low mood or other normal emotions during life can reactivate patterns of thinking that lead quickly into depressed ways of feeling about the self. Both CBT and medication are effective treatments for episodes of depression, with lower rates of relapse in those receiving CBT: 20–35 per cent relapse in CBT compared to 50–70 per cent for those treated with medication (Segal et al., 2002). Although effective, neither treatment offers complete protection from relapse. Medication is used to treat the episodes and as a long-term maintenance therapy, up to five years long, which is not acceptable to many people. The focus needed to change, therefore, from not just treating depression but also preventing relapse.

The three pioneers of MBCT, Zindal Segal, Mark Williams and John Teasdale (Segal et al., 2002), commenced with the development of an in-depth understand-ing of why people relapse after having effective treatment, and worked out that the key mechanism to prevent people relapsing into depression is 'decentering': the ability to step back from experience and thoughts. They worked closely with Jon Kabat-Zinn, who pioneered mindfulness-based stress reduction (MBSR) in the US. MBSR integrates Buddhist mindfulness meditation practices into a widely accessible group format, originally developed in medical settings (Kabat Zinn, 2001). The methods in MBSR and mindfulness practice provide a way of enabling the process of decentering; combining MBSR and CBT methods led to MBCT, now being evaluated for a wide range of physical and psychological problems (see Baer, 2006; Hofmann et al., 2010; Dunne, 2011).

DECENTERING AND DEPRESSION

Relapse was once thought to be because of unhelpful, dysfunctional attitudes or assumptions leaving individuals vulnerable to further depression. However, although depressed people do show increases on the dysfunctional attitude scale, scores return to normal when not depressed. Instead, relapse was related to changes in the relationship between the person and thinking. Studies inducing mood changes show that people vulnerable to depressive relapse find it harder to shrug off a negative mood than non-depressed people: that is, experience of depressed mood, sadness and negative thoughts tend to stick and become persistent. The experience of relapsing depression is familiar to many, with labels such as 'the black dog' or 'clouds descending' or 'falling back into the black pit', indicating a whole-body, whole-person experience.

People who have experienced episodes of depression in the past respond to life's difficulties in a particular way that can increase the likelihood of further episodes of depression (Segal et al., 2002), as the following case example illustrates.

CASE STUDY
Elaine

Elaine had experienced episodes of depression several times, often triggered by periods of stress and interpersonal difficulties. She was now settled in a new relationship, having started to live with her partner of several months. Elaine was hopeful that her life was changing for the better. Her partner, Jonathan, had been working hard for a promotion at work, and spent longer and longer hours there. Elaine was also working hard, partly because she did not want to come home to an empty house. She was coping fine until a minor argument with a colleague at work, after which she arrived home feeling upset and worn out. Thoughts went through her mind: 'I cannot get on with anyone; Jonathan's avoiding me, I'm so bad at relationships'. She remembered other times of feeling low and being alone, and exhaustion seemed to take over her body. She imagined Jonathan never coming home, and sitting in her empty house as the years stretch into the future. She felt a cloud of despair settling over her; 'Not again, I can never escape', and she sat, lonely and tearful. Even when Jonathan got back, she could not shake off her mood.

In this example, an avalanche of thoughts, emotions and body reactions come rushing down, maintained by memories of the same feelings in previous episodes of depression. As well as the negative thoughts, she experiences a flood of reactions unrelated to the original trigger: rather than just coping with her upset at work, she is overcome with memories and feelings about past struggles and depression. A mode of mind that configures negative mood, thoughts, images, memories, physical sensations is wheeled into place. Trigger events quickly lead to rumination and low mood, with all the accompanying pain of depression. Ruminating is used to solve the feelings, to 'work it out' in the head, but it backfires and sets off further painful reactions.

The task of preventing relapse was identified as enabling people to disengage from these toxic modes of mind, triggered by ordinary episodes of sadness or upset, and thus reduce the risk of tumbling back into depression. Rather than focusing on the content of thoughts, as in traditional CBT, it was necessary to step outside the thoughts and body reactions to 'decenter' from them. Decentering enables us to change not only the content of thinking but also to change our relationship to thoughts and experience, which is now seen as a central mechanism of change.

EXPERIENTIAL AVOIDANCE CAUSES MORE PROBLEMS

One way of coping with difficult experiences, feelings, bodily sensations, pain and adverse events is to shut off from them. This makes sense that we are hard-wired to get away from dangers, such as threats to our life or health. However, the mechanism that keeps us safe is over-applied to internal experience in the form of unwanted moods, thoughts or difficult bodily sensations, and to try to avoid these only creates secondary suffering and additional layers of problems. We can see from Figure 8.1 that primary pain, arising from our internal and external experiences, is then made worse by attempts to get rid of them.

Hayes et al. (1999) suggest that avoidance of unwanted experience is central across many psychological difficulties as well as chronic pain conditions; in contrast, the ability to connect with all experience, however difficult, is positively related to good therapeutic outcome. Trying to avoid our experience is, in the end, a fruitless activity: as Jon Kabat Zinn points out in his aptly named book, *Wherever You Go, There You Are* (2004). Avoidance reduces our ability to respond wisely to difficulties, and cuts us off from qualities of kindness, interest, compassion and warmth, all of which hold potential for literally changing our minds.

'Doing' versus 'being' mode

Most of the time, we are in 'doing' mode, focused on tasks, goals, plans, the future. Doing mode is necessary to life, to fulfilment and achievement: even those retreating from normal life are going through the tasks of living: getting out of bed, dressing, preparing food, eating and so on. When in doing mode, we are using particular areas of our brains as well as our bodies, essential to solving problems. 'Doing mode is entered when the mind registers discrepancies between an idea of how things are… and an idea of how things are wished to be, or how things ought to be' (Segal et al., 2002: 70) *I sit down to watch television, to relax for the evening, and remember that my chapter on mindfulness is not finished, the deadline fast approaching.* The discrepancy triggers discomfort and negative thoughts. *Oh no, I should have done it by now; my stomach churns, I feel tense and the sofa feels less inviting than usual.* The discomfort

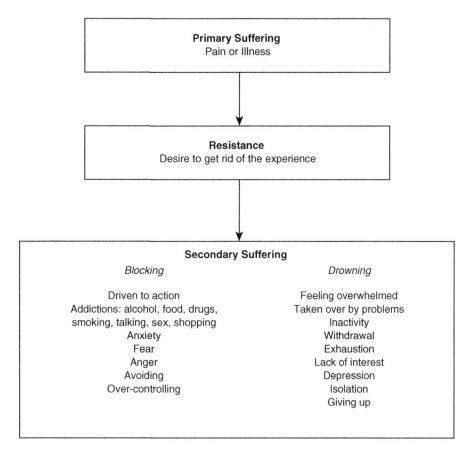

FIGURE 8.1   Primary and secondary suffering (Burch, 2008)

then triggers highly automatic and familiar processes designed to reduce the gap between the present state (unfinished chapter) and the desired state (completed work). *My discomfort propels me off the sofa and into my study where I switch on the computer and try to switch on my brain.* Once the 'doing mode' has solved the problems, it can switch off and allow the 'being mode' to take over.

However, doing mode cannot be applied to our emotions and moods: they cannot be solved so readily using the doing mind. In doing mode, thoughts are realities to be acted on; negative thoughts have to be acted on, using rumination or worry, or pushing them away to avoid the discomfort, which only serve to perpetuate the thoughts and mood. Instead of allowing us to be in the present, the focus goes to the future or past: whole minutes, hours, weeks and even lifetimes can pass with little awareness of what is actually going on right now. We can only too easily live in a state of mindless doing. Being mode, on the other hand, allows things to be as they are, seeing thoughts as mental events, experience as experience. Being mode is quieter, calmer, and uses very different parts of the brain. Both are in fact essential to healthy life, but being mode is too often the first to disappear at any sign of trouble. Mindfulness, at its essence, reconnects us with being mode, enabling the ability to live alongside problems, pain and discomfort. Being mode is highly centred in the present whereas doing mode tends to be future-centred. As we have noted before, we can become preoccupied with thinking of the future, and bringing our minds into the present moment can act as a healthy and balancing antidote.

MINDFULNESS

Despite being concerned with 'being', mindfulness has generated a vast amount of literature and scholarly work, confirmed by a quick search on Amazon and Google. However, it is a difficult topic to write about, without lapsing into concepts that are hard to articulate and may smack of new-age Utopia – peace, acceptance, gentleness, clear-sighted, multi-dimensional reality, experiencing sensation – hardly conducive to the hard-edged concepts of 'cognitive distortions', 'case formulation', 'negative automatic thoughts' we are used to in CBT. Mindfulness is an experience, a state of mind rather than a concept – in the way of trying to describe the awe of standing on top of a mountain, feeling profoundly moved by the beauty below, but being only able to find platitudes such as 'wow' and 'wonderful'. The best way to find out is to have a go oneself, learning by experience. Williams and Penman's (2011) book (with CD) is an excellent start. There are some brief exercises in the chapter as tasters, and sources of further information and training at the end to expand the summary below.

The central concept of mindfulness is that acceptance of one's situation can alleviate the battle inside the mind that often emerges when our expectation of how life should be does not match how life actually is. Being mindful involves sensing what is going on in any moment, even the judgements we make about what is going on, and noticing that these sensations, thoughts, images and feelings, come and go. 'Mindfulness means paying attention in a particular way: on purpose, in the present moment, and non-judgmentally … the simple act of recognising your thoughts (simply) as thoughts can allow for more clear-sightedness and a greater sense of manageability in your life' (Jon Kabat-Zinn, quoted in Segal et al., 2002: 40–41). Mindfulness involves cultivating awareness, practising a particular focus of attention, approaching experience with curiosity, openness and without judgement. There is no goal, no effort to 'get rid' of sensations, feelings or thoughts that are judged unacceptable. The experience of being in the moment involves letting go of judgements and goals. Readers are asked to work through this example:

> Right now, as you are reading this book, bring your attention to what is going on in your right foot. Notice any sensations, or absence of sensation, tingling or

numbness. Notice your reaction to being asked to pay attention to your foot – a feeling of irritation, curiosity, wanting to laugh. Notice any thoughts that go through your mind – 'What a daft thing to do', 'My foot is hurting/numb: what does that mean?', 'I must cut/paint my toenails' – or whatever else comes up for you. Notice what that moment feels like.

Mindfulness practice is kindly, steady and calm, and precise enough to notice all the varying qualities of experience. For example, pain arising from the body, such as lower back pain or headaches, may be viewed as a unitary and highly aversive experience. By mindfully paying attention in detail, we can explore the different textures and what they comprise, or find out that pain continually fluctuates and moves around. We may also notice that the pain is always accompanied by strong emotions, such as anger, disgust or fear, streams of thoughts and physical urges and sensations such as tension, as in Figure 8.1. The information gleaned in mindful attention can then be used to understand more about our habitual responses and enable us to make wiser and more helpful choices about how we respond to our experience.

Mindfulness tackles the very concept that our thoughts are 'true'. Thoughts are just thoughts but they exert a powerful effect on us. We tend to be unaware of the constant stream of thoughts, leaving little time for quiet. Disentangling from the mind's chatter, what one client described as 'a terrible soap opera, never ending and never having good outcomes', to realise that our thoughts, feelings and even sensations of pain, are 'just activities of the mind', is liberating, and for many, revolutionary.

Mindfulness allows things to be, just as they are, without changing anything – enabling, paradoxically, wise choices about 'What next?' for the next moment. Thoughts also change by themselves. The experience of stepping outside our thoughts, for a moment, brings them to a full stop – almost like our own experience of being watched will change how we behave (have a look at a group of children suddenly becoming aware that someone is taking a photo of them – they immediately change into different modes). Thinking patterns change by themselves.

Stop reading for a moment, and observe what is going through your head. Imagine that your thoughts are being projected onto a screen in front of you, or each thought is a lorry on a road and you are watching as they go past. Just notice they are there. You might want to note the content (thoughts about the chapter, your ideas about the chapter, thoughts about dinner, memories, worries), but don't latch on to any particular one. See your thoughts as events coming and going. Note how easily we grab onto one idea, particularly those with high emotion attached ('Oh no, I forgot to post that letter/answer that email/say how I am'). Notice that you might be resistant to the idea of stopping reading – I need to read this chapter and get on with the next thing in life. Just notice all this, as a kind and curious observer.

CBT AND MINDFULNESS – WORKING WITH THOUGHTS

> The endless battle of judgemental thoughts in my head had caused me so much pain that I'd go to great lengths to suppress them. I began to learn that, however many thought buses came past … I didn't have to catch any of them. I began to let the buses go by, just watching them . . . It seems like nothing, but its effects were huge. (Lewis, 2002: 92)

Mindfulness focuses on developing a different relationship to thoughts; rather than using evidence-gathering and answering back to decentre, as in CBT, mindfulness encourages bringing a different mind and quality of attention to thoughts. Thoughts are treated with kindly interest and gentleness – as but one of many aspects of our moment-to-moment experience.

> In this way, we can reduce some of the effort we expend in dealing with thoughts, as if they were telling the truth about the world or ourselves, the past, or the future. We also stop allowing ourselves to be controlled by them or, at least, we begin to see the tendency for that to happen emerge in the present moment. Once we see negative thoughts from this perspective, from behind the cascading waterfall, our emotional response to them will be different in subtle but important ways. (Segal et al., 2002: 252)

Mindfulness can be used in the service of traditional CBT, enabling clients to look clearly at all aspects of their experience and try out different responses. Mindfulness in therapy is, in essence, a willingness to go nose-to-nose with pain and accept it, as a vital first step towards change.

ACCEPTANCE AND MINDFULNESS

Acceptance involves intentionally turning towards and inviting in difficulties rather than pushing them away or striving to make things different, such as using safety behaviours as a means of coping with anxiety.

CASE STUDY
Simon

Simon had experienced panic attacks for years following a period of illness. He would feel, out of the blue, as though he was about to die: his heart raced, he became sweaty and he felt very detached from all around him. He went to great lengths to cope, but avoided being on his own, only going out of the house with his girlfriend, asking her for reassurance when he felt so bad. Using mindfulness, he turned towards these feelings when they occurred rather than run from them. Initially, this was terrifying for him, and he was concentrating on controlling his breathing under the guise of mindfulness. Very gently and for only moments at a time, he turned his attention to his breath without controlling it. He noticed that his breathing calmed itself down without him trying to control it. He then began to investigate, with curiosity rather than fear, the other sensations (sweating, dissociation) and found, again, that they passed as mysteriously as they arose. He began to be less fearful of his body, able to allow the sensations to come and go without, as he put it, 'powering into them'.

Being more open to experience, whatever it is, leads to a reduction in avoidance of experience, and in the necessity to control or get rid of unpleasant or difficult experience. For example, when traumatic memories come to mind, we habitually try to push them away, or think of something else, or ruminate about them, they can stay stuck and be allowed a great deal of potency over life. Also, if our thoughts and memories become 'truths', then we might allow them to predict the future, in a way which is not helpful: 'I remember last time I told a friend how upset I felt and she wasn't really interested, I felt so rejected and stupid, I better avoid letting other people know how I am feeling, never show my feelings and put on a brave face all the time.' By being able to take our experience moment by moment, being aware of the upset at the time rather than generalising into the future, such predictions become just thoughts and therefore not valid realities.

MINDFULNESS AND BEHAVIOUR

Mindfulness is not simply about acceptance and calm, being able to be with what is painful and difficult. It is centrally about behaviour, about what we do, how we respond to the challenges and difficulties life faces us with on a daily basis. Mindfulness makes the distinction between *reacting*, which is what we do when in doing mode, and *responding*, being able to choose between various responses based on awareness of what is going on right now.

CASE STUDY
Marie

Marie had always believed that when she started something, she must finish it. Not only finish it but do it to the best of her ability. She had been unwell for two years with chronic fatigue, pain and bouts of low mood. She had stopped working but found keeping up with the demands of house and family exhausting. Tidying up after the children had gone to school became a mammoth task, but she kept going until the house was 'up to scratch', then needed to sleep in the afternoons. During the mindfulness classes, she could see clearly the thoughts amassing in her mind as she did things around the house: 'I must keep going until it is all done'. It was a revelation to realise these were just thoughts: that she had a choice, moment by moment, about how she looked after herself, given her low energy. She began to pace herself, doing activities in a way that was in tune with her body rather than fighting it all the time, and found that she was able to introduce more activities just for her, and build up her confidence in herself.

LEARNING AND TEACHING MINDFULNESS

Mindfulness-based interventions include various methods for learning mindfulness, from formal meditation practice to awareness of activities in everyday life. MBSR and MBCT focus on formal meditation training, whereas mindfulness exercises in dialectic behaviour therapy (DBT) and ACT use shorter and less formal methods. Mindfulness is a simple concept, but is extremely difficult in practice, and so regular sustained practice is essential. Group participants commit to attending a regular course and engaging in both formal and informal practices on a regular basis. The skills learned during an MBCT course help participants to:

- Become aware of and able to step out of ruminative or unhelpful thinking patterns as they occur: a deliberate focus on the present-moment sensations in the body and breath redirects attention away from ruminative activity of the mind.
- Be aware of the 'pull' of automatic ways of reacting to unhelpful thinking, becoming aware of habitual patterns of the mind and choose to turn towards different responses.
- Recognise relapse-related processes in the mind and body.
- Discover and try out new ways to relate to depression-related experience, seeing thoughts and beliefs as simply events in the mind rather than realities, and use mindfulness to take appropriate action and look after oneself in a wise manner.
- Turn towards, befriend and engage with difficult and other aspects of experience to reverse judgemental and self-critical modes and habitual avoidance of experience (Crane, 2009; Williams & Penman, 2011).

STRUCTURE OF MBCT

MBCT is taught in eight, weekly classes of two hours each (see Table 8.1), with a one-day workshop halfway through the course. Each group is of 8–15 people, and they commit to regular, 45-minute daily home practice as well as attending all the groups. The sessions combine psycho-education, cognitive therapy and mindfulness meditation practices.

The meditation practices are drawn largely from Buddhist meditative traditions, including Vipassana and Insight meditation movements, as well as Theravadin and Zen Buddhist traditions. The meditations involve choosing a focus of attention, such as the breath, sensations from the body, sounds, eating or walking, and observing very carefully, without judging what is noticed. Participants are invited to notice when the mind wanders off, as it quickly does, into memories, fantasies and plans, then escort the attention back to the chosen focus, over and over again. Urges to move or scratch or give up the practice are also observed without necessarily being acted on. Practitioners are invited to hold an attitude of interest, curiosity and non-judgemental awareness, and when we inevitably rate our experience as 'pluses'

TABLE 8.1   MBCT programme

Session	Theme	Content
1	Introducing mindfulness. Mindfulness means paying attention, in the present moment, on purpose, without judgement. Automatic pilot.	Mindfulness of eating. Body scan.
2	Focus on the body. Recognising automatic patterns and chains of thought, emotion, sensation and action.	Body scan. Mindfulness of breath. Awareness of pleasant events.
3	Mindfulness of the breath: Awareness of experience through movement. Awareness of reactions as they occur.	Mindful stretches and yoga. Three-minute breathing space. Sitting meditation. Awareness of unpleasant events.
4	Staying present, using mindfulness to take a wider perspective on experience and relate to it differently.	Seeing and hearing meditations. Sitting meditation. Three-minute breathing space during difficulties. Education about cycles maintaining depression and problems.
5	Allowing experience to be as it is without trying to make it different. Acceptance allows us to see more clearly what, if anything, needs to change.	Introducing a difficulty into the practice: staying with, focusing on rather than pushing away. Extended breathing space, focus on difficulty.
6	Thoughts are not facts. Being aware of thoughts without seeing them as real gives flexibility of responses and interrupts automatic patterns of reaction.	Sitting meditation, awareness of thoughts. Understanding of moods and thoughts and alternative viewpoints. Using breathing space as 'first step'. Preparing home practice for end of course.
7	How best to take care of myself? Using breathing spaces to decide on wise action. Identifying relapse signatures.	Sitting meditation. Links between activity and mood. Pleasurable and mastery activities. Actions to deal with set-backs and relapse signatures. Mindful walking.
8	Using what has been learned to deal with future moods. Carrying on with regular mindfulness practice. Links to positive reasons to look after ourselves.	Body scan. Review of learning. Keeping up momentum. Concluding meditation.

Source: Segal et al., 2002

and 'minuses' ('Oh no, I'm thinking again, I'm not doing this right'), then treat such judgements as thoughts and return to focus. Mindfulness practice moves from specific focus, on breath or sounds, to non-judgemental awareness of the changing nature of experience – thoughts, sensations, emotions come and go.

In order to facilitate use of mindfulness in everyday life, the three-minute breathing space is a brief and portable meditation, which can be practiced regularly throughout the day and at difficult points, such as times when thoughts or feelings threaten to take over. The three-minute breathing space facilitates moving from 'reacting' to 'responding', enabling better choices about how to cope with what is going on. The three-minute breathing space involves three stages:

- *Awareness*: stepping out of 'automatic pilot', recognising current experience.
- *Gathering*: pulling attention to a point in the body, such as the sensations of breathing.
- *Expanding*: the attention to take in a wider sense of the body as a whole.

Taking a definite posture, sitting upright, with the back straight but not stiff, shoulders relaxed – allow the body to give the message of being awake and aware. Close your eyes, and become aware of what is going on for you right now. How are you feeling? What is going through your mind? Notice any sensations from your body. As best you can, just observing what is there, rather than trying to push away or changing anything.

Then, collecting your awareness by focusing on your breath, notice your belly moving in and out with each breath. Focusing on the entire in-breath and entire out-breath, closely observe the sensations of the breath moving in and out of the body.

The third step is expanding your awareness to take in a sense of your body sitting here, noticing the sensations of sitting, contact with the chair, any areas of tightness or tension, not trying to change anything but noticing what is there right now. When you are ready, open your eyes. (Summarised from Segal et al., 2002).

The instructions for the meditations are often given in a particular way, using the present continuous participle – 'noticing, moving, collecting' rather than the imperative 'notice, move, collect' – to emphasise present moment-by-moment experiencing. This way of phrasing also avoids a sense of effort and work, since direct instructions tend to give the message that there is a right and wrong way to do meditation. The instructor is inviting openness to all experience, whatever it is, particularly the experience of the mind going off in all directions regardless of the instructions to focus on one thing.

In the last few sessions of MBCT groups, ways of working with emotion are introduced. Although many people come along with problems with how they are feeling, the ability to use mindfulness to look at what can be overwhelmingly difficult is gradually built up across the first weeks of the course. For example, being able to focus on sensations in the body and sensations of breathing are first steps towards learning to stay with and accept experience, similar to discussion in Chapter 7. One works with emotion by observing the effect on the body, and allowing feelings to come and go, as in Figure 8.2.

CASE STUDY
Mahsa

Mahsa had been looking after her elderly mother for several years, and often found herself getting angry with her, but tried not to show it. She felt drained by the continual demands, and struggled with her mothers' frustration and irritability. Mahsa found her own anger unacceptable and had tried to keep it at bay. During MBCT meditation, however, she allowed herself to focus on it. Expecting to notice strong churning in her stomach and an anxious feeling, she was surprised when tears welled up, and her chest tightened with a hollow feeling inside. Tears flowed down her face as she watched her body respond with a huge feeling of loss in her heart. She recognised her feelings of grief, having lost her active and independent mother. She noticed relief, too, in allowing her sadness and grief to be expressed, and sat quietly with these feelings for the rest of the meditation.

1. Sit for a few minutes focusing on the sensations of breathing, then widen to take in the whole body.

2. Bring a difficulty to mind – something unresolved, unpleasant, perhaps where you feel upset, anger or guilt. When learning the method, it is best not to bring something overwhelmingly difficult but rather a moderate difficulty which can be focused on for a while.

3. Tune into any physical sensations evoked, and tune into these sensations in a spirit of warmth, kindness and welcome.

4. Watch the sensations moment to moment, staying with them, breathing into them, perhaps saying 'It's okay, whatever is here is here'.

5. If necessary, move the attention back to the breath periodically if it feels too much to focus on the body.

6. When the sensations no longer pull strongly for attention, return to the breath.

FIGURE 8.2   Inviting and receiving (abbreviated from Williams et al., 2007: 151–152)

CBT AND MBCT

The rationale and teachings of MBCT for preventing relapse in depression are based on a clear, cognitive behavioural formulation of the processes involved in triggering and maintaining depression: the tendency of the ruminative, problem-solving, doing mind to take over, triggering memories of previous mind-states and associated depression. The model is adapted for different groups of participants, such as those with chronic fatigue syndrome (Surawy et al., 2005; Rimes & Wingrove, 2011), chronic pain, addictions, health anxiety and other conditions, although the basic elements remain consistent across the models.

MBCT groups include explicit CBT elements. Participants are taught how thoughts affect how we feel, using thought diaries and in-group exercises and discussions. The effect of our mood on how we think can be illustrated by asking participants to consider their thoughts in two different conditions (Segal et al., 2002):

- *Condition 1:* You have had a quarrel with someone at work and are feeling quite down and upset. Later that day, you see another colleague in the office who rushes off quickly, saying she cannot stop. What goes through your mind? How do you feel?
- *Condition 2:* You have just come out of the bosses' office, having been praised for your work and are feeling good. Later, you see another colleague in the office who rushes off quickly, saying she cannot stop. What goes through your mind? How do you feel?

The kind of thoughts participants describe in condition 1 include being rejected or hurt, ruminating about what it all means, generalising thoughts such as 'Everyone has heard about the quarrel and taken against me', leading to further feelings of upset and rumination. In the second scenario, thoughts are more likely to be about the colleague's welfare, what was going on for her, and the event is quickly forgotten.

Other CBT elements include an explicit focus on ways of working with difficult thoughts, and the links between activity and mood, increasing nourishing and decreasing depleting activities. Once participants become aware of the patterns of their mind, by regular meditation and mindfulness practises, they are encouraged to introduce the step of 'wise action', being able to step out of automatic ways of reacting and ask 'How can I best take care of myself right now?' In addition, participants learn about their own 'relapse signatures' and develop a 'relapse prevention plan', as described in Chapter 10.

In contrast to the use of these methods in standard CBT, there is a different context that stresses a different quality to their use, one that perhaps tries to be closer to what might be called 'CBT in the key of being'.

TEACHING MBCT

MBCT is not merely a variant of CBT, so we cannot teach the approach simply by learning a few techniques. Teaching involves embodiment of mindfulness, and a commitment to both practising and living mindfulness is essential. Segal et al. (2002), describe how their initial response to mindfulness included concern about committing to regular practice themselves. This was resolved as they soon noticed the difference it made when instructors spoke from personal experience. In teaching mindfulness, teachers embrace a way of being and engaging: paying attention to experience with kindly interest. Things are much less likely to be pushed away, chased after or tuned out (Woods, 2009).

Mindfulness uses inquiry and dialogue as main teaching methods. Rather than giving instructions or answers, teachers offer and invite open conversations about what is happening in the room. They model openness to and interest in participants' experiences, and encourage participants to encounter a place of 'not knowing' – simply uncovering experience without trying to fix or shape the experience in any way. Acceptance is embodied in the way of teaching MBCT and other therapies using mindfulness, where the participant's experience is received in a spirit of openness, gentleness and respect, without having to fix it in any way or make things different.

It is a long journey from attending an initial group to being able to teach, and one not to be taken without considerable commitment of personal time and energy. Although some elements of mindfulness as a skill or technique have benefits in their own right, simply doing regular meditation practises, whilst essential, is not sufficient, since the pervasive habits we are working with are such an inherent and ingrained part of being human. Crane (2009) describes the following requirements for teaching:

- Development of awareness cultivated through formal and informal practice in daily life.
- Taking in, at a deeper-than-conceptual level, what it means to directly connect with experience through awareness and acceptance of moment-to-moment experience.
- An intention to underpin one's practice and life with an attitudinal framework of warm acceptance, non-striving and curiosity.
- Willingness to engage in a live exploration of what it is to be human and how suffering is caused.
- Be present with participants in the groups without moving in to try and fix things or give advice.
- Be prepared to be flexible in teaching people who are at very different stages and need different things.
- Be prepared to be compassionate towards the many difficulties expressed within the groups.

Before you reject the idea of teaching mindfulness and reach for a drink and the TV remote control, Crane goes on to point out that very many mindfulness teachers do not feel that they fully reach these principles, and that they are an ideal, not absolute. Teaching mindfulness involves holding the intention of keeping such ideas in mind, of keeping mindfulness fresh whenever possible, knowing that the very difficult task of being a human and living our complicated lives makes it hard to keep mindful.

MINDFULNESS AND OUR WORK AS CB THERAPISTS

Practising mindfulness ourselves may not only be of benefit to us and to our personal lives: it may well impact positively on our clinical work (Hick & Bien, 2008). Mindfulness is identified as a means of improving therapeutic relationships, to increase our ability to empathise with and tune into our clients, to listen fully without distraction and to impart acceptance, all of which are essential to fostering strong and effective therapeutic alliances. It may be that mindfulness is an active ingredient in therapy across a range of therapeutic methods. Mindfulness enhances self-reflection, seeing our thoughts and interventions as they arise, allowing mindfulness about the suitability of our work, moment by moment. Mindfulness facilitates a non-judgemental, accepting attitude, allowing suspension of judgements and negative perceptions of clients. It allows us to model equanimity towards difficult or distressing experience which might otherwise be avoided, allowing us to explore these experiences (O'Driscoll, 2009).

Mindfulness has been linked with increased empathy in a number of studies (summarised in Siegel, 2010), suggesting that as we understand our own internal, mental processes and we become more familiar with the internal sensations involved with empathy, we can more readily tune in to our clients. The concept of 'beginners mind', where we take each moment as it stands, as a new beginning, facilitates the process of seeing our clients without preconception or prejudice, without the mental filter of our own beliefs and experience (Morgan & Morgan, 2005). The impact of MBSR on healthcare professionals researched in a four-year study, showing positive physical, emotional, mental, spiritual and interpersonal changes, with an increased ability to deal with negative emotions, increased clarity of thought and improved self-reflection (Schure et al., 2008). Although it sounds almost too good to be true, my own experience is that, during periods of active use of mindfulness on a regular basis, I feel more in touch with what is going on, more in tune with my clients, able to sit and listen and stay with their experience in a clearer way and less muddied by the stress of life impinging all the time. Mindfulness does not prevent pain or self-inflicted suffering, nor stressful outbursts when trying to juggle all the various demands of life, but it does give me some tools for moving in that direction.

Does mindfulness lead to more effective work with clients? One small study suggests that teaching mindfulness (in this case Zen meditation) to trainees led to greater improvement in clients' experience and behaviour and lowered symptoms than in a control group of trainees (Grepmair et al., 2007).

EFFECTIVENESS OF MBCT

Mindfulness-based therapies have been shown to be effective across a broad range of chronic disorders and problems (Baer, 2003; Grossman et al., 2004; Allen et al., 2009; Chambers et al., 2009) with consistent and relatively strong levels of effect size across different studies. Improvements are shown in measures of both physical and psychological health and quality of life, such as depression, anxiety, coping style, pain and physical impairment. Several studies have replicated the original research looking at the efficacy of mindfulness-based psychological interventions in preventing relapse of major depression (Segal et al., 2002; Ma & Teasdale, 2004; Kuyken et al., 2009). A systematic review and meta-analysis (Chiesa & Serretti, 2009) concluded that MBCT as an adjunct to usual care is significantly better than usual care alone, an effect which continues when maintenance antidepressants are reduced. MBCT was shown to be valuable for reducing residual symptoms in major depression, and reducing anxiety in people with anxiety and bipolar disorders. Further studies show that MBCT is as effective as CBT groups for treating current episodes of depression (Manicavasgar et al., 2011). The effect size tends to reduce a little on three-year follow-up, suggesting the importance of regular booster sessions to facilitate continuing practice of mindfulness (Mathew et al., 2010).

Although research is proliferating, the methods are still in their infancy compared with other psychotherapeutic models. There is great potential, but mindfulness is not for everyone. MBCT is not a quick fix, takes time, energy and effort and may be so different from individuals' expectations of what psychological therapies should look like that it may be impossible to engage certain groups of people. The process of seeing and staying with experience can be overwhelmingly painful in the case of highly aversive experience or memories, such as trauma and abuse. One participant, with severe health anxiety, described being asked to be aware of his physical sensations as 'like being tied to a railway line when the express train is due'. He felt overwhelmed even at the thought of having to take a peep at his experience without being able to run away by using an array of safety behaviours. Another client known to us suffered a relapse as a result of a therapist using mindfulness approach with him, though the quality of this intervention appeared doubtful. Groups do not suit everyone, although the methods can be used with individuals, and it will be interesting to see case studies of how effective this is compared to the group programme. Mindfulness may well 'leak' into psychotherapy as a whole, becoming a common factor across different models that are taught as part of training in the complexities of working in psychotherapy, and thus move away from the current model of teaching and regular practise.

MINDFULNESS IN OTHER CBT-ORIENTED MODELS

In Chapter 6, we discussed the way ACT has used mindfulness-based interventions to help clients achieve psychological flexibility, especially through one of its key facets: facilitating 'contact with the present moment' (Hayes et al., 2004). Another similar development has been evident in DBT (Linehan, 1993; Robins et al., 2004).

Dialectics is a branch of philosophy that emphasises the balance of opposing ideas with the central dialect around acceptance and change: accepting the difficulties, validating how thoughts, feelings and behaviours make sense in the context of the individual's background, whilst being maladaptive and unhelpful, and therefore open to change. DBT (Linehan, 1993) was originally developed for people with 'borderline personality disorder': that is, those with complex problems of living, difficulties in managing emotion and often a history of suicidal or self-injurious behaviour, for whom other forms of psychotherapy, and CBT, had proved less helpful. It is a comprehensive approach, aiming to help many facets of the problems. The theories underlying the approach sees borderline personality problems arising from a combination of an emotionally vulnerable individual, with poorly developed abilities to manage emotion and a strongly invalidating environment: for example, the child's normal emotional responses and distress is invalidated, dismissed, contradicted and generally rejected. As children, they do not learn to label their inner experiences, regulate emotion or distress, or trust their private world of emotion. As adults, emotion becomes something to be feared, misunderstood, got rid of, causing immense difficulties in interpersonal relationships and a tendency to react dramatically, often in a self-harmful way, to feelings.

In DBT, there is a strong emphasis on the therapeutic relationship, in which the therapist balances accepting the client with an encouragement to change. The relationship validates and nurtures the individual, while at the same time encourages the client to make what are often radical changes to move towards a better and less harmful way of living. DBT includes many different methods (Swales & Heard, 2008) including elements of CBT, focused on changing thoughts and managing emotions:

- CBT strategies such as exposure, skills training, cognitive change methods;
- problem solving;
- skills training to help tolerate distress;
- mindfulness;
- increasing interpersonal skills;
- emotion regulation skills;
- commitment skills – pros and cons of change, playing devil's advocate;
- collaborative focus on behaviours that interfere with therapy, such as skipping sessions, not doing homework.

DBT is generally conducted in weekly skills-training groups as well as individual therapy and contact as needed, and a course of therapy takes around a year.

Mindfulness is a DBT module that facilitates the notion of 'wise mind' to enhance the individual's capacity to step out of a reactive mode, reacting rapidly and without thought or awareness to painful events, emotions or thoughts and bring mindful awareness to what might be a wise next step. For example, an argument with a friend may lead to an impulsive and dramatic attempt to get rid of the emotional pain and turmoil, such as lashing out at or harming the friend, self-cutting, bingeing on alcohol or food or suicidal behaviour. Instead, in DBT, the client learns how to identify strong emotion, sit with and hold it and decide on the most appropriate and helpful response: kindness and caring to the self, looking for support, a walk or thinking through how to manage the argument in the most constructive way. In this way, the therapy helps to increase awareness and understanding of inner experiences, thoughts and emotions, in a non-judgemental and validating way, and increase acceptance of what is happening moment by moment. Emotion then becomes less terrifying, more a normal part of life, giving the individual a choice of ways of responding. Observing and describing emotion just as it is and not acting on it, acts as a form of exposure, helping to normalise the range of human emotion as part of day-to-day experience and not something to be feared or got rid of. DBT is used in a number of different settings, including youth offending work, addictions services and chronic pain (Lynch & Cuper, 2010).

One apparent difference between the development of mindfulness practices in ACT and DBT is that there does not seem to have been the same emphasis given to personal practice in their respective literatures, certainly as compared to the MBCT literature, although it may be that this important aspect is covered in other ways within the practice communities supporting those models.

CONCLUSION

This chapter has given a brief introduction to mindfulness-based approaches, focusing on MBCT and its application to a number of clinical problems. Mindfulness is, at heart, a simple concept, that of being in the moment, open to experience just as it is without preconception or judgement. It is, however, a simple concept that is exceedingly difficult to put into practice, seeming to go so much against our natural tendency to want to do, achieve, move forward and solve problems. The chapter has discussed how such striving can be counterproductive in the area of mood and emotion, where the perhaps gentler and wiser philosophies of acceptance, being and non-judgement come into play. Mindfulness is not a technique or a quick fix, and can only be learned through experience of the methods, investing time to practice and absorb the concepts. It is not for everyone, but its proponents talk of both personal and professional gain: for many, even reading one book on the subject can begin to change ways of looking at the world, opening up possibilities of living more in the present and less in the future or past: in a lecture a few years ago, Tom Borkovec described walking through the door you are in rather than opening up all the other ones around you. The risk is that the current enthusiasm for mindfulness-based approaches sweeps conventional CBT to one side. MBCT, ACT and DBT all have their place, and none are a substitute for each other, but offer a choice of methods and approaches. CBT is essential first-line treatment for depression, and MBCT can strengthen the foundations and offer ballast against future storms. In terms of outcome, both MBCT and CBT groups can be effective for depression, but giving people a choice, and their preference for treatment-mode, may in itself prove to be therapeutic. We are in the middle of a storm of new ideas, methods, research and a great deal of interest, and it will be fascinating to see where it all gets to over the next decade.

FURTHER READING

Crane, R. (2009) *Mindfulness-based Cognitive Therapy*, London: Routledge.
Kabat-Zinn, J. (2001) *Full Catastrophe Living: How to Cope with Stress, Pain and Illness Using Mindfulness Meditation*. London: Piatkus.
Segal, Z., Williams, M., & Teasdale, J. (2002) *Mindfulness-based Cognitive Therapy for Depression: A New Approach to Preventing Relapse*. New York: Guilford Press.
Siegel, D. (2007) *The Mindful Brain in Human Development*. New York: Norton.
Williams, M., & Penman, D. (2011) *Mindfulness*: *A Practical Guide to Finding Peace in a Frantic World*. London: Piatkus.

9

Working with Assumptions, Core Beliefs and Schemas – Getting to the Heart of the Problems

The CBT model makes distinctions between automatic thoughts, conditional beliefs such as underlying assumptions and rules, and unconditional core beliefs and schemas. In this chapter we look in greater detail at how CBT tackles these deeper rules and beliefs that determine who we are and how we live in the world, which may be adaptive, or contribute to on-going difficulties. Although standard CBT guidelines recommend starting with NATs and working down to assumptions, then progressing to core beliefs and schemas, in practice working with thoughts, assumptions and beliefs often proceeds hand in hand, thoughts being embodiments of the assumptions and beliefs, sometimes in shorthand form, sometimes word for word. The same therapeutic interventions may work on different levels of cognition simultaneously. Working with assumptions and beliefs also often forms the part of therapy focused on maintaining change and preventing relapse after the end of therapy.

In contrast to conditional assumptions, core beliefs, derived from so-called 'early maladaptive schema', are unconditional, enduring beliefs about the self, others and the world, often formed in early experience, and often unhelpful. When entering the territory of core beliefs and schemas, we enter less-charted waters. Schema-focused therapy (SFT) is a newer version of CBT and is starting to have supportive research evidence (Arntz & van Genderen, 2009). It is also an area to enter once proficient in basic and standard methods of CBT, and is by no means necessary for many of the people we see in routine clinical practice.

This chapter is divided into two parts. First, we describe some of the tried and tested ways of working with assumptions and conditional beliefs to help clients to re-evaluate unhelpful rules of living and prevent relapse. Second, we go on to describe with unconditional core beliefs and schemas often related to long-term difficulties.

WORKING WITH ASSUMPTIONS AND BELIEFS: KEY ISSUES AND SKILLS

Working with clients' assumptions and beliefs is helpful for a number of reasons. As described in Part I, the CBT model emphasises the importance of assumptions and beliefs in the development and maintenance of psychological difficulties, hence directly targeting these can be vital to enable clients to change. Unhelpful assumptions make clients more vulnerable to relapse: although therapy may help them deal with present problems, unless the rules underlying the problems are also worked through, clients may experience similar problems again in future. Working with assumptions helps the client to develop skills for future problems.

Work focused on assumptions and beliefs requires a number of key therapist concepts and skills. Therapists and clients are explicit and collaborative: clients' rules are openly described, verbalised and examined as though they are hypotheses about the world rather than absolute rules (Young et al., 2003; Beck et al., 2004). Despite all the drawbacks clients' sets of rules may pose, their assumptions and beliefs may seem natural to them, fitting like comfortable old slippers. When therapists suggest that clients act or think against them, it may strike them as dangerous and anxiety provoking. It can, therefore, be threatening to have these beliefs challenged, and can imply that clients have 'got it wrong', sometimes for many years. Therapists need to proceed with empathy and sensitivity, working with, not against, clients. There should be no sense that beliefs are 'right' or 'wrong', or of having arguments. The therapist's task is to understand clients' viewpoints, however much we may disagree. We need to be aware of cultural differences in belief: Padesky and Greenberger (1995) quote examples of how easily therapists from one culture and/or gender can misinterpret and misdiagnose those from others, for example by accepting the therapist's cultural norms as healthy and diagnosing other standards as evidence of psychological problems. As we have noted of working with various issues, therapists should do belief work in ways adjusted to the needs of clients within their 'proximal zones of development' (Greenberg, 2011).

IDENTIFYING ASSUMPTIONS AND BELIEFS

Information for identifying a client's beliefs and assumptions comes from many sources, including themes that emerge in clients' ways of thinking. Clients avoid some issues because of personal 'rules' (Padesky & Mooney, 1998). For example, clients who always avoid talking in meetings may have 'if/then' rules about the meaning of looking anxious: 'If I show anxiety in a meeting, then I will sound stupid.' Similarly, if clients are overly rigid in their ways of life, underlying rules may operate: 'If I feel in control, then nothing bad will happen.' Clients who are always helpful, possibly irritatingly so, may assume that 'If I am *nice*, then people will like me'.

Guided discovery through Socratic Dialogue (GD/SD) is a key method for clarifying clients' assumptions. Asking questions, being curious, finding out what makes them think the way they do enables rules to be made explicit. Rather than accepting the client's thoughts at face value, guided discovery probes the underlying mechanisms. For example, instead of saying, with empathy, 'It sounds like you're scared of that happening' when a client is talking about the fear of fainting when anxious, the therapist enquires along the lines of 'What if that did happen … what would that mean?'. The therapist uses the downward-arrow technique (Greenberger & Padesky, 1995), a form of questioning, until clear rules emerge. The downward arrow peels the layers of meaning to identify what is beneath clients' specific fears. Questions are repeated several times until a 'bottom line' is reached. The aim is to clarify statements that make sense of clients' fears so that therapists can then respond with an empathic reflection such as 'If I believed x, then I would feel the same way'. Claudia, an adult education tutor, describes her terror of having panic attacks in front of her class.

CASE STUDY
Claudia

Claudia:	[*Describing panic*] I felt faint. I just knew I was going to pass out.
Therapist:	Suppose that you did faint … what would be bad about that for you?
Claudia:	I'd fall over in front of all these people.
Therapist:	And suppose you did that: what's the worst that could happen?
Claudia:	Well, I'd just be lying there like a complete fool …
Therapist:	Suppose that did happen. What would it mean to you?
Claudia:	It would mean I'm really out of control … I can't even stand up and do my job without completely messing up.
Therapist:	And if that were true, what would that mean?
Claudia:	It would just show what a fake I am.
Therapist:	Is this something that keeps coming back to you, some form of rule?
Claudia:	I guess I have to be in control. If I'm not in control, people will see me for what I am – a fake.

Using Imagery and Metaphor to Identify Assumptions and Beliefs

Verbal discussion cannot always reach assumptions or rules, particularly when the assumptions are charged with emotion, or if the individual has an intellectualising style or avoids emotion by excessive talking. Working with the client's images can be a powerful way of identifying meanings to the individual. The capacity to integrate imagery work into CBT has been greatly enhanced as a more transdiagnostic approach to emotions has developed in conjunction with advances in the science of imagery research (Hackman et al., 2011). Images are often more charged with meaning than are words, and therefore give more clues about underlying assumptions. Similarly when meaning is hard to identify, or during times of high emotion, finding metaphors for the experience can be helpful. These might include metaphors (Stott et al., 2010), common sayings or fairy stories or folk tales reflecting themes of goodness and badness (Blenkiron, 2005). One client described her black-and-white views of men in relationships, talked about looking for a 'Knight in shining armour', which the therapist unfortunately 'spoonerized' into 'A Shite in Knining Armour'. Although both initially laughed at the mistake, it led to an enlightening exploration of how one mistake could in her mind turn her knights into shites, and whether it is fair to judge someone totally on one aspect alone. Another client told his therapist that his frustration at not being able to solve his problems felt like 'being blown back round the Horn' – a reference to how many sailing ships[1] gave up trying to sail round Cape Horn because of the strength of the winds against them. Client and therapist subsequently used this metaphor to explore underlying rules ('Sometimes I am just up against a superior force and have to change tack'), and the client could decide when to persist and when to change tack. Another client had rules about needing to be needed and metaphors and images of 'the world on my chest', made up of 'continents' of other people's problems and 'seas' of their misery, causing episodes of chest pain and panic symptoms. By metaphorically deciding which parts of the world she wanted to visit, and those that could be left to themselves, she could begin to shrink the world and make it happier and more manageable for her.

Ways of getting in touch with images include asking 'Did you have a picture in your mind just then?'. Once the individual has come up with an image, the client can be asked to describe it in greater detail. Questions such as 'What is happening?', 'Who else is in the image?', 'What are they doing or saying?' can help the client to be more specific about the image. Once the image is identified, the types of questions in Figure 9.1 can be used to help the client to unpack and explore its personal meaning, implications and origins. Images can also be deliberately invoked.

MODIFYING AND REVISING ASSUMPTIONS AND BELIEFS

Simply identifying rules and articulating assumptions can enable clients to start changing: they see that it is unrealistic and unhelpful to hold such black-and-white views. Therapists can then encourage clients to look at grey areas between the black and white posed by assumptions, and this can offer more options rather than 'one true way'. For example, articulating the rule 'I have to do a perfect job at all

1. What can you see in the image?

2. What are you doing in that situation?

3. How are you feeling in that situation?

4. Who else is there? What are they doing?

5. What has happened just before/will happen just after what is happening now in the image?

6. What does this image mean?

7. What does how you are in this image say about you as a person?

8. What does how others are in this image say about other people or the world?

FIGURE 9.1   Questions for exploring clients' imagery

times' might change to 'It's good to aim high, but if it's not possible, then I'll lower my expectations'. The process of working with assumptions is similar to that described for challenging thoughts: the overall aim is for client to 'decentre' from unhelpful assumptions and empirically test them, to find out the relative 'truth' and helpfulness of the rules, and, if found not to measure up, to come up with alternatives (Padesky, 2004). Guided discovery, Socratic questions, diaries of negative thoughts and behavioural experiments all enable information to be gathered about clients' assumptions in order to test out their validity. Questions that can guide the client towards alternatives are shown in Figure 9.2, a version of which can be built into a cue card to work with when assumptions are activated.

- What is the assumption? What are my exact words to describe the rule, possibly stated as 'If … then'.

- In what way has this rule affected me? What areas of life has it affected; e.g., studying, work, relationships, leisure, domestic life?

- Where did the rule come from? What experiences contributed to its development? Rules make a lot of sense when first developed, but may need revision in the light of subsequent, or adult, experience.

- What are its advantages – In what ways has it helped me? What would I risk if I gave it up?

- What are its disadvantages – In what ways has it hindered me? What would I gain if I gave it up?

- In what ways is the rule unreasonable? In what ways is it a distortion of reality?

- What would be a more helpful and realistic alternative that would give me the pay-off and avoid the disadvantages? Is there another way of seeing things, which is more flexible, more realistic and more helpful, giving me the advantages of the assumption without the costs?

- What do I need to do to change the rule?

- How can I test out whether this is a better rule to live my life?

FIGURE 9.2   Questions to help the client discover alternative assumptions
(Beck et al., 1979, 1985; Burns, 1996)

Padesky (2004) makes a distinction between *trying to disprove old rules* by looking at the evidence on pros and cons, and *constructing new, more helpful rules* or adaptive assumptions. Key questions include: 'How would you like it to be?', 'In an ideal world, what rules work better for you?' (Mooney & Padesky, 2000).

Challenging Assumptions: Taking Risks

One powerful way of testing out rules is to devise behavioural experiments in which the individual does not act in accordance with the rule, but behaves as though a different rule is in operation, and tests out the consequences (Bennett-Levy et al., 2004). For example, Claudia's belief 'I must be in control all the time or it'll prove I'm a fake' could be tested with a series of experiments where she practises being slightly less 'in control' at work, occasionally preparing her lessons slightly less thoroughly than usual or feeling ill in class and having to sit down, to test out whether this proved that she was 'a fake'. She could also practise being more candid with colleagues about how she felt, or be more spontaneous in life and leaving some things to chance. If such initiatives pay off, then she might adapt the assumption to either 'I can be out of control sometimes' or 'Being in control can also include saying one does not feel very much in control'.

Whatever the outcome of the experiment, the client should learn something useful, and therefore experiments should as far as possible be experienced as 'no-lose' situations. Taking risks is, by definition, threatening, and clients often need support to try something new, with a good outcome whatever happens. Before doing an experiment for real, it can be helpful to go through the process using imagery, predicting possible difficulties and practising how these might be handled, thereby giving clients more sense of being in control and facilitating a good outcome. When revising rules that may have been in operation for a long time, experiments may need repeating many times, and in different ways, to reinforce the learning of new rules, also allowing adequate time for reflecting on results (Rouf et al., 2004).

Using Images to Modify Assumptions

Clients who can think and work 'in pictures' may find it helpful to use imagery to modify their assumptions. Although several texts on visualisation suggest that substituting a positive ending is a means of changing images, in CBT terms this may be counterproductive since merely looking at a 'happy ending' means that clients avoid looking at feared catastrophes in the images, and may actually prevent them from re-evaluating it and coming up with better alternatives. Often clients freeze negative images in time and do not look beyond them so that the negative meanings also stay frozen in time, and continue to 'invade' clients by intruding into their minds, like loop tapes or video players permanently on still-frame. Clients may need to experience what came next as images recede and 'heal'. If clients can hold and reflect on images, this may help to modify them, especially if they can move on from still-frame by projecting images forward in time, or can re-evaluate their reality. Images can help clients to experience and work with salient emotions, facilitating cognitive and emotional processing (Smucker & Dancu, 1999). Hackman et al. (2011) describe ways of working with images related to core beliefs and schemas. Stopa (2009) describes similar work in the field of trauma processing. In the example of Claudia, who only sees catastrophe arising from her fainting in front of the class, being out of control and seen as a fake, once she looked at her images and projected them forward in time, she understood that people would see that she was unwell and help her, and that they would not be very likely to think she was 'out of control', or judge her, for fainting and that most people would soon forget.

SCHEMA THERAPY AND WORKING WITH CORE BELIEFS

The Personality Domain in Therapy: A Dimensional and Categorical Approach

Beck's model began as a treatment of depression and gradually diversified out to other problems in therapy. Beck was not initially completely enthusiastic about working in psychiatric settings (Wills, 2009), but did then stay in that setting. One possible result of this was that research around his CBT model tended to focus on problems defined in the DSM (APA, 2000). When Young adapted the model to working with personality disorders he found that significant changes were required, adaptations that eventually evolved into a separate model of CBT: schema-focused therapy (SFT) (Young et al., 2003). Before describing schema-focused work, however, we should discuss the controversial label of 'personality disorder' – 'Axis II' disorders in the DSM (APA, 2000). This is necessary because, as we argued in earlier editions, there is a widespread tendency to associate personality disorder with being 'mad', 'bad' and 'hard to treat' (Sanders & Wills, 2005). In order to empower therapists to feel that they can help clients with problems in this area, we can abstract the small 'kernel of truth' in such categorical assertions but set it in the wider context of the dimensional aspects of these problems. In brief, the argument is that whilst there are some clients who i) completely fit descriptions contained in the label 'personality disorder', more clients have ii) some of the significant elements of them and can therefore be helped by schema-focused approaches. We should also add that even clients with a 'full diagnosis' are very rarely 'mad, bad and beyond treatment'.

In a classic book on critical thinking, Thouless (1953: 53) describes the 'problem of all and some' that bedevils many arguments. In brief, if you are arguing that 'all women like shopping', your opponent needs to find only one example of a woman who does not like shopping to destroy your proposition. Many arguments therefore descend to a more debatable question such as whether women 'usually', 'often', 'occasionally' or 'rarely' like to do this. Frequently up-to-date data on the question are lacking or not known to those debating it. As described of Socrates' debates in Chapter 5, the result is *aporia*, a gap in the knowledge. With this point in mind, let us consider some words from James Pretzer and Judith Beck as they write on adapting CBT to working with personality disorders. They are considering how various principles of cognitive therapy may need modification in such work:

> With clients who have straightforward Axis I disorders, a strong collaborative relationship is *usually* easy to establish. However, for clients with Axis II problems, the therapeutic relationship itself *often* becomes a focus of therapy … Clients with Axis I disorders *usually* do not have much trouble … (setting goals), but *many* clients with Axis II disorders have difficulty specifying goals and working to achieve them. (Pretzer & Beck, 2004: 305, my italics)

The authors are correct to use these relative terms but if we reversed them we could say that *some* clients with Axis II disorders might not need special CBT methods and *some* with Axis I problems might. We make this argument not to be perverse but because the result of it matches our clinical experience more accurately. This is not to argue that the categories described in Axis II are not meaningful or helpful. We have argued before that it is helpful to know what types of symptoms are likely to cluster together. The research on personality disorders does, amongst other things, suggest that they are common in everyday clinical samples (Cooper, 2008) but also that there are still major problems in reliable recognition (Westen & Shedler, 1999). Most psychological problems have widespread effects on the lives of clients. The key word is the definition of personality disorders is 'pervasive' – one might, of course, ask 'just how pervasive?'.

The significance of these arguments for the aspiring clinicians is that they do need to be aware that deeper, characterological issues may be lurking beneath more straightforward looking ones and that this may be the case more frequently than we have previously imagined. Therapeutic pessimism has dogged efforts in this area but there are now increasingly promising treatment options available. CBT has played a major role in the development of these options (Linehan, 1993; Young et al., 2003). Whilst new CB therapists might think first of referring on to where such options are available, they might also consider that they can develop some of the skills of schema-focused work with clients who exhibit at least *some* of the problems associated with the personality domain of therapy work – whom they are likely to see on a *reasonably regular* basis.

SCHEMA ISSUES – A MORE CONSTRUCTIVE APPROACH

At the end of this plea for therapists to look for what might be useful in the concept of 'personality disorder', we are still wary of the term itself. If it is consistently misunderstood and stereotyped among professionals, the term is likely to be similarly perceived among clients. Interestingly, therapists and clients in the USA appear more ready to adopt the term than in the UK. Fortunately, more user-friendly terms are emerging in CBT: schema issues and schema-focused therapy (Young et al., 2003).

The schema concept has a considerable history in psychology, for such a young science at least. The concept was probably first used by Bartlett (1932) and Piaget (1952). The term 'schema' referred then, as it does in Beck's work, to a 'pattern', in this case an enduring, deep cognitive structure or 'template' which is particularly important in structuring perceptions and building up 'rule-giving' behaviours. In Beck's initial work, there was a distinction between surface cognitions (automatic thoughts) and underlying cognitive structures (assumptions, core beliefs and schemas).

As we move into working with deeper levels of belief, it is useful to revisit the contexts and themes of cognitions from the surface thoughts through to core beliefs and schema, as the following examples illustrate:

1 *Negative automatic thought*: 'These people don't respect me.' The thought states that the people in this specific situation do not respect me. Despite the discomfort of this specific situation, however, it may be that in many other situations most people do, in fact, appear to respect me.

2 *Dysfunctional assumption*: 'If I work very hard, even though many people appear not to respect me, it may be possible to get some of them to respect me.'

3 *Core belief*: 'Nobody really respects me.' No matter what I do, however hard I try to please people by working hard, no matter how much I search, I can't seem to find any people who respect me.

4 *Early maladaptive schema*: A 'felt sense' of 'shame' in relationships that one counts for little or nothing. A consistent perception of indifference or violation from close significant others, most commonly parents, resulting in a profound sense of worthlessness which colours most situations one finds oneself in.

Core beliefs are therefore the central foundation of self-concept. Some writers use the terms 'schema' and 'core belief' interchangeably, but Young et al. (2003) distinguish between schemas as cognitive structures or modes, such as an 'unworthiness' schema, and core beliefs as specific content of the schema, such as 'I am unworthy', 'I don't measure up' or 'Others are better than me'.

YOUNG'S EARLY MALADAPTIVE SCHEMAS (EMS) AND 'LIFE TRAPS'

Young was an early associate of Beck's and the director of training at the Cognitive Therapy Center in Philadelphia in the early 1980s. Towards the end of the 1980s he began to develop a form of CBT that was suitable for clients with personality disorders. The work evolved as he realised that clients with personality issues did not always respond well to standard CBT. For example, a clinically significant feature of avoidant personality disorder (APD) would be clients' lack of close confiding relationships. The avoidance of intimacy might influence the therapeutic relationship, such as when clients do not trust the therapists' feedback (Beck et al., 2004) – a factor that could easily disrupt work on modifying unhelpful cognitions. Another example would be the over-compliant behaviour in dependent personality disorder (DPD), which could influence clients to give therapists what they think therapists want rather than developing what CBT requires: (evidence of all kinds, good and bad). Young et al. (2003) were aware of the difficulties surrounding the label of personality disorder and began to develop the 'schema-focused approach'. Rather than use the labels provided by the DSM (APA, 2000) classifications, they identified 18 early maladaptive schema (EMS) patterns in five general domains: disconnection and rejection; autonomy and performance; impaired limits; other-directedness; over-vigilance and inhibition. These schema patterns might be multifarious. Young's books carry self-rated inventories to help identify which schema issues might be active in a client's or one's own life. Schemas cluster within domains: for example, abandonment/instability and mistrust/abuse are schemas within the disconnection and rejection domain. The characteristics of schemas are shown in Figure 9.3.

Young and Klosko note that:

> Schemas are central to our sense of self. To give up our belief in the validity of a schema would be to surrender the security of knowing who we are and what the world is like; therefore we cling to it, even when it hurts us. These early beliefs provide us with a sense of predictability and certainty; they are comfortable and familiar. In an odd sense, they make us feel at home. (1994: 6)

A schema is a relatively enduring, deep cognitive structure that organises the principles of giving appraisal and meaning to experiences, especially in relation to rules of living, with regard to self, others and the world.

Schema are:

- unconditional;
- usually not immediately available to consciousness;
- latent and can be active or dormant according to the presence or absence of triggering events;
- neither 'good' nor 'bad' but may be considered functional or dysfunctional in how well they fit the client's actual life experiences and cherished life goals;
- compelling or non-compelling in the extent to which they are active and influential in the client's life;
- pervasive or narrow in the extent to which they influence the client's life, especially the number of areas in which they are active.

FIGURE 9.3 The characteristics of schema

In *Reinventing Your Life*, designed as a self-help book for clients, Young and Klosko (1994) use the more friendly term 'life traps' to describe schemas. The book also contains a simplified questionnaire to help clients identify which of the 11 specified life traps may play a role in their difficulties. It seems that Young changed the number of schematic patterns for a popularised version of his concepts rather than for theoretical reasons. Young, with various colleagues at the New York Cognitive Therapy Center, has continued to develop and research the model. *Schema Therapy: A Practitioner's Guide* (Young et al., 2003) represents the fullest attempt yet to spell out in more detail how the evolving schema-focused model might actually work in practice.

Young also clearly spells out the concept of schema maintenance. Early maladaptive schemas may be particularly rigid and resistant to change. This resistance will be reinforced by particular behaviours, thoughts and beliefs. For example, clients with mistrust schemas may well create almost impossible conditions of trust for others to comply with. Other people will inevitably not comply with impossible conditions – thereby reconfirming the client's original belief that other people cannot be trusted. Padesky (in Kuyken et al., 2009) uses the metaphorical term 'prejudice' to describe the operation of schemas. Like prejudices, schemas are not easily open to evidence that contradicts their assumptions. The prejudice model is a useful analogy for clients who are guided by their maladaptive schema, posing a question such as 'How much faith could a woman looking for personal advice have in a misogynistic adviser?'.

THE DEVELOPMENT OF SCHEMAS

Schemas develop from the way life events are evaluated. These views are then translated into ways of seeing self, others and the world at particular stages of development. Difficult or traumatic early experience is likely to be particularly influential, depending on the developmental stages the child is going through. For example, very early experiences (between birth and two years of age) can be conceptualised against Erikson's (1997) psychosexual stage of 'trust versus mistrust'. Experience of unreliable care during this period might result in the development of a 'mistrust schema'. Without some resolution, this schema could result in long-term difficulties in trusting others. A mistrust schema is a frequently met interpersonal difficulty for clients who experienced early difficulties, and this schema may be replayed within therapy itself.

Layden and colleagues (1993) have given CBT the valuable concept of 'The Cloud'. Very young children may be pre-verbal or have only limited verbal development and cannot encode and store experience in the ways of later life, when they will develop more sophisticated verbal processing and memory retention. Piaget (1952) describes early child thinking styles as 'pre-operational' (lacking the logical operations characteristic of later stages) and 'magical' (egocentric causal thinking).

These thinking styles might lead to 'black-and-white' thinking (reducing several categories to just two) and 'personalisation' (seeing oneself as more personally implicated than one is) in relation to the schema. However, recent neonate and infant research shows that very young children are extremely sensitive to visual, auditory and kinaesthetic cues in the environment. These perceptions then form the hazy mélange of 'felt sense' experience that Layden calls 'The Cloud'. Where there have been powerful early maladaptive experiences such as abuse, neglect or inconsistency, children learn that the world is not a good place and that others cannot be trusted. Since they are not able to completely understand the motives of caregivers, they may conclude that the only explanation for their predicament must lie in their own 'badness'.

When previously abused clients come into therapy as adults, such traumas may be relatively inaccessible mélanges of 'bad' visceral, fragmented memories. Because of the visceral haziness of 'The Cloud', such a child, and later adult, has few retrieval clues to access the memories, which means that they cannot be well processed, cognitively or emotionally. Like the 'fear structure' of Foa and Kozak (1986), the experiences may lie close to the surface of the mind and so can easily erupt as overwhelming emotion at any moment. As the matching memories themselves are not easily retrievable, the experience of overwhelming emotion may be all the more baffling and scary to clients and those around them.

CASE STUDY
Mary

Mary had strong schematic, childhood memories. In one of these, she was accused by her parents of having failed to discharge duties that most people would consider unfair impositions on a young child. She did not then have the sophisticated conceptual thinking that would have been necessary to defend herself and could only think of herself as 'unworthy of' her parents' trust. This and other similar incidents led to the development of an *unworthiness* schema that was now activated when she was unfairly criticised at work. The strong feeling that results from the triggering of this schema makes it difficult for her to respond in an adult fashion, so that, as in childhood, she experiences powerlessness and humiliation. Effectively, she has to deal with the stress of the actual current situation and, at the same time, with re-stimulated stress from memories of childhood. She might be able to deal with either stress on its own, but the combination of the two results in feeling overwhelmed.

CASE STUDY
Chrissie

Another client, Chrissie, had been feeling sad after getting caught in the rain one day. She couldn't see why this had upset her so much but, while processing the experience, recalled being left with painfully chapped legs from a wet nappy in a freezing house as her parents locked themselves in their bedroom and refused to come out to her.

The integration of schema work has been an important influence on the practice of CBT. For example, when therapists aim to help adult clients develop more flexible and functionally adaptable ways of thinking, they may be dealing with pre-verbal experience, which is perhaps impossible to deal with by conventional, highly verbal CBT interventions.

WHEN IS SCHEMA WORK APPROPRIATE AND INAPPROPRIATE?

Standard CBT works from the principle of parsimony – beginning work at the symptom level, especially with automatic thoughts. For example, Beck et al. (1979) stress that for depressed clients, hopelessness and difficulty in concentration can impair the capacity to enter into 'insight' work. Trying to 'work through' the depressive symptoms with cognitive techniques alone may not only prove inadequate but may even worsen the level of bad feelings. Such work becomes more possible as some of the symptoms of depression begin to lift. Blackburn and Davidson (1995) estimate that around 75 per cent of the intervention in standard CBT of depression is concerned with symptom-level work, typically working with behavioural responses to the passivity of depression and countering the negative automatic thoughts (NATs) of the depressed client. The remaining 25 per cent of treatment is with underlying issues and preventative strategies.

As therapy proceeds and therapists build up formulations, deeper core beliefs become evident. It may, of course, be that direct work on behavioural passivity and hopelessness also works on schematic beliefs such as 'I cannot act powerfully in my life'. As standard symptom-level work unfolds, most clients reveal previous experiences, including childhood experiences. CB therapists use formulations to fit all these pieces of information into the overall picture. Therapists may, for example, invite clients to explore childhood experiences and then ask 'What beliefs do you think developed from those experiences?'. It sometimes surprises therapists how easily clients can answer this question, describing clear, often stark, core beliefs that they were not previously consciously aware of. Schemas are unlikely to become a major focus of therapy, however, unless they keep coming up and demand to be put on the agenda so that therapists conclude that such underlying issues are likely to make the client vulnerable to relapse unless tackled therapeutically.

Where the client's functioning before the current problem was reasonably good, without marked personality issues, it may often be enough to unveil the core beliefs – to make clients aware of their existence and operation, particularly how they are activated and send disturbed feelings 'cascading' down to the symptom level. It may not always be necessary to work through core beliefs; the client's increased awareness of the beliefs can lead to changes, as the following example illustrates.

CASE STUDY
Keith

Keith, a 40-year-old IT worker, had been prone to depression and anxiety since adolescence. He became depressed again after his job was threatened by organisational changes. He had frequent NATs, such as 'I'm falling behind at work' and 'The others are way ahead of me'. Therapy was limited to a maximum of eight sessions. In the first six Keith used CBT techniques to challenge his NATs. His Beck depression inventory (BDI) score fell from 23 to 8 (from moderate to a non-clinical score). During these early sessions, Keith occasionally spoke about his childhood, usually rather reluctantly. He described his childhood as 'unremarkable' and it seemed difficult to link this with his worry-prone cognitive style. In session 6, the client and therapist went over this again to build a formulation together. Keith said, 'My parents didn't seem to worry about me ... maybe they didn't worry enough.' The therapist asked, 'Did that leave you to do all the worrying?' In session 7, Keith said that this question had stimulated him to write a formulation and handed over a long screed on his childhood experiences. The formulation was discussed in session 7 and in his 'blueprint' at the end of therapy, but not otherwise 'worked through'. Keith was happy to end therapy at the end of session 8. His feedback included comments about how helpful it was to explore the historical roots of his difficulties.

With the development of SFT come concerns about its use. Some therapists coming into CBT having practiced other models are more likely to believe that core beliefs and early experience are where the action is. They tend to want to dive into these areas early on in therapy, neglecting to fully explore maintenance cycles and day-to-day aspects of the client's problems, perhaps feeling that they are not doing 'real therapy' without bringing up the past.

SFT methods, as indeed is sadly true of many CBT methods, have not been much researched in their own right, partly because of the paucity of process research in CBT (Wills, 2010). Hazards can arise when we surface long-term core problems. Clients can be extremely vulnerable, and the risk is that difficult material is uncovered before the client has learned ways of coping with the consequences of uncovering such meanings. The downward arrow method is simple, but powerful, and often leads to pronounced emotional reactions, as clients unmask what they 'truly' believe but have been unaware of. Unpacking seemingly straightforward negative thoughts can lead to uncovering difficult and sensitive meanings, and if this is done prematurely, then clients may end up feeling much worse.

CASE STUDY
Clare

Clare, who had sought help for bouts of depression, felt terrible when she had a minor disagreement with someone at work. When she had told her supervisor that she had not understood her instructions, the supervisor was dismissive. Clare felt 'stupid' and 'useless' and also frightened that her supervisor now saw her as a failure. Reflecting on this in therapy, Clare saw that the supervisor's actions meant, to her, that she would 'always be alone' because 'once people find out how useless I am, they won't want to know'. Uncovering this meaning led Clare to feel much worse, bringing up many childhood memories of being severely reprimanded for small mistakes, and being punished by being left alone for long periods of time. For a while, she was left interpreting her world in terms of these beliefs, collecting examples in her mind, and remembering the past in terms of failures. However, another line that could have been taken to lift Clare's mood earlier on in therapy would have been to work with her assumption 'If people are stroppy with me, this means I've got something wrong', perhaps helping her to see that her supervisor was wrong to be so dismissive toward her. The supervisors' behaviour was perhaps her problem, not Clare's. Such work could have helped lift Clare's mood, rather than leading her to feel overwhelmed. Uncovering her underlying beliefs would have been valuable, helping her to understand and re-evaluate the meanings she was giving to day-to-day events.

James (2001) emphasises the need for therapists to think through the possible emotional consequences of accessing core beliefs, and suggests that hypotheses about core beliefs are brought gradually and sensitively into a course of therapy, not suddenly and confrontationally. Beliefs can be mood dependent. When depressed, clients may believe themselves to be useless and worthless. However, when feeling better, these apparently 'core' beliefs vanish, the person feeling once again reasonably well. Therefore, going in at the level of schemas can be counter-productive (James & Barton, 2004). In addition, therapists need to have sufficient skill and expertise, therapy time and supervision to do this kind of work.

In order to do core-belief work safely, James and Barton propose the following:

- Collaboratively decide with the client if, when and how to work on schemas.
- Start working early on in the session, allowing time for 'working through' any difficulties.
- Be mindful of the person's style of thinking. For example, if someone has a tendency to be black and white, the perspective may shift dramatically.
- Be mindful of how low mood leads to overgeneralised negative memories, so that the individual finds it difficult to remember things that offer a different perspective. For example, when low, Clare could not remember examples that counteracted her belief 'I am useless at relationships', whereas there were many examples of good friendships and relationships in her life that she was able to remember when less low.
- Work to enable the client to think more specifically and in detail about memories, and to be able to put things into context, before doing schema work. For Clare, this meant being able to see the supervisor's reaction in the context of the job situation (a stressed, open-plan office environment) and what was going on for the supervisor (recently split up with her husband) rather than automatically in terms of Clare.

Blackburn et al. (2001) observe that trainee CB therapists quickly become skilled at eliciting NATs and beliefs, but are less skilled at using methods to change such material, perhaps hoping that change will occur as a result of insight alone. We need to work with whatever thoughts come up in therapy, and be adept at methods of guided discovery and testing thoughts, so the client is not 'left hanging'.

The stepped-care approach is also useful in deciding when and where to start working at a 'deeper' level. Stepped care is a means of delivering services in the most parsimonious way, by starting with the simplest interventions and only using longer, more intensive or expensive forms of therapy where there is clear evidence for their effectiveness and where they are likely to serve the client's best interests (Richards, 2010b). Schema and core belief work is avoided as a first call of port for people with one episode of a problem, or someone with mild depression, or by less experienced therapists. However, it may be appropriate in the following situations:

- when there is clear trauma emerging from early and/or previous experience;
- with deeper 'themes' emerging strongly in the client's material;
- when early attempts to achieve some symptom relief have definitely not worked;
- when clients request longer-term therapy focused on early experience.

At the two ends of the continuum between work focused mainly on 'here and now' and that focused on 'there and then' underlying issues, there is a grey area of middle ground where these decisions about the foci and length of therapy are perhaps more difficult. Supervision is crucial to making decisions about the level at which to work.

TOOLS AND TECHNIQUES FOR WORKING WITH SCHEMAS

Ways of working with schema are gradually being developed, particularly through the work of Aaron and Judith Beck, Padesky, Young and Layden. As we have described earlier, schema networks may be difficult to access through language alone. Imagery techniques therefore have much to offer (Stopa, 2009; Hackman et al., 2011). Clients are asked to report significant images occurring at moments of difficulty or to induce images connected to their difficulties, which are explored for their inherent meanings. Therapist and client can transform the meanings and experience of imagery in ways that may prove more helpful to the client. Two-chair methods from Emotion Focused Therapy (EFT) can help reform the images and allow change in meaning as the next case example illustrates.

> **CASE STUDY**
> **Manesh**
>
> Manesh had struggled for years with depression related to underlying fears of being 'found out' and rejected but could not make sense of why this should be so. He articulated possible beliefs – 'People abandon me', 'I am going to be found out' – which were activated when feeling low. When he was one year old, he was left with his aunt for a few weeks while his mother was in hospital, but could not make sense of why this should have affected him. Although, rationally, he could tell himself that he was not abandoned – his mother had to go to hospital and it was not his fault – he still had an underlying sense that something bad would happen if he were not 'good'. In a two-chair dialogue, Manesh talked to his young self, allowed the younger self to express how upset he was, and comforted the child. This was an emotional turning point in therapy.

Continua work, positive data logs (Padesky, 1994; Padesky & Greenberger, 1995) and schema diaries (Young et al., 2003) enable old beliefs to be evaluated and weakened, and new beliefs to be constructed. In continua work the client is asked to map out how he sees himself in relation to others (Wills, 2008a). For example, with Sam, who holds the rigid belief 'I'm useless', the therapist would encourage him to define 'useless' more closely: 'What does it mean? Useless at what? What does the opposite concept, "useful", mean?'. Once the concepts have been discussed, Sam defines either end of the continuum: 0 and 100 per cent 'useful' (Figure 9.4).

The therapist then asks Sam to say where, realistically, he fits on the continuum. After he has located himself, therapist and client can begin to map out how different people register on the positive and negative criteria, allowing for more exploration of what those terms actually mean to him. For example, Mother Theresa, or other people who serve others all the time, might be seen as the most 'useful', but are these people Sam would want as close friends? If people are not 'useful' in any way, does this make them unacceptable human beings, or those worthy of help? The idea, as in standard CBT, is to try to 'stretch out' these inflexible categories, so that the client can begin to realise how invalid and counterproductive they may be.

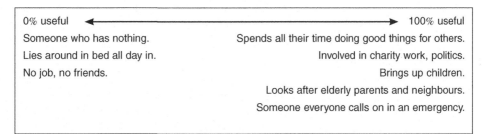

FIGURE 9.4 Continuum for the concept of 'useful'

Positive diaries encourage clients to keep a record of all the positive self-attributes and achievements they can detect in both their past and their present life. Often therapy starts focusing on episodes of negative thoughts and moods; with positive diaries we are aiming to highlight good aspects in the clients' lives. Initially, Sam found it hard to find evidence of being a 'useful, worthwhile person' and we needed to illuminate all the day-to-day actions that made up his life. Sam then started to notice how many times he interacted in a positive way with other people – chatting to the postman, holding the door for a colleague, making someone else laugh with a terrible joke – and how many times he achieved what he set out to do: 'I got up this morning; I got dressed. I put the rubbish out. I stayed at work all day, and finished two tasks I set out to complete.' Such activities would have previously been discounted; by keeping a diary over several weeks, Sam could begin to chip away at the notion of being 'useless'. Positive diaries provide powerful evidence to disconfirm the self-prejudice induced by maladaptive schema (Padesky & Greenberger, 1995).

Young et al. (2003) provide a comprehensive array of techniques specially adapted for SFT work. *Schema flashcards* are a valuable means of highlighting when the client's responses are being dictated by the activation of schemas as accompanying strong feelings make it difficult to appraise situations realistically. When clients notice that schemas or strong feelings are activated, schema flashcards written on postcards or in notebooks invite them to think, in the cool light of day, what is going on, and distinguish feelings arising from past beliefs from present realities.

Other cognitive interventions include 'life reviews' or 'historical tests of schemas', involving a process of drawing out a life history and trying to locate the development of core beliefs and schemas alongside it. Experiential techniques include 'schema dialogue', an adaptation of Beck's role-playing technique, where either therapist or client can take the role of either schema or anti-schema. Role-plays are particularly effective at helping clients to realise that there are 'two sides to the picture' and facilitate dialectical movement towards a new synthesis between polarised notions of 'good' and 'bad'. Behavioural interventions include collaboratively working on new behaviours that the client 'can try on for size': for example, 'acting as if' they did have more self-esteem. Another aspect of behavioural work can include behavioural pattern-breaking using experiments to test out forms of behaviours that would break with previous negative patterns.

Young and colleagues suggest that therapeutic relationships are central to SFT and that therapists can play the role of 'limited re-parenting' where they try to offer a therapeutic relationship that counteracts the schema by setting appropriate limits in interaction with the client. Consistency in therapists may, for example, counteract inconsistency in parenting. Such re-parenting can be helpful but, in our view, probably requires a good deal of therapeutic experience and should be approached with caution and monitored in supervision. Even experienced therapists need to take on board the comments of Arntz and van Genderen:

> [T]he therapist goes into this relationship *as if* he were a parent figure for the patient. Please note the words 'as if' … It is not the intention of this therapy for the therapist to become the parent but to model appropriate parental behaviours and reactions. (2010, p. 32)

RESPONDING TO SCHEMA ISSUES IN THE THERAPEUTIC RELATIONSHIP

How can therapists react when they become aware that clients have schema-based issues? First, they obviously need to be aware of the schema. This often comes about because the therapist experiences the counter-transferential 'push' and/or 'pull' of the schema. We have drawn up a brief résumé in Figure 9.5. Kahn (1991) develops a similar perspective in relation to how the humanistic and psychodynamic therapies are converging in their view of the therapeutic alliance. We would like the CBT voice to be heard more in this debate. Readers can use the template in Figure 9.5 to imagine how they would deal with the therapist's *countertransferential reaction* to a client, Wes.

CASE STUDY
Wes

The first sentence that Wes said in therapy was to ask what his therapist's qualifications were. This was neither an unusual nor unreasonable request. Wes, however, raised this question four times during the next eight sessions; every other session, in fact. On the last occasion he said 'Don't take this personally, but I'm not sure if you are a good enough therapist to work with me.' By this time it had emerged that Wes came from an indulgently 'laissez-faire' family on whom he was dependent but toward whom he felt perpetual anger. Visits home invariably resulted in him storming off before the expected time of departure. His current therapist was his fifth, most of whom Wes had 'provoked' (his own word) into terminating therapy with him. The therapist was determined to stay the course (20 contracted sessions) with him and not reject him, saying 'I know it's hard to know if I am the therapist for you but that's your question; I intend to stick around and do my work until you tell me otherwise.' The therapist rightly suspected that this would be a struggle and made sure that he took this to supervision regularly.

SOME RECENT DEVELOPMENTS IN SFT

Some recent major evidence on the effectiveness of SFT with one of its main target problems – borderline personality disorder (BPD) – has greatly advanced its cause (Arntz & van Genderen, 2009). Evidence on the use of dialectical behaviour

---

Phase I – Dealing with one's own countertransference reaction

1. **Do not retaliate**
    Schematic material can be very provoking and disheartening to the therapist. Remember that this is why the person needs therapy. It is just something that they do, not all of what they are that is the problem. Try to 'hold' the difficulty.

2. **Do not offer immediate 'easy' reassurance**
    Being a nice person, you will be very tempted to reassure the client: 'Of course, you can trust me .. .', '. . . I won't abandon you . . .'. If you do this, however, you run the danger of not seizing the moment and taking the chance to work with the schema while it is 'hot'. You may also be reacting like other people in the client's life – most usually in a schema-confirming way. Again, try to hold the difficulty and then open it for examination and 'working through'.

Phase II – Responding therapeutically

3. **Express empathy for the schema**
    'It's understandable that, given your circumstance, you've come to think that you can't trust people [i.e. in the case of a mistrust schema]. Most people who'd had those experiences would end up feeling that way.'

4. **Acknowledge the schema and suggest it is a problem that can be solved collaboratively**
    'In a way, it is good that it has come up now. It means that we can take the time to work out ways of stopping it from getting in the way of the things you want to do in your life.'

Figure 9.5 Schema issues and the therapeutic relationship

therapy (DBT) for treating BPD (Linehan, 1993) has always been promising, but the effectiveness of Young's SFT was recently tested against and found superior to a major alternative psychodynamic treatment in a clinical trial. Young has developed new aspects of SFT in the treatment of BPD in which he has identified the influence of 'modes' and has therefore developed mode-based treatment methods. The rationale and style of this type of treatment will be briefly described here. Readers can go to Young's major work (Young et al., 2003) and to Arnzt and van Genderen (2009) for fuller descriptions of this fascinating work in the area of what is probably the most commonly occurring problem in schema-focused work.

In order to formulate the major problems of BPD, Young et al. (2003) had to develop new ground in SFT. This was because many BPD clients present with multiple schema-based problems. It seemed to Young et al. (2003) that these schemas clustered into what he came to term 'modes': specifically, and in order of influence, the 'detached protector', 'punitive parent', 'abandoned child', 'angry child' and the 'healthy adult' modes. Understanding how the client can keep 'switching' between these modes helps to explain why Arnzt and van Genderen (2009: 12) describe SFT with BPD as being like 'playing chess with a pinball machine'.

CASE STUDY
Harry

Harry was a client in his 40s who had been severely sexually abused from the age of 8 until 14. He had been encouraged to go for therapy after talking to a priest about it. He was, however, deadly calm in therapy and insisted that he could not work out what all the fuss was about (*detached protector*). He talked about the abuse in matter-of-fact terms and complained that there were so many stereotypes of those who had been abused. The therapy seemed to be going nowhere over many months so that eventually the therapist suggested that they should look either at terminating or at alternatives. Harry reacted strongly and was successively hurt (*abandoned child*), then furious (*angry child*). When the therapist attempted to express empathy for his sense of hurt, Harry belittled himself by saying what a sad, pathetic 'specimen' he was (*punitive parent*).

It was only when he began to talk more about his mother, whom he suspected of colluding in his abuse, that therapy began to get closer to bringing out the weakest but potentially most curative part of the system, the *healthy adult*, into play, as the following schematic role play reveals:

Client: [*Trying to understand why he alone amongst his siblings had been abused*] … my sister always seemed to get things her way … and my brother was out of the picture …

Therapist: You say this in an almost matter of a fact way …

Client: Well it was the matter … it was the fact!

Therapist: [*Later*] Do you link this matter-of-factness with having to 'pull down your shutters', as you put it?

Client: If I reacted in any way to my mother, it would just goad her on … and with David [*his abuser*] he liked it when I showed pain … If I could stay icy calm, he would kind of give up in the end. It was the only way I could affect things.

Therapist: So how do you think you thought about all this as a child?

Client: It was just my bad fate – I didn't deserve anything better so all I could do was endure.

Therapist: Okay, so that's the way Child Harry thought, what about the Adult Harry? Is it possible to own the adult spirit of endurance without thinking you deserved to suffer?

Client: I hope so – I can see though that the way I shut things down with people leaves me empty … therapy has sown the idea that I might even deserve something better – may be.

With this kind of schematic role-play, CBT has come a long way from the more simple thought record work described in Chapter 5, yet in some ways the same type of manoeuvres are occurring at both levels of the work – but this time on a larger and more complex stage. Here, the negative cognitions cluster round an emotionally felt unworthiness and the alternative thoughts rest on the prospects of the Adult Harry finding a new way. Perhaps this is ultimately just a more emotionally and historically grounded form of GD/SD and therefore one that any therapist can reach toward as experience develops.

CONCLUSION

The tools and techniques of CBT discussed in Part II are many and varied, some unique to CBT, some borrowed from other models, including psychodynamic and emotion-focused therapy. We have stressed, however, that CBT, while using such techniques, is more than the sum of its parts, and must always be integrated with the CBT formulation and proceed within a good therapeutic relationship. This should ensure that techniques will impact on the deepest level of cognition possible, be that on assumptions, core beliefs or schemas.

A major overall aim of any technique in CBT is to target and modify clients' belief systems, a process guided by their individual formulations, which provide a sound understanding of what that belief system is, where it came from and how it works in practice. Thus, CBT becomes a dynamic therapy soundly based on an individual formulation, rather than a set of self-help techniques. In the words of Weishaar:

> Cognitive Therapy, viewed as a set of techniques, is not likely to be successful in treating the range of disorders confronting clinicians. Yet, Cognitive Therapy based in a theoretical framework, grounded in psychological literature, and presented within a sustaining therapeutic relationship has wide-ranging utility. (1993: 27)

If we are tempted simply to utilise techniques, we are missing key ingredients. On the specific question of working in schema-focused ways, it is important to acknowledge that there is a large 'grey area' concerning the presence of 'schemas' and/or 'personality disorders' in clients and in people – therapists included – in general. Whilst some CB therapists have tried to make hard and fast divisions between 'standard' and 'schema-focused' CBT, we think that the situation is best seen as being characterised by a number of different mixes of the two approaches distributed on a continuum. The significance of this view is that CB therapists may well find themselves working with schemas in both medium- and short-term work as well as in long-term work (Young et al., 2003). The fact that CB therapists are now better equipped to work flexibly is one of the most exciting developments of CBT today.

FURTHER READING

Arntz, A., & van Genderen, H. (2009) *Schema Therapy for Borderline Personality Disorder* (trans. J. Drost). Chichester: Wiley.

Beck, A. T., Freeman, A., Davis, D., & Associates (Eds) (2004) *Cognitive Therapy of Personality Disorders*. New York: Guilford Press.

Greenberger, D., & Padesky, C. (1995) *Mind Over Mood*. New York: Guilford Press. (Chapter 9)

James, I. A. (2001) Schema therapy: the next generation, but should it carry a health warning?, *Behavioural and Cognitive Psychotherapy*, 29: 401–407.

McGinn, L. K., Young, J. E., & Sanderson, W. C. (1995) When and how and to do longer-term therapy without feeling guilty, *Cognitive and Behavioural Practice*, 2: 187–212.

Young, J., Klosko, J., & Weishaar, M. E. (2003) *Schema Therapy: A Practitioner's Guide*. New York: Guilford Press.

NOTE

1 Including Captain Bligh's ship, the *Bounty*.

10

Process Difficulties and Endings in CBT

We frequently encounter clients who feel bad about some aspects of parenting their children, usually exhibiting the tendency to be overly self-critical. We have both said to these clients that, given the number of things that can go wrong with parenting, it often seems like a miracle that anyone gets it even half right. When one thinks about the number of things that can go wrong in therapy, it seems similarly miraculous that we therapists get as many things right as we do. Nonetheless, it is helpful to have some tools for looking at what we are getting right and wrong in our practice so that we can both play to our strengths and minimise the effects of our errors on clients. As we described different aspects of CBT in our succeeding chapters, we have already noted how things can go wrong with specific interventions. Here we focus more how these different problems affect the underlying processes of therapy.

We begin this chapter by offering a template for the 'perfect case' as it moves through the different phases of therapy. We then move through each of the succeeding phases and examine representative ways in which things can go wrong and have all too human and imperfect effects on the therapy. We cannot be comprehensive in a single chapter and readers can turn to Chigwedere et al. (2012) for excellent book length coverage of many of the same issues. We put slightly greater weight on problems in ending therapy because the general issue of ending has not yet been discussed in this book.

THE PERFECT CASE

CASE STUDY
Rosanna

Rosanna noticed that she had been feeling low for a few weeks. She decided this was probably just feeling a bit low after the exertions of Christmas and New Year but when the feelings ran on into March, she began to wonder if something more significant was happening to her. She talked it over with her partner, who was sympathetic but said that he had noticed that she had seemed flat for quite a while and wondered if she should go to see her general practitioner (GP). Rosanna also talked it over with a close friend at work, who said that when she had felt similarly a few years ago she had obtained help from a CB therapist who worked in a local specialist therapy centre. Rosanna's partner also thought that sounded like a good idea, and so she called the centre and actually spoke to a therapist. The therapist sounded nice and explained things well. She explained that if Rosanna wanted an emergency appointment one could be arranged that week but otherwise an appointment would be offered for 2–3 weeks' time. Rosanna felt that she could wait and the therapist made a few suggestions of things that she could do in the meanwhile: read some self-help materials and think about what she wanted to discuss at the first session.

During the first few sessions, Rosanna found the therapist easy to talk to and was surprised by the number of worries that she found herself telling her. The therapist thought that her worries might be the kernel of her problems. She was spending more and more time worrying, and that had got her down. Rosanna said that both her mother and father were worriers and that she had vowed that she didn't want to go that way herself. She realised that her current worry period coincided with her mother having serious health problems, during which her father had also become quite down.

Rosanna felt better after surfacing these worries but found that persistent anxiety feelings still troubled her. During the active therapy period, which lasted 14 weeks, Rosanna and her therapist worked on helping her to accept the anxiety feelings and to try to use them positively to work out solutions for some of the things that worried her. She managed, for example, to talk to a manager at work about some changes in her role that had made her work less satisfactory. This led to some improvement. She was able also to negotiate with her partner about how he could help more at home as she had to do more looking after her parents.

Rosanna and her therapist reviewed how things were going in their 10th session. Rosanna felt that they could begin a tapering-off process so that sessions 11, 12 and 13 were fortnightly and then there was a month gap between 13 and the final session. Rosanna felt that things had improved considerably and she now wanted to manage things for herself.

At a follow-up session six months later, Rosanna reported that her mother was now dying and she had experienced some negative feelings again. Over the next year or so, Rosanna emailed the therapist twice, first to say that her mother had died and then to say that though she still felt grief, she had managed things quite well.

PERFECTION AND DIFFICULTIES

We use the perfect case above now to discern the different stages of therapy and the difficulties that can arise when things do not go perfectly, as indeed they have a habit of doing (see Table 10.1).

Before Therapy

From a process perspective, we can see the lead-up to therapy as a stage in which there is a large group of actors, including the potential client and all those involved in his or her situation, slowly morphing into a dynamic small, usually dyadic, group that sets about establishing the therapeutic bond. In the ideal scenario, everything about this narrowing down is okay – all feel good about it. Those who gave advice before step back slightly, at least enough to give the therapy a chance to do its stuff. They want it to work and they wait in hope that the client, made better, will return from 'therapy world' – 'that land of which we know so little' – whilst maintaining positive contact, interested, friendly but non-intrusive.

In practice this means assembling a lot of ducklings in a nice tidy row. People often have mixed feelings about sending close ones off to be 'cured': does it mean that they have 'failed'? Will the client come back 'cured' but changed in some way inimical to them? We have learnt to expect that at some stage it is likely that clients will deliver a message from a significant other about these issues. Recent such messages have included 'My wife says you are doing a good job' and 'My partner (a counsellor, as it happens) says that a good therapist would have been more sensitive about x'. Sometimes a whole host of helpers – including professional ones – emerge in the background and some may interfere or even sabotage the work of others. We have both had cats that turned out to be feeding from at least ten other households: some clients are like that – they just attract helpers by the dozen, and those helpers can then get in each other's way. Sometimes the best decision is for the therapist to withdraw

1. What function does this client's difficulties with therapy have for him or her?
2. Is there anything in the formulation that throws light on this?
3. How might some of the client's beliefs be feeding into these diffficulties?
4. What might the client fear might happen if he/she accepts the therapist's interpretation?
5. How might the client be misunderstanding therapist suggestions?
6. What skills might the client lack that may hinder his/her collaboration?
7. What factors in the client's environment might be limiting the client's attempts to change?
8. Does the formulation need to change in view of any 'resistance'?
9. What more do I need to understand to make sense of the situation?

FIGURE 10.1 Question for reviewing therapy that feels 'stuck'

TABLE 10.1 Difficulties in therapy at different stages

	Perfect case	Difficulties
Before therapy	Symptoms recognised early. Family and work support idea of therapy. Appropriate referral is made. Quality service is available reasonably quickly.	Lack of recognition by CL and/or others leads to exacerbation of condition or suboptimal time for therapy. Errors are made in referral process. Agency is of poor quality. Long waiting time.
Assessment	CL can articulate problems and symptoms.	CL is shy or ashamed of problems, feelings etc. CL cannot articulate key problems and symptoms.
Formulation	TH can recognise syndromes and problem patterns TH is clear thinking and open. CL can accept and understand the basics of formulation.	TH fails to recognise key aspect of problem. TH is muddled or limited or stereotyped in approach to formulation. Formulation is over-focused on negatives. CL pretends to understand when doesn't. CL does not understand.
Early therapy: engagement	First impressions are good. Personal compatibility. Similar relationship rules.	Things get off on wrong foot. Personal and/or schematic mismatches. Mood interferes.
Treatment: structure and techniques	CL can use a degree of structure. TH can structure therapy flexibly. TH explains CBT methods clearly. CL can understand basics of techniques and ask questions and clarify them. TH sets appropriate homework. Few difficulties arise in the therapeutic relationship and those that do are dealt with effectively.	Client finds structure difficult or oppressive. TH finds structuring difficult. TH does not prepare for sessions. TH does not take enough care in introducing techniques and methods. CL cannot ask questions or express reservations. Heart/head difficulties in cognitive work. Behavioural work does not take enough account of context. Emotional work pursues wrong emotions. CL can't or won't do homework. Relationship breakdowns. Schema mismatches. Lack of trust, therapist retaliates – lacks interpersonal skills.
Endings and relapse prevention and follow-up	CL is prepared for ending. Ending is discussed. Generalisation of benefits of therapy is discussed. Procedure in the event of relapse is discussed. Follow-up arrangement is made. Follow-up arrangement is adhered to and things seem to be going well.	CL wants to 'cut and run'. CL is afraid to finish. CL sees ending as abandonment. Just seeing each other has become a comfortable rut. Ending is hurried or just 'peters out'. CL is ashamed to admit on-going problems. CL disappears.

Note: CL = client, TH = therapist

or to content himself with playing a co-ordinating role. Ideally we would have case conferences, but they involve a lot of professional time that can rarely be spared.

Other issues may include the appropriateness of referrals themselves. We have spoken to parents trying to refer children because the parents seem to be over-reacting to relatively minor symptoms. Therapists are faced with deciding whether to 'buy' such referrals and may decide to try to help in some other way. At the other end of the spectrum, there are referrals from clients who have delayed coming to therapy for various reasons and who are now coming at a non-optimal time. Early in the book, we have given examples of students who have exam anxiety appearing a week before important exams. 'Better late than never' of course holds true here, but the context has implications for how treatment can be formulated and planned.

It is difficult for individual therapists to be highly proactive when dealing with some of the problems at this stage because they tend to occur before we are aware of or have any direct responsibility for clients. It does, however, remind us that as members of agencies working with the public we do have some responsibility for helping our agencies develop policies and working styles that offer some help to the public and to other professionals to understand our service and how to make appropriate referrals to it. Furthermore, we also have some kind of wider professional duties that transcend even the ways of our own agency. In Chapter 12, we will describe how one of the many fascinating issues that arises in relation to the Improving Access to Psychological Therapies (IAPT) project concerns pathways between existing services. In some ways, increasing access heightens awareness of the clients who *still* do not get a service. We need to be aware of a natural human tendency to 'cherry pick' clients who look like they may do best in therapy and of the fact that such attitudes may condemn others to the proverbial 'revolving door' that still greets some, perhaps even many, clients. As one develops as a mental health professional, one becomes increasingly aware that one is required to act in a professional way in many situations other than sitting in a therapy room with clients.

CASE STUDY
Ron and Mary

Ron and Mary called an independent CB therapist when they discovered that their young son had a developmental disorder. They had looked up information on the Internet and had found research findings that CBT helped with this disorder. They were willing to pay 'whatever it takes' for the therapist to take on their son. After carefully listening to their descriptions, the therapist felt certain that the needs of the child would be better catered for by on-going NHS care. In a succession of further calls over several weeks, the therapist researched what services were available and coached Ron and Mary on how to approach their initially unhelpful GP and then on how to research various options within their local NHS services. This did eventually lead to a starting point for help for their son. Ron and Mary were extremely grateful to the therapist, not so much for the information and the hours of his unpaid work that finding it involved, but more for the fact that someone had listened and taken their concerns seriously and had refrained from showing them to that 'revolving door'.

Table 10.2 sets out the difficulties and solutions for each stage of therapy.

Assessment and Formulation

There are two key processes that cohere during the assessment phase: first, ensuring that clients are in the right place at the right time; and having ascertained that, secondly, asking the right questions to obtain the information needed to draw up the most helpful formulations and treatment plans.

On the therapist side, there is an emphasis on 'knowing enough' to be able to make effective interventions. A strong theme that has arisen in studies of difficulties that students experience during CBT training is the sheer volume of material that they feel they are expected to learn. The growth of CBT books, concepts and treatments has been truly astounding in recent years and this growth factor may be what underlies the potential fragmentation of the model. Expansion has come as CBT has expanded its scope and has needed to add more elements to deal with the inevitable variations that arise. There is, however, a countervailing tendency – transdiagnostic approaches to formulation and treatment – that may be poised to ride to our rescue. These theoretical considerations may at first sound rather remote from the day-to-day work of therapists and their difficulties, but in fact they are not. When a difficulty arises with a client, therapists are often facing two sets of opposite questions. First, is there something that I don't know about this kind of client or problem? If so, how do I go about finding out about it? Second, is there something that I already know that I am not applying? Essentially these two lines of enquiring lead to two possible reactions – 'try something new' or 'back to basics' – and readers will find frequent references to these two responses as we proceed through this chapter. Readers will find a heartening emphasis on basic CBT concepts and techniques in Barlow et al.'s (2011a) transdiagnostic protocol – a cutting edge development in the treatment of a wide range of emotional disorders (see also Chapter 11).

On the client side, the main difficulties arise when clients are not able easily to give the information that is required for a full assessment and formulation phase. In earlier chapters we noted that clients sometimes cannot access thoughts or may lack vocabulary for expressing feelings or insight or honesty to describe their behaviours accurately. The main solutions to these difficulties lie in therapists adopting a patient approach to teasing out information and then showing the ability to fit formulations to clients' understanding. The purpose of formulation is not so much to build the truest and most prize-winningly psychological document of all time but to

TABLE 10.2 Difficulties and solutions

	Difficulties	Solutions (examples)
Before therapy	Lack of recognition by CL and/or others leads to exacerbation of condition or suboptimal time for therapy. Errors are made in referral process. Agency is of poor quality. Long waiting time.	Be sensitive to fears of relatives. Feed back to referrers. Be proactive in agency processes.
Assessment	CL is shy or ashamed of problems, feelings etc. CL cannot articulate key problems and symptoms. TH fails to recognise key aspect of problem.	Help with vocabulary of feeling.
Formulation	TH is muddled, limited or stereotyped in approach to formulation. Formulation is over-focused on negatives. CL pretends to understand when doesn't or does not understand. Difficult to establish goals, e.g., CL blames others.	Test formulation – explain symptoms? Understanding of client? Put back blaming comments to client. Contract – written goals. Agree to differ on goals.
Early therapy: engagement	Things get off on wrong foot. Personal and/or schematic mismatches. Mood interferes. Technique predominates over empathy. Unsure what interventions to use.	Monitor first/early contacts – raise if necessary. Return to basic techniques. Return to empathy. Client feedback – monitoring. Use ESTs in combination with clinical judgement.
Treatment: structure and techniques	Client finds structure difficult or oppressive. TH finds structuring difficult. TH does not prepare for sessions. TH does not take enough care in introducing techniques and methods. CL cannot ask questions or express reservations. Heart/head difficulties in cognitive work. Behavioural work does not take enough account of context. Emotional work pursues wrong emotions. CL can't or won't do homework. Relationship breakdowns. Schema mismatches. Lack of trust, therapist retaliates – lacks interpersonal skills. Lack of progress.	Ask client about agenda-setting – pass more responsibility to client. Return to key principles/concepts – basis for transdiagnostic protocol (Barlow). Look for creative variations. Return to basics. Review goals in light of life changes.
Endings and relapse prevention and follow-up	Unexpected, premature ending. CL wants to 'cut and run'. CL is afraid to finish. CL sees ending as abandonment. Just seeing each other has become a comfortable rut. Ending is hurried or just 'peters out'. CL is ashamed to admit on-going problems. CL disappears.	Contact or leave/ let be – use formulation. Experiment with 'time out' of therapy.

Note: CL = client, TH = therapist

devise something that helps therapists and clients orient interventions in a way that can also be mapped helpfully for the client. In this text we have frequently discussed how our whiteboards often play a crucial role at this stage. If readers have not yet used a whiteboard or similar then they may find it worth trying. As we have also discussed many times, we can't always know precisely what clients do take from formulation but it is likely to involve literally 'seeing' their experience in another, decentred form. There is also likely to be less of the 'road to Damascus' experience than that of a gradual building up to insight. Watching a formulation evolve on a piece of paper or whiteboard would probably facilitate an experience of building up. The whiteboard just has the advantage of size and perspective.

CASE STUDY
Karla

Karla would have been the 'go to' actress for the role of 'mad scientist' in any am-dram production. She was a brilliant engineer and very much her own woman. She had always had obsessive compulsive disorder (OCD) tendencies and when her company sidelined her and then made her redundant, she became very depressed. Reflecting on her professional demise, she was sure that her brilliant and unconventional ideas had become less and less acceptable as her company became more and more 'cool and corporate'. She was great fun to have as a client but applied the same stream of brilliant ideas to formulation – taking the board marker to write in yet another line of dazzling psychological insight. Eventually she and her therapist sat looking at a whiteboard equivalent of a Jackson Pollock painting. After trying to sum it up for a while, they both started giggling. In her dramatic Slavic accent, Karla said, 'I complicate things, don't I?' The therapist replied, 'Yes. How can we simplify them?' Those two lines were in fact her formulation and treatment plan.

Early Therapy: Engagement

We highlighted earlier the key role that 're-moralisation' seems to play in therapy generally but crucially in early therapy (Ilardi & Craighead, 1994). As the therapeutic process is centred on forming a working alliance and starting to work at this stage, there are likely to be re-moralising aspects to both these factors. First impressions are known to play a big part in interpersonal appraisals of other people, so on the one hand it is again likely that they are powerful in therapy. On the other hand, one is reluctant to conclude that therapists should rely on making good first impressions as it is in the nature of things that this will not always occur. Idiosyncratic aspects of personal judgements can't really be legislated for. It is worth bearing in mind that clients will often feel nervous about a first meeting; there may after all, be more at stake for them. This can lead to a degree of caution and/or over-talkativeness in some, both of which can result in awkwardness in early interactions. Within CBT structure, the emphasis on feedback is helpful to therapists, who should obviously be particularly interested in the client's impressions and feedback on the first meeting. If awkwardness in interaction persists into several meetings, the therapists can look at what is emerging in the formulation for clues on what is going on and how to respond to it. Other response options include talking about the client as part of on-going supervision and/or conducting a review on 'how things are going' with the client. We suggested formats for doing this at various stages of therapy in Chapter 4.

Another aspect of early therapy is that therapists will be introducing clients to the classic structural and technical aspects of CBT. How, for example, are they responding to filling out any of the measures that you might be asking them to complete? We have noticed that measure-completing behaviours often carry clues about other aspects of the client's life: very slow deliberation may be linked to obsessional tendencies, whilst excessive concern about 'getting it right' may be linked to worry or social anxiety. Similarly, early encounters with drawing out vicious cycles and/or using thought records will reveal much about the client's capacity to name emotions and access thoughts. Any difficulties arising in these matters are usually best dealt with by gentle and flexible therapist responses, slowly testing out the boundaries of the client's proximal zone and finding the right dose of CBT for this particular client. Sometimes a more fundamental level of resistance may become evident, and this could prove a longer-term obstruction to progress. It is nevertheless usually wise to refrain from any more direct interpersonal inter-vention, such as using immediacy or meta-communication, as discussed in Part I, until one is sure that problems are just not part of a process whereby clients adapt to the unfamiliar 'land' of therapy.

CASE STUDY
Grace

Grace was a nurse who came to the UK from Africa. All went quite well until she took on a job that required her to do hydrotherapy with patients. She showed extreme phobic reactions to water and was unable to do this work. Her manager took quite a hard line with her and eventually she reluc-tantly agreed to have 'therapy' for her phobia. She was a very reluctant client and would only speak single words to her therapist at first. It took a few sessions for the following salient facts to emerge. First, she thought the therapist was part of a disciplinary system, designed to make her do her duties. Second, as a child she had to wade across four rivers to get to school. One day an unex-pected water surge in one of the rivers drowned her best friend and nearly drowned her. Third, Grace had no motivation whatsoever to change her phobia. The therapist was then able to write to her employers suggesting that in light of these facts she be reassigned to different duties and offered exposure therapy when and if she did ever want to work on her phobia. These suggestions were accepted. Grace was delighted to return to work and has yet to request any further therapy.

Treatment: Structure and Techniques

It is during this stage of therapy that CBT takes on it most characteristic form and when techniques are likely to be used in familiar ways. Even so, as earlier, there is a delicate balance between getting the right structure to facilitate therapeutic work, implementing techniques with interpersonal sensitivity matched to the client's needs, and tending to the therapeutic relationship in light of what starts to unfold in the therapeutic process. All these factors are relevant to building on or refining the re-moralising foundations laid down in the opening manoeuvres, described in the previous section.

CBT training studies (Wills, 2006b, 2008b) have found that trainees find implementing CBT structure one of the most challenging aspects of training, whilst at the same time they also report that achieving structure in their practice was the greatest gain in training. One study (Wills, 2008b) found that structuring the early part of sessions was more difficult than the later part. Trainees often forgot to set agendas but rarely forgot to set homework. This seemed to be a function of a self-consciousness that decreased as sessions unfolded and trainees became more comfortable. Therapists do seem to be prone to negative beliefs about the aversive affects of structuring on clients, so that a good way to sort this is to have an overt collaborative discussion on how to implement structural elements with clients. Clients usually find structure helpful and will typically give therapists a mandate to use a structure compatible with their personal needs. This discussion can also clarify the expectation that clients will gradually take over more responsibility, for example, for setting agendas as therapy proceeds. An overtly stated expectation has much more chance of being met. Some clients have an aversion to structure, that perhaps reminds them of bad experiences of home or school so that extra care needs to be taken to hit the optimal mix of leading and following with them (Castonguay & Beutler, 2006). This extra care is very justifiable therapeutically because for them getting that kind of balance in an important personal relationship can itself act as a corrective emotional experience.

Clients who need the finely tuned response in structuring described above may, however, encounter therapists who, for whatever reason, have a strong need of structure themselves. Thus, the scene is set for a classic personality or schema mismatch. The signs of this might be quite subtle and small at first, so that neither party is aware of them. As time progresses there may, however, be escalation of the problem as 'complementarity' and 'pulling' occur: the more unstructured the client tries to be, the more the therapist will press the structure button. This then sets up the need for more active interventions, including immediacy, meta-communication and therapy reviews in session and in supervision.

If therapists begin to feel that therapy has got stuck, it is useful to have some reflection time, and in supervision to review the therapy, including the positive and negative aspects of interventions and relationship factors experienced so far.

Cory Newman (2002) suggests questions especially well suited to therapists' reflection processes at these times. He suggests that therapists should use them for solo reflection before going into either supervision or a client review. A set of similar questions appeared in Figure 10.1, and is used in the worked client example below.

CASE STUDY
Callum

Callum had suffered a trauma after he and his girlfriend were viciously robbed during extended holiday travel in Africa. He had 'put the attack behind him' and enrolled on a university course on his return. All had gone well until a few weeks before his final exams when he had suddenly started feeling intense anxiety. It was then that he finally presented himself for therapy. Callum wanted the therapist to help him master the anxiety for his finals. Whilst both agreed that his anxiety was linked to the trauma, they also considered that it might be unwise to open up a trauma story so close to the exams. It was agreed, therefore, to make anxiety management the main focus and review the role of the trauma later. The next weeks were a bumpy ride, with Callum repeatedly asking for reassurance that he was not going to 'break down'. The therapist used the review questions in Figure 10.1 to explore why the client, despite a wealth of evidence, could not reassure himself. The answer came in the conjectured response to question 4: 'What might happen if ... this client were to rely on his own judgement to reassure himself?' 'He may fear that his judgement was shown to be flawed and cannot be relied on.' Exploring this question with him, the therapist found that Callum felt that his poor judgement had exposed him and his girlfriend to the attack. This enabled a new focus on 'learning from mistakes and bad experiences' that ultimately helped the client both to cope with his exams and to begin the process of 'working through' his trauma.

In the example of Callum, problems arose really because of an incomplete formulation. There are also many reasons why therapy runs aground for technical reasons, and we have discussed some of the main ones in the earlier chapters of this Part of the book. Cognitive restructuring can make logical sense, for example, but still not help clients to feel better. Efforts to enhance emotional sensitivity in CBT are major feature of the current CBT scene and are likely to feature heavily in its on-going development. Therapists should not, however, be over-hasty in decisions to try new interventions when older ones do not seem to be working. Another major tactic is to return to basics, both double-checking that one is using techniques in recommended ways and also realising that at times over-learning and persistence is needed to overturn long-standing habits (Leahy, 2003). When techniques do begin to fail, however, there are often knock-on effects in the therapeutic relationship, so once again the questions suggested in Figure 10.1 can come to our aid.

Endings and Relapse Prevention and Follow-up. CBT is frequently time-limited, focused on the goals that clients identify, and the success, or otherwise, in meeting those goals. CBT's reputation for being a short-term therapy leaves it open to the criticism that it does not always get to the root of problems and potentially leaves clients stranded at the end. In this section, we look at the issues surrounding ending therapy, and ensuring that clients feel neither that their core difficulties have not been solved, nor left high and dry when therapy finishes. We discuss how to assess when to finish, the stages of ending, the value of offering follow-up sessions, and ways of helping people prepare for future difficulties and writing a 'blueprint' for long-term coping. We also look at what happens when endings do not go according to plan; when the client abruptly terminates; when the client does not feel any better at the end of therapy; or when other unresolved issues derail satisfactory endings.

ENDINGS IN CBT

Beck originally developed cognitive therapy for depression in 12 to 20 sessions, and research evidence has shown that the therapy can be, and often is, effective in this kind of timeframe. This relatively short-term aspect has made CBT popular where time and resources are constrained, for example, therapy settings in the National Health Service (NHS). Counsellors in the NHS have often had to work in shorter timeframes even than this. In IAPT, low-intensity work is at the fewer-sessions end of the spectrum whilst high-intensity work is close to lengths advocated by Beck. The brief nature of CBT means that client and therapist are likely to work efficiently: 'Being under sentence of termination doth most marvellously concentrate the material' (Dryden & Feltham, 1992: 152). A short timeframe would normally allow for full work at the symptom level and a certain amount of work on assumptions with some reframing of beliefs, depending on the kinds and length of problems the client brings to therapy. However, a short timeframe would probably allow only limited schema-focused work — held to take considerably longer periods of therapy. For example, if a client's main goal is to get rid of panic attacks and be able to go out more, then short-term work can be effective, and both helping the client with the presenting problem and, directly or indirectly, changing some beliefs or improve self-esteem. For depression, short-term work can alleviate the current episode, and equip the person with methods for dealing with future episodes. If the client has long-term, enduring difficulties in many areas of life, although good work can be done in short-term therapy, it is probably necessary to work also with schemas in longer therapy.

Whether short- or long-term therapy is needed can to some extent be estimated during assessment and taken into account when setting goals. Ending therapy is therefore a phase of therapy that, in fact, starts right at the beginning when negotiating a contract with the client (Wills, 2006a). During goal-setting, ending is signalled, for example, by asking the client to think about questions such as 'How will your life be different once therapy is finished?'. Depending on organisational context, therapists may give clients a specific number of sessions: in the region of 6 to 20 for anxiety, 12 to 20 for depression and so on. Whether the therapy is likely to last one month or two years, it is important to be explicit about the dates when reviews happen, as well as being explicit about the likely time-scale of therapy and therefore of ending. Both client and therapist need frequent reminders of where the therapy has got to, including looking at progress made and forward to future sessions. It is helpful to remind the client how many sessions are left at every session; incorporating reviews every few sessions serve as reminders without appearing too much like a number-cruncher. Some clients have difficulties ending things and working through these difficulties may help them, perhaps for the first time, to have the experience of a satisfactory ending to an important relationship. Whatever the number of sessions, reviews every six sessions or so enable both client and therapist to check that they are on course. Sometimes it may even be appropriate to end somewhat ahead of schedule.

Another important characteristic of CBT is that it aims to help clients to become their own therapists, by teaching them ways of helping themselves across a range of problems. Although, when working as any type of therapist, our clients are at the centre of our professional lives, the therapy may not be so central to the client's life, and learning occurs outside sessions. 'A therapist who views himself as responsible for helping the patient with every problem risks engendering or reinforcing dependence and deprives the patient of the opportunity to test and strengthen her skills' (Beck, 1995: 269). A key advantage of CBT lies in its ability to transfer the benefits of work during therapy to the client's life after therapy. Such generalisation and transfer of learning can be major factors in preventing relapse. The message throughout therapy is that the real work is a function of what goes on between as well as within sessions, expressed as a concentration on homework and practising therapeutic gains across different situations. CBT has key advantages in stopping the 'wash-out' of gains over time (Hollon, 2003). Therefore, ending therapy concerns what clients learned and how they will cope with difficulties in the future.

Leading on from the 'learning' function of CBT are ways in which ending therapy might be difficult for some clients: for example, those whose hopelessness prevents them generalising from sessions or those with issues of dependence who believe themselves incapable of coping alone. Thus, the stage of ending requires both identification of and working through such issues. Therapists too may have issues about ending with some clients, for instance where pressures from workplace constraints mean that they only offer fixed numbers of sessions, thereby ending with some clients earlier than they would like; feeling they have not done a 'good enough job'; where there are unresolved relationship issues; or where endings press therapists' personal buttons.

The Process of Ending

Termination is more than an act signifying the end of therapy; it is an integral part of the process of therapy and, if properly understood and managed, may be an important factor in the instigation of change (Yalom, 1975: 365).

Ending therapy can represent real or symbolic losses, and how it is handled can make a difference to outcome. Endings can be planned and known from the beginning and go as planned but, not uncommonly, therapy ends prematurely if the client terminates early and unexpectedly, or the therapist changes jobs or geographical area; illness or unexpected life events can also interrupt therapy. Despite the importance of endings in therapy, and clinical experience of 'messy' endings, they seem surprisingly under-discussed in the CBT literature, with the exceptions of Persons (2008), Safran and Muran (2000) and Judith Beck (1995). Beck and colleagues pertinently remind us of the importance of handling endings well: 'Because cognitive therapy is time-limited, the problems associated with termination are usually not as complex as those associated with longer forms of treatment. However, much of the benefit of cognitive therapy can be lost through inappropriate or inept closure' (1979: 317).

One way of handling endings in CBT is to conceptualise them as processes that need appropriate time and attention, rather than sudden cessations of activity, with four main tasks (Horton, 2006):

1 Seeking resolution of issues around ending.
2 Exploring ways of consolidating learning and change.
3 Identifying obstacles to maintaining changes.
4 Evaluating the outcomes and effectiveness of therapeutic process and relationship.

Having good formulations of clients' beliefs and assumptions is an invaluable aid in predicting and working with potentially difficult endings in therapy. On approaching ending, therapists can ask themselves: 'What does this client's formulation tell me about how the client is likely to see ending?' The client's response to ending can be identified and worked with in a collaborative way, and be seen as the opportunity for one last piece of crucial therapeutic learning. For example, beliefs concerned with dependency on others are likely to be activated during the ending of therapy, particularly if client and therapist have formed a good therapeutic relationship. For other clients, where therapy has been less helpful, beliefs such as 'No one can help me' may be activated and strengthened. If such issues have already emerged, as they would in good therapy, then they will already have been incorporated into the formulation and will have shown themselves in attempts to predict the course of therapy. For some clients, these predictions can be valuable as they allow the therapist to offer them the chance to make a deliberately good end to therapy. Having been an elusive experience for them in other relationships, this can prove a valuable learning experience and an excellent way to finish therapy.

Ending therapy involves assessing the client's readiness for closure, addressing and resolving remaining issues, bringing about appropriate detachment from the relationship, and consolidating what has been gained and learned during therapy so that the client can carry on making gains afterwards. The extent to which each of these stages is emphasised depends on the individual client and the therapy situation.

Assessing When to End CBT

The usual criteria for when to stop therapy are when the allocated number of sessions has been completed and, ideally, the client feels better about the presenting problems, is acting differently in life, or at least working in that direction, and can predict and prevent future difficulties. The client's goals for therapy and the extent to which they have been met are the main guiding factors, and the simplest, and most collaborative, way of assessing when to end therapy is to ask the client. It is important, however, that the goals are realistic. Therapy is not likely to resolve all problems, remove all symptoms or result in 'complete cure', and clients may continue to have symptoms that led them to therapy in the first place. It is also not realistic to expect never to feel anxious, low or angry again. Therefore one goal of therapy may have been to be more accepting of emotions and distress. This may be particularly important for people who do not easily express or experience feelings, who may be feeling significantly more emotionally fluid since starting therapy, perhaps noticing and expressing emotions in a way that was previously uncharacteristic.

Therapists can begin ending therapy by increasing the time between sessions. Even when good progress has been made, clients often wish to have a period of consolidation before ending. The therapist and client may meet weekly during the initial stages of therapy, but may then spread out the sessions to every two or three weeks. In addition, clients are encouraged to see the therapist for follow-up sessions approximately three, six and twelve months after ending. Spacing sessions in this way enables the client to have more time between sessions in which to practise and consolidate gains made during therapy. This also allows potential difficulties to arise before therapy has ended.

There are times when the desirability of ending is less clear. Clients may have doubts about ending therapy or may want to end therapy 'early', when important issues are left dangling. Some people may want to stop, understandably, at the point of feeling better, perhaps wanting to avoid looking at underlying issues in case further work makes them feel worse. The client may 'give up' on therapy before giving it a full try. In this case, therapist and client can work out the pros and cons of both ending and continuing (Beck, 1995) in order, collaboratively, to arrive at a decision. Towards the end of therapy therapists can act as 'devil's advocates' for the client: clients can put forward the arguments in favour of ending therapy and how to cope in future, and therapists can challenge these, to help the client clarify issues in ending therapy.

Dealing with Unresolved Issues and Ending the Therapeutic Relationship

During the final stages of CBT, clients may identify issues that still remain unresolved, requiring collaboration in working out how best to deal with these issues. It may be possible to negotiate additional sessions; it may be more appropriate to look for other sources of help, such as group therapy or social support. Some clients may bring important issues to the last session, with the flavour of a 'parting shot', leaving the therapist puzzled, frustrated or annoyed, which may mean that therapy ends with an 'unfinished' feeling. It may be that these issues were too difficult or threatening for the client to work with before, or they may have been brought up as a way of continuing the therapeutic relationship. It is important to try to discuss what has happened and offer some understanding in terms of the client's formulation.

The end of the therapy relationship may evoke a variety of feelings including loss and grief, and Safran and Muran (2000) note that ending therapy can activate specific interpersonal schema, such as that of abandonment. Addressing and discussing these feelings is an important part of the stage of ending therapy, enabling the client's reactions to be understood as part of the overall formulation. The client can be encouraged to look at any similarities between ending therapy and other endings, and invited to think about how they usually handle saying goodbye, and whether they wish to try a different way of ending this relationship.

CASE STUDY
Joanna

Joanna found ending any relationship difficult. The feelings evoked in her seemed unbearable. She tended to leave without saying goodbye, promising to get in touch before a friend left and then not contacting her. She left relationships at the first sign that things were wrong. Her beliefs included: 'People always abandon me eventually', 'There's no point in saying goodbye. They'll go anyway'. Her way of coping with endings avoided the pain of confronting her loss, but led to great dissatisfaction and a feeling of something missing. Towards the end of the allocated therapy, Joanna, predictably, started to miss appointments. Given the pressures in the NHS to discharge people who do not attend (DNA) appointments, the therapist was initially tempted to give up on Joanna, thus confirming her beliefs. However, she persisted in contacting her after missed appointments to offer another. When Joanna returned she could explore her feelings around ending, and identified how she could try out a different approach to ending this time. Both therapist and client devised ways to say more satisfactory 'goodbyes' that they could try in therapy.

Ending the relationship can also be a positive experience for people who have learned something about themselves and the nature of relationships through the relationship with the therapist. It may offer healing opportunities for clients to work out ways of being assertive. The relationship may have been an opportunity to be honest about difficulties, when these could be discussed with the other person without being judged. This sort of experience allows clients to examine ways in which they can be honest in other relationships. During the ending phase, some clients may find it valuable to reflect on the nature of the therapeutic relationship and what has been learned about other relationships. Some may not have ever experienced a really satisfactory end to any relationship ever before.

It is also important to discuss why change happened, and how the client attributes responsibility for change. A client who says 'If it wasn't for you ...' or 'You've made me so much better' may give the therapist a self-satisfied glow. However, this should be used not to boost therapist self-esteem but as an opportunity to attribute progress to the client. One response to such praise might be to ask the client the proportion of the work in therapy done by the client versus therapist, or the amount of time the client has been tackling the problems (24 hours a day, 7 days a week) versus the amount of time the therapist has put in (10 hours). Dismissing their own contribution to therapy may relate to clients' beliefs about powerlessness, therefore endings can be used to enable clients to develop alternative beliefs. Another response to ending therapy may be for the client to feel angry about the need to seek 'professional help' in the first place. Although such a response to coming for help is often looked at during the early stages of therapy, sometimes the client may have found the process of therapy to have made sense in a way that leads them to question 'Why couldn't I do it for myself?'. Such responses, as for other responses to ending therapy, need careful attention.

The ending of therapy is a stage for the therapist as well as the client. If the therapist has found the client particularly difficult to work with, or therapy has not been particularly helpful, they may feel a sense of disappointment at not being able to help, or relief at finishing with the client. Alternatively, sometimes it is difficult for us to end therapy at the point at which the client is improving or becoming

CASE STUDY
Paul

Paul presented with depression and difficulties at work and questioned what he was doing with his life. During his first session, he was angry at 'having' to see the therapist, thought it was pointless 'just talking about things', and simply wanted Prozac. At the end of the first session, he reported that despite his misgivings he had found talking helpful, and was a bit more hopeful that he could sort things out. He turned out to be an easy and rewarding client to work with: he took to CBT with ease, devouring self-help books, and began to make long-overdue changes to his life. He could make use of the depression, looking back and seeing it as a valuable indicator that he needed to take stock. The therapist felt sad at ending therapy with him, partly because he represented an 'easy' case among a sea of more complex clients, and partly because, on reflection, the therapist realised that some of the issues he was successfully tackling, with the flavour of a 'mid-life crisis', were those that she, too, felt were close to her own heart.

more emotionally accessible and therefore more rewarding to work with, or where a client's developmental stage is mirroring one's own, as shown in the next example.

Therapists' feelings, both positive and negative, are best dealt with during supervision, giving opportunities to end therapy successfully for the therapist as well as the client. Sometimes, issues in ending are systemic: both authors have sometimes struggled to avoid endings being driven by the needs of clients on our waiting lists.

Preparing for the Future: Long-Term Coping

As therapist and client begin to reach the end of therapy, they begin to review progress made and what implications the gains or lack of gains have for the ending of therapy. CBT, as we have discussed, stresses its active, self-help oriented nature. To a large extent, the therapy moves from more therapist activity in the early stages, to more client activity later on. Handing over the reins of therapy is completed in the end stages. Ideally, the client will have practised new ways of seeing things, of thinking or of acting in different situations, enabling therapy gains to be generalised to a wide range of situations. Clients benefit from specific reminders of progress. Pen-and-paper activities of CBT enable clients to collect written information in a therapy notebook, along with session tapes, handouts and books. Flashcards give clients reminders of key points during the therapy, as shown in Figure 10.2.

Another model used in practice is a 'positive cycle', such as that shown in Figure 10.3. The early stages of therapy focused on Elaine's negative spiral, the factors maintaining her low mood and negative feelings about herself. Later we drew up a positive spiral, incorporating things she needed to do in order to carry on feeling well and keeping on improving her self-esteem and accepting herself. She stuck the positive cycle on her fridge, as a reminder of the direction she wanted to stay facing.

Reminder of what I have learnt

- There are times when I'm anxious, but try and swim along with it: nothing awful is going to happen.

- I've been anxious many times and it's felt like something bad is going to happen, but it never has.

- I know nothing bad is going to happen because during therapy I faced my worst fear – going into a public place and feeling really anxious – and still, nothing bad happened. Nobody noticed, nobody is judging me.

- Even if I feel anxious and sick, I'm not going to be sick.

- Even if I did feel very ill, it would not be a complete disaster: other people would help.

- Don't get out of the habit of doing things: keep going despite how I feel. Make friends even if it is a bit frightening.

I KNOW I CAN DO THINGS
DON'T DWELL ON HOW I FEEL ALL THE TIME
DON'T DWELL ON THE SLIGHTEST MISTAKE I'VE MADE
IMAGINE PUTTING ALL THE WORRIES IN MY HEAD IN A RUBBISH BIN
IF I DON'T FEEL LIKE DOING SOMETHING, DO IT ANYWAY, AS AN EXPERIMENT

FIGURE 10.2   Therapy flashcard

The method of 'point counterpoint', similar to rational role play (Cromarty & Marks, 1995), can test whether someone is able to fully challenge old thoughts and assumptions. Therapists take the voice of the old assumption or belief ('I'm rubbish if I make mistakes', 'I've got to worry all the time to prevent bad things happening', 'I'm useless') and clients argue back from a new perspective, giving a counterpoint to each negative point the therapist voices. This needs to be done with compassion and humour, so we are not labelling clients, merely giving voice to what they used to say about themselves. By hearing the negative view, and coming up with a different perspective, the client can practise what needs saying when the old voices come back (Mooney & Padesky, 2000).

Although CBT aims to help clients to learn approaches that can be applied across many different situations, successful therapy does not, unfortunately, always guarantee an easy, problem-free life. Therapists and clients may, however, be reluctant to bring up the thorny issue of what happens if things do go wrong: therapists wanting to engender hope, and clients preferring not to think about future problems. But given that progress is rarely in a straight line, and that most people have some form of setback at some stage, knowing what to do is crucial.

One useful strategy is to help clients to find ways so that they do not turn a setback into a disaster, 'building a floor' under their feet that will limit how far they

A: Negative Cycle

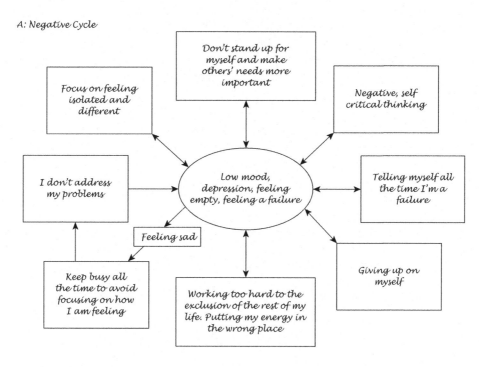

B: Positive Cycle

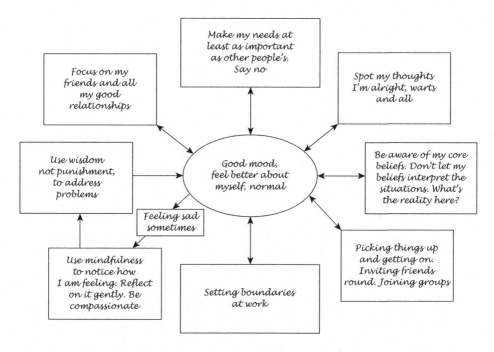

FIGURE 10.3 Elaine's Negative and Positive Cycles

can fall. Setbacks do not necessarily mean relapses; relapse does not necessarily mean that clients are back to square one. Models of the process of change are valuable in highlighting the organic nature of change, and how we move through stages. Prochaska (2000) describes six stages:

1 *Pre-contemplation*: when we are not aware of the problem.
2 *Contemplation*: when we become aware and think about it.
3 *Preparation*: working out what to do and when to do it.
4 *Action*: doing something about it.
5 *Maintenance*: keeping up progress.
6 *Relapse*: when the change begins to slip.

Relapse is normal. Should clients experience problems again therefore rather than viewing themselves as being back to square one, it is helpful to look at how they can get back on to track, identifying the need for change and what to do in order to change. Other models include the Lewin-Kolb learning cycle (Bennett-Levy et al., 2004), which highlights the importance of reflection time as well as preparation and action in making changes.

Blueprints

During the process of ending therapy, clients can be asked to work on a 'blueprint', or first-aid book, of how beneficial change will be maintained and how future problems may be handled. Judith Beck describes the process:

> The therapist encourages the patient to read through and organise all her therapy notes so she can easily refer to them in future. For homework, she may write a synopsis of the important points and skills she has learned in therapy and review this list with the therapist ... The therapist prepares the client for setbacks early in treatment. Nearing termination, the therapist encourages the patient to compose a coping card specifying what to do if a setback occurs after therapy has ended. (1995: 278)

Working on a blueprint involves at least two sessions for clients to think through questions and work on them with therapists, as shown in the blueprint in Figure 10.4.

The stages of working on a blueprint involve inviting the client to think about what kind of difficulties may be encountered in future. What kind of problems led up to the client requesting help? Is it likely that these problems will recur? If so, what can be done? What are the early signs of problems? Who else may be able to help? The client can be encouraged to carry on working on the issues identified

Issue	Action
What have I learned?	Modifying my thoughts can change my feelings. I don't necessarily need tablets. I can challenge my thoughts: they are just thoughts, not facts. Don't slump into depression – do something. Recognise the early signs and do something about them. Allow myself to receive support from my family.
How can I build on this? What's my plan of action?	I can define how I want to be: more light-hearted. I can learn to worry less. I can actively plan more enjoyable activities: go to the cinema; go for walks at weekends. Get my work–home life in balance. Don't allow myself to stay in bed and ruminate.
What will make it difficult for me to put this plan of action into practice?	Taking work home. Not going to work feeling fresh. Getting into a cycle of 'no time', 'no motivation'. Not spotting the early signs.
How will I deal with these difficulties?	Keep on reviewing the costs and benefits of positive and negative actions and thoughts. Ask J. to remind me of what I need to do and to help spot the early signs.
What might lead to a setback? For example, stresses, life problems, relationships and so on.	Problems at work. Ill health.
If I do have a setback, what will I do about it?	Seek help early from family and friends, GP, therapist. Read the self-help books and reminders of therapy. Read this blueprint! Re-start activity scheduling and writing down thoughts.

FIGURE 10.4   CBT blueprint (worked example – see Alec's formulation at www. sagepub.co.uk/wills3)

during therapy or after therapy has ended. An important goal is for clients to become their own therapists and be able to use informal support networks rather than automatically relying on professional help. An example of a 'self-therapy' session is given by Judith Beck (1995), where the client sets aside time to conduct a session with herself, incorporating the usual structure of agenda, reviews, and so on.

Offering Follow-up Sessions

Many therapists will routinely offer clients one or more follow-up sessions after therapy has ended in order to review progress and work on difficulties. Offering follow-up sessions may be valuable, particularly for those clients with long-term difficulties. Therapist and client need to decide whether to arrange regular reviews, regardless of how the client is feeling, or more open access: that is, clients being able to contact therapists to 'touch base'. However, continuing contact with therapists may be a means for the client or therapist to avoid saying goodbye and deal with feelings of loss, or avoiding issues of dependency. We need, therefore, to be aware of possible difficulties as well as potential benefits of offering follow-up sessions.

Sudden Endings

The progression of therapy through the beginning, middle and end stages often involves satisfactory completion of each stage. However, we have all experienced clients who suddenly terminate therapy, leaving a sense of incompletion for the therapist and uncertainty about 'where we went wrong'. Such feelings imply that there is an ideal way for therapy to end, contravened by the client who just disappears, implying that the client has ended before the therapist thinks they 'should'. In a truly collaborative relationship, the client's wishes regarding termination are those on which decisions are made: thus, if the client wants to end, the therapist respects this decision and is able to deal with his or her own issues accordingly. The client's wishes to end therapy can be openly discussed, the pros and cons of ending weighed up, and the therapist can encourage the client to give honest feedback. Should the therapist want to carry on where the client wishes to end, it is possible that client and therapist are working from different formulations: the therapist may believe that schema-driven issues are at the root of the problems and need to be worked on before ending, while the client might be happy to feel a bit better and get back to 'coping'.

The client's formulation can be used to analyse sudden endings: for example, the client who has learned not to trust people, developing the belief that 'No one can really help you anyway', is likely to translate whatever happens in therapy in terms of the belief; thus, one difficult or unproductive session may lead to schema confirmation and the end of therapy. The desire to end therapy can, ideally, be both understood and handled using the case formulation.

The 'sudden death' ending requires careful handling. When clients simply disappear we need to think about our responsibilities to follow up these people. Again, returning to the client's formulation, 'walking in their shoes' and carefully discussing and reviewing previous sessions may help us to understand what is going on. Sudden ending may be a way for the client to cope with the ending, or may be a way of communicating with the therapist, as in the earlier example of Joanna. The client may be acting out interpersonal strategies, part of which may be to suddenly disappear only to suddenly reappear later on. Whether or not we take the active step of contacting the client may depend on the client's particular issues. For example, following the disappearance of a client who believed 'Nobody really cares about me', the decision to pursue him was well justified by his successful re-entry into therapy. People who default from therapy, ending abruptly and not responding to letters or phone calls, can haunt us for some time: what has happened to the client? Is he or she alright? Did I do something wrong? Could I have done better? Such issues are best taken to supervision where they often prove a source of valuable clinical learning.

Relapse Prevention and Relapse Signatures

CBT has focused on relapse prevention for many psychological problems, and the evidence suggests that relapse following CBT is lower than following other forms of therapy or pharmacotherapy (Hollon, 2003; Butler et al., 2006). As discussed earlier, the ending stage of therapy involves looking at what might happen should clients feel they are going back to square one, or seemingly insurmountable difficulties begin to arise. However, relapse can and does occur, possibly associated with the re-emergence of core issues following successful work with the client's presenting problems such as depression. One way of seeing relapse prevention for these clients is to enable them to view difficulties as equivalent to chronic conditions such as diabetes, which, when looked after properly, have less impact on the individual's life than when ignored. A car analogy may be helpful: a yellow light indicates that the oil is low, but it is more helpful to check and top up the oil on a regular basis than to just use the warning sign. Similarly, if clients react in a certain way when particular beliefs and assumptions are triggered, and remain vulnerable to relapse, regular maintenance is crucial. Such maintenance may be in the form of regular booster sessions, regular self-reviews by the client to identify the early warning signals and respond quickly rather than waiting until a serious problem develops.

One of the keys in preventing serious relapse is to identify early signs, and intervene by putting action plans and blueprints into practice before problems escalate. Studies of people with repeated episodes of depression show that the process of becoming depressed can become increasingly autonomous: one slight hint of what depression feels like and the person will switch mode and escalate into depression (Segal et al., 2002). As part of mindfulness-based cognitive therapy (MBCT), identifying these early markers, or 'relapse signatures', while the mood is still stable, can enable the person to take action to stop switching mode by choosing one of the skills he or she has been practising (Segal et al., 2002). Such relapse signatures for depression may include:

- becoming more irritable;
- withdrawing and not wanting to see people;
- changes in sleep and eating patterns, tiredness;
- a reduction in exercise;
- not dealing with work and things that may come up;
- putting off deadlines.

Segal et al. (2002) stress that each person's signature is unique, and being aware of these signs, without becoming hyper-vigilant for them, is important. However, they also stress that while it is easy when feeling well to list these warning signs, when depressed, the person may not see the point of heeding them at all, or doing anything about the problem: 'I'm back to square one'. Therefore, it is also important to work out how clients and people close to them to detect the early signs of relapse. Segal and colleagues suggest three questions that need clear answers, to aid relapse prevention:

- 'What in the past has prevented me from noticing and attending to these feelings (e.g., pushing them away, denial, distraction, alcohol, arguments, blaming others)?'
- 'How can other family members help in my warning system for detecting relapse?'
- 'If depression strikes, how can I look after myself to get me through this low period?'

CONCLUSION

We have, in this chapter, given a flavour of the difficulties which may arise in CBT and a flavour of the way in which a CBT therapist might set about solving such difficulties. Some arise from the tasks and methods of CBT; other issues, to do with the interpersonal nature of the encounter, are likely to be familiar across all therapies. The philosophy behind problem resolution may be expressed as 'Occam's Razor' – in CBT terms, the best solution is one that gives the most benefit for the least effort, and therefore the simplest. We have stressed the importance of an approach to dealing with difficulties that starts at the simplest level and the importance of collaboration at whatever level the difficulties occur. At times this means acknowledging our own contribution to the encounter: in the words of Albert Ellis (Dryden, 1991), being willing to be an FFHB – a 'fucked up, fallible human being' – at times of dealing with difficulties is essential (and these authors, Wills and Sanders, frequently compete with each to see who can be more of an FFHB than the other)[1]. If a therapist can be 'real' and admit to mistakes or uncertainties, this can be both a powerful model and a means of challenging assumptions or schemas within sessions.

The end of CBT is a stage that starts right at the beginning and ends with the process of follow-up sessions. Ideally, ending the meetings between therapist and client is not an end to therapy, since the aim is for clients to become their own therapists and to generalise learning to other situations or problems – perhaps taking aspects of their therapists with them on the journey. Learning associated with ending therapy works both ways: ending with each of our clients giving us the chance to reflect on the work we did and did not do, to reflect on the formulation we developed and evolved and, most importantly, to reflect on how we might consolidate or change our practice as a result of the journey with each individual client. Blueprinting and relapse prevention are thus helpful notions for both client and therapist.

FURTHER READING

Chigwedere, C., Tone, Y., Fitzmaurice, M., & McDonough, M. (2012) *Overcoming Obstacles in CBT*. London: Sage.
Newman, C. F. (2002) A cognitive perspective on resistance in psychotherapy, *Journal of Clinical Psychology*, 58(2): 165–174.
Safran, J. D., & Muran, J. C. (2000) *Negotiating the Therapeutic Alliance: A Relational Treatment Guide*. New York: Guilford Press.

NOTE

1 Bookmakers have long since refused to take bets on this contest.

PART III
CBT IN CONTEXT

11

Applications of CBT

Padesky (1998) has said, possibly with tongue in cheek, that learning cognitive therapy was easy when she trained because there was at the time, in the late 1970s, only one 'application' to be learned – that of Beck et al.'s (1979) seminal work on the cognitive therapy of depression. Aspirant CB therapists taking this remark too literally might experience heart sink when considering the number of applications to be learned now. In any current CBT conference, there will be a bewildering array of symposia on many different areas of application. It appears that there is no problem known to human kind that CB therapists will not turn their hand to fixing. Cognitive-behavioural models and therapy interventions have been developed in many areas, as shown in Table 11.1, and such work has been invaluable in helping people with problems such as panic, depression, obsessive-compulsive disorder, eating disorders or sleep disorders, and many others.

Therefore, when learning CBT, we have to learn not only the general principles but also its application to particular problems. Each application is based on similar overall principles, but, in line with 'cognitive specificity', has significant variations on the exact way such principles are actually applied. Further complications arise because clients often present with more than one problem, co-morbidity of different psychological difficulties being the norm rather than the exception. Whatever mélange of issues clients arrive with, we need to tease out the strands and apply the methods applicable to the most germane problems. A sea change, 'the transdiagnostic turn' in the forms of transdiagnostic formulations (Harvey et al., 2004) and treatments (Barlow et al., 2011a), is, however, taking place and is likely to be helpful to CB therapists. Transdiagnosis raises the possibility of stressing commonalties in problem areas with treatment effects running across disorders and allowing refined treatments based on well-established generic CBT principles.

In this chapter we explain some key features of the concept of 'applications of CBT'. We show such principles in action for the two most common reasons people seek psychological help, anxiety and depression, as separate problems and as

Table 11.1   Applications of Cognitive Behavioural Therapies

CT/CBT has been developed for people with the following types of problems:	CT/CBT is applied in the following types of settings:
Anxiety problems:	Mental health
	In patient
• Panic	Primary care
• Agoraphobia	Medical settings
• Social phobias	Elderly
• Simple and complex phobias	Child and adolescent
• Health anxiety	Youth work
• General anxiety	Forensic
• Worry	Education
	Social work
Post-traumatic stress disorder	Probation
Obsessive-compulsive disorder:	Human resources
	Employee assistance programmes
• Obsessive rituals	Life coaching
• Obsessive thoughts	Individual therapy
Depression – moderate	Groups
	Couples
	Families
Long-term, chronic depression	Bibliotherapy
Treatment-resistant and recurrent depression	Self-help groups
Post-natal depression	On-line resources
Suicidality	Telephone
Deliberate self-harm	Email
Survivors of childhood sexual abuse	
Health anxiety	
Somatisation	
Unexplained medical symptoms	
Adjustment to chronic health problems	
Chronic pain	
Chronic fatigue syndrome	
Skin disorders	
Trichotillomania	
Medical problems – e.g., rheumatoid arthritis	
Sleep problems	
Eating disorders	
Relationship problems	
Sexual problems	
Psychotic disorders	
Manic depression	
Hearing voices	
Delusions	
Hallucinations	
Complex personality problems	
'Personality disorders'	
Drug and alcohol problems	
Dual diagnosis	
Anger, hostility, violence	
Stress	
Learning disability	
ADHD	
Autism and Asperger's syndrome	
Stuttering	

transdiagnostic issues. Some other general principles will then be used to illustrate how to work with common psychological processes, drawing on examples from the ever-widening web of CBT applications. We look at some of the settings in which CBT might be applied, including group work, couples and the growing area of self-help, bibliotherapy and using on-line resources and discuss the pros and cons of using therapy protocols. At the end of the chapter we list a number of texts on application to different problems. One message we wish to give readers, particularly those new to the approach, is that we do not all have to be experts on all these therapy variations. Good CBT therapists will know where to find out about how to work with particular clients and can usually implement variations fairly quickly. Both authors have worked in various settings and, therefore, had to become familiar with many human conditions. In our experience, however, clients can tolerate the fact that their therapists will not always completely understanding every aspect of their difficulties, provided that therapists express the desire to find out more about them and have confidence that they can do so. Our experience is that the stance of 'Let's find out about this together' is a good starting point with clients and begins the process of collaboration. We start, therefore, with general principles of application.

THE CONCEPT OF APPLICATION

A defining feature of CBT is how it has built on empirically researched models of psychological problems such as anxiety and depression (Salkovskis, 2002). Clark (1996) describes how development of CBT models starts with clinical observation or insight. For example, Beck's early work was based on his observation of specific negative thoughts in depressed patients. Clinical and non-clinical research is then used to build up understanding of the cognitive, emotional and behavioural 'architecture' of the problem. Treatment interventions are devised to impact on the psychological mechanisms that cause and maintain these problems. As these interventions are tried and tested; they build into whole models of intervention that are in turn tested for efficacy. Therapists in the field are encouraged to use the interventions only when good levels of confidence in treatment have been achieved.

Many emotional disorders have separate and unique cognitive profiles and, therefore, have formulations that are generic to many clients with those disorders. As we have stressed earlier, however, these generic and transdiagnostic formulations and treatment have to be 'individualised' to the unique client in question, allowing for a specific and individual formulation and therapy plan for each client. Each problem has both similarities and differences, illustrated here by using examples from anxiety and depression. The development of CBT perhaps had to begin by isolating problems in order to work out precise interventions but has now reached the stage where it can build on the commonalties that have emerged in these separate problem formulations and treatments. These commonalties may now be the bases on which a more transdiagnostic approach is built.

CBT MODELS OF ANXIETY AND DEPRESSION

The standard, basic CBT models of depression and anxiety are shown in Figure 11.1. Putting the two generic formulations for anxiety and depression alongside each other helps us to see that the two models have many basic similarities. They trace out, for example, similar patterns of influence between the thoughts, feelings and behaviours. There is also different content in the levels of cognition, and significantly different types of problematic behaviours that would need to be targeted in order for maintenance cycles to be disrupted, broken down and modified.

COGNITIVE CONTENT AND PROCESSES IN DEPRESSION

At the deepest level of cognition – schema and core beliefs – depression-linked content is most characterised by themes of loss and defeat (Beck et al., 1979). Themes of loss have wide meaning for depressed clients. They may concern the loss of something specific like a partner, health or a job or career. The sense of loss can, however, reach beyond objective loss to a sense of loss of faith in oneself or even the loss of having any sure sense of self at all. Given the strong links between

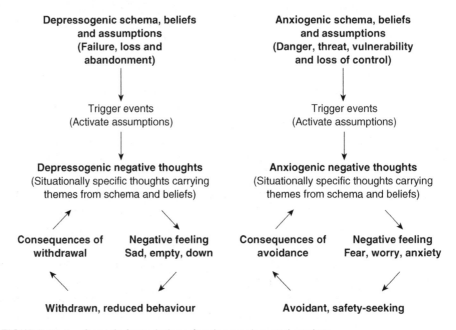

FIGURE 11.1   Generic formulations for depression and anxiety

depression and loss, it is perhaps surprising that the CBT literature has had comparatively little to say about grief and bereavement. Beck et al. (1979) describe the 'cognitive triad' where a negative concept of self combines with a negative sense about the world and hopelessness – a lack of faith in the future. Hopelessness is seen as particularly powerful in determining the strength of depression. Most people can tolerate negative feelings about themselves and their lives in the short term, provided that they see 'light at the end of the tunnel'. Negative feelings become intolerable, however, if there is no belief in release from suffering in the future. Hopelessness is also linked with increased danger of self-harm and suicide, and so should be specifically assessed and targeted in therapy.

Beckian CBT has links with evolutionary theory (Wills, 2009). In brief, an evolutionary perspective on depression suggests that, after defeat, there is survival value in withdrawing resources from previously invested objects, followed by a period of 'hibernation'. For example, common sense often supports the idea that it is not necessarily wise to rush into finding a new partner after the failure or loss of a relationship. Conventional wisdom – not always wrong in these matters – suggests that there is danger of acquiring an ill-chosen new partner 'on the rebound'. Equally, if a business is failing, at some point it will be right to 'cut one's losses' and withdraw from the enterprise. In general, we allow for people in such situations to be 'a bit down' and withdrawn, at least for a while. Problems result not so much from initial negative reactions, but when the person in effect stays asleep when the spring arrives.

Beck and Emery (1985) suggest that evolutionary mechanisms often have on–off mechanisms. They are switched on for a while to cope with short-term emergencies but once the immediate emergency has passed, they are then switched off. The problem with depression is that the deeper or more long-lasting it becomes, the harder it can be to switch it off in this way. Linking psychological problems with evolution fits with CBT's aim to de-stigmatise many of the 'psychiatric' conditions.

As well as factors connected to cognitive content, there are also distinctive cognitive processes such as rumination that reinforce the operation of the vicious cycle in depression. Rumination is a deliberative thinking style that keeps going over and over negative events. Sometimes clients believe that if they keep going over and over things, they will somehow eventually find 'the answer' – a process targeted in Wells' (2009) metacognitive therapy. Ruminative patterns are reinforced by the fact that the depressed person withdraws from many aspects of previously normal routines, for example by going out less and seeing fewer people. In the absence of other activity, clients' daytime hours may become filled with ruminative thought. At night, sleep, often already disrupted, becomes further disrupted by rumination, staying awake and going over life issues. In addition to rumination, there are other well-known cognitive effects of depression: 'transdiagnostic' processes (Harvey et al., 2004) such as difficulty in concentration, negative attentional bias and a negative, globalised memory, often described as making memories 'depressing and fuzzy'.

COGNITIVE CONTENT AND PROCESSES IN ANXIETY

The salient cognitive content of anxiety concerns the appraisal of threat and danger and the preoccupation with reaching safety. The experience of anxiety is often linked to unbalanced ways of thinking:

- overestimating the likelihood of occurrence of negative events;
- overestimating the cost of negative events;
- underestimating how the person may cope with negative events;
- underestimating rescue factors – how others may help, for example.

These four factors can be put into an equation (Salkovskis, 1996):

$$\text{\textbf{Anxiety}} = \frac{\text{Perceived likelihood that threat will happen} \times \text{Perceived cost/awfulness}}{\text{Perceived ability to cope} + \text{Perceived rescue factors}}$$

The more likely and the more awful the threat is perceived, the greater the anxiety. Anxiety may, however, be lessened by the appraisal of one's coping abilities and/or the possibility of 'rescue'. The more clients appraise such mediating benefits as likely, the less anxiety there will be. For example, for clients with health anxiety, health risks, such as having a brain tumour, may be seen as highly unlikely but the cost of illness is seen as so extreme, combined with the sense that there would be no help available, so that anxiety becomes uncontrollable.

Underlying beliefs in anxiety often show preoccupation with the self as vulnerable and with being unable to get help from a world seen as indifferent and dangerous. One anxious client picked up on the survival metaphor often attached to anxiety by describing his fears of work colleagues as 'predators, circling round the sheepfold looking for stray lambs to devour'. Sometimes these negative conceptions may relate to schemas and core beliefs picked up in early experiences during which the client's caretakers dwelt on the dangers of life (Chorpita & Barlow, 1998).

Assumptions and rules of living stress the benefits of being vigilant and seeking safety so that control and avoidance are therefore common. Anxious people often mentally and physically prepare for possible catastrophes, however unlikely. Anxious clients see the threats of imminent danger happening, most classically in panic attacks, and their negative automatic thoughts (NATs) often reflect this sense of threat. Imagery is particularly potent in anxiety, so that thinking a danger might happen can lead to powerful images experienced as if that danger *were* happening now. In social anxiety, for example, clients think that others are scrutinising them critically. Clients' attention is so monopolised by negative images that the evidence of the images of what other people are *imagined* to be doing is more compelling than the evidence of what those people are *actually* doing.

It has become clearer that the core cognitive processes in anxiety lie in the way that anxiety sufferers pay attention to supposedly potentially dangerous situations. Metacognitions that stress the positive functions of anxiety and worry (e.g., 'If I worry a lot about my course work, I will get a higher grade') have been shown to play a key role in the maintenance cycle of many types of anxiety (Wells, 2009).

BEHAVIOURAL RESPONSES IN DEPRESSION AND ANXIETY

The different types of cognitive content and processes in anxiety and depression link to different types of problematic behaviours. The major behavioural features of depression are those of social withdrawal, isolation and physical atrophy. Behavioural interventions are therefore focused on 'activation' (Martell et al., 2001). In anxiety, problematic behaviours are more likely to be avoidant and safety-seeking actions. Interventions are usually based on helping anxious clients to confront situations they have been avoiding and to drop the safety-seeking behaviours that may prevent them from disconfirming their fearful beliefs about the outcomes of such situations. Avoidance also occurs in depression – in a different form, especially avoiding exertion and social contact. The time perspective is helpful in understanding lack of activity: it seems that the depressed persons adapt to past loss, but, at the moment of brief contemplation of future action, have automatic closing-down reactions, probably motivated by the desire to avoid further defeat and loss (Emery, 1999).

GENERIC MODELS AND INTERVENTIONS IN DEPRESSION AND ANXIETY

While there are variations in the schemes of formulation models, all fundamentally differentiate between current maintenance cycles of the problem and underlying mechanisms of the problem. This section describes ways of working with each of the maintenance cycles for depression and anxiety, and then with a common approach to underlying material.

Depression

Emery has suggested that relatively brief CBT of depression:

> ... is foremost an educational approach to treatment. It involves teaching clients two things: 1) concepts that can help them better understand and cope with depression, and 2) specific skills that enable them to confront and master the symptoms of depression and the dysfunctional beliefs that predispose them to this disorder ... The heart of the programme is teaching two main skills: the ability to act differently and think differently ... This programme uses two tools to bring about this correction: the action schedule and the thought record. (1999: 5)

The weekly activity diary (see Figure 6.3) can be a good place to start the therapy of depression, in that the method immediately targets behavioural activation and also engages with clients' thinking processes. Activity schedules are used both retrospectively, looking at previous patterns, and prospectively, planning future new patterns, as described in Chapter 6. When first using this technique, therapists can make the mistake of asking clients to plan the week ahead immediately: it seems generally better to get the client to plan flexibly and for just a day or two ahead, less daunting and with more 'doable' tasks for clients. Emery (1999) suggests that clients who have planned some days ahead can be encouraged to write or say intentional sentences about what they will do that day: 'Today I will get up by 9am and be dressed and ready to go out by 10 am. I will visit my friend for coffee, and take my library books back'; 'Tomorrow, I will go to the job centre to make an appointment and then walk around the park'. These statements can reinforce the client's intention to act. They may also carry meta-meaning, sometimes representing a shift from a 'why bother' frame of mind to a 'can do' frame of mind. This cognitive shift indicates that, despite looking like a behavioural intervention, activity diaries also hold the potential for cognitive change and behavioural experiments (Emery, 1999).

CASE STUDY
Mike

Mike was a young client who had become understandably depressed following a serious illness. During his slow recovery, he frequently felt a sense of self-disgust because 'I never do anything'. A retrospective schedule for his previous two days, however, revealed that Mike worked on both days, cleaned the house, met a friend for a drink, read two chapters of a novel and watched a TV film. The therapist had to admit that Mike had exceeded his own activity level in those two days. Thought records completed by Mike continually revealed perfectionist demands that he 'should' fill his days with achievement and he judged himself harshly when he didn't do so. His father had belonged to an extreme Protestant sect that held the belief that 'The Devil makes work for idle hands'. In this way, the seemingly straightforward behavioural task of monitoring activities served to identify other issues maintaining the depression, and lead to cognitive work, identifying and modifying underlying assumptions.

With greater understanding of cognitive processes in depression, including those processes linked to relapse for people who experience repeated episodes of depression, come newer ideas such as mindfulness-based cognitive therapy (MBCT) (Segal et al., 2002). Mindfulness training is based on the idea that depressive relapses often relate to changes in clients' relationship to their thoughts, and on enabling the clients to take different relationships to their thinking, to avoid relapse. MBCT maintenance programmes for the prevention of depressive relapse consist of eight weekly group sessions, each lasting two hours, consisting of psycho-educational elements, cognitive therapy and mindfulness meditation (see Chapter 8).

As described in Chapter 8, MBCT groups have significantly lower relapse rates and seem particularly effective with the most vulnerable people – those who had had three or more previous episodes. MBCT appears to be an exciting and valuable development, and the ideas can be incorporated into individual therapy (Fennell, 2004).

CASE STUDY
Yasmin

Yasmin was an overseas student suffering from dysthymic depression. She was particularly troubled by negative rumination over whether she should give up her course and return home. This was obviously a legitimate concern, yet it was a cycle she had been through many times, indicating that the key problem was a pattern of ruminating in search of certainty in an inherently uncertain situation. Thought record-based exploration of her thoughts floundered on the fact that the relevant evidence of having or not having her PhD would not emerge for many years. After this realisation, Yasmin was, however, able to experiment in taking a more mindful approach to these ruminations with some success.

Anxiety

Interventions for anxiety focus on clients' cognitions about future, supposedly dangerous, events and on over-activated behaviours orientated towards avoidance and safety seeking. Cognitive work faces the epistemological difficulty that, unlike events that have happened, events in the future are harder to assess and obtain evidence for. We have already seen, however, the four components of the anxiety formula: appraising the likelihood and costs of both attack and rescue determine the degree of anxiety and how a change in any one of them can result in lessening it. Therapists can therefore be particularly alert to any of these factors evident in clients' cognitions, reviewing them in thought records and/or testing them using behavioural experiments.

There will, however, be issues that will be intrinsically harder to deal with by cognitive interventions or behavioural experiments. These issues may include realistic fears about serious illness so that, for many, putting any attention on the thought of them would be likely to lead to anxiety. People's worries may concern realistic events: dying, for example, is something we are all certain to do at some stage; the world is in some areas a very dangerous place, and environmental disasters, terrorism and terrible unexpected accidents can and do occur. When working with clients where worry is a central feature, such as generalised anxiety disorder (GAD), many therapists describe trying to dispute the indisputable, stuck in a blind alley of remote possibilities. The worry is fully understandable and in a sense indisputable so that it may be better to think of ways of either 'achieving closure of the worry' or taking attention from it.

The problem with worries is not so much in the content of them as in the interminability of worry process. After a while, the worry process feeds on itself. Cognitive responses to anxiety, GAD and worry have been immensely strengthened by the addition of strategies that focus on accepting anxiety processes rather than working to undermine or change the content of anxious cognitions (Orsillo & Roemer, 2011). Such strategies include worry management (Butler & Hope, 1995), attentional and metacognitive training (Wells, 2009) and mindfulness strategies (Roemer & Orsillo, 2009).

Worry management strategies such as Butler and Hope's 'worry decision tree' offers a set of pragmatic steps that brings one out of the worry. The method invites clear definition of the problem and offers paths that lead to either acting to counteract the worries (doing something) or seeing that one can accept them and let them be (accept and distract). Precisely identifying what the worries are, in so many words, is important because global, amorphous beliefs possess greater ability to 'stick around', whereas precise thoughts carry the seeds of action and thereby their own resolution. For example, being 'scared all the time' is paralysing, whereas 'worrying about how we will pay the mortgage' suggests the utility of a plan to 'make the mortgage payments'. Another way to manage worry is to accept it. Hayes et al. (1999) have highlighted the role of acceptance of problems as a first stage in the change process. It can be helpful to, as it were, let the worry into the house, give it a cup of tea and then wave it farewell. Such acceptance resonates well with mindfulness, a method and approach that will prove as valuable in anxiety as in depression.

Avoidance is common in anxiety. Traditionally, avoidance is tackled by the principle of 'facing the fear' by using graduated exposure: a stepwise approach to feared objects by using a hierarchy of situations, starting with the easiest and proceeding to the more difficult. This procedure is probably best known through the step-by-step desensitisation such as used in phobias or agoraphobia: going to the front door; going down the path; walking to the gate; walking to the post box; walking to the shop and so on. Such exposure work can mesh in with behavioural experiments aimed at testing out beliefs, thereby facilitating behavioural and cognitive change. The example below shows how the idea of a hierarchy can be used in a very different type of situation: recovering from trauma.

Although graduated exposure programmes, like the one above, have been strongly associated with behavioural aims – getting Cathy driving again – a CBT approach seeks also to capitalise on the cognitive potential of what can be seen as a series of

---

CASE STUDY
Cathy

Cathy was involved in a lethal motorway pile up. Although she was not hurt and initially seemed to have got over the accident well, about a month after her recovery she started showing strong trauma symptoms with flashbacks, anxiety and avoidance. She could not get into a car. She lived in a new housing estate built on the assumption that inhabitants would use car travel on the nearby motorway. An initial hierarchy succeeded in getting Cathy into a car quite quickly, but then it emerged that she got very strong trauma symptoms when near a motorway. She had to get out of the car and walk home. The therapist introduced another graduated programme. Together they devised a programme with 15 steps. The first was to drive near to and look at the motorway. The second was to drive on a bridge over the motorway. The third step was to stop on that bridge and look at the motorway. Subsequent steps involved driving short distances on the motorway between exits that were close to each other. These steps gradually built up to longer driving trips along the motorway, culminating in a final step of getting to the town, about 70 miles away, to which Cathy had been driving on the day of her accident. It took her about three months with lots of ups and downs to complete this programme. It ended with a lovely therapeutic moment when she telephoned the therapist to say that she had, literally and metaphorically, 'made it'.

---

behavioural experiments. The cognitive gain implied in the small but telling phrase 'made it' shows how engaging with activities like a programme has significant impact on self-concept. As part of running this graduated step programme, Cathy was encouraged to work on her negative automatic thoughts as she tried to complete various steps. These negative thoughts ranged from reasonable and possibly true fearful thoughts such as 'Other cars will beep their horns at me because I am going so slow' to catastrophic predictions like 'I'll never get off this motorway alive'. Cathy found it helpful to work through these types of thoughts after the event but had only limited success in being able to challenge them at the time of driving on the motorway. She was, however, able to find something that in retrospect had combined elements of both distraction and mindfulness.

Besides its traditional place towards the behavioural end of the CBT spectrum, it is interesting that Barlow et al.'s (2011a) transdiagnostic treatment for *emotional disorders* builds emotional and cognitive awareness to facilitate a final phase of more general *emotional exposure*.

Although we have, in this book, made a distinction between 'standard' and 'schema-focused' CBT, in our experience the distinction between the two different therapies may not always be completely clear. Many clients bring along at least elements of issues influenced by underlying beliefs. The therapy with Cathy and Mike within the format of 'standard CBT' had such moments, and we give these as examples of the way in which underlying beliefs influence the way standard CBT might be conducted.

CASE STUDY
Mike

We mentioned earlier the problems created by Mike's father's inflexible religion. Mike was closer to his mother and was devastated when she died when he was 18 years old. He had just started university and experienced severe loneliness and unhappiness there, compounded by the fact that his father remarried within a year of his mother's death. Mike had never really talked through his feelings about his mother's death, believing that he had to be 'brave' and conquer these sad feelings. As he reviewed his depressed feelings in therapy, he increasingly noted the similarity of these feelings with those that he had felt at the time of his mother's death. It seemed helpful to give him space to talk about this. The issue raised itself again, however, as therapy drew towards its concluding sessions. The therapist had thought that Mike had not particularly 'bonded' with him but noted signs of increasing distress as ending therapy was discussed. Further exploration of this revealed that Mike did have schematic feelings about abandonment. He had 'held back' in the relationship, as he had in other relationships, but still felt a sense of loss as termination of therapy approached. Mike related these feelings and behavioural patterns to the death of his mother. This new material allowed a particularly meaningful focus for ending therapy so that some of these feelings could be worked through in a way that allowed Mike to negotiate his needs, for example, by defining his preferred level of follow-up contact.

CASE STUDY
Cathy

About halfway through the graduated programme with Cathy, she rang the therapist to say that her sister had told her that she must tell him something. Cathy wouldn't say what this was on the telephone but said that she would explain at the next session. In the session, half an hour passed without Cathy referring to the call. When the therapist asked about it, however, she said that she had been sexually abused as a child. Within the spectrum of abuse, these experiences were at the less severe end. The abuser, who was an uncle, did not proceed far with his advances. The experiences had happened twice before her parents had confronted the abuser, leading to immediate cessation of abuse. Nonetheless, memories of these events had come into Cathy's mind after her motorway accident. It turned out that she had experienced a number of other traumatic incidents, for example, one with a 'prowler'. Cathy had developed a style of dealing with worries by saying that she didn't have them – 'I am laid back. Nothing gets to me'. And yet she also had issues consistent with a 'vulnerability schema'. She and the therapist worked out that only traumatic worries could break through this screen of being 'laid back'. As well as working on motorway driving therapy they also revisited traumatic memories via imagery and reconstructive narrative work (Stopa et al., 2009).

TRANSDIAGNOSTIC FORMULATION IN CBT: A DIFFERENT VIEW OF APPLICATION

CBT models have evolved for specific problems or 'disorders', implying, as described earlier, that in order to help people with these problems, we have to know about specific applications. However, as highlighted throughout the book, many common processes operate across the psychological problems, and knowledge of these processes, how to spot them and how to intervene, gives CB therapists a wide repertoire of helpful skills across a number of problems. While processes are common, how they are expressed in terms of particular problems depends on the person's current concern and focus. For example, the main concerns in eating disorders are shape and weight; in worry and GAD, clients are concerned about the impact of worrying thoughts and their safety within the world; and in OCD, the concerns are around responsibility and contamination. Harvey et al. (2004) clearly summarise a transdiagnostic approach, and this is reassuring in the face of a bewildering sea of applications. This transdiagnostic approach offers the potential of moving on from having to learn discrete series of applications by developing transdiagnostic protocols that can be adapted to individual clients using case formulation (Persons, 2008). David Barlow and colleagues (2011a) have established an efficacious protocol that is based on similar emotional constructs as those described in Chapter 7, and can be used over a wide spectrum of emotional disorders. Rather than having to learn a multitude of different methods and approaches, understanding common processes such as attention, memory, patterns of thinking, avoidance and safety behaviours, and how to work with these, give a wide repertoire, toolbox and modes of understanding to client difficulties. Fitting these processes to client profiles leads to individually formulated and planned CBT. We now describe one common process, that of self-focused attention, how it is formulated and used in social anxiety.

SELF-FOCUSED ATTENTION

Attending to internal cues rather than the external world, and paying attention to information consistent with one's beliefs rather than objective reality, is seen in many problems. Clients in the midst of panic attacks often focus only on internal sensations of a racing heart and sweating; and when depressed, negative thoughts and memories are attended to while other, more comforting or positive aspects of the environment or life are not seen. By paying attention to internal mood states and to information consistent with beliefs, clients miss other information useful to aid disconfirmation of negative beliefs and reinforce learning new beliefs. Clients stuck in self-focused attention are also more likely to make internal attributions to events, such as blaming themselves for external problems such as setbacks at work, which may in any case be out of their control.

Working with attentional processes can enable clients to redirect their attentional resources to external information and thereby break the cycle of overly attending to internal stimuli. Methods such as attention training and mindfulness enable clients to focus more widely, without judgement. Methods such as positive data logs, experiments to collect information from the environment and thought records also aim to help broaden attention and attend to previously ignored information. Thus, where attention is seen as a core, maintaining process, a range of methods can be valuable.

Self-focusing Interventions in Social Anxiety

Wells (2009) and Clark and McManus (2002) have developed robust models of the way clients with social anxiety function in social situations and the central role taken by 'self-focused attention' or 'self-consciousness'. Self-consciousness may be thought of as an interacting cognitive subsystem (Teasdale, 1996) involving a series of complex triggering mechanisms between thoughts, emotions, physical sensations and behaviours. All these phenomena continuously reinforce a sense of self-consciousness, keeping it firmly in place.

CASE STUDY
Ellie

Ellie was a person who generally thought of herself as quite confident. However, she suffered from periodic intense anxiety and worry and had taken selective serotonin reuptake inhibitor (SSRI) medication on and off for years. She had recently been appointed as a science lecturer and her duties included giving demonstrations of scientific procedures to students. Ellie found these demonstrations generally difficult, especially when mature students were present. She and the therapist drew up a formulation presented in Figure 11.2.

Knowledge of the CBT model of social anxiety not only allows such formulations to be drawn up, but also establishes a common language for the problem and therapy:

Therapist:	So, when you are presenting, do you feel quite self-conscious?
Ellie:	Yeah, that's it, exactly. Mmm. Not half!
Therapist:	And it's hard to act naturally then.
Ellie:	Yes, I feel so tense … like it is already going all pear shaped and it kind of goes from bad to worse. I'd like to just run out but I can't. I have to tough it out.
Therapist:	So the CBT model suggests the feeling of self-consciousness drives the whole thing. So if we can lessen that, we might lessen the whole anxiety reaction?
Ellie:	Well, yeah … but it is something that I have had for a long time. I'm not sure how easy it will be to change that.

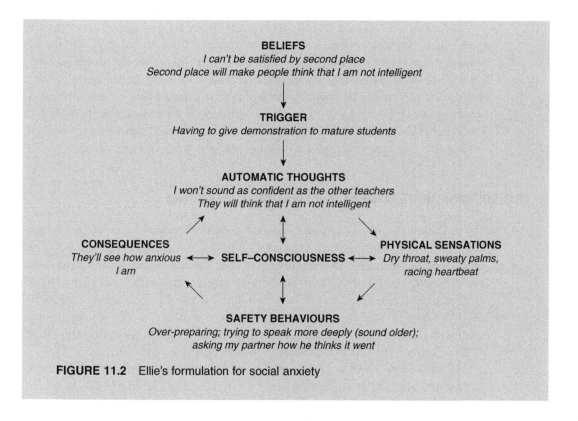

FIGURE 11.2   Ellie's formulation for social anxiety

Self-focused attention drains attention from observing external events and this may be one reason why socially anxious clients are so convinced that people in their environment are critically examining them. When they are in the mode of self-consciousness, their perceptions are dominated by internal fearful images and they consequently do not pay enough attention to what is actually going on in the environment. Behavioural experiments are then often directed to getting clients to observe their environment more directly. There are, of course, always likely to be at least some fashionistas who may critically examine one from top to toe. In general, however, the presence of critical people is usually balanced by others who may be quite favourable and by many more who may be relatively indifferent. Ellie learned to make more neutral appraisals of how people were reacting to her demonstrations and also that she could be more direct at asking for feedback. The greatest moment of emotional change, however, seemed to come when she experimented with dropping safety behaviours, especially seeking reassurance from her partner.

During demonstrations, Ellie thought 'The students think I'm hopeless at this' and 'They'll all fail their exams' or 'They'll think that I am not intelligent'. This latter thought seemed to be the 'hot' one and related back to competitive siblings in childhood. Ellie realised that she was extremely focused on herself and her own performance during her demonstrations, and so could not provide any convincing evidence that her thoughts were true. She also realised that she consulted her partner for reassurance. This could only be a *safety behaviour* because the partner was not present at her demonstrations so his reassuring evidence could not carry much weight. Ellie found that when she dropped this behaviour she instantly felt much better and could quickly reassure herself more. Other experiments involved paying attention externally to see how her students were, in fact, reacting.

TRANSDIAGNOSTIC TREATMENT FOR EMOTIONAL DISORDERS

David Barlow's work to develop a unified protocol for transdiagnostic treatment of emotional disorders (Barlow et al., 2011a) offers an intriguing synthesis of many of the specific treatment interventions described above for anxiety and depression. His protocol has, however, been tested and found efficacious with all the main anxiety disorders (except simple phobias) and the main presentations of depression. We have already discussed transdiagnostic aspects of psychopathology but a treatment approach is also justified by high levels of comorbidity within this range of disorders and the fact that treatment effects generalise across them.

The unified protocol is based on a transdiagnostic formulation, and a related treatment consisting of eight treatment modules as shown in Figure 11.3.

The formulation begins by indicating that emotional problems begin within the mechanisms of emotional regulation and dysregulation, as argued in Chapter 7. Strong negative feelings are regarded as normal and functional and the problem in emotional disorders lies not in them as such but in the way that certain individuals respond to them – by using maladaptive emotional regulation strategies. These strategies consist of lack of emotional awareness, cognitive appraisals that amplify negative emotions, lack of awareness of 'acting out' of negative emotions by using emotionally driven behaviours (EDBs), intolerance of negative emotions, and a lack of skills in handling both internal and external emotion-provoking situations. Each of these aspects of emotional dysregulation is tackled by one of five treatment modules designed to promote a core client skill, as shown in Figure 11.3. The five treatment modules are preceded by two other modules designed to prepare the client for therapy and are followed by a final module, focused on relapse prevention. A therapist guide (Barlow et al., 2011a) supports the treatment along with a client workbook (Barlow et al., 2011b), complete with client materials and measures.

As might be expected from the comparatively recent dates of these publications, research assessment of the treatment approach is still underway at the time of writing. Preliminary analysis of existing trials suggests that, even with relatively conservative assumptions, the unified protocol is 'at least comparable to (effect sizes of) those reported in similar trials of existing CBT evidence-based protocols'

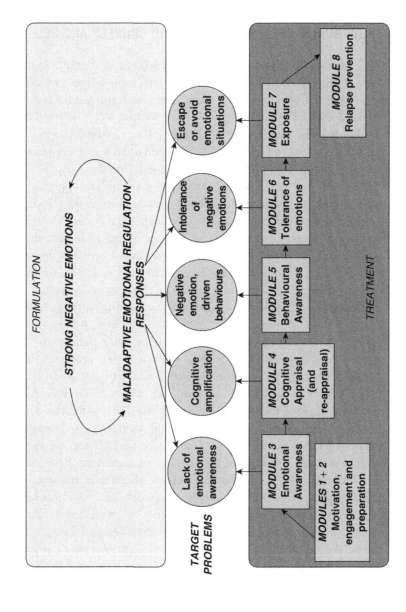

FIGURE 11.3 Transdiagnostic formulation and treatment of emotional disorders

(Barlow et al., 2011a: 4). The great promise of the approach also lies in the economy of effort for training and dissemination implicit in the transdiagnostic element and its wide applicability.

BEYOND INDIVIDUALS: CBT WITH GROUPS AND COUPLES AND SELF-HELP

CBT initially developed as an individual form of therapy, and one-to-one work remains the traditional model. However, to limit access to CBT in this format is demanding of resources, and even after the Improving Access to Psychological Therapies (IAPT) programme there are waiting lists – demand often exceeds supply. We describe the development of IAPT in our final chapter, but here focus on the development of CBT outside the individual therapy format.

Group work is an obvious and well-used method of delivering therapy, and CBT works well in this setting. As well as learning and applying specific and effective methods, there are general factors across group work (Dryden, 1998; Yalom & Leszcz, 2005) which can, for some people, make it preferable to individual therapy: instillation of hope, finding that one is not alone with difficulties, sharing others' experiences, and translating an individual painful problem into a common, shared understanding. Group therapy is effective: for example, for many people with anxiety problems, group work can be as effective as individual therapy (White & Freeman, 2000). Jim White's work involves setting up large 'stress control' groups (structured, didactic groups of up to 50 people) with very much an educational flavour. Participants are encouraged to 'become their own therapists' and are actively discouraged from talking about their own problems in the group. While necessary for large group work, avoiding problem discussion helps focus on anxiety-reduction methods and solutions rather than difficulties. Although IAPT has not been implemented in Scotland,[1] White (2010) described the wide range of proactive, creative and community-based services that developed as the STEPS project in Glasgow, including stand-up comedy based on mental health issues. Large, day-long workshops on anxiety management have shown good results (Brown et al., 2000), and that they are as effective as the small-group format. As well as applications for anxiety, group work can be effective for people with depression, low self-esteem, schizophrenia, sleep disorders, chronic fatigue syndrome, medical problems, pain, anger difficulties and many other problems, and can be used in settings such as in-patient, primary care or education. For further details of group CBT, we recommend White (2000) and Bieling et al. (2006).

There is good evidence to show that self-help bibliotherapy is effective (Frude, 2004). Self-help materials can be useful to clients on long waiting lists, instilling hope and beginning clients on the process of helping themselves, and may reduce the number of sessions. In addition to self-help books, the Internet and computer technology provide a rich resource which is beginning to show effective results, such as the Overcoming Depression programme developed by Chris Williams (2006) and Marks et al.'s (2004) Fear-fighter programme.

Results from group therapy and self-help are encouraging, but can they replace individual work or is it a case of 'dumbing-down' therapy? The evidence to date is that while many clients can find groups helpful, these may not be appropriate for everyone. Individual work is more helpful for clients who are depressed, those with complex difficulties and those with OCD (Morrison, 2001), although it may be that group work has a place for these people while they wait for individual therapy. Groups probably have higher dropout rates than individual work, and face the challenge of being relevant to mixed groups with a variety of individual problems. Depending on the setting, it can be difficult to recruit sufficient numbers to groups without some clients having a long wait until groups are ready to run. With self-help methods such as bibliotherapy and computer-assisted packages, there may be issues around maintaining motivation or the therapeutic effects of other people's interest in overcoming the difficulties. It may be that a combination of self-help with some therapist contact, as and when needed, is sufficient for many clients. This solution addresses the problem of diluting effectiveness while increasing access to resources. IAPT has been inspired by the idea that a range of different types and intensities of service can allow clients to find the paths to healing that most suit them.

USING PROTOCOLS IN CBT

As the applications have widened, so too have the number of protocols and manualised guidelines for working with different problem areas. An early protocol within CBT was Beck's manual for depression (Beck et al., 1979), where the specific approaches and methods were detailed so that all therapists could use identical methods. Beck started the quest to know what works and why, so the methods could have general applicability. The development of applications of CBT and research into their effectiveness has followed this tradition of a degree of manualisation and standardisation of the stages and methods of therapy. Therapist protocols are necessary for research trials so the therapists in the trial can ensure that they are all offering the same procedures. Without this uniformity, the trial is not a fair test of the therapy model. After successful trials, protocols can be published so that other therapists can work to guidelines that have been shown to be successful for specific problems. For example, Leahy and Holland (2000) describe up-to-date protocols and structured therapy plans for the main anxiety problems and depression; Steketee (1999a, 1999b) offers similar protocols for obsessive-compulsive disorder. Padesky and Greenberger (1995) describe protocols for using their manual 'Mind over Mood' with people with a variety of problems including anxiety, depression, anger and personality issues. The core features of CBT are common to many of the problems, but differences lie in the way the problems are formulated and in the specific interventions used.

In many ways, the idea of a standard approach for standard problems is reassuring: therapists can know they are using tried and tested methods and people receiving the therapy know they are getting what is deemed best, and most effective, practice for their particular difficulties. However, the area of protocols is by no means a clear one, and their effectiveness and value in therapy remains controversial and we should note that Beck himself has said 'You cannot do cognitive therapy by manual anymore than you would do surgery by manual' (Norcross et al., 2005: 140).

The main controversies are around standard versus individualised therapy, and now between transdiagnostic and condition-specific treatments. At the heart of CBT is the development of individual client formulations that guide understanding of the client and the direction of therapy; against this, we have the development of effective, specific protocols for specific problems. How do we, as therapists, balance these two apparently contradictory ways of working?

PROTOCOLS VERSUS INDIVIDUAL FORMULATION

Some therapists and counsellors, particularly those not trained in CBT, feel alarmed by the idea of protocols and manuals for conducting therapy, given that their philosophy and training are geared towards treating each client as an individual with individual problems. The idea of protocols implies that there is a correct way to work with clients and that this way is separable from the client's individuality.

The protocol debate centres around the finding that there are certain active ingredients that have been shown to be effective for clients with anxiety problems such as phobias and OCD, and without which the therapy may be less effective (Barlow et al., 2011a). Giving therapists free reign to design their own therapy for the individual may mean that such active ingredients are left out. For example, people with specific phobias are by definition scared of the thing that they are phobic about and do not want to be exposed to their fears. They may predict 'I couldn't do it' or 'I'll be overwhelmed with anxiety'. Therapists can find it difficult to go against compassion and encourage clients to do something that they fear will make them worse, but challenging these fears, both for ourselves and our clients, may be necessary to helping them overcome specific fears and phobias.

CASE STUDY
Nicola

Nicola was in her early thirties when her therapist first saw her and had been phobic of spiders for most of her life. The phobia was having an increasing impact on her life, meaning that going to strange places was difficult, she had to check out rooms she went in and felt uncomfortable being at home on her own in case spiders appeared and she would not be able to deal with them. Nicola was also troubled with periods of low mood during which her phobia would get much worse. She had been for counselling and help many times, often focused on her mood, building self-esteem, understanding how her fears may be important to her relationships, looking at the origins – work which she found had given her valuable insights but had not tackled the phobia.

Nicola simply refused to do any exposure work with spiders. We spent several sessions in preparation, formulating her difficulties and fears, attempting to decatastrophise her predictions about herself and spiders. However, she would not do the exposure work and remained very phobic. She asked her GP to refer her several times, each time really wanting to make a fresh try, but each time she would cancel or not turn up and the unemployed spiders would be returned to their webs. Nicola reported that therapy had been helpful for many things, but no progress was made on her phobia without the exposure work. Therefore, if we take as a successful outcome symptom reduction, the therapy could not work without the active ingredient of contact with spiders.

Research on protocol-based therapy has mostly been conducted within research trials and clients with complex and multifaceted difficulties more common in clinical practice would not be included in such research. Nicola may have felt better, been more proactive in her life and developed greater self-esteem, but not following the therapy protocol would mean that she would be in the 'treatment failure' group. So, the protocol versus individual therapy debate needs to take into account what the meaning of good outcome is. Beutler (2009) shows that manualised treatment does not show superiority over individualised therapy using informed clinical decision making. He also argues that advocacy of protocol-based treatment only maintains the chasm between therapy research and practice. As we have argued before, following protocols to the letter seems a highly implausible way to proceed with clients who can be so varied. The resolution of this 'old chestnut' argument seems then to lie in the detail of what effects result from various levels of deviation from set lines of treatment. There is increasing agreement that this kind of detail can only emerge from small-scale, process-oriented research acting alongside models of outcome research. This type of thinking echoes Persons' (2008) call that CBT should be based on combining knowledge from empirically supported interventions (ESTs) and clinical judgement, based on formulation.

The formulation approach to CBT is based on the concept that, although ideas can be helpfully gleaned from general models and protocols, in the end the treatment of the individual client will be best formulated according to an individual assessment of that client. This is reflected in CBT theory that emphasises the fact that people will react to events, including the experience of having CBT, according to their idiosyncratic cognitive frameworks. Given that clients often present with complicated issues, it can feel good for therapists to go into sessions with a framework for both understanding and working with the client. This framework can act both as a map to locate where we are and as a rudder to guide us forward. If, for example, clients disabled by panic attacks can experience a marked reduction in attacks from a manualised, six-session, protocol-based therapy, then it makes sense for therapy to proceed along standard lines rather than to spend many sessions building up a detailed formulation. Protocols, however, should never lead us to impose ideas or activities on clients. It should help us to negotiate individual approaches to clients based on general principles. The art and skill of CBT may well lie in being able to develop models and therapy plans which are unique to individuals in all their idiosyncrasies, and yet follow methods and approaches that have been found to be helpful for specific problems. This combination of the general and particular is the science and art of CBT. This debate is set to go round some new turns as more transdiagnostic protocols become available, setting up no doubt new controversies and issues in time.

CONCLUSION

The development of CBT appears to be a show that will run and run. This chapter has shown how CBT developed around specific applications of its concepts and interventions to specific problem areas. While the chapter has of necessity had to adopt a limited focus on what might be regarded as the 'classical applications' of CBT, the model itself has spread to ever-wider areas. Even within the relatively narrow confines of these classical applications, however, it can be seen that innovation is the name of the game, with major new developments coming on stream every three to four years. This is all exciting in many ways, but the dizzy rate of change and the increasing amount of desirable knowledge for working in the various provinces of CBT raises questions on how much specialisation or transdiagnostic approaches or both will be called for. Answers on a postcard please.

FURTHER READING

Barlow, D. H., Farchione, T. J., Fairholme, C. P., Ellard, K. K., Boisseau, C. L., Allen, L. B., & Ehrenreich-May, J. (2011a) *Unified Protocol for Treating Emotional Disorders: Therapist Guide*. New York: Oxford University Press.
Beck, A. T., Reinecke, M. A., & Clark, D. A. (2003) *Cognitive Therapy Across the Lifespan: Theory, Research and Practice*. Cambridge: Cambridge University Press.
Clark, D. M., & Fairburn, C. G. (Eds) (1997) *The Science and Practice of Cognitive Behaviour Therapy*. Oxford: Oxford University Press.
Freeman, A., Pretzer, J., Flemming, B., & Simon, K. M. (2004) *Clinical Applications of Cognitive Therapy* (2nd ed.). Boston, MA: Kluwer Academic.

Friedberg, R. D., & McClure, J. M. (2002) *Clinical Practice of Cognitive Therapy with Children and Adolescents*. New York: Guilford Press.

Grant, A., Mills, J., Mulhern, R., & Short, N. (2004) *Cognitive Behavioural Therapy in Mental Health Care*. London: Sage.

Morrison, A. P. (2003) *Cognitive Therapy for Psychosis: A Formulation-based Approach*. London: Brunner-Routledge.

Tarrier, N., Wells, A., & Haddock, G. (Eds) (1998) *Treating Complex Cases*. Chichester: Wiley.

NOTE

1 Scotland has also been innovative in implementing 'mental health first aid' (see www.smhfa.com).

12

CBT and IAPT

I believe that we must renounce the aim of creating a positive feeling of happiness through any kind of social legislation. (Max Weber, quoted in Scaff, 1989: 135)

The era of medical omniscience – when 'doctor knew best' – began to erode as it was realised that many commonly accepted medical treatments were not nearly so effective as people imagined (Pickering, 1996). A concerted effort to have a more rigorous approach to effectiveness was pursued by strategies that eventually cohered in 'evidence-based treatment'. Although the term itself does not seem to have been used before the 1990s, Claridge and Fabian (2005) see the modern approach to effectiveness in medicine beginning with Archie Cochrane's 1972 publication, *Effectiveness and Efficiency: Random Reflection on Health Services.* Cochrane came to value reliance on evidence when he was a doctor dealing with an epidemic with very limited resources in a prisoner-of-war (POW) camp in Salonika during 1941. There was an outbreak of jaundice amongst the prisoners and Cochrane decided to experiment by giving a small portion of his tiny store of yeast to patients on one ward but not on the other. When the patients fed yeast showed a significant improvement on the third day, he persuaded the German authorities to supply more and eventually overcame the outbreak (Cochrane, 1984). He refined his 'evidence-based' approach over the years and his work led to the foundation of the systematic reviews of the Cochrane Collaboration (founded in 1993, after his death). Systematic reviews began by examining the research on physical medicine but eventually included both psychiatric treatment and psychological therapy. Whilst we have expressed concern about some of the difficulties in working out the exact meaning of meta-analyses and systematic reviews for work with individual clients, such research can be regarded as being more reliable as a guide for service provision to whole populations.

CBT tended to show up well in effectiveness and efficacy research and thus began to attract support at the more institutional and governmental level from the early 1990s onwards. In the USA, the 'Chambless Report' of 1996 (Chambless et al., 1996) offered a list of empirically supported treatments (ESTs) in the field of psychological therapy: 12 of the 15 treatments fell within the CBT fold at that stage (Roth & Fonagy, 2004). We should note, however, that neither the Chambless nor the subsequent American Psychological Association (APA) reports were intended as guides for treatment provision by insurance companies or anyone else but as guides for including effective interventions in the training of clinical psychologists. It was never claimed that other treatments, not included in the lists, were *ineffective*. In the UK, CBT increasingly featured in government reports as ESTs and 'treatments of choice' (Department of Health, 2001). Development of actual CBT services, however, was still slow – funding for psychological therapy being as ever hard to come by. A new factor emerged in the form of 'happiness research'. The work of Richard Layard for the Centre for Economic Performance (see below) in particular argued that if effective treatments for problems like anxiety and depression (CBT, for example) could be made much more available, it could increase the nation's happiness quotient. Layard was actually an economist and a Labour peer with good political connections. He extended his argument by hypothesising that expanding therapy services could help to reduce loss of workdays and the cost of sickness benefits – thereby making money available for psychological therapy services. These ideas were eventually formulated into *The Depression Report* (Centre for Economic Performance, 2006), and this overtly advocated the plan that eventually became the Increasing Access to Psychological Therapy (IAPT) initiative. We opened this chapter with Max Weber's pessimistic view of social policies designed to increase happiness in Germany in the early 20th century; the jury is still out on such efforts in the early 21st century.

The IAPT programme began in 2006 with demonstration sites in Doncaster and Newham focusing on psychological services for adults of working age. In 2007, 11 IAPT Pathfinder projects began to explore work in developing services for other groups with more specific vulnerabilities: 'older people, children and young people, offenders, new mothers, black and ethnic minority communities, people with long-term conditions or medically unexplained symptoms' (Department of Health, 2008: 1). On World Mental Health Day, 7 June 2007, the then Health Secretary, Alan Johnson, announced a major extension of funding, worth £173 million, between 2008–2011. This money would support the development of IAPT services in 34 Primary Care Trusts and regional training programmes to support staffing them. These services are now up and running and helping large numbers of clients. Clark et al. (2009) reviewed the clinical outcomes for the two pilot demonstration sites and found them to be as effective as expected – with 55–56 per cent of clients showing significant improvement and 5 per cent improved employment situations. Glover et al. (2010) reported on outcomes in the 32 other sites after one year of operation. These outcomes were not quite as good as in the pilot sites and also showed significant variations between different teams and areas. Further research is now exploring what might be the reasons for these variations. These later results are somewhat disappointing, but perhaps need to be viewed in light of a large project that will inevitably have some difficulties in implementation. Despite recession from 2008 and a change of government in 2010, the future of IAPT seems relatively secure. The Conservative–Liberal Democrat Coalition government has signalled support and further development, especially to ensure that choice of therapy is extended to other models beyond CBT (Brindle, 2011).

THE STRUCTURE OF IAPT

IAPT has been constructed according to the principles of a 'stepped care' policy (Bower & Gilbody, 2005). This principle involves treatment organised in a series of steps, ranging from minimal 'low intensity' interventions toward more extensive 'high intensity' ones. Provision begins with the simplest interventions and only uses more complex interventions when the simpler ones prove inadequate: it thus represents the LIFT ('least intervention first treatment' or 'least intrusive first treatment') principle. 'High intensity' of interventions is therefore reflected in more complex and longer treatments (see Figure 12.1).

The stepped care principle has the potential to address some of the most difficult problems that have plagued the therapy field for many years. First, it has been known that only a very small percentage of those who could benefit from psychological therapy ever get anywhere near it (Lovell & Richards, 2000; Frude, 2004). An effective allocation system matched by gradually increased funding could really make in-roads into this problem. Second, practitioners of psychological therapy

---

Access into the scheme: Access was initially only by GP referral, then became a self-referral system. Low intensity worker – Psychological Wellbeing Practitioner (PWP) – telephones and assesses the client for the most appropriate treatment from the following options:

Step 1: Pure self-help, including bibliotherapy, CDs and DVDs.

OR

Step 2: Low-intensity interventions by telephone (occasionally face-to-face) – delivered by PWP. Limited to single method, usually 5–8 'contacts', e.g., of behavioural activation.

OR

Step 3: High-intensity interventions delivered by HI intensity therapist or counsellor – up to 14–16 usually face-to-face sessions of CBT or counselling. May also have access to specialist PTSD treatment.

OR

Other steps: May lead into services outside IAPT, e.g., CMHT, crisis interventions, trauma service, long-term psychotherapy.

FIGURE 12.1 Stepped care in IAPT

have been consistently disadvantaged by a professional debate about what is the 'best' therapy, often conducted in highly partisan terms. Advocates of treatment have often advocated throwing long-term treatments at problems that have been shown to be more amenable to short-term treatments and vice versa. The stepped care format represents the first substantial system of regulated rational access into a range of treatment services. A stepped care system has the potential for clients to 'feel their way into' a wide range of services until they find the right match for their needs. IAPT is of course only a start – and, as we shall see, this point of view is already a common one amongst IAPT workers. As we shall also see, there have already been surprising twists and turns in its brief period of evolution.

Critics of IAPT have frequently pointed to the following issues:

1   The narrow focus on CBT in the project, including the lack of choice to patients/clients.
2   The narrow focus on the problems of anxiety and depression.
3   The encouragement to use supposedly 'simple' models such as CBT leads to 'de-skilling' of the therapist workforce.
4   The imperative for clients to 'get back to work' reinforces the oppressive nature of the capitalist economic system.

The following section describes the experience of people employed in IAPT and particularly focuses on their views on the above issues in light of that experience.

THE EXPERIENCE OF WORKING IN IAPT

During the period of writing this book, 20[1] people employed in different roles from eight different IAPT project areas in the South West of England have been interviewed. The interviews were analysed using 'line-by-line' framework analysis (Ritchie & Lewis, 2003) to generate main themes. The emergent themes are presented in Figures 12.2 and 12.3 later in this chapter, alongside discussion and reflections on what seem to us to be key issues. It is not claimed that these views are representative.

WHO IS WORKING FOR IAPT?

The sample was a convenience sample generated by contacting people known to be working in IAPT and then being given contact details for other IAPT workers who had agreed to be interviewed. Twelve were women and eight men, and their ages ranged from 25 to 56. Seven were involved in low-intensity roles, seven in high-intensity CBT roles, two combined some aspect of management with actually doing therapy work. Finally, one was an Operational Lead, facilitating the day-to-day operations of a therapy team, and one a Clinical Lead, more concerned with strategic planning, audit and supervision. There were also two trainees who were still completing training and working with only limited caseloads.

Other people linked to IAPT but not interviewed include service managers and staff working for NHS and partner services administration.

The psychological wellbeing practitioners (PWPs) (low-intensity workers) were significantly younger than the other types of worker, ranging from 25 to 31, and had all worked in what they described as 'graduate mental health' jobs before coming into IAPT. They had typically worked in mental health projects for specific patient groups (e.g., adolescents or the chronically unwell). Six of the seven PWPs were women, and one described the people who filled the PWP role as 'psychology graduates who are quite ambitious'. The psychological therapists (high-intensity workers) were more evenly split between male and female and were older, ranging from trainees in their thirties to veteran practitioners in their fifties. They came from a wide range of backgrounds, usually either from counselling and/or NHS backgrounds.

WHAT DO THEY DO IN IAPT?

PWPs, initially called 'low-intensity therapists' (LI), occupy a key position in IAPT services – exercising a strong influence over which clients come into the service and, following the parsimony principle, carrying out the majority of the work at the lower intensity levels. They mostly work sitting at a computer, often typing the client's responses on to an electronic form as they talk on the telephone. Initial assessment calls are termed 'triage' – the aim is to determine the type and priority of patients' treatments based on the nature of their problems. If the client is allocated to Step 2 (on-going low-intensity therapy by telephone), then this intervention will be conducted by PWPs themselves. Such an intervention as low-intensity behavioural activation will be completed in 5–8 sessions. The PWP is encouraged not to deviate from this one single intervention other than in exceptional circumstances. In contrast, high-intensity (HI) psychological therapists work in ways that are closer to conventional therapy: meeting face-to-face with the client and, in the case of CB therapists, following relatively orthodox CBT protocols and structured sessions. They are allowed and mostly use 14–16 sessions but can also be permitted up to 14–16 more sessions in appropriate circumstances. HI therapists are also usually involved in supervising LI practitioners. Within a team there are two levels of management: one an operations manager, who also usually does some HI therapy, oriented towards the day-to-day running and morale of the team; and the service manager, who has an overview of the service offered by the team and acts as the bridge to the external NHS structure – usually to the local Trust but in some areas to third-sector organisations such as Turning Point.

WHAT DO THEY LIKE ABOUT WORKING IN IAPT?

Interviewees were encouraged to reflect on both what they liked about working for the IAPT service as a whole and about their part in it. Answers were generally characterised by a tone of idealism and *mission*:

> I find that there is a really wide range of people to work with and it is great to be involved in working towards providing a universally accessible service. (101, HI therapist)

This was especially so amongst some of the older therapists, with a sense that this had been an objective towards which they had been aiming for some time:

> I almost feel that this is my generation of therapists' World War II – like we have been called to fight on the front line. (105, HI therapist)

> Under the NHS there will always be struggles for resources. Nye Bevan said that back in the 1950s 'We'll never meet the need of every person but we'll have a damn good try, like!' (103, HI therapist/Operations Manager)

The last quotation was delivered in a Welsh Valleys accent and the respondent was born within 10 miles of Bevan's constituency. A major aspect of the mission is *the democratisation of therapy* through the extension of access:

> IAPT has opened up this therapy to an awful lot of people – we have had 10,000 people in the last year. People are getting what was not available before and that's a good thing. (302, LI practitioner)

For many, this has meant that they are encountering types of client that they may not have met before, mainly because such clients may not have had access to therapy services in the past:

> Many are experiencing therapy for the first time … the range is wide and that is stimulating for me … [Compared to social work] … IAPT clients feel like they are more ready to start working on their problems. (101, HI therapist)

It is the 'stepped care' system that allows this to happen. The following comments on that system come from a therapist who has moved from continental Europe:

> I think that the Stepped Care model is a really good approach because it is based on scientific evidence that if the severity is not very high people can be helped by low-intensity interventions – this makes it possible for them to go through and get a good service … not many countries have that … I think it is a big step forward and I like it very much. (102, HI therapist)

As noted earlier, many critics have focused on the 'imposition' of CBT via IAPT, but actually respondents unanimously stressed the value of *choice* and believed that IAPT *is* now establishing more choice, including access to other models of therapy, including brief psychodynamic and interpersonal therapy:

> The good thing is the choice because it is not just about CBT ... IAPT is expanding to include other therapies and in our area there is a lot of choice – and that is positive. (301, LI practitioner)

> Okay, CBT came first – it was the most ready to run if you like. It has always used masses of self-help materials for example. But I think it is great that other things are coming on board ... actually CBT has done them a favour ... it has challenged them – 'Come on then, show us you too can do!'. (104, HI therapist)

Some respondents contrasted this kind of access with the service available from private practitioners:

> I have heard that there has been a reduction in private therapy referrals. I am not surprised because I have heard that some of them charge £85 a session – even as high as £110 ... and then there are some therapists who are charlatans – at least in IAPT there are checks and therapists are supervised. (201, HI therapist trainee)

True to the principle of 'collaboration' in CBT, many respondents described going to some lengths to provide a 'patient-centred' service:

> Certainly we are trained in a very patient-centred way – it was very much put to us that we were guiding people in self-help and making choices – it is not supposed to be prescriptive. (302, LI practitioner)

> The patient-centred thing can even go too far the other way at times – some will virtually say that they want you to decide for them ... and then there are people who make what seem like crazy choices but you have to respect that ... their genuine choice is the primary principle at stake. (303, LI practitioner)

This emphasis on collaboration argues against the earlier-mentioned criticism that IAPT would be 'corralling' clients back into the workforce against their will.

IAPT workers at all levels strongly connote and value the *atmosphere of mutual support* that they receive from colleagues. This was especially strong amongst the PWPs, perhaps because they are working together in the same room and, as will be described later, in somewhat difficult situations:

> Just dealing with the calls is quite stressful but the support we get from each other is really outstanding – we often turn to others in the room for help and they never make you feel stupid for asking – that is just so important, especially when you are just starting. (306, LI practitioner)

The quality of support within and between levels was also widely commented on and with it a sense of professional respect between colleagues:

> They are very good in my team – when you make a decision they will back you up … we are taken seriously when we make clinical decisions – they treat us as someone who knows what he is talking about – that is a thing I really enjoy. Coming from another country and having worked in that country's mental health system I find it a phenomenal idea to have something like IAPT. (102, HI therapist)

Liked aspects of working in IAPT are set out in Figure 12.2.

WHAT DON'T THEY LIKE ABOUT WORKING IN IAPT?

Low- and high-intensity practitioners tend to report different aspects when describing the less-positive elements of IAPT. Whilst both groups of staff report issues that might be termed 'mission shortfall' (i.e., groups of clients who 'fall between' services and clients, such as children, who fall outside the present IAPT remit[2]) low-intensity workers describe more dissatisfaction with their actual *day-to-day working conditions* than high-intensity therapists. All the PWPs reported that they do not like having to sit in front of a computer all day:

> Sitting in front of a computer all day – I don't think that I'll ever get used to that – I get headaches and the others do too … and there is not any other part of your job that is away from the computer – I mean usually if you do admin or something then you get to post the letters but we don't even get that. (301, LI practitioner)

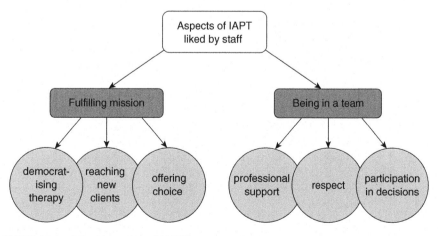

FIGURE 12.2   Liked aspects of IAPT

> [B]ecause of number of contacts we have to do it is very much sitting and typing … you can be there for 8 hours staring at a computer and I get headaches. (302, LI practitioner)

> The computers make the room so hot – luckily it is a nice room but now I associate it with headaches and I seem to get them every day pretty well. (304, LI practitioner)

Some have complained about this to management and there has been some response but only at the level of 'work-station assessment' by health and safety staff, but there does not seem to be a more structural awareness of the problem: 'attrition' of LI staff has now been identified as a major problem. These problems are unfortunately very familiar from workplace studies of 'call centres' (Smith et al., 2006) – see later discussion – as is the issue of how 'telephone-based' practitioners can achieve *career progression* (Taylor et al., 2002):

> The PWP role is not developing as much as it should be – as yet – although I have seen a number of Band 6 posts for Senior PWPs in certain NHS places. There is a lot of frustration about what the future role will be because they obviously hired a lot of people who are psychology graduates who are quite ambitious. They are now recruiting non-graduates for the low-intensity posts because they think they are more likely to stay in the role. (301, LI practitioner)

> When we were hired we seemed to be told that we would be able to go through to HI but now they have put a halt to that because not enough PWPs are staying in post – they have said that no PWPs will be considered for HI posts until they have been in the post for 2 years whereas others from the outside can come into HI posts with fewer qualifications and experience than us. (307, LI practitioner)

Staff turnover is a problem in many fields of telephone-based work and one factor seems to be the potential for *a sense of alienation* and of not being valued (Holman, 2002):

> [PWP] is an important role because most clients are put onto Step 2 first – unless they have another service before … Step 2 is the starting point for most peoples' journey into the service … [but] … Sometimes there's a perception that … [Low intensity] … is a kind of 'watered down' version of the service – just someone to go to in order to get to 'proper therapy' as it were. I don't think that is the case – it can be very effective in its own right. I have come across people who have been told that it is just a watered down version. (302, LI practitioner)

> I just get the feeling sometimes that we are the 'donkeys' of the service – they give us all this stuff about how valued we are but when push comes to shove it is us

that is keeping it all going and some of us can't see a way on from here right now. (306, LI practitioner)

I have observed PWPs working on the telephone and been impressed by the sensitive and skilled way help was offered:

I was naive when I started in IAPT and didn't realise that I would not be doing face-to-face work. But there are lots of skills involved as well as the listening skills on the phone. (301, PWP)

I did find it difficult at first but you do adapt to it funnily enough … you do pick up more of the nuances of peoples' voices and the silences. (302, PWP)

PWP work is quite closely controlled by the protocols they are required to follow but few interviewees mentioned that as a limitation or problem. Perhaps because of a point made by a high-intensity therapist – also required to follow protocols, though to a lesser extent:

I mean I practiced CBT in a much freer way for years and yes I do sometimes think that if I wasn't working in IAPT I would go a different way with some of the clients but then I think that that would lengthen things out and if I did that too much I'd end up seeing fewer clients and that's not the name of the game here … I minded that at first but now there is even a bit of freedom in thinking that I don't have to chase down everything. (106, HI therapist)

It was interesting that high-intensity workers often expressed particular admiration for the PWPs – perhaps in a slightly guilty way at times:

I think that the PWPs are incredibly skilled – we are so lucky to have them but in my heart of hearts, I do think that I'm glad that I don't have to do their work – basically I really don't think I could do that. (107, HI therapist)

When I came into the job I really didn't understand what the PWPs did so the first thing I did was spend a lot of time with them … they were training me … I phoned a client and the PWPs gave me feedback on how I did … also they saw me as vulnerable … there was pleasure in that and they'd laugh at me (and my mistakes) … I realised how incredibly hard they worked and how very skilled they are in terms of typing and their empathy and to listen to them doing all that and still be working well after 7 and 8 contacts sometimes. They seem like the little boy with his finger in the hole in the dam at times. (103, Operations Manager/ HI therapist)

In terms of the criticisms interviewees made about aspects of the IAPT mission that remained unfulfilled, the main theme was that some clients get *lost in the system* because of gaps between IAPT and other mental health services. One PWP, however, made a telling additional critical point about systemic aspects of this factor:

> It should be a stepped care system but if ... they are not right for IAPT then we refer them back to the GP who then has to refer them to the psychological recovery service – that is, not stepped care because they have to go back whereas in stepped care they should come in and then go on until they find the right place for them. (302, LI practitioner)

This view suggests the desirability of a single point of entry – a 'one-stop shop' – for people seeking psychological therapy. We have also noted that such an entry point would be well complemented by a greater degree of choice for the clients. As noted before, IAPT workers tend to favour choice and would like to see more of it. A final point of IAPT self-criticism concerns the *economic mission of IAPT*: to 'get people back to work', to put it one way, or 'help them find employment' put another way, for their own well-being but also to secure the Layard rationale for the project – that funding for the service should be covered by the subsequent saving in benefits. Whilst many respondents accepted that the economic situation from 2008 onwards was hardly favourable to such an aim, this part of the IAPT plan seemed relatively underfunded compared to other parts – especially given that much of the funding had come from the Department of Work and Pensions:

> I know it is hard to help people get jobs these days but I think it has not been enough to the forefront. In our area there was just one guy working on employment and he left quite quickly ... they took ages to replace him. I just wonder if it has been prioritised enough. (108, HI therapist)

Disliked aspects of working in IAPT are set out in Figure 12.3.

CONCLUDING DISCUSSION: IAPT – 'DEMOCRATISED THERAPY' OR 'CALL CENTRE THERAPY' OR BOTH?

Support for the idea that IAPT was helping to 'democratise' the therapy field was a strong and consistent element in the responses of project workers to questions about their experiences of working there. Though the word 'democratisation' is not often mentioned in official IAPT literature, there is an obvious link between this notion and the idea of 'increasing access to therapy'.

The word 'democracy' has two parts. The part coming from 'demos' suggests that it should encourage the participation of 'the people' on the widest possible basis. The part coming from 'cracy' ('rule') in this context suggesting perhaps that the service should be 'ruled' by choice of options – in a 'democratic' way that encourages clients

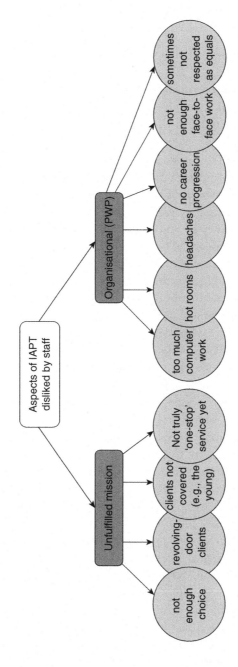

FIGURE 12.3 Disliked aspects of IAPT

to 'vote for' the service they wanted. IAPT workers highlighted different strands of the project when making the case that democratisation was in fact taking place:

1 IAPT is a free service at the point of access – especially compared to private practice.
2 IAPT is dealing with a high volume of clients – many of them had not received services before.
3 IAPT is a de-stigmatising service.
4 IAPT is run in a patient-centred way.
5 IAPT is developing further options to increase client choice.

In a world seemingly dogged by cynicism, the IAPT workers in the interviews showed a refreshing streak of idealism. Rather than being disillusioned by what many in other public services often perceive as the 'bullshit bingo'[3] of the official ideology behind big projects, they were notably whole-hearted in their support of much of it. Furthermore, they by and large thought that significant progress had been made in this particular aspect of the development of the service. If anything, they tended towards a militant stance on the need for yet more to be done to include, de-stigmatise and offer greater choice to the widest possible range of clients.

As ever, those in pursuit of general ideals need to pay attention to the 'devil in the details' of implementation. Neil Frude (2004) has commented that the choices confronting those who wish to 'give therapy away' often seem like choices between 'giving Rolls Royce cars to the few' and 'giving smart cars to the many'. Therapy services, like all services, exist within economic frameworks and it is unlikely that taxpayers will support long-term funding of open-ended therapy services for whoever wants them. There does, however, seem to be public support for a significant increase of services from the very low base that has prevailed historically. A major feature of recent economic development in many societies has seen increased pressure to contain costs by 'rationalising services' to achieve cost-effectiveness. Within manufacturing there have been increases in mechanisation and computerisation of production that increase productivity but have limited workers' 'labour power'. Since World War II, many of these processes have spread to service industries, most notably fast-food restaurants, where 'Mcdonaldisation' holds sway (Ritzer, 1996). In more recent decades, similar processes have crept into office and clerical work, accelerating further falls in the status of these posts. Call centres and online services have already made significant in-roads in traditional middle-class areas of employment such as banking, legal advice, insurance and sales. Here workers often perform a combination of telephone and online work where the answers to questions put to customers may be controlled by algorithms (set patterns of response) stored in computers, including elements of 'false fraternisation' ('Have a nice day') and 'suggestive selling' ('Do you need any house insurance at the moment, Sir?'). Could these developments ever show themselves in the 'caring professions' amongst whom skilled interpersonal face-to-face interaction has always been held as the sine qua non of the work? Some elements of call-centre organisation were seen in the development of NHS Direct, where, as Smith et al. comment:

> For the first time nurses ... [were] ... confined behind desks – a situation that allows management to exercise far more control ... etc. (2006: 591)

Before Frank began these interviews, the earliest description that he heard of working in IAPT said that it was 'just like working in a call centre'. Has the drive to increase access then also opened the possibility of call-centre organisation? If so, what should be our response?

Holman et al. (2003) point out that there are differences between call centres based on 'mass service' and 'high-commitment service' models. Mass service is oriented towards cost reduction and highly simplified work tasks. High-commitment service is oriented towards quality of service and a more nuanced approach to what might be the required skills for the individual worker. Mass service models are associated with greater work stress and staff turnover. High-commitment models exert less time pressures and allow workers to adapt and develop previous work skills to the context they are now working in. Smith et al. (2006), for example, show how nurses working in NHS Direct can use their clinical skills to 'over-ride' the computer algorithms they are expected to follow. This allows the nurses to experience greater work satisfaction and this in turn contributes, with other factors, to limit staff turnover. Bennett-Levy et al. have argued, apparently in the context of LI CBT that, 'CBT now largely resides within the materials, rather than within the therapist' (2010: 13). It is unclear what exactly is being claimed here, in that all therapy models to some extent follow a 'script' that is, however, implemented in more or less 'tight' ways. Whilst wanting to resist the authors' sentiments, one must concede that in IAPT the balance has shifted several steps further towards 'tight implementation'.

Even in high-commitment service models, however, there are factors that suggest the possibility that such technical changes may eventually act as the 'thin end of a wedge' of a technological 'iron cage' (Scaff, 1989) which could herald increased 'de-skilling' of workers and hence to worker alienation. In particular, technological changes associated with both telephone and computer work greatly facilitate the intensification of managerial control via performance monitoring. Holman et al. (2003) suggests that performance monitoring is a double-edged sword: at its best and most helpful it can enhance worker empowerment and productivity, whilst at its worst and most intrusive it is strongly associated with stress and alienation (Holman, 2002). Sociologists have also pointed out the particular stresses of 'emotional labour': work that involves dealing with and conveying appropriate emotions connected to the work transactions in progress (Holman et al., 2003). There can, for example, be a cost to maintaining 'service-correct' responses to a 'customer' who is driving one round the bend, and the instant recordable responses of telephone calls and 'flaming' (instant negative responses) emails may well raise whole new workplace problems, previously unknown in the helping professions. To people like ourselves who have spent a lifetime conducting face-to-face reflective therapy, it can be easy to retreat into a 'good old days' perspective and just be grateful that we don't have to perform in this new style of working. Yet we know that these are long-term trends in work organisation and will have to be dealt with in psychological therapy services just as much as they will elsewhere. Whilst it is good to 'put the services where the clients are', we also need to ensure that the work of therapy remains fulfilling for those who perform it. Most of us are both producers and consumers with interests that both parties get a 'fair deal'. One might even see this as yet another way in which therapy is 'democratic': we all, clients and therapists, consumers and producers, have to deal with certain common problems that make us part of the same humanity – thank goodness. Neither should we take acceptance of this reality as a reason to be passive and do nothing: as the TUC booklet on call centres says to call-centre workers, 'It's your call' (TUC, 2001).

I will conclude this chapter with a quotation from David Holman et al. that exactly captures what in our view is required for our response to these changes in the styles of delivering psychological therapy:

> This dynamic understanding of call centres means that managers do have a choice in how they run and organise call centres, and that well-being can be designed into call centres … the lessons from other types of organisation are that worker knowledge, when it is called upon, often improves the design of customer service, technology and HR practices … Perhaps it is time that customer service advisers are given greater opportunity to engage in the design of call centre technologies and practices. (2003: 131)

There was some evidence in my interviews that this was happening in at least some IAPT teams:

> It's been great to be in on the start of the team and in a completely new office because they really did consult us about a lot of things and you really did get the feeling that even though you were only operating on the bottom, low intensity, rung of the service, your voice really was listened to and what you said could have an influence in the way that things were arranged. (306, LI practitioner)

It would be a good resolution for all of us to do all we all can to ensure that this was the norm in our bright new, shining service.

FURTHER READING

Bennett-Levy, J., Richards, D., Farrand, P., Christensen, H., Griffiths, K. M., Kavanagh, D. J., Klein, B., Lau, M. A., White, J., & Williams, C. (Eds) (2010) *Oxford Guide to Low Intensity CBT Interventions*. Oxford: Oxford University Press.
Cochrane, A. (1984) Sickness in Salonika, *British Medical Journal*, 289: 1726–1727.

NOTES

1   A further aim is to conduct more interviews and produce a report independently of this book.
2   No respondents mentioned the omission of older clients.
3   This term includes concepts such as 'Stakeholders' Empowerment, 'Blue Skies Thinking' and 'Investors in People' etc.

Epilogue: Of Books and Waves and Lives

We began writing the first edition of this book, *Cognitive Therapy: Transforming the Image*, in 1995. We had both just finished training in CBT on the famous Oxford course and were full of missionary zeal to spread the word on this surprisingly straight-forward and effective, yet also subtly challenging, form of therapy that we had learnt. We wanted others to share the excitement with us and were clear about what we wanted to say and duly set about writing it. Towards the end of our training we had just begun to hear of the schema-focused model and could see that CBT was set to keep changing. As time went on we heard of even more new developments in CBT and these seem to keep coming, but nonetheless when we were asked to write a second edition, subsequently called *Cognitive Therapy: an Introduction*, around 2002, we were surprised at the sheer amount of material that we eventually had to include, and struggled with how to adapt some previous material and indeed chapter structure to do so. It was not only CBT that was throwing up changes and challenges – so were our lives. As we were thinking about the second edition, Diana was waiting to have a heart and lung transplant and amazed us all by the way she kept writing in spite of her situation.[1] New developments in CBT suddenly became named as *waves* around this time and we just managed to make a first mention of them in this second edition. Just after the successful reception of the new edition, we were also delighted to attend a book launch in 2006 for Diana's book about how she journeyed to her new heart and lungs. We will soon be attending a party for the 10th anniversary of the 'new Diana'. Frank has been adjusting to 'retirement' from the University of Wales and attaining his PhD at the age of 60. Tranmere Rovers avoided relegation on the last day of the season twice – anxiety time!

In the years building up to this third edition, the waves of CBT have continued to mount and roll up on to the shore with regular monotony. One of the author's has entered a 40th year in practice. Despite the fact that Larry Beutler, with his tongue firmly in his cheek, has argued that one attains competence after 40 years, this author still finds many new things to learn and try with each new day of practice – lifelong learning indeed. The world of therapy no longer seems so straight-forward, and the challenges of writing this edition have indeed been mighty. Major new developments in CBT continued to be evident right up to the final few weeks of writing – it almost feels that the 'paint' of the book is not yet dry. At times it has seemed impossible to comprehend that the CBT model would not fall apart from the sheer stress of accommodation.

The changes that have struck us the most are those of mindfulness and emotion-focused work in CBT. When Frank was first engaging with CBT in the early 1970s, it seemed that the world was at the start of a long march away from experientially and emotionally based modes of therapy. The excesses of the encounter group movement and the 'far out' forms of therapy only added to this trend. An American author recalls turning from humanistic therapy because Fritz Perls' nude marathons in 1969 secretly repelled him! We wonder now if that long march towards cognition and rationality has reached its high-water mark and a movement back the other way is starting. We kind of hope it has, but we hope also that we will not 'throw the baby out with the bath water'. So much has been learnt and so many steps forward taken, and the signs are that these lessons will not be lost. Whilst we were writing this edition, we were interested to learn of changes in other models too: for example, the evolution of the emotion-focused model that one could argue overlaps with emotion-focused changes to the CBT model, and the briefer and more empirically based models now being built on psychodynamic principles. It seems to us that a spirit of competition and cooperation prevails between therapy models – often, as one of IAPT interviewees said, goading each other to 'do their stuff'. Also evident was much work that has been quietly progressing over decades – such as behavioural activation models and the transdiagnostic unified protocol from Barlow and colleagues – without much fanfare of being 'the latest thing' of the newest wave. Despite having to weigh and assess all these new developments, we have ended the process as CBT loyalists. We think that the basic model and paradigm still hangs together as both a way of understanding clients and a good-value guide to what may help them most. Whilst we find much in new developments to admire, use and learn more about, we believe that we have in this book been able to demonstrate a mode of CBT practice that incorporates much from exciting new developments but also retains much of the reassuring strength of the original parsimonious model. We look forward to hearing from our readers whether they agree with this assessment.

Frank Wills
Diana Sanders
January 2012

NOTE

1 She has written a remarkable book, *Will I Still be Me? A Journey Through a Transplant*, about her experiences, including her use of mindfulness and CBT in her recovery (Sanders, 2006) – available from Amazon.

Appendix: Cognitive Behaviour Therapy Resources

There are a huge number of books and other resources on cognitive therapy and CBT. Included in this Appendix are some of the ones we have found useful. It is now very easy to find information on the Internet and we also list a few of the websites we know about and use, but each one will direct you to many other resources. A search for 'cognitive therapy' produces 1,430,000 hits on Google and 4,065 books on Amazon, so happy surfing and reading!

CLASSIC TEXTS WITH HISTORY AND ORIGINS OF COGNITIVE THERAPY

Beck, A. T. (1976/1989) *Cognitive therapy and the emotional disorders.* New York: Penguin.
Beck, A. T., & Emery, G., with Greenberg, R. L. (1985) *Anxiety disorders and phobias: a cognitive perspective.* New York: Basic Books.
Beck, A. T., Rush, A. J., Shaw, B. F., & Emery, G. (1979) *Cognitive therapy of depression.* New York: Guilford Press.

GENERAL

Beck, J. S. (1995) *Cognitive therapy: basics and beyond.* New York: Guilford Press.
Bennett-Levy, J., Butler, G., Fennell, M., Hackman, A., Mueller, M., & Westbrook, D. (2004) *The Oxford guide to behavioural experiments in cognitive therapy.* Oxford: Oxford University Press.
Clark, D. M., & Fairbun, C. G. (Eds) (1997) *The science and pratice of cognitive behaviour therapy.* Oxford: Oxford University Press.
Dryden, W. (Ed.) (2012) *Cognitive behaviour therapies.* London: Sage.
Dryden, W., & Branch, R. (Eds) (2012) *The CBT handbook.* London: Sage.
Hawton, K., Salkovskis, P., Kirk, J., & Clark, D. (1989) *Cognitive behaviour therapy for psychiatric problems.* Oxford: Oxford University Press.
Leahy, R. L. (2003) *Cognitive therapy techniques: a practitioners guide.* New York: Guilford Press.

Padesky, C. A., & Greenberger, D. (1995) *Clinician's guide to mind over mood*. New York: Guilford Press.

Persons, J. B. (2008) *The case formulation approach to cognitive behaviour therapy*. New York: Guilford Press.

Wells, A. (1997) *Cognitive therapy of anxiety disorders*. New York: Wiley.

Wills, F. (2008) *Skills in cognitive behaviour counselling & psychotherapy*. London: Sage.

APPLICATIONS

Beck, A. T., Reinecke, M. A., & Clark, D. A. (2003) *Cognitive therapy across the lifespan: theory, research and practice*. Cambridge: Cambridge University Press.

Bruch, M., & Bond, F. W. (1998) *Beyond diagnosis: case formulation approaches in CBT*. Chichester: Wiley.

Clark, D. M., & Fairburn, C. G. (Eds) (1997) *The science and practice of cognitive behaviour therapy*. Oxford: Oxford University Press.

Grant, A., Mills, J., Mulhern, R., & Short, N. (2004) *Cognitive behavioural therapy in mental health care*. London: Sage.

Salkovskis, P. M. (Ed.) (1996) *Frontiers of cognitive therapy*. New York: Guilford Press.

Sanders, D., & Wills, F. (2003) *Counselling for anxiety problems*. London: Sage. (Also available as eBook.)

Wells, A. (2009) *Metacognitive therapy for anxiety and depression*. Chichester: Wiley.

'THIRD WAVE' CBT BOOKS

Gilbert, P. (2009) *The compassionate mind: a new approach to life's problems*. London: Constable Robinson.

Hayes, S. C., Strosahl, K. D., & Wilson, K. D. (1999) *Acceptance and commitment therapy: an experiential approach to behaviour change*. New York: Guilford Press.

Hayes, S. C., Follette, V. M., & Linehan, M. M. (2004) *Mindfulness and acceptance: expanding the cognitive-behavioural tradition*. New York: Guilford Press.

Segal, Z. V., Williams, J. M. G., & Teasdale, J. D. (2002) *Mindfulness-based cognitive therapy for depression: a new approach to preventing relapse*. New York: Guilford Press.

SELF-HELP BOOKS

Burns, D. D. (1999a) *The feeling good handbook* (Rev. ed.). New York: Penguin.

Burns, D. D. (1999b) *Feeling good: the new mood therapy* (Rev. ed.). New York: Avon Books.

Butler, G., & Hope, T. (1995) *Manage your mind: the mental fitness guide*. Oxford: Oxford University Press.

Fairburn, C. G. (1995) *Overcoming binge eating*. New York: Guilford Press.

Farrington, A., & Dalton, L. (2004) *Getting through depression with CBT: a young person's guide*. Oxford: Blue Stallion (www.oxdev.co.uk).

Greenberger, D., & Padesky, C. (1995) *Mind over mood*. New York: Guilford Press.

Gurney-Smith, B. (2004) *Getting through anxiety with CBT: a young person's guide*. Oxford: Blue Stallion (www.oxdev.co.uk).

Harris, R. (2008) *The happiness trap*. London: Robinson.

Holdaway, C., & Connolly, N. (2004) *Getting through it with CBT: a young person's guide to cognitive behavioural therapy*. Oxford: Blue Stallion (www.oxdev.co.uk).

Young, J. E., & Klosko, J. (1994) *Reinventing your life: how to break free from negative life patterns*. New York: Penguin Putnam.

Also, the Constable and Robinson 'Overcoming' series:

Butler, G. (1999) *Overcoming social anxiety and shyness*. London: Constable and Robinson.

Davies, W. (2000) *Overcoming anger and irritability*. London: Constable and Robinson.

Espie, C. A. (2006) *Overcoming insomnia and sleeping problems*. London: Constable and Robinson.

Fennell, M. (1999) *Overcoming low self-esteem*. London: Constable and Robinson.

Gilbert, P. (2000) *Overcoming depression*. London: Constable and Robinson.

Herbert, C., & Wetmore, A. (1999) *Overcoming traumatic stress*. London: Constable and Robinson.

Kennerley, H. (1997) *Overcoming anxiety*. London: Constable and Robinson.

Kennerley, H. (2000) *Overcoming childhood trauma*. London: Constable and Robinson.

Silove, D. (1997) *Overcoming panic*. London: Constable and Robinson.

Veale, D., & Willson, R. (2005) *Overcoming obsessive-compulsive disorder*. London: Constable and Robinson.

Booklets are available from Oxford Cognitive Therapy Centre on a variety of problems including depression, low self-esteem, phobias, health anxiety and obsessive compulsive disorder: www.octc.co.uk

WEBSITES

British Association for Behavioural and Cognitive Psychotherapy – www.babcp.com

Compassion focused therapy – http://compassionatemind.co.uk

Contextual Psychology (ACT) website – http://contextualpsychology.org

Oxford Mindfulness – www.oxfordmindfulness.org

Training, accreditation, conferences, therapists; valuable links including NICE guidelines and computer-assisted packages: Oxford Cognitive Therapy Centre – www.octc.co.uk

Training, workshops, supervision, therapists and so on: The Oxford Development Centre – www.oxdev.co.uk

Workshops, bookshop, training and therapy: The Beck Institute for Cognitive Therapy and Research – www.beckinstitute.org

Information about training, bookshop, resources and so on: International Association for Cognitive Psychotherapy – www.cognitivetherapyassociation.org

European Association for Behavioural and Cognitive Psychotherapies – www.eabct.com

An umbrella organisation for CBT in Europe: Jeffrey Young's website with resources on schema therapy – www.schematherapy.com

The Australian Association for Cognitive and Behaviour Therapy (AACBT) – www.psy.uwa.edu.au/aacbt/

Christine Padesky's website for workshops, training and resources – www.padesky.com

CBT Arena – www.cbtarena.com

Resources for professionals and academics and links for professional organisations: The National Association for Cognitive-Behavioural Therapists – www.nacbt.org

JOURNALS

Behavioural and Cognitive Psychotherapy: published by Cambridge University Press for the British Association for Behavioural and Cognitive Psychotherapies.

Behaviour Research and Therapy: published by Elsevier.

Journal of Cognitive Psychotherapy: official publication for the International Association of Cognitive Psychotherapy, published by Springer.

Cognitive Behaviour Therapist: published by Cambridge University Press.

Cognitive Therapy and Research: published by Springer.

Cognitive and Behavioral Practice: published by the Association for Advancement of Behavior Therapy (AABT).

Cognitive Behaviour Therapy: formerly *Scandinavian Journal of Behaviour Therapy*, published by Routledge.

VIDEOTAPES AND CDS

The Theory and Practice of CBT: tapes and CDs showing:

1 Christine Padesky doing cognitive therapy are available from: www.padesky.com
2 Frank Wills doing CBT are available from: http://counsellingdvds.co.uk

References

Alford, B. A., & Beck, A. T. (1997) *The integrative power of cognitive therapy*. New York: Guilford Press.

Allen, M., Bromley, A., Kuyken, W., & Sonnenberg, S. (2009) Participants' experiences of mindfulness-based cognitive therapy: 'It changed me in just about every way possible', *Behavioural and Cognitive Psychotherapy*, 37: 413–430.

Allen, N. N., Blashki, G., & Gullone, E. (2006) Mindfulness-based psychotherapies: a review of conceptual foundations, empirical evidence and practical considerations, *Australian and New Zealand Journal of Psychiatry*, 40(4): 285–294.

American Psychiatric Association (APA) (2000) *Diagnostic and statistical manual of mental disorders* (4th ed., Text Revision). Washington, DC: American Psychiatric Association.

Arntz, A., & van Genderen, H. (2009) *Schema therapy for borderline personality disorder* (trans. J. Drost). Chichester: Wiley.

BABCP (2001) *Minimum training standards for the practice of CBT*. London: BABCP.

Baer, R. A. (2003) Mindfulness training as a clinical intervention: a conceptual and empirical review, *Clinical Psychology: Science and Practice*, 10: 125–143.

Baer, R. A. (2006) *Mindfulness-Based treatment approaches: clinician's guide to evidence base and applications*. Burlington, MA: Academic Press.

Baer, R., & Kreitemeyer, J. (2006) Overview of mindfulness- and acceptance-based treatment approaches. In R. Baer (Ed.), *Mindfulness-based treatment approaches: clinician's guide to evidence base and applications* (pp. 3–27). London, Academic Press.

Bannister, D., & Fransella, F. (1986) *Enquiring man: the psychology of personal constructs* (3rd ed.). London: Routledge.

Barker, P. (1992) *Regeneration*. London: Penguin.

Barlow, D. H., Farchione, T. S., Farchinone, C. P., Ellard, K. K., Boisseau, C. L., Allen, L. B., & Ehrenreich-May, J. (2011a) *Unified protocol for treating emotional disorders: therapist manual*. New York: Oxford University Press.

Barlow, D. H., Farchione, T. S., Farchinone, C. P., Ellard, K. K., Boisseau, C. L., Allen, L. B., & Ehrenreich-May, J. (2011b) *Unified protocol for treating emotional disorders: workbook*. New York: Oxford University Press.

Bartlett, F. C. (1932) *Remembering*. New York: Columbia University Press.

Batchelor, A., & Horvath, A. (1999) The therapeutic relationship. In M. Hubble, M. Duncan, & S. Miller (Eds), *The heart and soul of change: what works in therapy* (pp. 133–178). Washington, DC: American Psychological Association.

Bayne, R. (1997) *The Myers-Briggs indicator: a critical review and practical guide*. London: Nelson-Thornes.

Beck, A. T. (1976/1989) *Cognitive therapy and the emotional disorders*. New York: International Universities Press.

Beck, A. T. (1991) Cognitive therapy as the integrative therapy, *Journal of Psychotherapy Integration*, 1: 191–198.

Beck, A. T. (1996) Beyond belief: a theory of modes, personality and psychopathology. In P. M. Salkovskis (Ed.), *The frontiers of cognitive therapy* (pp. 1–25). New York: Guilford Press.

Beck, A. T., Rush, A. J., Shaw, B. F., & Emery, G. (1979) *Cognitive therapy of depression*. New York: Guilford Press.

Beck, A. T., & Emery, G., with Greenberg, R. L. (1985) *Anxiety disorders and phobias: a cognitive perspective*. New York: Basic Books.

Beck, A. T., Epstein, N., Brown, G., & Steer, R. A. (1988) An inventory for measuring clinical anxiety: psychometric properties, *Journal of Consulting and Clinical Psychology*, 56(6), 893–897.

Beck, A. T., Steer, R. A., & Brown, G. K. (1996) *BDI-II Manual* (2nd ed.). San Antonio, TX: Harcourt Brace.

Beck, A. T., Reinecke, M. A., & Clark, D. A. (2003) *Cognitive therapy across the lifespan: theory, research and practice*. Cambridge: Cambridge University Press.

Beck, A. T., Freeman, A., Davis, D. D., & Associates (2004) *Cognitive therapy of personality disorders* (2nd ed.). New York: Guilford Press.

Beck, A. T., Steer, R. A., Brown, G. K., & Weissman, A. (1991) Factor analysis of the dysfunctional attitude scale in a clinical population, *Psychological Assessment*, 3(1): 478–483.

Beck, A. T., & Steer, R. A. (1993) *Beck Anxiety Inventory Manual*. San Antonio, TX: Harcourt Brace.

Beck, J. (1995) *Cognitive therapy: basics and beyond*. New York: Guilford Press.

Beitman, B. D. (2003) Integration through fundamental similarities and useful differences among the schools. In J. Norcross & M. Garfield (Eds), *Handbook of Psychotherapy Integration* (pp. 202–230). Oxford: Oxford University Press.

Bennett-Levy, J. (2003) Mechanisms of change in cognitive therapy: the case of automatic thought records and behavioural experiments, *Behavioural and Cognitive Psychotherapy*, 31: 261–277.

Bennett-Levy, J. (2006) Therapist skills: a cognitive model of their acquisition and refinement, *Behavioural and Cognitive Psychotherapy*, 34: 57–78.

Bennett-Levy, J., Butler, G., Fennell, M., Hackman, A., Mueller, M., & Westbrook, D. (2004) *The Oxford guide to behavioural experiments in cognitive therapy*. Oxford: Oxford University Press.

Bennett-Levy, J., & Thwaites, R. (2006) Self and self-reflection in the therapeutic relationship: a conceptual map and practical strategies for the training, supervision and self-supervision of interpersonal skills. In P. Gilbert & R. Leahy (Eds), *The therapeutic relationship in the cognitive behavioural psychotherapies* (pp. 255–281). London: Routledge.

Bennett-Levy, J., Richards, D., Farrand, P., Christensen, H., Griffiths, K. M., Kavanagh, D. J., Klein, B., Lau, M. A., White, J., & Williams, C. (Eds) (2010) *Oxford guide to low intensity CBT interventions*. Oxford: Oxford University Press.

Beutler, L. E. (2009) Making science matter in clinical practice: redefining psychotherapy, *Clinical Psychology: Science and Practice*, 16(3): 301–317.

Bieling, P. J., McCabe, R. E., & Antony, M. M. (2006) *Cognitive behavioural therapy in groups*. New York: Guilford Press.

Blackburn, I. M., & Davidson, K. (1995) *Cognitive therapy for depression and anxiety* (2nd ed.). Oxford: Blackwell Scientific.

Blackburn, I. M., James, I. A., Milne, D. L., Baker, C., Standart, S., Garland, A., & Reichelt, F. K. (2001) The revised cognitive therapy scale (CTS-R): psychometric properties, *Behavioural and Cognitive Psychotherapy*, 29: 431–446.

Blenkiron, P. (2005) Stories and analogies in cognitive behavioural therapy: a review, *Behavioural and Cognitive Psychotherapy*, 33(1): 45–60.

Bower, P., & Gilbody, S. (2005) Stepped care in psychological therapies: access, effectiveness and efficiency, *British Journal of Psychiatry*, 186: 11–17.

Bowlby, J. (1969) *Attachment and loss* (vol. 1: Attachment). London: Hogarth Press and the Institute of Psychoanalysis.

Bowlby, J. (1973) *Attachment and loss* (vol. 2: Separation, anxiety and anger). London: Hogarth Press and the Institute of Psychoanalysis.

Brewin, C. R., Dalgleish, T., & Joseph, S. (1996) A dual representation theory of posttraumatic stress disorder, *Psychological Review*, 103: 670–686.

Brewin, C. R. (2006) Understanding cognitive behaviour therapy: a retrieval competition account, *Behaviour Research and Therapy*, 44: 765–784.

Brewin, C., & Holmes, E. A. (2003) Psychological theories of PTSD, *Clinical Psychology Review*, 23: 339–376.

Brindle, D. (2011) An equal footing for mental health, *Guardian* newspaper, 2 February.

Brown, J. S. L., Cochrane, R., & Hancox, T. (2000) Large-scale health promotion stress workshops for the general public: a controlled evaluation, *Behavioural and Cognitive Psychotherapy*, 28(2): 139–151.

Bruch, M., & Bond, F. W. (1998) *Beyond diagnosis: case formulation approaches in CBT*. Chichester: Wiley.

Burgess, M., & Chalder, T. (2005) *Overcoming chronic fatigue syndrome*. London: Constable-Robinson.

Burns, D. D. (1999a) *The feeling good handbook* (Rev. ed.). New York: Penguin.

Burns, D. D. (1999b) *Feeling good: the new mood therapy* (Rev. ed.). New York: Avon Books.

Burns, D. D., & Auerbach, A. (1996) Therapeutic empathy in cognitive-behavioral therapy: does it really make a difference? In P. M. Salkovskis (Ed.), *Frontiers of cognitive therapy* (pp. 135–164). New York: Guilford Press.

Butler, A. C., Chapman, J. E., Forman, E. M., & Beck, A. T. (2006) The empirical status of cognitive behavioral therapy: a review of systematic reviews, *Clinical Psychology Review*, 26(1): 17–31.

Butler, G. (1999) *Overcoming social anxiety and shyness*. London: Constable and Robinson.

Butler, G., & Hope, T. (1995) *Manage your mind: the mental fitness guide*, Oxford: Oxford University Press.

Carey, T. A. & Mansell, W. (2009) Show us a behaviour without a cognition and we'll show you a rock rolling down a hill, *The Cognitive Behaviour Therapist*, 2: 123–133.

Carey, T. A., & Mullan, R. J. (2004) What is Socratic questioning? *Psychotherapy: Theory, Research, Practice, Training*, 41(3): 217–226.

Carlson, R. (1997) *Don't sweat the small stuff.* New York: Hyperion.

Carroll, L. (1865/1998) *Alice's Adventures in Wonderland.* London: Penguin Classics.

Casement, P. (1985) *On learning from the patient.* London: Tavistock.

Castonguay, L. G., & Beutler, L. E. (Eds) (2006) *Principles of therapeutic change that works.* Oxford: Oxford University Press.

Centre for Economic Performance (2006) *The depression report: a new deal for depression and anxiety disorders.* London: London School of Economics.

Chambers, R., Gullone, E., & Allen, N. B. (2009) Mindful emotion regulation: an integrative review, *Clinical Psychology Review*, 29(6): 560–572.

Chambless, D. L., Sanderson, W. C., Shoham, V., Bennett Johnson, S., Pope, K. S., Crits-Christoph, P., Baker, M., Johnson, B., Woody, S. R., Sue, S., Beutler, L., Williams, D. A., & McCurry, S. (1996) An update on empirically validated therapies. *The Clinical Psychologist*, 49: 5–18.

Chiesa, A., & Serretti, A. (2009) Mindfulness-based stress reduction for stress management in healthy people: a review and meta-analysis, *Journal of Alternative and Complementary Medicine*, 15(5): 593–600.

Chigwedere, C. (2010) Self-practice and self-reflection as an alternative to traditional personal therapy in CBT training. Paper presented at the BABCP Annual Conference, Manchester, July.

Chigwedere, C., Tone, Y., Fitzmaurice, B., & McDonough, M. (2012) *Overcoming obstacles in CBT.* London: Sage.

Chorpita, B. F., & Barlow, D. H. (1998) The development of anxiety: the role of control in the early environment, *Psychological Bulletin*, 124(1): 3–21.

Ciarrochi, J. V., & Bailey, A. (2008) *A CBT practitioner's guide to ACT.* Oakland, CA: New Harbinger.

Claridge, J. A., & Fabian, T. C. (2005) History and development of evidence-based medicine, *World Journal of Surgery*, 5: 547–553.

Clark, D. A., & Beck, A.T. (2002) *Clark–Beck obsessive compulsive inventory manual.* San Antonio, TX: Psychological Corporation.

Clark, D. A., & Beck, A. T. (2010) *Cognitive therapy of anxiety disorders: science and practice.* New York: Guilford Press.

Clark, D. A., & Beck, A.T. (2012) *The anxiety and worry workbook.* New York: Guilford Press.

Clark, D. M. (1986) A cognitive approach to panic, *Behaviour Research and Therapy*, 24: 461–470.

Clark, D. M. (1996) Panic disorder: from theory to therapy. In P. M. Salkovskis (Ed.), *The frontiers of cognitive therapy* (pp. 318–344). New York: Guilford Press.

Clark, D. M., & Fairburn, C. G. (Eds) (1997) *The science and practice of cognitive behaviour therapy.* Oxford: Oxford University Press.

Clark, D. M., Layard, R., Smithies, R., Richards, D. A., Suckling, R., & Wright, B. (2009) Improving access to psychological therapy: initial evaluation of 2 UK demonstration sites, *Behaviour Research and Therapy*, 30: 1–11.

Clark, D. M., & McManus, F. (2002) Information processing in social phobia, *Biological Psychiatry*, 51(1): 92–100.

Cochrane, A. L. (1972) *Effectiveness and efficiency: random reflections on health services.* Oxford: Nuffield Trust.

Cochrane, A. L. (1984) Sickness in Salonika, *British Medical Journal*, 289: 1726–1727.

Cooper, M. (2008) *Essential research findings in counselling and psychotherapy: the facts are friendly.* London: Sage.

Crane, R. (2009) *Mindfulness-based cognitive therapy: distinctive features,* Hove: Routledge.

Cromarty, P., & Marks, I. (1995) Does rational role-play enhance the outcome of exposure therapy in dysmorphophobia? A case study, *British Journal of Psychiatry*, 167(3): 399–402.

Davies, W. (2000) *Overcoming anger and irritability.* London: Constable and Robinson.

De Rubeis, R. J., Brotman, M. A., & Gibbons, C. J. (2005) A conceptual and methodo-logical analysis of the non-specifics argument, *Clinical Psychology: Science and Practice*, 12(2): 174–183.

Department of Health (2001) *Treatment choice in psychological therapies and counselling: evidence based clinical practice guidelines.* London: Department of Health.

Department of Health (2008) *The IAPT pathfinders: achievements and challenges.* Published only as a PDF at www.dh.gov.uk/publications

Dobson, K. S., Hollon, S. D., Dimidjian, S., Schmaling, K. B., Kohlenberg, R. J., Gallop, R., Rizvi, S. L., Gollan, J. K., Dunner, D. L., & Jacobson, N. S. (2008) Randomised trial of behavioural activation, cognitive therapy, and anti-depressant medication in the preven-tion of relapse and recurrence in major depression, *Journal of Consulting and Clinical Psychology*, 76(3): 468–477.

Dozois, D. J. A., Dobson, K. S., Ahnberg, J. L. (1998) A psychometric evaluation of the Beck depression inventory–II, *Psychological Assessment*, 10(2): 83–89.

Dryden, W. (1991) *A dialogue with Albert Ellis: against dogmas.* Buckingham: Open University Press.

Dryden, W. (1998) *Developing self-acceptance: a brief, educational, small group approach.* Chichester: Wiley.

Dryden, W. (2006) *Getting started with REBT.* London: Taylor and Francis.

Dryden, W., & Feltham, C. (1992) *Brief counselling.* Buckingham: Open University Press.

Dunne, J. (2011) Toward an understanding on non-dual mindfulness, *Contemporary Buddhism: An Interdisciplinary Journal*, 12(1): 71–88.

Eells, T. D. (1997) *Handbook of psychotherapy case formulation.* New York: Guilford Press.

Egan, G. (1975) *You and me: the skills in communicating and relating to others.* Monterey, CA: Brooks Cole.

Egan, G. (2002) *The skilled helper* (7th ed.) Monterey, CA: Brooks Cole.

Ehlers, A., & Clark, D. M. (2000) A cognitive model of post-traumatic stress disorder, *Behaviour Research and Therapy*, 36(4): 319–345.

Elliott, R., Watson, J. C., Goldman, R. J., & Greenberg, L. S. (2004) *Learning emotion-focused therapy.* Washington: APA.

Emery, G. (1999) *Overcoming depression.* Oakland, CA: New Harbinger.

Epstein, S. (1998) *Constructive thinking: the key to emotional intelligence.* Westport, CT: Praeger.

Erikson, E. (1997) *The life cycle completed.* New York: Norton.

Fairburn, C. G. (1995) *Overcoming binge eating.* New York: Guilford Press.

Farrington, A., & Dalton, L. (2004) *Getting through depression with CBT: a young person's guide.* Oxford: Blue Stallion (www.oxdev.co.uk).

Fennell, M. J. V. (1989) Depression. In K. Hawton, P. M. Salkovskis, J. Kirk, & D. M. Clark (Eds), *Cognitive behaviour therapy for psychiatric problems* (pp. 169–234). Oxford: Oxford Medical.

Fennell, M. (1999) *Overcoming low self-esteem.* London: Constable and Robinson.

Fennell, M. J. V. (2004) Depression, low self-esteem and mindfulness, *Behaviour Research and Therapy,* 42: 1053–1067.

Ferster, C. B. (1973) A functional analysis of depression, *American Psychologist,* 28(10): 857–870.

Flecknoe, P., & Sanders, D. (2004) Interpersonal difficulties. In J. Bennett-Levy, G. Butler, M. Fennell, A. Hackman, M. Mueller, & D. Westbrook (Eds), *The Oxford guide to behavioural experiments in cognitive therapy* (pp. 393–412). Oxford: Oxford University Press.

Foa, E., & Kozak, M. J. (1986) Emotional processing of fear: exposure to corrective information, *Psychological Bulletin,* 99: 20–35.

Frank, J. D. (1971) *Persuasion and healing: a comparative study of psychotherapy.* Baltimore, MD: Johns Hopkins University Press.

Freeman, A., Pretzer, J., Flemming, B., & Simon, K. M. (2004) *Clinical applications of cognitive therapy* (2nd ed.). Boston, MA: Kluwer Academic.

Freud, S., & Breuer, J. (2004) *Studies in hysteria.* London: Penguin.

Friedberg, R. D., & McClure, J. M. (2002) *Clinical practice of cognitive therapy with children and adolescents.* New York: Guilford Press.

Frude, N. (2004) A book prescription scheme in primary care, *Clinical Psychology,* 39: 11–18.

Gendlin, E. (1981) *Focusing.* New York: Everest House.

Gendlin, E. (1998) *Focusing-oriented psychotherapy: a manual of experiential method.* New York: Guilford Press.

Gilbert, P. (2000) *Overcoming depression.* London: Constable and Robinson.

Gilbert, P. (2007) Evolved minds and compassion in the therapeutic relationship. In P. Gilbert & R. L. Leahy (Eds), *The therapeutic relationship in the cognitive behavioural psychotherapies* (pp. 106–142). London: Routledge.

Gilbert, P. (2009) *The compassionate mind: a new approach to life's problems.* London: Constable Robinson.

Gilbert, P. (2010) *Compassion-focused therapy (distinctive features).* Hove: Routledge.

Gilbert, P., & Leahy, R. L. (Eds) (2007) *The therapeutic relationship in the cognitive behavioural psychotherapies.* London: Routledge.

Glover, G., Webb, M., & Evison, F. (2010) *Improving access to psychological therapy: a review of progress made by sites in the first roll out year.* Stockton on Tees: North East Health Public Health Observatory.

Grant, A., Mills, J., Mulhern, R., & Short, N. (2004) *Cognitive behavioural therapy in mental health care.* London: Sage.

Greenberg, L. S. (2011) *Emotion-focused Therapy.* Washington: American Psychological Association.

Greenberger, D., & Padesky, C. (1995) *Mind over mood.* New York: Guilford Press.

Grepmair, L., Mitterlehner, F., Loew, T., Bachler, E., Rother, W., & Nickel, M. (2007) Promoting mindfulness in psychotherapists in training influences the treatment results of their patients: a randomized, double-blind, controlled study, *Psychotherapy and Psychosomatics*, 76: 332–338.

Grossman, P., Niemann, L., Schmidt, S., & Walach, H. (2004) Mindfulness-based stress reduction and health benefits: a meta-analysis, *Journal of Psychosomatic Research*, 57: 35–43.

Guidano, V. F., & Liotti, G. (1983) *Cognitive processes and emotional disorders: a structural approach to psychotherapy*. New York: Guilford Press.

Gurney-Smith, B. (2004) *Getting through anxiety with CBT: a young person's guide*. Oxford: Blue Stallion (www.oxdev.co.uk).

Hackman, A., Bennett-Levy, J., & Holmes, E. A. (2011) *Oxford guide to imagery in cognitive therapy*. Oxford: Oxford University Press.

Harvey, A., Watkins, E., Mansell, W., & Shafran, R. (2004) *Cognitive-behavioural processes across psychological disorders*. Oxford: Oxford University Press.

Hawton, K., Salkovskis, P., Kirk, J., & Clark, D. (1989) *Cognitive behaviour therapy for psychiatric problems*. Oxford: Oxford University Press.

Hayes, S. C. (1984) Making sense of spirituality, *Behaviorism*, 12: 99–110.

Hayes, S. C. (1993) Analytic goals and the varieties of scientific contextualism. In S. C. Hayes, L. J. Hayes, H. W. Reese, & T. R. Sarbin (Eds), *Varieties of scientific contextualism* (pp. 11–17) Reno, NV: Context Press.

Hayes, S. C. (2004) Acceptance and commitment therapy, relational frame theory, and the third wave of behavioural and cognitive therapies, *Behaviour Therapy*, 35: 639–665.

Hayes, S. C., Follette, V. M., & Linehan, M. M. (2004) *Mindfulness and acceptance: expanding the cognitive-behavioural tradition*. New York: Guilford Press.

Hayes, S. C., with Smith, S. (2005) *Get out of your mind and into your life: the new acceptance and commitment therapy*. Oakland, CA: New Harbinger.

Hayes, S. C., Masuda, A., Bissett, R., Luoma, J., & Guerrero, L. F. (2004) How empirically oriented are the new behavior therapy technologies? *Behavior Therapy*, 35(1): 35–50.

Hayes, S. C., Strosahl, K. D., & Wilson, K. D. (1999) *Acceptance and commitment therapy: an experiential approach to behaviour change*. New York: Guilford Press.

Hays, P. A. (1995) Multicultural applications of cognitive-behaviour therapy, *Professional Psychology: Research and Practice*, 26(3): 309–315.

Heesacker, M., & Mejia-Millan, C. (1996) Change processes and their application in counselling. In W. Dryden (Ed.), *Research in Counselling and Psychotherapy: Practical Applications* (pp. 49–78). London: Sage.

Herbert, C., & Wetmore, A. (1999) *Overcoming traumatic stress*. London: Constable and Robinson.

Hick, S. F., & Bien, T. (2008) *Mindfulness and the therapeutic relationship*. New York: Guilford Press.

Hofmann, S., Sawyer, A., Witt, A., & Oh, D. (2010) The effect of mindfulness-based therapy on anxiety and depression: a meta-analytic review, *Journal of Consulting and Clinical Psychology*, 78(2): 169–183.

Holdaway, C., & Connolly, N. (2004) *Getting through it with CBT: a young person's guide to cognitive behavioural therapy*. Oxford: Blue Stallion (www.oxdev.co.uk).

Holman, D. (2002) Employee well-being in call centres, *Human Resources Management Journal*, 12(4): 35–50.

Holman, D., Wall, T. D., Clegg, C. W., Sparrow, P., & Howard, A. (Eds) (2003) *The new workplace: a guide to the human impact of modern working practices*. Chichester: Wiley.

Hollon, S. D. (2001) Behavioral activation treatment for depression: a commentary, *Clinical Psychology: Science and Practice*, 8(3): 271–274.

Hollon, S. D. (2003) Does cognitive therapy have an enduring effect?, *Cognitive Therapy and Research*, 27(1): 71–75.

Hollon, S. D., Stewart, M. O., & Strunk, D. (2006) Enduring effects of cognitive behavior therapy for depression and anxiety, *Annual Review of Psychology*, 57: 285–315.

Hopko, D. R., Lejuez, C. W., Ruggiero, K., & Eifert, G. (2003) Contemporary behavioral activation treatments for depression: procedures, principles and progress, *Clinical Psychology Review*, 23: 699–717.

Horton, I. (2006) Structuring work with clients. In C. Feltham & I. Horton (Eds), *Handbook of counselling and psychotherapy* (2nd ed.) (pp. 118–126). London: Sage.

Howard, K. I., Lueger, R. J., Maling, M. S., & Martinovich, Z. (1993) A phase model of psychotherapy outcome: causal mediation of change, *Journal of Consulting and Clinical Psychology*, 61: 678–685.

Hubble, M., Duncan, B., & Miller, S. (1999) *The heart and soul of change: what works in therapy*. Washington, DC: American Psychological Association.

Ilardi, S. S., & Craighead, E. W. (1994) The role of non-specific factors in cognitive behaviour therapy for depression, *Clinical Psychology: Science and Practice*, 1(2): 138–155.

Inskipp, F. (1996) *Skills training for counselling*. London: Cassell.

Ivey, A. E., D'Andrea, D. D. J., & Ivey, M. B. (2011) *Theories of Counselling and Psychotherapy* (7th ed.). Thousand Oaks, CA: Sage.

Izard, C. E. (1971) *The face of emotion*. New York: Appleton-Century-Crofts.

Jacobson, N. S., & Christenson, A. (1996) *Integrative couple therapy*. New York: Norton.

Jacobson, N. S., & Gortner, E. (2000) Can depression be de-medicalised in the 21st Century: scientific revolutions, counter-revolutions and the magnetic field of normal science. *Behaviour Therapy and Research*, 38: 103–117.

Jacobson, N. S., & Margolin, G. (1979) *Marital therapy: strategies based on social learning and behavior change principles*. New York: Brunner Mazel.

James, I. A. (2001) Schema therapy: the next generation, but should it carry a health warning?, *Behavioural and Cognitive Psychotherapy*, 29: 401–407.

James, I. A., & Barton, S. (2004) Changing core beliefs with the continuum technique, *Behavioural and Cognitive Psychotherapy*, 32: 431–442.

James, I. A., Blackburn, I. M., & Reichelt, F. K. (2000) *Manual of the revised cognitive therapy scale*. Newcastle Upon Tyne: Newcastle Cognitive & Behavioural Therapies Centre.

Jeffers, S. (1997) *Feel the fear and do it anyway*. New York: Simon and Schuster.

Johnstone, L., & Dallos, R. (2006) *Formulation in psychology and psychotherapy: making sense of people's problems*. London: Routledge.

Kabat-Zinn, J. (2001) *Full catastrophe living: how to cope with stress, pain and illness using mindfulness meditation*. London: Piatkus.

Kabat-Zinn, J. (2004) *Wherever you go, there you are: mindfulness meditation for everyday life*. London: Piatkus.

Kahn, M. (1991) *Between therapist and client: the new relationship*. New York: Freeman.

Kanter, J. W., Busch, A. M., & Rusch, L. C. (2009) *Behavioural activation (distinctive features)*. Hove: Routledge.

Katzow, A. W., & Safran, J. D. (2007) Recognising and resolving ruptures in the therapeutic alliance. In P. Gilbert & R. L. Leahy (Eds), *The therapeutic relationship in the cognitive behavioural psychotherapies* (pp. 90–105). Hove: Routledge.

Kazantzis, N., Deane, F. P., Ronan, K. R., & L'Abate, L. (Eds) (2005) *Using assignments in cognitive behaviour therapy*. New York: Routledge.

Kazantzis, N., & Ronan, K. R. (2006) Can between sessions (homework) assignments be considered a common factor in psychotherapy?, *Journal of Psychotherapy Integration*, 16(2): 115–127.

Keijsers, G. P., Schaap, C. P., & Hoogduin, C. A. (2000) The impact of interpersonal patient and therapist behaviour on outcome in cognitive behavioural therapy: a review of empirical studies, *Behaviour Modification*, 24(2): 264–297.

Kelly, G. (1955) *The psychology of personal constructs*. New York: Norton.

Kennerley, H. (1997) *Overcoming anxiety*. London: Constable and Robinson.

Kennerley, H. (2000) *Overcoming childhood trauma*. London: Constable and Robinson.

Kiesler, D. J. (1996) *Contemporary interpersonal theory and research: personality, psychopathology and psychotherapy*. New York: Wiley.

Kirk, J. (1989) Cognitive behavioural assessment. In K. Hawton, P. M. Salkovskis, J. Kirk & D. M. Clark (Eds), *Cognitive behaviour therapy for psychiatric problems* (pp. 13–51). Oxford: Oxford Medical.

Kohlenburg, R. J., Kanter, J. W., Bolling, M. Y., Parker, C. R., & Tsai, M. (2002) Enhancing cognitive therapy for depression with functional analytic psychotherapy: treatment guidelines and empirical findings, *Cognitive and Behavioural Practice*, 9: 213–229.

Kuyken, W. (2006) Evidence-based formulation: is the emperor clothed? In N. Tarrier (Ed.), *Case formulation in cognitive behaviour therapy* (pp. 12–35). Chichester: Wiley.

Kuyken, W., Padesky, C. A., & Dudley, R. (2009) *Collaborative case conceptualisation*. New York: Guilford Press.

Laing, R. D. (1970) *Knots*. Harmondsworth: Penguin.

Lao-Tzu (1993) *Tao Te Ching* (trans. S. Addiss & S. Lombardo). Indianapolis, IN: Hackett.

Layden, M. A., Newman, C. F., Freeman, A., & Morse, S. B. (1993) *Cognitive therapy of borderline personality disorder*. Boston, MA: Allyn and Bacon.

Le Doux, J. (1996) *The emotional brain: the mysterious underpinnings of emotional life*. New York: Simon & Schuster.

Leahy, R. L. (2001) *Overcoming resistance in cognitive therapy*. New York: Guilford Press.

Leahy, R. L. (2003) *Cognitive therapy techniques: a practitioner's guide*. New York: Guilford Press.

Leahy, R. L. (2005) *The worry cure: 7 steps to stop worry from worrying you*. New York: Crown.

Leahy, R. L. (2007) Schematic mismatch in the therapeutic relationship. In P. Gilbert & R. L. Leahy (Eds), *The therapeutic relationship in the cognitive behavioural psychotherapies* (pp. 229–254). Hove: Routledge.

Leahy, R. L. (2011) *Emotional regulation in psychotherapy*. New York: Guilford.

Leahy, R. L., & Holland, S. J. (2000) *Treatment plans and interventions for depression and anxiety disorders*. New York: Guilford Press.

Leahy, R. L., Tirch, D., & Napolitano, L. A. (2011) *Emotional regulation in psychotherapy: a practitioner's guide*. New York: Guilford Press.

Leijssen, M. (1996) Characteristics of a healing inner relationship. In R. Hutterer, G. Pawlowsky, P. F. Schmid, & R. Stipsits (Eds), *Client-centred and experiential psychotherapy towards the nineties* (pp. 225–250). Leuven, Belgium: Leuven University Press.

Lewinsohn, P. M. (1974) A behavioral approach to depression: the psychology of depression: contemporary theory and research. In R. J. Friedman & M. M. Katz (Eds), *The psychology of depression: contemporary theory and research* (pp. 318–331). Oxford: Wiley.

Lewinsohn, P. M., & Graf, M. (1973) Pleasant activities and depression, *Journal of Consulting and Clinical Psychology*, 41(2): 261–268.

Lewis, G. (2002) *Sunbathing in the rain: a cheerful book on depression* (p. 92). London: Flamingo.

Linehan, M. M. (1993) *Cognitive-behavioural treatment of borderline personality disorder.* New York: Guilford Press.

Liotti, G. (2007) Internal working models of attachment in the therapeutic relationship. In P. Gilbert & R. L. Leahy (Eds), *The therapeutic relationship in the cognitive behavioural psychotherapies* (pp. 143–162). London: Routledge.

Lomas, P. (1987) *The limits of interpretation.* Harmondsworth: Penguin.

Longmore, R. J., & Worrell, M. (2007) Do we need to challenge thoughts in cognitive behaviour therapy?, *Clinical Psychology Review*, 27: 173–187.

Lovell, K., & Richards, D. (2000) Multiple access points and levels of entry (MAPLE): ensuring choice, accessibility and equity for CBT services, *Behavioural and Cognitive Psychotherapy*, 28: 379–391.

Luoma, J. B., Hayes, S. C., & Walser, R. D. (2007) *Learning ACT: an acceptance and commitment therapy skills training manual for therapists.* Oakland, CA: New Harbinger.

Lynch, T. R., & Cuper, P. (2010) Dialectical behavior therapy: cognitive and behavioral theories in clinical practice. In N. Kazantzis, M. Reinecke, & A. Freeman (Eds), *Cognitive and behavioral theories in clinical practice* (pp. 218–243). New York: Guilford Press.

Ma, S. H., & Teasdale, J. D. (2004) Mindfulness-based cognitive therapy for depression: replication and exploration of differential relapse prevention effects. *Journal of Consulting and Clinical Psychology*, 72: 31–40.

Macran, S., & Shapiro, D. (1998) The role of personal therapy for therapists: a review. *British Journal of Medical Psychology*, 71: 13–25.

Manicavasgar, V., Parker, G., & Perich, T. (2011) Mindfulness-based cognitive therapy vs cognitive behaviour therapy as a treatment for non-melancholic depression, *The Journal of Affective Disorders*, 130(1–2): 138–144.

Marks, I. M., Kenwright, M., McDonough, M., Whittaker, M., & Mataix-Cols, D. (2004) Saving clinicians' time by delegating routine tasks to a computer: a randomised controlled trial in phobia/panic disorder, *Psychological Medicine*, 34: 9–17.

Martell, C., Addis, M., & Dimidjian, S. (2004) Finding the action in behavioural activation: the search for empirically supported interventions and mechanisms of change. In S. C. Hayes, V. M. Follette, & M. M. Linehan (Eds), *Mindfulness and acceptance: expanding the cognitive-behavioural tradition* (pp. 152–165). New York: Guilford Press.

Martell, C. R., Addis, M. E., & Jacobson, N. S. (2001) *Depression in context: strategies for guided action.* New York and London: Norton.

Mathew, K. L., Whitford, H. S., Kenny, M. A., & Denson, L. A. (2010) The long-term effects of mindfulness-based cognitive therapy as a relapse prevention treatment for major depressive disorder, *Behavioural and Cognitive Psychotherapy*, 38(5): 561–576.

McCullough, J. P. (2000) *Treatment for chronic depression: cognitive behavior analysis system of psychotherapy*, New York: Guilford Press.

McCullough, J. (2001) *Skills training manual for diagnosing and treating chronic depression: cognitive behavioural analysis system of psychotherapy*. New York: Guilford Press.

McCullough, J. P. (2006) *Treating chronic depression with disciplined personal involvement*. New York: Springer.

McGinn, R., Young, J. E., & Sanderson, W. C. (1995) When and how to do long-term therapy and not feel guilty, *Cognitive Behavioural Practice*, 2: 187–212.

McKay, M., Wood, J. C., & Brantley, J. (2007) *The dialectical behavior therapy skills workbook: practical DBT exercises for learning mindfulness, interpersonal effectiveness, emotional regulation and distress tolerance*. Oakland, CA: New Harbinger.

Mikulincer, M., & Shearer, P. R. (2007) *Attachment in adulthood: structure, dynamic, and change*, New York: Guilford Press.

Mooney, K., & Padesky, C. (2000) Applying client creativity to recurrent problems: constructing possibilities and tolerating doubt, *Journal of Cognitive Psychotherapy*, 14: 149–161.

Moorey, S., & Greer, S. (2002) *Cognitive behavioural therapy for people with cancer*. Oxford: Oxford University Press.

Morgan, W. T., & Morgan, S. T. (2005) Cultivating attention and empathy. In C. K. Germer, R. D. Siegel, & P. R. Fulton (Eds), *Mindfulness and Psychotherapy* (pp. 73–90). New York: Guilford Press.

Morrison, N. (2000) Schema-focused cognitive therapy for complex long-standing problems: a single case study, *Behavioural and Cognitive Psychotherapy*, 28: 269–283.

Morrison, N. (2001) Group cognitive therapy: treatment of choice or sub-optimal option? *Behavioural and Cognitive Psychotherapy*, 29(3): 311–332.

Morrison, A. P. (2003) *Cognitive therapy for psychosis: a formulation-based approach*. Philadelphia, PA: Brunner-Routledge.

Nathan, P. E., & Gorman, J. M. (2007) *A guide to treatments that work* (3rd ed.). London: Oxford University Press.

Newman, C. F. (2002) A cognitive perspective on resistance in psychotherapy, *Journal of Clinical Psychology*, 58(2): 165–174.

Norcross, J. C. (2002) *Psychotherapy relationships that work: therapist contributions and responsiveness to patient need*. New York: Oxford University Press.

Norcross, J., Levant, R., & Beutler, L. E. (2005) *Evidence-based practices in mental health: debate and dialogue on the fundamental questions*. Washington, DC: American Psychological Association Press.

O'Donoghue, W. T., & Fisher, J. E. (2009) *general principles and empirically supported techniques of cognitive behavior therapy*. New York: Wiley.

O'Driscoll, A. (2009) The growing influence of mindfulness on the work of the counselling psychologist: a review, *Counselling Psychology Review*, 24: 16–23.

Oatley, K., & Laird-Johnson, P. N. (1987) Towards a cognitive theory of emotion, *Cognition and Emotion*, 1(1): 29–50.

Orsillo, S. M., & Roemer, L. (2011) *The mindful way through anxiety*. New York: Guilford.

Ost, L. G. (2008) Efficacy of the third wave of behaviour therapies: a systematic review and metaanalysis, *Behaviour Research and Therapy*, 46: 296–321.

Overholser, J. C. (1993) Elements of the Socratic method: II. Inductive reasoning, *Psychotherapy: Theory, Research, Practice, Training*, 30(1): 75–85.

Padesky, C. A. (1993) *Socratic questioning: changing minds or guided discovery?* Paper given at the Congress of the European Association of Behavioural and Cognitive Therapies, London.

Padesky, C. A. (1994) Schema change processes in cognitive therapy, *Clinical Psychology and Psychotherapy*, 1: 267–278.

Padesky, C. A. (1996) Developing cognitive therapist competency: teaching and supervision models. In P. M. Salkovskis (Ed.), *Frontiers of cognitive therapy* (pp. 266–292). New York: Guilford Press.

Padesky, C. A. (1998) Keynote speech, European Association for Behavioural and Cognitive Psychotherapies, Cork, September.

Padesky, C. A. (1999) *Therapist beliefs: protocols, personalities and guided exercises.* Audio CD, Newport Beach, CA: Center for Cognitive Therapy. (Available from www.padesky.com)

Padesky, C. (2004) *Socratic questioning in cognitive therapy and guided discovery: leading and following clinical workshop.* Audiotapes. Newport Beach, CA: Center for Cognitive Therapy. (Available from www.padesky.com)

Padesky, C. A., & Greenberger, D. (1995) *Clinician's guide to mind over mood.* New York: Guilford Press.

Padesky, C., & Mooney, K. (1998) *Between two minds: the transformational power of underlying assumptions.* Cork: EABCT Workshop.

Persons, J. B. (1989) *Cognitive therapy in practice: a case formulation approach.* New York: Norton.

Persons, J. B. (2008) *The case formulation approach to cognitive behaviour therapy.* New York: Guilford Press.

Persons, J. B., Gross, J. J., Etkin, M. S., & Madan, S. K. (1996) Psychodynamic therapists' reservations about cognitive-behavioral therapy: implications for training and practice, *Journal of Psychotherapy Practice & Research*, 5: 202–212.

Piaget, J. (1952) *The origins of intelligence in children.* New York: International Universities Press.

Pickering, W. (1996) Does medical treatment mean patient benefit?, *The Lancet*, 347: 379–380.

Pierson, H., & Hayes, S. C. (2007) Using acceptance and commitment therapy to empower the therapeutic relationship. In P. Gilbert & R. L. Leahy (Eds), *The therapeutic relationship in the cognitive behavioural psychotherapies,* Hove, East Sussex: Routledge, pp. 205–228.

Popper, K. R. (1959) *The logic of scientific enquiry.* London: Hutchinson.

Power, M. (2010) *Emotion-focused cognitive therapy.* Chichester: Wiley.

Power, M., & Dalgleish, T. (2008) *Cognition and emotion: from order to disorder,* Hove: Psychology Press.

Pretzer, J., & Beck, J. (2004) Cognitive therapy of personality disorders, in R. L. Leahy (Ed.), *Contemporary cognitive therapy: theory, research and practice* (pp. 299–318). New York: Guilford.

Prochaska, J. O. (2000) How do people change, and how can we change to help many more people? In M. A. Hubble, B. L. Duncan, & S. D. Millar (Eds), *The heart and soul of change: what works in therapy* (pp. 227–255). Washington, DC: American Psychological Association.

Psychological and Educational Films (1986) *Three approaches to psychotherapy: Richard.* Corona del Mar, CA: Psychological and Educational Films.

Rachman, S. (1997) The evolution of cognitive behaviour therapy: science and practice of cognitive behaviour therapy. In D. M. Clark & C. G. Fairburn (Eds), *Science and practice of cognitive behaviour therapy* (pp. 3–26). New York: Oxford University Press.

Rachman, J. (2003) *The treatment of obsessions.* Oxford: Oxford University Press.

Rennie, D. L. (1998) *Person-centred counselling: an experiential approach.* London: Sage.

Richards, D. A. (2010a) Behavioural activation. In J. Bennett-Levy, D. Richards, P. Farrand, H. Christensen, K. Griffiths, D. Kavanagh, B. Klein, M. A. Lau, J. Proudfoot, L. Ritterband, J. White, & C. Williams (Eds), *Oxford guide to low intensity CBT interventions* (pp. 141–150). Oxford: Oxford University Press.

Richards, D. A. (2010b) Access and organization: putting low intensity interventions to work in lcoinical services. In J. Bennett-Levy, D. Richards, P. Farrand, H. Christensen, K. Griffiths, D. Kavanagh, B. Klein, M. A. Lau, J. Proudfoot, L. Ritterband, J. White, & C. Williams (Eds), *Oxford guide to low intensity CBT interventions* (pp. 19–34). Oxford: Oxford University Press.

Rimes, K. and Wingrove, J. (2011) Mindfulness-based cognitive therapy for people with chronic fatigue syndrome still experiencing excessive fatigue after cognitive behaviour therapy: a pilot randomized study, *Clinical Psychology and Psychotherapy*, 39: 235–241.

Ritchie, J., & Lewis, J. (2003) *Qualitative research practice: a guide for social science students and researchers.* London: Sage.

Ritzer, G. (1996) *The Macdonaldisation of society.* Thousand Oaks, CA: Pine Forge Press.

Rivers, W. (1918) The repression of war experience, *The Lancet*, 2 February. (Available as free download at http://net.lib.byu.edu/estu/wwi/comment/rivers.htm)

Robins, C. J., Schmidt III, H., & Linehan, M. M. (2004) Dialectical behavior therapy: synthesising radical acceptance with skilful means. In S. C. Hayes, V. M. Follette, & M. M. Linehan (Eds), *Mindfulness and acceptance: expanding the cognitive-behavioural tradition* (pp. 30–44). New York: Guilford Press.

Roemer, L., & Orsillo, S. M. (2009) *Mindfulness and acceptance-based behavioral therapies in practice.* New York: Guilford Press.

Rogers, C. R. (1957) The necessary and sufficient conditions of therapeutic personality change, *Journal of Consulting and Clinical Psychology*, 21: 95–103.

Roth, A., & Fonagy, P. (2004) *What works for whom? A critical review of psychotherapy research* (2nd ed.). New York: Guilford Press.

Rouf, K., Fennell, M., Westbrook, D., Cooper, M., & Bennett-Levy, J. (2004) Devising effective behavioural experiments. In J. Bennett-Levy, G. Butler, M. Fennell, A. Hackman, M. Mueller, & D. Westbrook (Eds), *The Oxford guide to behavioural experiments in cognitive therapy* (pp. 21–58). Oxford: Oxford University Press.

Ryle, A., & Kerr, I. (2003) *Introducing cognitive analytic therapy.* Chichester: Wiley.

Safran, J. D. (1998) *Widening the scope of cognitive therapy.* Northvale, NJ: Aronson.

Safran, J. D., & Muran, J. C. (2000) *Negotiating the therapeutic alliance: a relational treatment guide.* New York: Guilford Press.

Sage, N., Sowden, M., Chorlton, E., & Edeleanu, A. (2006) *CBT for chronic illness and palliative care.* Chichester: Wiley.

Salkovskis, P. M. (1996) Anxiety, beliefs and safety seeking behaviour. In P. M. Salkovskis (Ed.), *Frontiers of cognitive therapy* (pp. 48–74). New York: Guilford Press.

Salkovskis, P. M. (2002) Empirically grounded clinical interventions: cognitive-behavioural therapy progresses through a multi-dimensional approach to clinical science, *Behavioural and Cognitive Psychotherapy*, 30: 3–10.

Salkovskis, P. M., Forrester, E., Richards, H. C., & Morrison, N. (1998) The devil is in the detail: conceptualising and treating obsessional problems. In N. Tarrier (Ed.), *Treating complex cases: the cognitive behavioural approach* (pp. 46–60). Chichester: Wiley.

Sanders, D. (2006) Psychosomatic problems. In C. Feltham & I. Horton (Eds), *Handbook of counselling and psychotherapy* (2nd ed.) (pp. 442–449). London: Sage.

Sanders, D., & Wills, F. (2003) *Counselling for anxiety problems.* London: Sage.

Sanders, D., & Wills, F. (2005) *Cognitive therapy: an introduction.* London: Sage.

Scaff, L. A. (1989) *Fleeing from the iron cage: culture, politics and modernity in the thought of Max Weber.* Berkeley, CA: University of California Press.

Schure, M. B., Christopher, J., & Christopher, S. (2008) Mind-body medicine and the art of self-care, *Journal of Counselling and Development*, 86: 47–56.

Segal, Z. V., Williams, J. M. G., & Teasdale, J. D. (2002) *Mindfulness-based cognitive therapy for depression: a new approach to preventing relapse.* New York: Guilford Press.

Seligman, M. E. P. (2003) *Authentic happiness: using the new positive psychology to realise your potential for lasting fulfilment.* New York: Free Press.

Shapiro, F. (2001) *Eye movement desensitisation and reprocessing: basic principles, protocols and procedures* (2nd ed.). New York: Guilford Press.

Siegel, D. (2007) *The mindful brain in human development.* New York: Norton.

Siegel, D. (2010) *The mindful therapist: a clinician's guide to mindsight and neural integration.* New York: Norton.

Silove, D. (1997) *Overcoming panic.* London: Constable and Robinson.

Simmons, M., & Wills, F. (2006) *CBT skills in practice* (DVD/video). Newport: University of Wales Newport (UWN).

Simmons, M., & Wills, F. (2009) *CBT for depression: behavioural activation and cognitive change.* Newport: University of Wales Newport (UWN).

Skinner, B. F. (1953) *Science and human behaviour.* Oxford: Macmillan.

Smith, C., Valesschi, R., Mueller, F., & Gabe, J. (2006) Knowledge and the discourse of labour process transformation: nurses and the case of NHS Direct for England, *Work, Employment and Society*, 22: 581–599.

Smucker, M. (2005) Imagery rescripting and reprocessing, *Encyclopaedia of Cognitive Behavior Therapy*, Part 9: 226–229.

Smucker, M., & Dancu, C. V. (1999) *Cognitive behavioral treatment for adult survivors of childhood trauma: imagery rescripting and reprocessing.* Northvale, NJ: Jason Aronson.

Sroufe, L. A. (1996) *Emotional development: the organisation of emotional life in the early years.* New York: Cambridge University Press.

Steketee, G. (1999a) *Overcoming obsessive-compulsive disorder: therapist protocol.* Oakland, CA: New Harbinger.

Steketee, G. (1999b) *Overcoming obsessive compulsive disorder: client protocol.* Oakland, CA: New Harbinger.

Stopa, L. (Ed.) (2009) *Imagery and the threatened self: perspectives on mental imagery in cognitive therapy.* Hove: Routledge.

Stott, R., Mansell, W., Salkovskis, P., Lavender, A., & Cartwright-Hatton, S. (2010) *Oxford guide to metaphors in CBT: building cognitive bridges.* Oxford: Oxford University Press.

Sullivan, H. S. (1954) *The interpersonal theory of psychiatry.* New York: Norton.

Surawy, C., Roberts, J., & Silver, A. (2005) The effect of mindfulness training and mood and measures of fatigue, activity and quality of life in patients with chronic fatigue syndrome on a hospital waiting list: a series of exploratory studies, *Behavioural and Cognitive Psychotherapy*, 33(1): 103–110.

Swales, M. A., & Heard, H. (2008) *Dialectical behaviour therapy: distinctive features.* London: Routledge.

Tarrier, N. (2006) *Case formulation in CBT: the treatment of challenging and complex cases.* London: Brunner Routledge.

Tarrier, N., Wells, A., & Haddock, G. (Eds) (1998) *Treating complex cases.* Chichester: Wiley.

Taylor, P., Mulvey, G., & Hyman, J. (2002) Work organization, control and the experience of work in call centres. *Work, Employment and Society*, 16(1): 133–150.

Teasdale, J. (1996) Clinically relevant theory: integrating clinical insight with cognitive science. In P. M. Salkovskis (Ed.), *The frontiers of cognitive therapy* (pp. 26–47). New York: Guilford Press.

Teasdale, J. (2004) *Mindfulness and the third wave of cognitive-behavioural therapies.* Keynote address, Congress of the European Association of Behavioural and Cognitive Therapies Conference, Manchester.

Teasdale, J. D., Segal, Z. V., & Williams, J. M. G. (2006) Mindfulness training and problem formulation, *Clinical Psychology: Science and Practice*, 10(2): 157–160.

Thorne, B. (2003) *Carl Rogers.* London: Sage.

Thouless, R. H. (1953) *Straight and crooked thinking* (Rev. ed.). London: Pan Books.

Tolan, J. (2006) *Skills for person-centred counselling and psychotherapy.* London: Sage.

Toner, B., Segal, Z. V., Emmott, S. D., & Myran, D. (2000) *Cognitive-behavioural treatment of irritable bowel syndrome.* New York: Guilford Press.

Townend, M. (2005) Inter-professional supervision from the perspective of both mental health nurses and other professionals in the field of cognitive behavioural psychotherapy, *Journal of Psychiatric and Mental Health Nursing*, 12(5): 582–588.

Trade Union Congress (TUC) (2001) *It's your call: TUC call-centre workers' campaign.* London: TUC.

Truax, C. B. (1968) Reinforcement and non-reinforcement in Rogerian psychotherapy, *Journal of Abnormal Psychology*, 71: 1–9.

Tsai, M., Kohlenburg, R. J., Kanter, J. W., Kohlenburg, B., Follette, W. C., & Callaghan, G. M. (2009) *A guide to functional analytic psychotherapy: awareness, courage, love and behaviourism.* New York: Springer.

Twohig, M. P., Hayes, S. C., & Masuda, A. (2006) Increasing willingness to experience obsessions: acceptance and commitment therapy as a treatment for obsessive-compulsive disorder, *Behavior Therapy*, 37(1): 3–13.

Van der Kolk, B. (1994) The body keeps the score: memory and the evolving psychobiology of post-traumatic stress, *Harvard Review of Psychiatry*, 1(5): 253–285.

Veale, D., & Willson, R. (2005) *Overcoming obsessive-compulsive disorder.* London: Constable and Robinson.

Vickers, S. (2006) *The other side of you*. London: Harper Perennial.

Waddington, L. (2002) The therapy relationship in cognitive therapy: a review, *Behavioural and Cognitive Psychotherapy*, 30(2): 179–191.

Watson, D. L., & Tharp, R. G. (2007) *Self-directed behavior* (International Students Edition). Belmont, CA: Thomson.

Wegner, D. M. (1994) Ironic processes of mental control, *Psychological Review*, 101(1): 34–52.

Weishaar, M. E. (1993) *Aaron T. Beck*. London: Sage.

Wells, A. (1997) *Cognitive therapy of anxiety disorders*. New York: Wiley.

Wells, A. (2000) *Emotional disorders and metacognition*. Chichester: Wiley.

Wells, A. (2006) Cognitive therapy case formulation in anxiety disorders. In N. Tarrier (Ed.), *Case formulation in cognitive behaviour therapy* (pp. 52–80). Hove: Routledge.

Wells, A. (2009) *Metacognitive therapy for anxiety and depression*. Chichester: Wiley.

Westbrook, D., Kennerley, H., & Kirk, J. (2007) *An introduction to cognitive behaviour therapy: skills and applications*. London: Sage.

Westen, D., & Shedler, J. (1999) Revising and assessing Axis II: Part I: developing a clinically relevant and empirically valid assessment method, *American Journal of Psychiatry*, 156: 258–272.

White, J. (2000) *Treating anxiety and stress: a group psycho-educational approach using brief CBT*. Chichester: Wiley.

White, J. (2010) The STEPS model: a high-volume, multi-level, multi-purpose approach to address common mental problems. In J. Bennett-Levy, G. Butler, M. Fennell, A. Hackman, M. Mueller, & D. Westbrook (Eds), *Oxford guide to low intensity CBT interventions* (pp. 35–52). Oxford: Oxford University Press.

White, J. R., & Freeman, A. (Eds) (2000) *Cognitive-behavioral group therapies for specific problems and populations*. Washington, DC: American Psychological Association.

Whitehead, E. E., & Whitehead, J. D. (2010) *Transforming our painful emotions*. Maryknoll, NY: Orbis.

Wilkins, P. (2006) Personal and professional development. In C. Feltham & I. Horton (Eds), *Handbook of counselling and psychotherapy* (2nd ed.) (pp. 158–165). London: Sage.

Wilkinson, A., Meares, K., & Freeston, M. (2011) *CBT for worry and generalised anxiety disorder*. London: Sage.

Williams, C. (2006) *Overcoming depression and low mood: a five areas approach* (2nd ed.). London: Hodder Arnold.

Williams, M., & Penman, D. (2011) *Mindfulness: a practical guide to finding peace in a frantic world* (with CD). London: Piatkus.

Williams, M., Teasdale, J., Segal, Z., & Kabat-Zinn, J. (2007) *The mindful way through depression*. New York: Guilford Press.

Wills, F. R. (2006a) Cognitive counselling: a down to earth and accessible therapy. In C. Sills (Ed.), *Contracts in counselling* (pp. 29–40). London: Sage.

Wills, F. (2006b) CBT: can counsellors fill the gap?, *Healthcare Counselling and Psychotherapy Journal*, 3: 6–9.

Wills, F. (2008a) *Skills for cognitive behaviour therapy and counselling*. London: Sage.

Wills, F. (2008b) *Therapeutic attitudes and the acquisition of competence during CBT training*. Unpublished PhD thesis, University of Bristol.

Wills, F. (2009) *Beck's cognitive therapy: distinctive features*. London and New York: Routledge.

Wills, F. (2010) *Yada, yada, yada: finding the missing bit of CBT – a call for more practitioner research*. A paper given at the Annual Conference of the British Association of Behavioural and Cognitive Psychotherapies (BABCP), Manchester, July.

Wills, F. (2012a) Assessment and formulation in CBT. In W. Dryden & R. Branch (Eds), *The CBT handbook* (pp. 101–124). London: Sage.

Wills, F. (2012b) CBT skills. In W. Dryden & R. Branch (Eds), *The CBT handbook* (pp. 125–140). London: Sage.

Wills, F. (2012c) Beck's cognitive therapy. In W. Dryden (Ed.), *Cognitive behaviour therapies* (pp. 25–48). London: Sage.

Wills, F., & Sanders, D. (1997) *Cognitive therapy: transforming the image*. London: Sage.

Wilson, K. G., & Sandoz, E. K. (2008) Mindfulness, values, and therapeutic relationship in acceptance and commitment therapy. In S. F. Hick & T. Bien (Eds), *Mindfulness and the therapeutic relationship* (pp. 89–106). New York: Guilford Press.

Woods, S. L. (2009) Training professionals in mindfulness. In F. Didonna (Ed.), *Clinical handbook of mindfulness*. New York, Springer.

Worthless, I. M., Competent, U. R., & Lemonde-Terrible, O. (2002) And finally … cognitive therapy training stress disorder: a cognitive perspective, *Behavioural and Cognitive Psychotherapy*, 30: 365–374.

Wright, J. H., Basco, M., & Thase, M. E. (2005) *Learning cognitive behavior therapy: an illustrated guide*. Washington, DC: American Psychiatric Association.

Yalom, I. D. (1975) *The theory and practice of group psychotherapy* (2nd ed.). New York: Basic Books.

Yalom, I. D., & Leszcz, M. (2005) *Theory and practice of group psychotherapy*. New York: Basic Books.

Young, J. E., & Beck, A. T. (1980) *The cognitive therapy rating scale manual*. Philadelphia, PA: Center for Cognitive Therapy, University of Pennsylvania.

Young, J. E., & Beck, A. T. (1988) *The cognitive therapy rating scale manual* (Revised ed.). Philadelphia, PA: Center for Cognitive Therapy, University of Pennsylvania.

Young, J. E., & Klosko, J. (1994) *Reinventing your life*. New York: Plume.

Young, J. E., Klosko, J., & Weishaar, M. E. (2003) *Schema therapy: a practitioner's guide*. New York: Guilford Press.

Index

Made in the USA
Coppell, TX
11 May 2021